US Environmental Policy in Action

"Rinfret and Pautz's title offers a unique, concise, and highly readable overview of contemporary environmental policy and politics in the United States. It comes at an opportune time as longstanding policies and programs face more opposition than ever before from political ideologues and vested economic interests. What we most need at present is a clear understanding of the problems that we face, the most viable policy alternatives for addressing them, and the kinds of programs that offer the greatest promise. Students will find the authors' innovative coverage of the practical challenges of successful policy development and implementation a refreshing alternative to conventional texts."
—Michael E. Kraft, *Professor Emeritus, Political Science and Public and Environmental Affairs, University of Wisconsin-Green Bay, USA*

"Anyone interested in environmental policy will applaud this updated edition of *US Environmental Policy in Action*. In this engaging book, Rinfret and Pautz provide a careful and rich analysis of key policy developments in the field, but also explore how environmental policy is shaped through rulemaking, evolves during implementation, is influenced by interest groups and front-line staff in state environmental programs, and is evaluated. By doing so, students and scholars alike gain a greater appreciation for the context in which environmental policy occurs and the conditions under which it may succeed. This outstanding book is a must-read for those seeking a deeper understanding of environmental policy in the United States."
—Denise Scheberle, *Clinical Teaching Professor, School of Public Affairs, University of Colorado Denver, USA*

"The second edition of *US Environmental Policy in Action* illustrates the challenging nature of environmental problem and the difficult choices confronting policymakers. The authors' most important contribution is to focus on those at the front lines of environmental policy—the rule writers, inspectors, businesses, and policy analysts, who are typically overlooked in the literature."
—Robert Duffy, *Professor, Political Science, Colorado State University, USA*

Sara R. Rinfret · Michelle C. Pautz

US Environmental Policy in Action

Second Edition

Sara R. Rinfret
University of Montana
Missoula, MT, USA

Michelle C. Pautz
University of Dayton
Dayton, OH, USA

ISBN 978-3-030-11315-5   ISBN 978-3-030-11316-2   (eBook)
https://doi.org/10.1007/978-3-030-11316-2

Library of Congress Control Number: 2018967759

This Palgrave Macmillan imprint is published by the registered company Springer Nature
Switzerland AG
The registered company address is: Gewerbestrasse 11, 6330 Cham, Switzerland

To our students—they hold the keys to our environmental future.

PREFACE

Understanding environmental issues and problems is incredibly complicated because of the encompassing nature of the topics and the increasing politicization of these issues. At its most basic level, environmental issues concern the air we breathe, the water we drink, and the land and resources we live on and use to sustain our lives. Although we both share a passion for these issues from different places—Sara is an avid outdoorswoman and Michelle is most definitely not, we are both committed to understanding complex environmental issues and working with our students to tackle incredible challenges. Most importantly, we are keenly interested in how policy works on the front-lines, not just in the halls of Congress. This orientation, coupled with our passions for learning and teaching, motivated the first edition of this book.

The second edition of this book finds the United States grappling with environmental issues in a way that we have not witnessed in our history. As you may already be aware, environmental issues were not always so contentious and divisive. In fact, the passage of most of our modern environmental laws—predominantly in the 1960s and 1970s—came about during highly charged times, but during a period in which consensus was possible and action essential.

Since those formative decades, we have seen American environmental policy become increasingly political under the Trump administration. Given the political climate surrounding environmental issues, it is essential that we have meaningful and productive dialogue around these challenges that affect all of us and not talk past one another in heated rhetoric. We hope this book provides a foundation for some of those conversations as those conversations have to be grounded in an understanding of environmental policy history and environmental policy in action.

There are many wonderful environmental policy texts available but what sets this one apart and what makes it particularly useful in today's discussions of these issues is our emphasis on the "doing" of environmental policy. Often environmental policy texts focus at the highest levels of our government—notably the federal level—and discuss policy from that vantage point. Although we discuss environmental policy at the federal level, we take the conversation a step further and discuss implementation on the front-lines. Our emphasis on this action orientation stems from both our professional experiences working in environmental policy and regulation but also our academic backgrounds in public administration. It is important to understand how and why Congress passed the Clean Air Act in 1970, for example, but it is equally important to understand how that law is implemented today through the work of air inspectors and members of the regulated community and what nearly five decades of experience and additional research and data mean for safeguarding the quality of the nation's air. Additionally, we incorporate stories of individuals on the front-lines of environmental policy implementation to enhance our understandings of these issues. With these deeper understandings and richer contexts, we hope to move the conversation forward in a productive manner about what the government should and should not do as it concerns the environment.

With this approach to environmental policy action, this book is intended for readers coming to the subject from a variety of contexts. For students in environmental studies and sustainability studies programs, this book will aid an understanding of the governmental and policy side of these issues. For students in political science and public administration, this book will help in applying core concepts in these fields to the environmental realm. For students in the natural sciences and engineering, this book will assist in explaining why seemingly obvious solutions to environmental challenges go unpursued in environmental policy.

Ultimately, our take on environmental policy issues comes from the passion and energy our students have shown us over many years and across institutions when it comes to tackling these very present and intense issues before us. We hope that this book helps advance understanding of environmental issues and helps chart a path forward because inaction is action, and inaction—particularly in this policy area—can have significant and lasting negative ramifications for us and generations to come.

Dayton, USA   Michelle C. Pautz
Missoula, USA   Sara R. Rinfret
November 2018

ACKNOWLEDGEMENTS

As is the case with the environmental issues we discuss in the following pages, the number of people who contributed to and supported our efforts developing and writing this book is significant. Therefore, while our names adorn the cover of this book, it is essential that we acknowledge a wonderful group of colleagues, friends, and family members that helped bring this book to fruition in its first edition and were equally essential in the revisions and additions for the second edition.

First and foremost, we must acknowledge our students who motivate us, challenge us, and sustain our passion for this topic and our hopes for future generations alive. We have both taught at a variety of institutions over many years and we continue to be impressed by our students who crave understanding in the hopes of making the world just a little bit better for the future. A number of students have helped us with various aspects over the course of both editions, including Emily Kaylor, Taylor Pair, Susan Weaver, and Jeff Cook. Jeff, a former student of Sara's, recently completed his Ph.D. in political science at Colorado State. He was instrumental in re-working Chapter 8. His passion for understanding the next generation of environmental policy should not go unnoticed and we thank him for his willingness to push us to revise and update.

In addition, our respective institutions and colleagues have been supportive of our work. At the University of Dayton, the colleagues in the Department of Political Science have been very supportive and encouraging, especially Dr. Grant Neeley who is a wonderful department chair. And members of the Ryan C. Harris Learning and Teaching Center, led by

Dr. Deb Bickford, Associate Provost for Academic Affairs, have been invaluable. At the University of Montana, Sara is indebted to the encouragement and support from her colleagues Anthony Johnstone, Andrea Vernon, Adam Brewer, Christina Barsky, Sam Panarella, and Brock Tessman. And colleagues at other institutions, including Dr. Denise Scheberle and Dr. Michael Kraft, have been supportive mentors throughout my career.

Each of us is supported by wonderful friends and family members who must be mentioned.

Sara could not have written this second edition without mentioning the support of family and colleagues. Her interests and passion for environmental policy come from living in the American West. The support of her parents to move west for graduate school was a life-changing experience, of which she is forever fortunate. Countless hikes and runs with her husband, Bob, provided an appreciation for the natural beauty of Arizona and Montana and its importance to the future of environmental policy. He has also supported countless revisions and editions. I am extremely fortunate to have learned from the best and brightest minds in the discipline from Northern Arizona University and Colorado State University—Drs. David Schlosberg, Jacqueline Vaughn, Chuck Davis, Sandra Davis, and Robert Duffy.

Most importantly, my students continue to inspire me. I am unbelievably humbled by and honored to work with so many students over the last decade. Their commitment to providing solutions for environmental problems is insurmountable, yearning to learn more and ask how. To my students that worked numerous hours to write their own plans to meet the University of Montana's carbon goals, thank you. This was not an easy endeavor and you each saw the politics behind policymaking firsthand. Regardless, our students are the future to our environmental success. As educators, we must continue to push ourselves and our students to discuss a variety of solutions to address the very real and imminent environmental problems of today and tomorrow.

Michelle must acknowledge teachers, mentors, colleagues, and friends and family. My abiding interest in environmental policy regulation started as a young girl interested in marine mammals, and this curiosity led to several transformative experiences as an undergraduate at Elon University. In the same year, I took environmental policy with Dr. Sharon Spray and environmental economics with Dr. Doug Redington. These courses convinced me that there was nothing I wanted to study more than environmental issues. I then had the good fortune to intern with what was then the North Carolina Department of Environment and Natural Resources thanks to Dr. Chalmers Brumbaugh. My passion for these issues only intensified as Dr. Betty Morgan helped me find my way to graduate studies in public administration at Virginia Tech. There, with the guidance of Dr. Karen Hult, Dr. Larkin Dudley, and the late Dr. John Rohr, I was able to continue my work in this area. I owe these educators and mentors an incredible debt for helping me find my path.

In addition to these individuals, the love and support of my friends and family are essential. Sara and I first met on a panel at the Midwest Political Science Association conference many years ago, and a productive professional relationship as well as a friendship has evolved that I am grateful for. Friends have enthusiastically listened to my ramblings about my research pursuits and writing for more hours than is fair, especially Danielle, Kurt, and Kris. But through all of it, Steven has stood next to me, challenging me when needed, listening with patience and kindness, and encouraging me always. Being married to an academic is not easy and Steven is the patient and supportive partner I never even knew I needed. Quite simply, I cannot imagine my life without him. And his grace and encouragement is accentuated by the love and support of our wonderful four-legged girls. Sydney and Victoria have grown accustomed to my long hours of research and writing and sit with me when they would probably rather be doing something else. Their supportive looks and occasional snores are so often just what I need. And while Mackenzie is getting used to hours spent reading and writing, her unwavering love of life is inspiring. And to Emma and Ellie whose paws are gone from this world, but who are forever in my heart, I owe them so much.

CONTENTS

LIST OF FIGURES

List of Tables

Environmental Policy in Practice

Contents

Lessons from *The Lorax*

Dr. Seuss's *The Lorax* presents readers with a choice: protect the land for future use, or develop the land for monetary gain. The story unfolds as a young boy attempts to understand what caused the extinction of the beautifully colored Truffula Trees. He discovers that the trees were cut down in order to produce Thneed needed for various products. Eventually, Thneed was overproduced, causing the natural landscape to become dark and dreary—a wasteland where no one wanted to live because of all the pollution. This story reminds us what happens when we make environmental choices; cutting down trees has costs and benefits.

© The Author(s) 2019   1
S. R. Rinfret and M. C. Pautz, *US Environmental Policy in Action*,
https://doi.org/10.1007/978-3-030-11316-2_1

The story of *The Lorax* struck a chord with former administrator of the US Environmental Protection Agency (EPA), Lisa Jackson; she hoped that the book, which was turned into a feature film in 2012, would help us understand the importance of protecting the environment (Nakashima 2012). During her time at the EPA, Jackson always kept a copy of *The Lorax* in her desk to remind her of the importance of protecting the environment (Boyle 2010). Even though the *Lorax* is a children's story, it serves as an essential lesson for modern-day environmental policymaking—"Unless someone like you cares a whole awful lot, nothing is going to get better. It's not" (Suess 1998).

The United States continues to confront a host of environmental issues that range from protecting the gray wolf in Wyoming, preventing drinking water contamination in Flint, Michigan to endeavoring to preserve biodiversity and combating climate change. Although the environmental problems we confront are more complex than those in Dr. Seuss's *The Lorax*, the choices they present are no less stark. The following pages unpack these challenges by exploring environmental policy in the United States.

We begin our conversation about environmental policy by defining key terms. First, a basic dictionary definition of "environmental policy" is necessary. The word "environment" encompasses our natural surroundings and includes how it is affected (e.g., pollution, water, sanitation). Here we define environmental policy as one area of public policy that the government is called to address by its citizens. More specifically, environmental policy is government action related to the natural environment.

Environmental policy is also about making tough choices. It is difficult because it can pit individuals against one another. The American public might be vehemently opposed to shutting down a coal company Colstrip, Montana that releases harmful pollutants because it means a loss of jobs for the community; however, that same public also wants a clean environment. Environmental policymaking is difficult because it brings together an enormous array of actors—institutional (Congress, the President, and the Courts) and noninstitutional actors (media, interest groups, political parties, and the public). All of these actors have their own perspectives and their own agendas.

In addition, environmental decision-making is challenging because the information age has brought us a deluge of material. Discerning fact from fiction can be frustrating and overwhelming. Historically, institutional actors, if they did not have the requisite information to make a decision, relied upon scientific or policy experts to inform and help them make the best, most informed choice. However, the temptation for institutional actors is to bypass outside expertise and advance their own decisions with information readily available from the click of a button from the first set of results from an Internet search. Moreover, for politicians, the temptation is to base choices increasingly on how they might help secure reelection (Jacobson 2012). For instance, if an elected member of Congress' congressional district has the highest unemployment rate in the United States, the goal is not going to be to shut down the local coal mining facility because jobs are needed; and this takes precedence over protecting the environment. However, what if this coal mining company's chemicals end up in the local water supply and kill thousands of citizens? As this example suggests, environmental policy is about difficult choices.

The focus of this introductory chapter is, first, to present a few environmental dilemmas (e.g., air pollution, water contamination, garbage disposal, and species protection) in order to examine the choices that the United States has made about these issues. Then, we introduce the reader to the central theme of our book: we need to pay attention to the doers of environmental policy, as they are the people on the front-lines of environmental policy, implementing society's choices.

With the term "front-lines," we are referring to the people who implement or carry out environmental policy on a daily basis. These individuals on the front-lines include environmental rule-writers, who translate congressional statutes into actionable policy, and environmental inspectors, who ensure that your neighborhood waste management company is complying with federal law to ensure that your waste is properly stored. They also include members of advocacy groups who urge collective action as well as policy analysts who provide the important facts and analysis we need to make decisions. Further, we cannot overlook those businesses that cooperate with rule-writers and environmental inspectors to protect the environment (Pautz and Rinfret 2013). The argument we make in this book is simple: in order to understand environmental choices made in the United States, we need to pay attention to the doers of environmental policy, many of which occupy the so-called fourth branch of government (i.e., the bureaucracy).

ENVIRONMENTAL DILEMMAS AND CHOICES

We offer a snapshot of environmental challenges (e.g., air pollution, climate change, hazardous and solid waste, etc.) and the choices the United States has made to address some aspects of these issues. These choices by no means indicate that these environmental issues have been resolved. The goal here is to introduce our readers to some examples, leaving the remaining pages of the book to fill in the details. So many of the challenges presented here continue to evolve and have no conclusion. After all, environmental policy evolves daily and with Republicans controlling the White House and the Senate and Democrats controlling the House of Representatives after the 2018 midterm elections, there will be even greater need for our institutional actors to bargain and compromise regarding the future of environmental policy.

Clean or Dirty Air?

Prior to the 1970s, the air quality in the United States was often defined as unhealthy or simply dirty because of the pollution that filled the air in many of our major cities, such as Los Angeles (Andrews 2006). Among the culprits of the dirty air were six major toxic pollutants: sulfur dioxide, nitrogen dioxide, carbon monoxide, particulates, lead, and ozone (Andrews 2006). These six pollutants are of concern because of their impact on the health and well-being of humans; but, what are the origins of these pollutants? For instance, carbon monoxide (the most common of the six) is colorless and odorless and is a product of burning fossil fuels (including running your car), and when there is too much of it in the air, it can cause an array of cardiovascular problems and even visual impairment.

Because of such concerns, Congress decided to establish air quality standards with the passage of the Clean Air Act (CAA) of 1970, which created National Ambient Air Quality Standards (NAAQS). The EPA, in implementing the NAAQS, established limits for the aforementioned six pollutants and continues to enforce these standards across the country (Kraft 2017). Going back to our example of carbon monoxide, the NAAQS standards forced car manufacturers to devise ways to produce cars that are cleaner burning. The EPA suggests that, when examining these six areas of pollutants that lead to poor air quality, significant improvements have been made over time. The EPA reports that, from

1980 to 2017, air quality in the United States has improved because the agency set standards that were required to be met; if not, fines resulted (US EPA Air Quality Trends 2014). To demonstrate some of these improvements, the EPA's longitudinal study of carbon monoxide from 1980 to 2017 reports a decrease by 77% (US EPA Air Quality 2014).

Cleaning up dirty skies may not seem to be a difficult choice, as evidenced earlier; however, challenges still exist today. For instance, why has Congress not passed new legislation to combat climate change? "Climate change" is the term explaining that the Earth is warming and, according to the EPA, the Earth's temperature has increased by 1.6 degrees Fahrenheit over the last century. Accordingly, the logical question then becomes: what has caused the temperature increases? The vast majority of scientific research supports the conclusion that human activities—through the burning of fossil fuels—have released significant quantities of carbon dioxide, posing a threat to human health. However, some US politicians, including Senator Jim Inhofe (R-OK), argue that the warming of the Earth is a natural occurrence, not a human-made one, and scientists should not be trusted to make these determinations. Some members of Congress agree with Senator Inhofe, and do not see the value in pursuing climate change policy because the consequences will be realized well after their life expectancy.

The choices we have available here are to either believe or not believe the science. Does climate change exist? As President Obama noted in his 2014 State of the Union address: "climate change is a fact." For some, though, the answer is not this simple.

Is It Really Drinkable?

Much like breathing clean air, it seems unfathomable that you could not drink the water from your faucet at home. However, safe drinking water has not always been available in the United States—and today there are still concerns about the tap water in Flint, Michigan. In 1976, Congress passed the Safe Drinking Water Act (SDWA). The SDWA established national standards to protect our drinking water from naturally occurring or human-made contaminants that might be found in drinking water. The US EPA works with state and local governments to ensure safe drinking water from the more than 160,000 public and private drinking water suppliers in the United States. Keep in mind that the SDWA does not regulate private wells that serve fewer than 25 individuals

(US EPA Drinking Water 2014). However, the United States does have some of the cleanest tap water in the world, which ensures we do not fill our drinking glasses with chromium or chlordane (Andrews 2006).

Threats to our drinking water still exist (McLendon 2014). One of the problems with the SDWA is that it does not regulate "nonpoint" sources, which include runoff from farms (e.g., cow manure), construction, or stormwater runoff (e.g., you are washing your car and the soap goes into the nearby drain). Thus, our water can still become polluted from sources that are classified as nonpoint because the exact origin cannot necessarily be determined. Let us hypothesize that a nearby river necessary for a town's water supply has high traces of fecal matter. The presumption is that the source of the contamination could be from the adjacent yogurt factory that has thousands of cows grazing in close proximity to the river. However, there are also several large farms alongside the river. Therefore, how could someone determine definitively the source of the drinking water contamination? One option would be to blame all of the farms, or at least the one closest to the drinking water facility. We know that contaminants upstream travel downstream, but how do you determine who is responsible? It is not an easy answer.

The SDWA routinely monitors and tracks only 91 contaminants. Yet, there are new chemicals manufactured each day and we are unaware of their effects on our tap water. For instance, methyl cyclohexane methanol (MCHM), a black licorice-smelling chemical that is used to clean coal, is not on the list of 91 routinely monitored contaminants. In 2014, a water treatment plant near Charleston, West Virginia found this chemical in the water (Levitz et al. 2014). Ingesting this chemical can cause vomiting and other flu-like ailments, but much is still unknown about MCHM.

MCHM's scary counterpart, TTHM (trihalomethanes—used in disinfection byproducts) was found in Flint, Michigan's drinking water supply in 2015. The City of Flint's testing showed high levels of lead in the drinking water supply—104 parts per billion. The acceptable EPA rate is fifteen parts per billion. These high levels of lead sparked a state of emergency declaration ordered by then President Obama. The argument in 2018 is that Flint's drinking water is still unsafe (Kennedy 2016).

The question driving these incidents is whether or not the EPA, or state equivalent, should be required to examine and test every single chemical ever manufactured, which would take significant amounts of time and resources.

Taking Out the Trash

No one—except *Sesame Street*'s Oscar the Grouch—likes trash, but few people think about it once the local garbage collector picks it up weekly and drives it away. However, there are safeguards—just as with the air we breathe and the water we drink—to protect us from solid waste through the Resource Conservation and Recovery Act (RCRA) of 1976.

Prior to the 1970s, the customary approach to taking out the trash was to dump it cheaply—often, in the ocean or burning it in a dumpsite (Andrews 2006). Obviously, these practices were not environmentally friendly and, with the creation of RCRA, Congress required the EPA to develop criteria for the safe disposal of hazardous waste. For instance, former EPA administrator William Ruckelshaus tried to implement "Mission 5000" to close 5000 out of the 14,000 reported dumps across the United States and convert into sanitary landfills. Ruckelshaus fell short of this mission, but, over time, all dumps had been closed and converted to sanitary landfills (Andrews 2006). By the 1980s, RCRA became even more stringent because of two horrific stories of hazardous waste disposal in Love Canal, New York and Times Beach, Missouri. Congress was disappointed with the EPA during these hazardous waste crises and amended the RCRA in 1984 to enact more stringent provisions requiring rapid EPA action (Kraft 2017). More specifically, the Comprehensive Environmental Response and Liability Act (CERCLA) of 1980 was set up to help provide the cleanup of previous toxic dumping sites.

According to the EPA, Americans generated about 250 million tons of trash in 2011 and, of this trash, 87 million tons were either recycled or composted (US EPA Wastes 2014). However, since 1960, these waste totals have increased by almost 60%, which is burdening local landfills that are on the brink of capacity in urban areas such as New York City, where expansion is limited (US EPA Wastes 2014). Many Americans do not consider the disposal of our daily trash as a crisis because we pay a monthly flat fee and it is easily taken away from our homes.

Regardless, the United States is facing a solid waste problem because landfills are full and finding new space is problematic—after all, who wants a landfill built next door. But, what are our choices in addressing our overcrowded landfills? One option is to provide incentives or more stringent policies that mandate recycling and composting to help alleviate overcrowding concerns. Another option is to charge Americans based upon their monthly use—the less you throw away, the less you get charged. Alternatively, all elementary and high school students could be required to take a class on the best practices of how to reduce the waste we generate. These options could be plausible, but are probably impossible because Americans hate to be required to do something.

Why Should We Care About Plants and Animals?

Apart from assuring that air and water are clean and the land is safe for humans, the United States has also been active in protecting the environment for plants and animals. On December 28, 2018, the United States celebrated the forty-fifth birthday of the Endangered Species Act (ESA) of 1973. The United States is one of the few countries that has national legislation to protect animals and plants from becoming extinct. Under the ESA, the U.S. Fish and Wildlife Service (USFWS) has the authority to protect and list endangered and threatened animals and plants. To date, the USFWS, through the ESA, has been able to protect approximately 99% of all species and plants that have been placed on the endangered or threatened lists from becoming extinct (Environment News Service 2014). The Trump administration is considering ways to weaken the ESA by adopting language to provide leniency for effected businesses (Resnick 2018).

Nonetheless, the ESA, like many other environmental laws, can spark controversy. For instance, what if you want to build a new golf course, but are told you are unable to do so because the building plans would inhibit the nests of the California Condor? Or, what happens when the USFWS determines that a species has met its population threshold and hunters determine in Wyoming that they will shoot and kill gray wolves to protect their livestock? The ESA is a noteworthy piece of legislation, but it has not come without controversy, particularly in western parts of the United States (Rinfret 2009).

As noted in the opening pages of this chapter, environmental policy is created through the efforts of various institutional and noninstitutional actors. As we have seen in a few of the aforementioned dilemmas, environmental issues can and do result in difficult choices. These choices have become even more difficult because of congressional gridlock—the inability of congressional policymakers to reach a compromise. Gridlock is problematic because many of the lingering challenges, ranging from climate change to what to do with overcrowding landfills, affect the daily lives of Americans; no one wants water that we cannot drink because of a chemical spill. Even with gridlock in Congress, environmental choices and policy are being made through a less obvious means.

While it is true the federal government creates environmental law for states and local governments to implement, this does not mean they are unimportant. With any environmental law, states must implement federal policy. States, however, can exceed federal minimum requirements or if there is not a federal policy (i.e., 10th amendment), states can create their own. California, for example, routinely sets much stronger environmental policies than the federal government does. In 2013, California created its own cap and trade system to reduce its greenhouse gas emission levels. Although touted by environmentalists as a work in progress, the California Supreme Court ruled it is not an unconstitutional tax on businesses. By way of comparison, the United States Congress has failed to adopt a national level cap and trade system.

Environmental policymaking is also made by bureaucrats in government agencies. For example, environmental rule-writers in the USFWS used legislation like the ESA designate critical habitat to protect the polar bear in Alaska. There are also thousands of government regulators who work for state-level environmental agencies such as the Montana Department of Environmental Quality. These state-level regulators monitor the local coal company, for example, to ensure the correct scrubber on its smokestack so the company does not pollute the air we breathe.

Plan of the Book

The chapters in this book are designed around one central theme: to better understand the doing and implementing of environmental policy through the often unnoticed actors on the front-lines. This is not to say that we disregard the more prominent actors, but we emphasize those actors who are often overlooked or absent from other textbooks. We argue that this focus is especially important in an era of congressional gridlock or lack of policy action for the environment at the most macro levels. Accordingly, this book addresses several elements missing in existing texts: (1) explanations and discussions of policy implementation from an institutional perspective, (2) illustrative case studies explaining foundational concepts, and (3) voices sections in each chapter so that readers can connect theory with practice.

In order to provide a solid foundation for our readers, Chapter 2 focuses on establishing a context in which environmental policy is made. This chapter begins by considering the history of environmental protection in the United States, starting with the conservation and preservation movements in the late nineteenth and early twentieth centuries. We focus on the modern environmental movement in the 1960s and overview the social and political movements that culminated in more than two dozen major environmental laws, which continue to provide the backbone of US environmental policy today. Within his conversation, we trace public opinion on environmental matters, past and present.

The final section of the chapter explores the role of scientific knowledge and information in environmental policy discussions. American society is seemingly more skeptical about scientific information than it was in the past; such skepticism impacts public discourse on environmental matters. Transmission of scientific knowledge is important, as the various perspectives on environmental issues increasingly debate the science itself, rather than debating what should be done in response to the science. Many of the insights we can draw contemporarily about environmental issues can be understood by how American society views scientific information. These discussions of public opinion and science help contextualize our look at the role Rachel Carson had in spurring a national focus on environmental concerns through her ability to communicate complex scientific information to the general public, notably through *Silent Spring*. The case study in this chapter considers the still ongoing drama in Flint, Michigan and the safety and quality of the drinking water in this city.

Chapter 3 builds on these foundations by delving into the process of policymaking in the United States. We begin with an overview of public policy and explore the stages heuristic model as a framework for understanding how policy is made. To help illustrate the realities of making environmental policy, we then review the stages model's shortcomings in understanding environmental policy. We use this discussion to demonstrate that environmental policy is not, often, made in the neat, linear fashion many would think; rather, it is a complex process that is often messy, vague, and unpredictable. After demonstrating the complexity of the policymaking process, we consider the various factors that influence the crafting of policy. Our case study in this chapter explores the policymaking process by using Superfund as an example. For our voices section, we examine the efforts of Governor Moonbeam, also known as

Governor Jerry Brown, to challenge his congressional colleagues to fight for the environment.

Chapter 4 delves into the key institutional (or official) actors and their impact on US environmental policy. More specifically, this chapter provides an in-depth discussion of how Congress, the courts, and the presidency have shaped environmental policy in the twenty-first century. In particular, we offer a brief overview of how each of the three branches of government has been instrumental in crafting the US environmental policy regime and how each of the players' roles has ebbed and flowed in recent decades. These perspectives are captured with our voices section on Senator James Inhofe (R-OK), and our chapter case study documents why congressional committees serve as the gatekeepers to US policymaking.

Chapter 5 examines the instrumental role that a variety of "unofficial actors" (i.e., interest groups, the media, and lobbyists) have played in shaping environmental policy in the United States. To understand the remarkable impact that groups can play in policymaking, the chapter begins with the voices of Women's Voices for the Earth, an organization devoted to sound the alarm on harmful toxins in women's feminine products. Detox the Box demonstrates how the work of grassroots interests can affect change on the front-lines of environmental policy. The closing section of the chapter uses the case of Daniel McGowan to determine whether the actions of this unofficial actor should be classified as environmental terrorism.

How vague policy language is translated into rules and regulations for organizations and individuals to follow is the focus of Chapter 6. The rulemaking process is frequently ignored in environmental policy discussions; however, it is through this process that policy is put into action. We begin this chapter with lessons from our voice, former EPA administrator Scott Pruitt. Then, we provide an overview of the rulemaking process, from the pre-proposal stage to rule finalization in the *Federal Register*. To document the nuts and bolts of the rulemaking process, the case study for this chapter examines corporate average fuel economy (CAFE) standards and how presidential changes can engender regulatory rollbacks. As our case study and voices section demonstrate, rulemaking is important, especially environmental rulemaking, but politics can affect progress.

Crucial to understanding environmental policy on the front-lines is investigating how environmental policy is implemented. Chapter 7 turns to the regulatory environment and begins by discussing the nature of command and control regulations and how they are the primary tool of environmental policy. In particular, we draw connections from earlier chapters as we discuss the governing and economic contexts that shape the implementation of environmental policy. As in Chapter 6, we focus on the actors in environmental policy in this chapter by highlighting the role of environmental inspectors, particularly the inspectors at the state level. These inspectors are the government officials who are responsible for the implementation of environmental regulation every day. We look at who these individuals are and what their experiences and challenges are like. For the case study in this chapter, we focus on the story of a regulated facility, its perspective, and the perspective of its environmental regulator. In our voices section, we explore the stories of a state air pollution control inspector, which enables our readers to gain a thorough understanding of what it is like to be an inspector. This discussion helps us understand the individuals who are responsible for protecting the environment on a daily basis.

Figuring out if environmental policy is working is more critical now than ever. Chapter 8 provides an overview of how environmental policy is evaluated and the complexities of its evaluation. Much of policy evaluation has to do with the quantification of various variables, which is understandably complex in this policy realm. We consider how this is done, with a significant portion of this chapter devoted to both understanding how cost–benefit analysis and risk assessment are conducted. Our chapter voice and case challenge the contemporary notions of cost–benefit analysis through an examination of environmental justice. Our voices section notes the important work of Matthew Tejada. Our case study examines longitudinal research on commercial hazardous waste, defining for the reader, the intricate details of environmental justice in the United States.

Chapter 9 explores the natural resource and energy policy nexus that often defines environmental policy in the American West. This chapter begins with the voice of Representative Raul Grijalva and a family vacation to Grand Canyon National Park. This introductory story gets at the heart of the interconnectedness of natural resource and energy policy. The majority of public lands are managed by federal agencies (e.g., BLM, USFWS, USFS, NPS). Yet, within these lands are resources that could be used for energy development in the United States The chapter concludes with the case of the Dakota Access Pipeline to the true complexities of the actors involved trying to influence public policy outcomes.

Discussions of environmental policy often focus on pollution, natural resources, and energy. The role of food production and consumption on these areas is significant, so Chapter 10 focuses on food policy. The chapter begins with a look at former First Lady Michelle Obama's White House vegetable garden as indicative of the complexities and intersectionality of food and the environment. Then the chapter goes on to discuss food production and consumption in the United States, along with the role of the government in providing dietary guidance to Americans. Nutrition labels on food products sold in the United States are a piece of the government's role in protecting public health and ensuring food safety. The role of food in our society and the cultural trends around the topic are also investigated. The case study in this chapter explores the challenges of creating regulations for the national school lunch program.

Finally, Chapter 11 looks at environmental policy, past, present, and future. The chapter offers three overarching characteristics of environmental policy today: (1) hyper-partisanship, (2) gridlock at national level, and (3) emerging questions about the role of government in environmental protection. The chapter notes that uncertainty abounds about the government's role in environmental protection. This does not mean environmental issues will halt government action, but instead, demand solutions for growing consequences we face. Accordingly, we identify five needs for the future of environmental policy in action.

Chapter Wrap-Up

Overall, this textbook provides a comprehensive look at the creation, implementation, and evaluation of environmental policy. Understanding environmental policy is not just a function of political science that many traditional environmental policy textbooks emphasize. We continue where many textbooks leave off with discussions about the roles of political institutions and we build on this conversation with an examination of how environmental policy is implemented and evaluated from the ground up.

Therefore, we examine the processes of implementation and evaluation along with the often-neglected actors who are critical to these aspects of environmental policy (i.e., environmental inspectors and rule-writers). Such an examination is particularly important as most environmental policymaking is done via alternative means because of persistent congressional gridlock. Nevertheless, as the Lorax says, "It is not about what it is. It's about what it can become" (Seuss 1998).

SUGGESTED RESOURCES
Readings and Websites

Andrews, Richard L. *Managing the Environment, Managing Ourselves: A History of American Environmental Policy.* New Haven, CT: Yale University Press, 2006.

Fifth Assesment Report. "Intergovernmental Panel on Climate Change." Accessed October 15, 2018. http://www.ipcc.ch/report/sr15/.

Seuss, Dr. *The Lorax.* Nashville, TN: Randall House Publishers, 1998.

Films or Videos

Before the Flood. Directed by Fisher Stevens. 2016. Appian Way, Dune Entertainment.

The Future of Energy: Lateral Power to the People. 2016. Directed by Brett Mazurek.

The 11th Hour. Directed by Leila Conners and Nadia Conners. 2007. Appian Way, Greenhour, and Tree Media Group. DVD.

The Lorax. 2012. Chris Renard and Kyle Balda. Los Angeles, CA: Universal Studio. DVD.

REFERENCES

Andrews, Richard L. *Managing the Environment, Managing Ourselves: A History of American Environmental Policy.* New Haven, CT: Yale University Press, 2006.

Boyle, Lisa Kass. "Earth and the Balance of Power What the Citizens United Ruling Means for the Environment." *Huffington Post*, February 6, 2010. http://www.huff-ingtonpost.com/.

Environmental News Service. "Celebrating 40 Years of Endangered Species Success." Accessed January 30, 2014. http://ens-newswire.com/2013/12/31/celebrating-40-years-of-endangered-species-act-success/.

Jacobson, Gary C. *Politics of Congressional Elections.* Upper Saddle, NJ: Pearson, 2012.

Kennedy, Merritt. 2016. https://www.npr.org/sections/thetwo-way/2016/04/20/465545378/lead-laced-water-in-flint-a-step-by-step-look-at-the-makings-of-a-crisis.

Kraft, Michael E. *Environmental Policy and Politics.* 5th edition. New York: Longman, 2017.

Levitz, Jennifer, Cameron McWhirter, and Valerie Bauerlein. "West Virginia Begins to Lift Water Ban." *Wall Street Journal*, January 14, 2014. http://online.wsj.com/.

McLendon, Russell. "How Polluted Is U.S. Drinking Water?" Accessed January 30, 2014. http://www.mnn.com/earth-matter/translating-uncle-sam/stories/how-polluted-is-us-drinking-water.

Nakashima, Ryan. "The Lorax: Green Commerical Tie-Ins for Dr. Suess Film." *Huffington Post*, February 8, 2012. http://www.huffingtonpost.com/.

Pautz, Michelle C., and Sara R. Rinfret. *The Lilliputians of Environmental Regulation: The Perspectives of State Regulators*. New York: Routledge, 2013.

Resnick, Brian. 2018. https://www.vox.com/energy-and-environment/2018/7/20/17594908/endangered-species-act-trump-proposal-change-weaken.

Rinfret, Sara R. "Changing the Rules: Federal Environmental Rulemaking." PhD dissertation, Northern Arizona University, 2009.

Seuss, Dr. *The Lorax*. Nashville, TN: Randall House Publishers, 1998.

US EPA. "Air Quality Trends." Accessed January 30, 2014. http://www.epa.gov/air-trends/aqtrends.html.

———. "Drinking Water." Accessed January 20, 2014. http://www.epa.gov/epawaste/nonhaz/municipal/index.htm.

———. "Wastes-Non Hazardous." Accessed January 20, 2014. http://www.epa.gov/epawaste/nonhaz/municipal/index.htm.

The Development and Context of American Environmental Policy

Contents

Rachel Carson, the Biologist Who Galvanized a Movement

Rachel Carson was a marine biologist who worked for the U.S. Fish and Wildlife Service and is widely credited with galvanizing the modern environmental movement with the publication of her book *Silent*

© The Author(s) 2019   17
S. R. Rinfret and M. C. Pautz, *US Environmental Policy in Action*,
https://doi.org/10.1007/978-3-030-11316-2_2

Spring. Her role in fundamentally altering the nation's pesticide industry seemed unlikely given her roots and her gender. Born in rural Pennsylvania, not too far from Pittsburgh, in 1907, Carson spent much of her early years exploring her family's farm. She loved to read and write stories about the natural environment. This led to her original intention to study English at the Pennsylvania College for Women (now known as Chatham University), but she changed her major to biology. She graduated in 1929 and then went on to Johns Hopkins University where she studied zoology as a part-time student while working in a lab to earn money for tuition. When she completed her master's degree in 1932 she had planned on continuing her education and earning a doctorate, but ended up returning home to help her family during the Great Depression. Just a few years later, her father died suddenly, worsening the family's financial situation. Carson then went to work in a temporary position for the U.S. Bureau of Fisheries, writing scripts for a radio program to educate people about marine life. During this time, she also published her own essays on related topics. Over time, her position at the Bureau of Fisheries evolved to where she analyzed data on fisheries and wrote brochures for the public and she eventually came to supervise a small group of writers within the agency, which eventually became known as the U.S. Fish and Wildlife Service.

In 1945, Carson wrote for the first time about the new, revolutionary pesticide, dichlorodiphenyltrichloroethane, better known as DDT. It would be almost two decades before she wrote a book about the subject. During the intervening years, Carson wrote a lot about the ocean and marine life, including the books *The Sea Around Us* and *The Edge of the Sea*. Her writing became prolific enough and spurred enough speaking engagements that Carson was able to resign from the USFWS to write full time. By the late 1950s, Carson was following developments around DDT and its widespread use in agriculture and began writing about it and its harm to the environment and public health. These efforts culminated in the publication in 1962 of *Silent Spring*. The thrust of her book was that pesticides can have negative effects on much more than their intended target through the food chain. She also accused the chemical industry of lying about the effects of its product.

As you might imagine, the book was highly criticized and ignited a firestorm upon publication. She was by no means the first to discuss the dangers of DDT—a pesticide that has been since banned in the

United States—but her book became a best seller and sold millions of copies. The scientific community reviewed her work and supported her research and analysis, but the chemical industry responded very negatively to the book (as might be expected). Ultimately, Congress was spurred into action. Her book was written in a manner that was accessible to scientists and the general public alike. It was serialized in *The New Yorker* and featured in the Book of the Month program. News media covered the book and the debate it sparked. Carson was already ill from breast cancer and its treatments and she died in April 1964.

Her efforts to convey complex scientific information to the general public are widely credited with leading to the ban of DDT and catapulting environmental concerns to the forefront of the nation's attention in the 1960s. She persisted in her efforts and forever changed how Americans thought about pesticides and the environment more broadly.

To understand the challenges of environmental policy today, and to place in context the role of Rachel Carson (along with many others), we have to start at the beginning. By reviewing the development of environmental policy in the United States, we understand better the context of environmental policymaking today. More specifically, this chapter will explore the history of environmental policy in the United States, examine in greater detail the American public's evolving opinion on environmental issues, and consider how society deals with complex scientific and technical issues. Without this understanding, it would be difficult to understand our present challenges in environmental policy.

As we explore the historical context of environmental policy in this chapter, several important themes emerge. First, notice that the US government, albeit at different levels (e.g., federal, state, and local), has been involved in environmental policy for a long time. Our look at environmental policy's history will begin with Colonial America, despite the common misconception that the United States only waded into environmental policy in the 1960s. Second, we focus on how the government's role in environmental matters has ebbed and flowed over time due to the ever-changing mood of the American public and political leadership and this is likely to continue in this policy area. Third, since the 1990s, the traditional means of making environmental policy—notably, con-gressional action—have largely stalled for reasons we will discuss. But this does not mean that environmental policy action is not happening as there are alternative pathways. These less obvious means of policymak-ing are growing in their use. The major themes of the development of environmental policy will define environmental policy into the future. Accordingly, we begin by investigating the first efforts of governmental action regarding the environment before turning to public opinion and public discourse on science.

HISTORICAL EVOLUTION OF US ENVIRONMENTAL POLICY

Most people think that the US government first became involved in environmental matters during the 1960s, alongside the other major social movements of the era. This is not the case. Although it was not called environmental policy or thought of in this manner, colonial Americans passed important local ordinances that are essential to our understanding of our relationship with the environment. In this section, we take a chronological approach to investigating the history of environ-mental policy and draw some conclusions about each time period.

Colonial America

Even before the United States formally existed as a country, its colonial residents demonstrated some concern over the environment and aware-ness of the need for its health. As early as 1626, colonists in Plymouth (in Massachusetts Bay Colony) passed ordinances limiting the harvesting and sale of timber (Andrews 2006; Nash 1990; Vaughn 2007). This is not to say that these early settlers were environmentalists as we might think of today, because they did try to control nature and fundamen-tally alter it; however, there is some indication that these early Americans thought overharvesting needed to be curbed along with maintaining nat-ural spaces. In 1681, William Penn set aside lands in Pennsylvania to be kept natural, and Massachusetts followed suit in 1691 (Vaughn 2007). Moreover, other colonies took various steps to preserve some of their own resources. For example, there were hunting bans in Massachusetts and measures to protect coastal waterfowl in New York. Similarly, Connecticut passed laws to protect its game animals. It is also worth not-ing that many of the nation's founders, including George Washington and Thomas Jefferson, were concerned with the health of the environment on their own estates, as evidenced by their frequent mentions of these matters in correspondence and journals. To summarize early America's concern with the environment, we can conclude that there were some limited and local government efforts to address environmental concerns about the use of natural resources.

Nineteenth Century

As the eighteenth century gave way to the nineteenth, the United States began to establish itself and to grow both in terms of population and territory. The acquisition of new territories spawned quests to explore these newly incorporated lands and the explorers' tales of their adventures captivated Americans. Lewis and Clark began their famous expedition westward in 1804, and trips to explore and settle lands continued throughout the century.

Furthermore, changing landscapes dominated the young country in different ways, particularly toward the end of the century. The late 1800s saw dramatic population shifts as industrialization enticed many Americans to leave rural, agrarian lifestyles for urban centers where jobs in factories offered a way to move up in society. With large numbers of people living in urban areas, concerns arose that anyone might expect when lots of people live near one another in a confined space—garbage, waste, and other sanitation issues. Cities across the country, including Philadelphia, New York, Boston, Chicago, and St. Louis, saw significant rises in their populations, and had to confront new challenges. Not only were there concerns about growing numbers of people living together in urban areas, but the reasons many people moved to cities—factory jobs—brought even more environmental challenges. These factories and tanneries contributed to concerns over environmental impacts of these operations (Andrews 2006).

The end of the nineteenth century brought a variety of reform movements, often encapsulated in the broader moniker of the Progressive Era. Demands for improved working conditions, increased sanitation, prohibition of alcohol, and other social reforms abounded. It was also during this time that the formal, academic study of public administration—the doing of government—emerged, as government was increasingly called upon to address societal ills.

With this foundation, we better understand how concerns about the environment came about in the 1800s, because they were often couched within broader movements focused on public health conditions and the increasing desire for outdoor recreation. As germ theory[1] emerged along with new understandings of the need for sanitation, worry over the emissions from factories and their dumping of wastes also surfaced. In addition, as people's lifestyles evolved when they left rural areas for urban ones, there was increasing desire for recreation in open spaces. In particular, hunting and other activities in the natural environment were fashionable, particularly for the well-to-do in society. Magazines such as *The American Sportsmen* and *Forest & Stream* expressed concern over the quality and quantity of game and fish stocks for sportsmen. These instrumental motivations for environmental health parallel other motivations.

Intrinsic reasons also explain the growing focus on environmental issues. The term ecology was first coined in the late 1800s. Published in 1854, Henry David Thoreau's *Walden* details his two years living in a small cabin on Walden Pond in Massachusetts. In his writing, Thoreau describes his observations about nature and the growing disconnect between humans and nature. His book was initially slow to find a wide readership, but over time it did, contributing to the growing focus on nature. George Perkins Marsh wrote *Man and Nature* in 1864, which called for planting measures to thwart erosion and for the protection of songbirds in response to the impact of human activity on the natural environment. Other ways of noting human connection with the environment are exemplified in the First Arbor Day in 1872 and the creation of the Sierra Club by John Muir in 1892.

The federal government, furthermore, took a number of actions to signal that environmental issues—albeit not necessarily characterized as such—were an area of emphasis. Congress passed the Homestead Act in 1862 that permitted people to receive 160 acres of public lands if they lived on it and worked the land. More than 250 million acres of public lands were converted to private ownership as a result of this law (Kraft 2011, 91). In 1871, the US Fish Commission[2] was created, and it was the first federal agency responsible for the conservation of a specific natural resource (Vaughn 2007, 12). Although George Catlin first proposed the

---

[1] Germ theory is the idea that diseases are caused by various micro-organisms and sanitary conditions can help stem the ill effects of such organisms.

[2] This commission later became the U.S. Fish and Wildlife Service.

idea of a national park in the 1830s, it was not until the 1870s that the first national parks were created. Two million acres spanning across three states near the upper Yellowstone River were set aside to form Yellowstone National Park in 1872. Sequoia, Kings Canyon, and Yosemite National Parks were created shortly thereafter. Rounding out some of these highlights was the creation of large subsidy programs to ranchers, farmers, and mining companies to encourage resource development.

By the close of the nineteenth century, it would be difficult to define as a movement any of the actions described earlier surrounding the natural environment and its health, but the beginnings of interest in environmental and resource issues is evident. These starts, however, gave way to a more concerted movement in the early 1900s.

Early Twentieth Century: 1900s–1930s

The turn of the twentieth century brought with it the definitive beginnings of an environmental movement in the United States. The origins of this movement center on the debate between conservationists and preservationists, which is still evident today. Accordingly, we begin with an overview of this debate and then continue through the entire century and the birth of the modern environmental movement.

The first few decades of the twentieth century can be encapsulated by the conservation and preservation movements and the tension between the two. Conservationists, led by Gifford Pinchot (who would go on to lead the U.S. Forest Service) embraced the idea that natural resources could be used in a sustainable way that would allow for the growth and development of society. Advocates of conservation emphasized the efficient use of resources for development and took an instrumental view of nature. Such a view indicates that nature is valued because one sees value for human use of it. In other words, one might value the wellbeing of nature because she wants to ensure plenty of healthy fish in the nearby pond for fishing.

In contrast, preservationists sought to preserve wilderness and natural resources from any development other than for recreation and education. An oft-cited preservationist is John Muir who founded the Sierra Club—the first major environmental organization—in 1892. The preservationists believed that the environment had value in its own right—intrinsic value. In other words, the fish in the aforementioned pond have value because they are fish—unrelated to a person's interest or use of those fish. However, generally speaking, the conservationists dominated government action regarding the environment. President Theodore Roosevelt was a champion of the conservation movement; his passion for the natural environment began as a young man who loved studying nature, and this love was manifested in his desire to better understand it by perfecting his hobby of taxidermy. He was an avid sportsman and spent a good deal of time out West camping, hunting, and exploring.

The debates between conservationists and preservationists are contextualized in the broader social and economic context of the early twentieth century. As noted earlier, in the late 1800s, public health and sanitation concerns emerged, and the first local government laws were passed dealing with pollution, which was increasingly recognized as a public health issue. Chicago and Cincinnati were the first cities to approve air pollution laws and, by 1920, more than three dozen cities had similar laws (Kraft 2011, 92). However, it was not until 1952 that the first state—Oregon—passed state air pollution laws (Kraft 2011, 92; Portney 2000; Ringquist 1993). In addition, the dust bowls of the 1930s brought attention to drought and erosion. These severe dust storms caused major damage to America's prairie and farmlands, particularly in the erosion of topsoil. Finally, a number of environmental organizations continued to emerge, including the National Audubon Society in 1905, the National Parks Association in 1919, the Izaak Walton League in 1922, the Wilderness Society in 1935, and the National Wildlife Federation in 1936 (see Chapter 5 for more information on environmental organizations).

As we already indicated, most of the federal government's actions during these decades were focused on land management and the conservation of the nation's natural resources. In 1903, President Theodore Roosevelt created a Public Lands Commission to help the development of land and, then, in 1905, Roosevelt tapped Gifford Pinchot to run the newly created Forest Service. A few years later, the White House convened a Conference on Resource Management organized by Pinchot that attracted more than 1000 leaders for a few days in May 1908 (Vaughn 2007, 14). This meeting concluded with the recommendation that the president created a National Conservation Commission to catalog the nation's natural resources, which was done. By the following year, 41 states had created similar state-level agencies. Moreover, this conference discussed forest, soil, and water management issues. In 1916 the National Park Service was created. Subsequent presidents continued to oversee the creation of new national forests and other laws to protect particular species.

As the country grappled with the Great Depression, President Franklin D. Roosevelt was largely concerned with economics and social policy; however, components of the New Deal focused on natural resource issues. In particular, the Tennessee Valley Authority, created in 1933, sought to provide low-cost energy to Americans. Other programs included the Soil Conservation Service and the Civilian Conservation Corps, which addressed a variety of environmental concerns and put Americans to work during the height of the Depression.

Furthermore, there were a number of congressional actions during the 1930s that are notable. In 1934, the Taylor Grazing Act was passed to address overgrazing on America's grasslands and, 2 years later, the Flood Control Act delegated to the Army Corps of Engineers the responsibility for developing and implementing policies to protect watersheds and improve flood control. Federal government actions along these lines were firmly in the purview of government action by the outbreak of World War II (Vaughn 2007, 15).

Mid-Twentieth Century: 1940s and 1950s

The end of World War II saw great changes in American society. Success on the war front and emergence from dire economic circumstances left the American population much more hopeful, optimistic, and proud. Although the Harry Truman and Dwight D. Eisenhower administrations were far more concerned with national security threats and the spread of communism, environmental issues surfaced on the national scene. Eisenhower maintained, however, that pollution issues were a state and local government matter rather than a federal issue (Sussman et al. 2002, 4). With peace and economic growth, Americans began to focus on leisure, recreation, and quality-of-life concerns. Americans flocked to the national parks in pursuit of recreation and leisure. More than 30 million people toured national parks in 1950, compelling the government to grow the parks system (Vaughn 2007, 15).

Although the federal government's concerns were largely focused elsewhere, there are two notable federal environmental laws passed during this time period: the Federal Water Pollution Control Act of 1948 and the Air Pollution Control Act of 1955. Although neither law was much of a success, these laws signal the first attempts of the federal government to enact legislation aimed at addressing the growing pollution problem in the United States. The Federal Water Pollution Control Act was intended to prevent and mitigate water pollution, mostly through delegation of responsibilities to the states, as it was widely presumed that states were responsible for water quality. The law did little to stem pollution, as it did not require any direct reductions in pollution to the nation's waterways. Congress largely gutted and rewrote the act in the early 1970s because it was so ineffective, and the new act became the modern Clean Water Act (CWA). In addition to concerns over the quality of water, air quality was also a concern by the mid-1950s. Smog and soot were increasingly problematic in major metropolitan areas, including Los Angeles. Again, Congress responded by passing the 1955 Air Pollution Control Act, which was the first federal legislation intended to address air pollution. The act stipulated that air pollution was a threat to public health, but it did little to address air pollution, as the law mostly called for government research into the effects of air pollution and methods of reducing it.

Examining these two decades reveals that the federal government was tepidly entering into the arena of environmental concerns, although its emphases clearly lay with national security threats. What is important to note about the decades preceding the birth of the modern environmental movement is the emergence of a citizenry increasingly able to turn its attention to quality-of-life issues—such as pollution—as the dire economic circumstances of the 1930s and World War II gave way to economic growth and prosperity in the 1950s.

The Birth of the Modern Environmental Movement

The 1960s in America are synonymous with a tumultuous period of significant social change. The increasingly affluent population made significant educational advancements and emphasized quality-of-life concerns alongside conflict abroad. The Civil Rights Movement and the Women's Movement, along with many others, toppled traditional societal norms. Moreover, conflict in Southeast Asia escalated, and the United States soon saw itself embroiled in a war in Vietnam. These events and movements compelled distrust in the establishment, particularly governmental organizations and corporations, and this distrust grew and permeated many aspects of life.

Growing concerns regarding the environment mounted as well. In particular, rapidly advancing scientific and technical knowledge led to concerns over the effects of seemingly benign, everyday things like pesticides. As discussed in the chapter's opening story, Rachel Carson, a biologist wrote the book *Silent Spring* (published in 1962), which was intended for the lay audience and detailed the dangerous effects of pesticides, dichlorodiphenyltrichloroethane (DDT) in particular, on wildlife and led to a considerable public panic. This book is widely credited with galvanizing the modern environmental movement, as it topped bestseller lists and led to the ban of DDT. Other notable books of this decade underscored the need to reconceptualize the relationship between society and nature, including Paul Ehrlich's *The Population Bomb*.

Before one thinks that it was only books that changed the public discourse on environmental concerns, rest assured that numerous focusing events spurred the public as well. For example, the Cuyahoga River in Cleveland, Ohio was, at one time, so polluted that sections of it could not sustain fish life. In addition, there were numerous instances in the 1950s and 1960s when the river literally caught on fire from all the toxic sludge. A fire was so bad in 1969 that the Cuyahoga River was featured in *Time* magazine. Two major oil spills off the coast of Santa Barbara, California, in early 1969—just days into Richard Nixon's administration—captured the attention of the media. These events, featured prominently in the news, helped solidify the public's demand for governmental action.

Although these particular events occurred in the latter part of the decade, the federal government increasingly took action over the course of the entire decade. In 1963, the first Clean Air Act (CAA) was passed, and subsequently amended in 1967; it authorized public hearings on air pollution issues. The following year (1964) saw the passage of the Wilderness Act that set aside tracts of public lands and barred development so as to preserve some lands in their natural condition. Furthermore, in 1964, the Land and Wildlife Conservation Fund Act was enacted, which coordinated local, state, and federal government efforts to acquire and develop lands. Other pieces of federal legislation include the Water Quality Act passed in 1965, the Endangered Species Preservation Act in 1966, and the Wild and Scenic Rivers Act and National Trails Act, both in 1968.

Arguably, the most significant piece of federal legislation came in 1969 with the passage of the National Environmental Policy Act

(NEPA). The purpose of NEPA is "to declare a national policy which will encourage productive and enjoyable harmony between man and his environment; to promote efforts which will prevent or eliminate damage to the environment and biosphere and stimulate the health and welfare of man; to enrich the understanding of the ecological systems and natural resources important to the nation; and to establish a Council on Environmental Quality" (NEPA 42 USC § 4321). This statute is a key environmental law that (1) establishes national environmental policy goals, (2) requires the federal government to analyze the environmental impacts of proposed projects and devise ways to mitigate negative environmental impacts, and (3) creates the Council on Environmental Quality within the White House. NEPA is largely a procedural environmental law that requires any federal executive agency to review how proposed agency action may impact the environment. Therefore, if an agency is considering a new program or project, such as building a highway, the agency has to study the environmental impacts it might cause and conduct an environmental assessment (EA) or, if the impacts are more significant, produce an environmental impact statement (EIS). Without delving into a lot of detail about these procedures here, suffice it to say that the research and investigation that coincides with the preparation of such statements can significantly alter an agency's course of action so as to lessen its environmental impact.

The 1960s saw the emergence of the full-fledged modern environmental movement, born of the broader social unrest of the time period, numerous focusing events, and a ramping up of governmental action as it related to the environment. These first steps toward a comprehensive national environmental policy laid the groundwork for the 1970s—arguably, the most productive decade ever of environmental policymaking (and Table 2.1 summarizes the major environmental laws).

The 1970s: The Development of Modern Environmental Regulation

The beginning of the 1970s continued the momentum of the previous decade regarding environmental protection. Almost all major environmental laws, federal environmental agencies, and mainstream environmental interest groups appeared during this decade. Moreover—and of particular interest contemporarily—most of the governmental action regarding the environment enjoyed broad, bipartisan support from politicians and citizens alike.

Table 2.1 Major environmental laws

Year	Environmental law
1969	• National Environmental Policy Act
1970	• Clean Air Act Amendments
1972	• Federal Water Pollution Control Act Amendments (better known as the Clean Water Act)
	• Federal Insecticide, Fungicide, and Rodenticide Act
	• Marine Mammal Protection Act
1973	• Endangered Species Act
1974	• Safe Drinking Water Act
1976	• Resource Conservation and Recovery Act
	• Toxic Substances Control Act
	• National Forest Management Act
	• Federal Land Policy and Management Act
1977	• Clean Air Act Amendments
	• Surface Mining and Reclamation Act
1980	• Comprehensive Emergency Response, Compensation, and Liability Act (better known as Superfund)
1986	• Emergency Planning and Community Right to Know Act
	• Superfund Amendments and Reauthorization Act
1990	• Clean Air Act Amendments
	• Oil Pollution Act
	• Pollution Prevention Act

Two pivotal events in 1970 demonstrated the nation's determination to protect the environment. The first Earth Day was celebrated on April 22, 1970 by millions of Americans and it continues to be celebrated annually. Rosenbaum (2011) describes the first event as the "Big Bang of U.S. environmental politics" (7). Senator Gaylord Nelson (D-Wisconsin) founded Earth Day by calling for an environmental teach-in. Earth Day events were held around the nation. At the end of the same year, the US Environmental Protection Agency (EPA) was created by President Richard Nixon via executive order. Nixon recognized the need for a single agency to coordinate and oversee a coherent national environmental policy and he appointed William Ruckelshaus was the agency's first administrator. President Nixon was not a passionate environmentalist, but he realized the importance of responding to the public's demand for environmental action and building momentum in Congress; therefore, he took action. These two events in the same year set the trend for the decade, and signaled the national emphasis on environmental protection.

In addition to these happenings, key focusing events kept the nation's attention on the health of the environment. The 1973 Arab oil embargo brought energy policy center stage as the Organization of Petroleum Exporting Countries (OPEC) voted to cut oil production by 5% and Saudi Arabia halted oil exports to the United States because of US support of Israel, thus leading to gasoline shortages in the United States. Toward the end of the decade, a neighborhood in Niagara Falls, New York became the go-to example of what happens when hazardous chemicals are buried beneath ground and, then, an elementary school is built atop the contaminated ground. This environmental disaster, known as Love Canal, led to the passage of legislation designed to clean up environmental hazards (for more on Love Canal, see Chapter 3). In 1979, the Three Mile Island Nuclear Generating Station near Middletown, Pennsylvania experienced a partial nuclear meltdown, heightening concerns about the safety and reliability of nuclear power. With these events and growing government action, numerous environmental organizations got their start in the 1970s. For instance, the League of Conservation Voters, the Natural Resources Defense Council, Save the Bay, Greenpeace, and Public Citizen all started during this time.

With the tremendous focus on the environment, the federal government embarked on its most productive decade of environmental policymaking ever, with many of the laws falling under the purview of the newly created US EPA. In 1970, the Air Pollution Control law, passed 15 years earlier, was dramatically overhauled and became the CAA that is still the guiding federal law on air quality today. The CAA mandated, for the first time, federal air pollution standards and put in place a regulatory structure to ensure that the laws were enforced. Under the CAA, both mobile (e.g., vehicle) and stationary (e.g., industrial) sources of air pollution would be subjected to emissions limits. In addition, four major regulatory programs were started under the CAA: the National Ambient Air Quality Standards (NAAQS), State Implementation Plans (SIPs), New Source Performance Standards (NSPS), and the National Emissions Standards for Hazardous Air Pollutants (NESHAPs).

Just two years later, a similar overhaul of the 1948 Federal Water Pollution Control law was passed and became the modern CWA in 1972. Much like the dramatic overhaul that came with the 1970 CAA, the 1972 CWA completely restructured the federal government's approach to ensuring water quality. Waste could no longer be discharged from a point source (e.g., pipes into bodies of water) without a permit to ensure certain emissions limits were followed. The CWA set national water quality goals and established the National Pollution Discharge Elimination System (NPDES). In addition, a grant program was established under this law to fund the building of wastewater treatment plants around the nation. Similar to the CAA, the CWA included enforcement provisions that would ensure the limits would be followed, unlike the environmental legislation from prior decades. It is worth noting that President Nixon vetoed the CWA, citing economic and inflation concerns, but the Congress easily overrode the presidential veto.

Additional laws enacted during this decade merit mention. In 1972, the Coastal Zone Management Act was passed that gave grants to states to establish coastal zone management plans. The Marine Mammal Protection Act and the Federal Environmental Pesticides Control Act were also passed the same year. In 1973, the Endangered Species Act was passed that mandated the government list certain species as threatened or endangered in an effort to protect species from extinction. The passage of the Safe Drinking Water Act that provided the first federal standards protecting the quality of the nation's drinking water came in 1974. President Gerald Ford begrudgingly signed this law although it enjoyed broad support in Congress.

In 1976, Congress passed the National Forest Management Act, the Federal Land Policy Management Act (FLPMA), the Toxic Substances Control Act (TSCA), and the Resource Conservation and Recovery Act (RCRA). The last two laws require a little elaboration. The TSCA requires chemical substances to be tested to ascertain their environmental impacts before being sold on the open market, and the Act permits the EPA to regulate or ban any substances that pose "an unbearable risk of injury to health or to the environment." The RCRA continues to be the key law governing hazardous wastes in this country; RCRA requires national standards for the treatment, storage, and disposal of hazardous waste and takes a "cradle-to-grave" approach regarding such hazards.

The last few years of the decade saw the election of the first avowedly environmental president, Jimmy Carter. Unlike his predecessors, President Carter portrayed himself as an environmentalist, and expectations for his presidency were high. During his time in the White House, the Surface Mining Control and Reclamation Act was passed in 1977 that established the first federal standards for strip mining operations and required restoration of lands that were mined. Amendments to both the CAA and CWA were passed and, in the last days of his administration, the Comprehensive Environmental Response, Compensation, and Liability Act (CERCLA) was passed. In October 1977, the Department of Energy was created to bring together the disparate energy programs in various governmental agencies.

By the end of the 1970s, the United States had an impressive statutory and regulatory framework from which to protect the nation's environment. For the first time, federal agencies were devising environmental standards that, if not met, would have real consequences for those that violated them. Concerns over the environment were, clearly, here to stay and the nation seemed committed to doing what it could to improve and protect the health of the environment. Nonetheless, with more than 10 years of experience trying to ensure environmental protection, Americans began to see the challenges with their regulatory structure and have experience with the costs associated with such protection.

The 1980s: Changing Course with Environmental Protection

The productivity of the 1970s provided the United States ample opportunity to gain significant experience implementing an array of environmental protection measures. This familiarity led to growing debates over the best approach to environmental policy in the United States in the 1980s that have continued developing ever since. In particular, key themes include the disintegration of the bipartisan consensus that produced the major statutes just a handful of years prior, intensification of arguments about costs and economic considerations associated with environmental protection, and debate over the role of government in this policy arena. Although much of the foundation of environmental policy remained intact throughout the 1980s, significant steps were taken to undo policies, and approaches were reassessed during this decade.

For the first time, the environmental movement was put on the defensive with the election of Ronald Reagan as president in 1980, as his administration signaled a major shift in the nation's approach to the environment. Whether one concludes that this was the first administration hostile to the environment or if President Reagan was emphasizing economic concerns before environmental ones or somewhere in between, his administration fundamentally altered environmental policy. Several key changes defined his approach, and we will take each in turn.

The Reagan administration emphasized that government should be limited and devolved to the most local level possible. In other words, governmental action should be kept closest to the people. This meant that programs were divested from federal government control to the states for administration, and hopefully devolved even further, to local control. This aligns with a traditional conservative point of view on the role of government. In terms of environmental policy, Reagan determined that, with divestiture to the states, the size and scope of the federal bureaucracy could be cut, particularly the US EPA. During Reagan's administration, the EPA's budget was initially slashed 11% and further reductions were advocated (Layzer 2012, 104). Other environment and natural resources agencies were cut too, including the Fish and Wildlife Service, which saw a 28% cut between 1981 and 1983 (Layzer 2012, 105). These budget cuts coincided with significant personnel cuts in agencies. The amount of money the federal government authorized for environment and natural resource programs fell from $17.9 billion in 1980 to between $12 and $15 billion for most of the 1980s (in constant, 1994 dollars) (Layzer 2012, 131). As these cuts persisted, Congress—spurred, in some measure, by outrage among the American public—scaled back some of the proposed cuts.

Second, and related to pushing government to its most local levels, the Reagan administration embraced a broad view that government's role in society should be much smaller and more limited. More specifically, government regulation should be kept at a minimum and this policy tool should only be employed when absolutely necessary. This fundamental view on government was coupled with a belief that economic growth was stifled, rather than enhanced, by government involvement in the market. Therefore, Reagan took various steps to ensure that any government regulation and its effects were minimized. Perhaps, the best example of Reagan's policies in action is Executive Order 12291 that required federal agencies to conduct a regulatory impact analysis on any new regulation and submit it to the Office of Information and Regulatory Affairs for review. This order was designed to ensure that the benefits to society exceeded the costs of any regulatory action taken (Shabecoff 1981). The changes made to the adoption of government regulations formalized the White House's role in the process and allowed it to influence regulatory efforts. This Executive Order remained in effect during the administration of both Reagan and his successor, George H.W. Bush. Subsequent administrations have modified Reagan's executive order, but largely left it in effect.

The efforts to curb the federal government's role in environmental protection were met with resistance, particularly into Reagan's second term in the White House. With time, Americans and environmental groups mobilized to stymie the administration's efforts to curb and repeal environmental actions. Reagan's first EPA administrator, Anne Gorsuch Burford (mother of Supreme Court Justice Neil Gorsuch), who was a champion of Reagan's approach to government, regulation, and its role in the environment, was ultimately forced out of her position. As a result, William Ruckelshaus returned to the helm of the EPA as her successor. James G. Watt was Reagan's selection to head the Department of Interior; he was a controversial figure because he was branded as hostile to environmental protection as he advocated the use of federal lands for timber harvesting, expanded grazing, and various other commercial interests. In addition, several significant events during the 1980s reminded Americans of the destruction being done to the environment. By the mid-1980s, depletion of the Earth's protective ozone layer was front-page news and it galvanized international action to curb the effects of ozone-depleting materials such as chlorofluorocarbons (CFCs). Moreover, in 1984, a gas leak at the Union Carbide plant in Bhopal, India, exposed more than half a million people to methyl isocyanate gas and other chemicals. In 1986, a nuclear power plant in Chernobyl, in present-day Ukraine, suffered a catastrophic nuclear meltdown.

During Reagan's two terms in the White House, every major environmental statute that came up for renewal was, indeed, reauthorized, including the Hazardous and Solid Waste Amendments in 1985, Superfund Amendments in 1986, the Federal Insecticide, Fungicide, and Rodenticide Act Amendments in 1988, along with amendments to the CWA. Additionally, the Emergency Planning and Community Right to Know Act (EPCRA) was passed in 1986 (part of the Superfund reauthorization) that requires local governments and communities be provided information about chemical hazards in the area so the community can plan for emergency situations.

By the end of the 1980s, environmental issues no longer enjoyed the broad bipartisan support that had defined them in past years, as the nation had experienced environmental regulation for several decades, and conflicting perspectives on the role of government in regulation, the economy, and the environment had solidified. Reagan had shaped the foundation of the Republican Party's position on the environment as skeptical and resistant to governmental efforts because of concerns over economic implications and overreach of the government. However, it should be noted that although there were many environmental issues that were not addressed during this time period (e.g., climate change, acid rain, toxic pollution) and the federal government's approach to environmental issues shifted, the government still had a clear role in environmental protection and the worst fears expressed with Reagan's election were not realized (Shabecoff 1989). These outcomes were in part the result of the concern of Americans, and efforts of environmental groups capitalizing on these concerns saw their membership rosters swell to record levels. Congress was left trying to strike a balance between governmental protection of the environment without negative effects on the economy. This decade fundamentally changed the nation's approach to the environment as cost concerns gained substantial footing against environmental concerns.

The 1990s: Stagnation

The last decade of the twentieth century saw continued evolution in how the federal government responded to environmental issues. Reagan's vice president, George H.W. Bush, became president, in part, on a campaign to be an environmental president and, after his one term in office, hopes were high for Bill Clinton's administration, as longtime environmentalist Al Gore was his vice president. Despite hopes and expectations, the 1990s increasingly saw environmental issues take a backseat to other more dominant domestic and international concerns, as these issues moved down the nation's priority list despite punctuations from a few major events. Consider this decade in two parts defined by the Bush and Clinton presidencies.

By the early 1990s, our understanding of environmental issues had grown and developed tremendously since the decade that first saw major environmental policy action. In particular, the advances in science and technology helped us understand the global and interconnected dimensions of these issues and, in 1989, the spill of the Exxon Valdez in Prince William Sound, Alaska, provided a poignant reminder.

On March 24, 1989, the Exxon Valdez oil tanker ran aground off the coast of Alaska due to human error and negligence, spilling approximately 11 million gallons of oil into the pristine ecosystem—the worst environmental disaster in the United States until the explosion on the Deepwater Horizon drilling platform in the Gulf of Mexico in 2010.

Containment and cleanup of the Exxon Valdez spill was hindered by the difficulty in accessing the site. Hundreds of thousands of animals died, and the long-term effects to the environment are still being studied today. This incident led directly to the passage of the Oil Pollution Act of 1990. Other significant events of this decade included the United States's involvement in the first Gulf War, when Iraqi forces invaded neighboring Kuwait. The petroleum industry of this region was significantly impacted by the war, and massive oil-field fires were frequent and devastating.

During George H.W. Bush's campaign for the presidency in 1988, he declared that he would be an "environmental president" but, ultimately, he never truly fulfilled that promise, which is explainable. In large part, his four years in the White House were marred by other events and dominating concerns, including the aforementioned Gulf War. However, "his administration ended the pernicious impasse of the Reagan years with important, if episodic, new policy initiatives" (Rosenbaum 2011, 11). President George H.W. Bush favored market solutions to environmental issues, just as his predecessor did; however, he did appoint more environmentally friendly officials to head major environmental programs, including William Reilly to run the EPA. Nonetheless, federal budgets did not reflect any fulfillment of Bush's campaign promise to be an environmental president. There were some increases to environmental dimensions of the federal budget, but those increases did not match the statutory mandates for those agencies (Layzer 2012, 184).

There were some notable policy efforts, however. The 1990s saw major changes and improvements to air pollution with the passage of the CAA Amendments, including the acid rain allowance trading program. President Bush's leadership was essential to the enactment of the legislation that called for stricter motor vehicle emissions standards and established a market trading program, among others. As mentioned previously, the Oil Pollution Act was passed the same year, and 1992 saw the Energy Policy Act pass, which created a federal energy plan designed to reduce dependence on foreign oil, encourage energy efficiency, and promote conservation. Efforts at preventing pollution also gained traction with the passage of the Pollution Prevention Act.

Internationally, President Bush's leadership on environmental issues left much to be desired in fulfilling a promise to be an environmental president. In 1992, there was a follow-up summit in Rio de Janeiro coinciding with the twentieth anniversary of the Stockholm Declaration.

Bush faced criticism for his plans not to attend the Earth Summit, despite promises for the United States to lead globally on environmental issues. Only after pressure did Bush relent and lead the US delegation. The United States was a signatory to Agenda 21—a nonbinding statement of principles—but it refused to sign the Convention on Biological Diversity.

By 1992, the presidential campaign was in full swing and Bill Clinton ousted Bush after only one term in office. Although the environment did not feature prominently in the campaign, environmentalists were optimistic about this new administration because Al Gore, author of *Earth in Balance*, was the incoming vice president; Gore had previously established himself in the Senate as a champion of environmental issues. This optimism did not last long as the 1994 midterm elections brought Republican control to the Congress and the Republicans signaled their inclinations to oppose additional environmental regulations, particularly without careful considerations of costs associated with those protection efforts. Republicans focused their attention on lessening regulatory burdens, reducing paperwork requirements, and incorporating cost into decision making. However, interest in the environment quickly waned as other domestic priorities—particularly healthcare, crime, drugs, and urban infrastructure—dominated the policy agenda. The Clinton administration mobilized to stymie efforts at rolling back environmental laws and slashing budgets, including the use of the veto power. Clinton's reelection in 1996 signaled that his administration's priorities were here to stay, but scandal quickly overshadowed his remaining years in the White House.

Most governmental efforts at environmental protection never gained sufficient traction. Early in Clinton's first term, sweeping changes were proposed to public land policies, including the raising of grazing fees, but those proposals were immediately attacked. By the midterm elections in 1994, two new national parks in California, Death Valley National Park and Joshua Tree National Park, had been created. In 1996, the Food Quality Protection Act was passed that involved the EPA in determining health risks in food and mandating the agency to consider all of the ways in which consumers were exposed to chemicals, as well as determine a reasonable risk health standard. The Safe Water Drinking Act was reauthorized and the Sustainable Fisheries Act (also known as the Magnuson-Stevens Act) became law.

Besides legislative action, the Clinton administration did use executive power to focus attention on some facets of environmental concerns. In particular, Clinton's 1994 Executive Order 12898 was the first federal government action dealing with environmental justice concerns (see Chapter 8 for more about environmental justice). Another notable executive order was 12866, which Clinton used to replace Reagan's executive order mandating White House Office of Management and Budget review of agency rules. Clinton modified that requirement to mandate review of "significant regulatory actions."

In terms of agency action, Clinton's appointments to federal agencies generally pleased environmental interests. Bruce Babbitt became Secretary of the Interior and endeavored to shift the agency's focus to water conservation and away from dam building. He proved to be a very popular Cabinet member. Clinton tried to elevate the EPA to a cabinet-level agency, but that effort was defeated in Congress (Layzer 2012, 199). Carol Browner was Clinton's pick to head the EPA and under her leadership, the EPA promulgated new particulate matter and ozone standards. He pursued increases to the budgets of the EPA, Interior, and other environmental agencies.

In addition to some modest accomplishments at the domestic level, Clinton tried to renew the United States' involvement internationally on environmental issues. In 1993, the United States signed the Biodiversity Convention, but its ratification stalled in the Senate. Furthermore, the United States participated, under Vice President Gore's leadership, in the negotiations and drafting of the 1997 Kyoto Protocol on Climate Change. Although the United States did sign the convention, ratification by the Senate was not pursued, as Senate leaders made it clear that it would not pass.

In the final days of Clinton's tenure, significant executive actions were taken in an attempt to make last-minute efforts at environmental protection. Clinton used his powers under the 1906 Antiquities Act to make last-minute designations of national monuments, but the incoming administration put much of those efforts on hold.

The 1990s saw some renewed focus on environmental concerns; however, these concerns were often overshadowed by other priorities—both domestic and international—and by the trials and tribulations of the American political environment. Both Presidents Bush and Clinton spoke of being environmentally minded, but both presidents failed to meet expectations of their respective elections. Bush only served one term, thereby limiting the timeframe in which to accomplish significant environmental actions. He did help orchestrate major amendments to the CAA that were widely welcomed, but war in the Persian Gulf and the limits of a single term kept his accomplishments at a minimum. With two terms, Clinton had longer to achieve environmental policy objectives, but other domestic pursuits, politics, and the Monica Lewinsky scandal that consumed his last years in office left him with the label of "underachiever" in this policy arena.

The Early Twenty-First Century: Presidents Bush and Obama

The lack of rhetoric about the environment during the presidential campaign in 2000 proved to be indicative of the lack of emphasis on environmental issues in the United States in the first decade of the twenty-first century. Former Governor George W. Bush (R-Texas) and then-Vice President (former senator, D-Tennessee) Al Gore were the major party candidates for president in 2000, and neither candidate mentioned much about the environment during the campaign, as other issues dominated it. After a controversial election that ultimately ended with the Supreme Court's halting of ballot recounting in Florida, George W. Bush became president in January of 2001. Within months of taking office, the terrorist attacks on September 11 came to redefine politics and policy in the country and dramatically change the nation's priorities. Despite two very different presidents in the opening years of the century, the years following the attacks on 9/11 saw environmental concerns—along with many other policy pursuits—take a back seat to other issues, namely, national security and economic conditions. Accordingly, we examine the nation's approach to environmental policy in the 2000s through each presidency.

George W. Bush entered office promising to undo much of the Clinton-era policy and adjust the nation's approach to regulation. On his first day in office, President Bush issued a moratorium on regulations in development from the Clinton administration (which is often the case when new administrations take office), including the actions Clinton took under the Antiquities Act. In addition, Bush quickly retracted his campaign pledge supporting regulation of carbon dioxide emissions from power plants. Related to energy production, Bush tried repeatedly to open government lands to drilling and energy extraction, particularly in Alaska's Arctic National Wildlife Refuge (ANWR). Moreover, he wanted to open public lands in the West to expedited oil and gas leases to increase US production. In addition to this, he called for stricter cost–benefit analyses and more rigorous risk assessment for any new environmental regulation.

Regarding federal agencies and their activities, Bush took a number of significant steps, both regarding appointments and with his administration's involvement. Bush's appointments to key agencies generally went to individuals from the oil and natural gas industry or individuals who were pro-business advocates, as opposed to environmental advocates. The appointment of former New Jersey Governor Christine Todd Whitman to head the EPA was an exception, but she did not remain in the post long; public clashes between Whitman and the White House led to her resignation in 2003. At the end of her time at the EPA, Whitman complained of constant fights between the administration and environmental groups (Rosenbaum 2011, 14).

Subsequent EPA administrators during Bush's tenure included former Utah Governor Michael Leavitt who replaced Whitman and, then, in 2005, Stephen Johnson took over. Spencer Abraham was appointed Secretary of Energy and was a notable opponent of increasing fuel efficiency. Gale Norton was Bush's pick to lead the Interior Department, as she was a protégé of Reagan's Interior head, James Watt. She championed attempts to drill in ANWR.

Additional examples demonstrate the Bush administration's approach to environmental concerns throughout its tenure. The White House meddled rather publicly with the EPA. The much anticipated 2003 Draft Report on the Environment from the EPA was widely reported to be interfered with, including language changes that suited political purposes, rather than comporting with scientific research and evidence-based information. Bush followed in Reagan's footsteps and sought budgetary cuts to federal agencies working in environmental and natural resources pursuits. His first budget called for an 8% decrease in funding for environment and natural resource programs, including a 6.4% cut for the EPA (Layzer 2012, 266).

The Bush administration ultimately failed in its pursuit of stopping the EPA from regulating greenhouse gases (GHGs) under the CAA. The EPA, under direction from the White House, determined in 2003 that it was not statutorily authorized to regulate carbon dioxide and other GHGs; and the EPA quickly found this decision challenged in court. The Supreme Court ruled in 2007 in *Massachusetts v. EPA* (549 US 497) that the EPA was indeed authorized to regulate those pollutants under the Clean Air Act and did not have sufficient reasons not to regulate them.

Legislatively, Bush oversaw passage of several major initiatives that purported to be good for the environment. The 2003 Healthy Forests Restoration Act is demonstrative of administration efforts to reframe the debate about the environment and use terminology to suggest one end goal of protecting forests, whereas, in fact, statutorily pursuing other and less environmentally minded ends (Vaughn and Cortner 2005). In 2005, Vice President Cheney oversaw the controversial closed-door meetings that led to that year's Energy Policy Act. The Act was intended to increase the supply of energy, improve efficiency of energy, and accelerate research and development. However, it has been heavily criticized for its overreliance on increasing US energy production from fossil fuel sources at all costs—recall the earlier note about opening public lands for expedited oil and gas exploration. Customarily, companies have to apply for a permit that takes a while to be approved, but, under the Bush administration, these processes were being bypassed in order to increase the supply of oil and gas.

Toward the end of his time in office, Bush also signed into law the Energy Independence and Security Act of 2007, which was a follow-up to the 2005 Energy Policy Act, that emphasized energy efficiency and mandated an increase in the corporate average fuel economy (CAFE) standards to 35 miles per gallon by 2020, reflecting a significant increase over standards at the time.

Finally, the United States largely removed itself from international efforts at environmental protection during the Bush presidency. Citing the Kyoto Protocol on Climate Change as "fatally flawed," the White House formally withdrew the United States from the agreement. In addition, international meetings that focused on environmental and natural resource concerns were generally overlooked by the United States, and low-level delegations were sent to represent the country. Despite criticism, Bush elected not to attend the 2002 World Summit on Sustainable Development in Johannesburg, South Africa.

The nation changed forever because of events that unfolded during Bush's time in the White House. Moreover, with the nation's focus shifting to security concerns and military involvement in Afghanistan and Iraq, environmental concerns—along with many others—were neglected. During the 2004 campaign, environmental concerns were hardly mentioned in the presidential race between Bush and Senator John Kerry (D-Massachusetts). Furthermore, the 2008 campaign that brought

Senator Barack Obama (D-Illinois) to the White House to succeed Bush focused little on environmental matters.

The inauguration of President Obama brought with it a sense of optimism and change for the nation that had become deeply divided over many issues, particularly the involvement of US forces abroad in the War on Terror. Many observers looked to the new president with the hope that the country's policies on the environment would change, and a renewed focus on environmental protection and fighting climate change might come about. During his campaign, Obama indicated that he would pursue policy goals on the environment, and his initial actions in office fueled optimism, particularly coupled with the short-lived Democratic control of Congress. However, over time, the Obama administration focused its attention elsewhere.

Regarding federal agencies, Obama's appointees and directives of executive agencies marked a change from the previous administration. Obama appointed Lisa Jackson, the former head of the New Jersey Department of Environmental Protection, to oversee the EPA during his first term. The EPA quickly rescinded a number of regulations from the Bush administration, particularly new source review changes under the CAA. In addition, the EPA set to work on stricter mercury and hazardous air pollutant standards from coal-fired power plants. In 2010, the EPA began tracking, for the first time, the carbon dioxide emissions of large industrial polluters. Gina McCarthy replaced Jackson in 2013 as the EPA head when Jackson resigned. McCarthy had a long history of working in local, state, and federal environmental regulation. McCarthy's tenure in this role followed much of the same trajectory, particularly with regard to carbon emissions. McCarthy has served her entire career in environmental agencies, both state agencies and the US EPA. She got her start working in public health. Ken Salazar was appointed to head the Interior Department; his appointment was seen as only a moderate departure from the tenor of the Bush administration (Layzer 2012, 351). The Interior Department removed gray wolves from the endangered species list in Montana and Idaho, but not in Wyoming. Legal challenges were brought and the courts ruled against the administration, thus forcing the re-listing of the wolves in all the aforementioned states.

Legislatively, Obama was largely focused elsewhere, particularly on the nation's economy and its recovery from the Great Recession, healthcare, and ongoing national security concerns. The American Recovery and Reinvestment Act of 2009 was signed shortly after Obama came into office and, although its aims had little to do with environmental concerns, the Act provided more than $100 billion of spending on tax incentives and loan guarantees related to energy efficiency, renewable energy, and fuel economy. It remains to be seen if there will be demonstrable effects on the environment from this law, especially given steps the Trump administration has taken. Much of the challenge has been because governmental efforts were focused elsewhere, and an increasingly divisive Congress is stalling efforts. In 2010, Republicans regained control of the House and, although the Democrats maintained control of the Senate through the 2012 elections, they did not have a filibuster-proof majority. Further, environmental issues are increasingly proving to be a litmus test issue for candidates, as the partisan divide in Washington seems to grow.

Internationally, Obama promised to restore the United States as a key actor in international environmental efforts, and, more specifically, to curb the effects of climate change. The 2010 explosion and sinking of the Deepwater Horizon drilling platform in the Gulf of Mexico and the ensuing release of oil for three months brought renewed attention to the extraction of oil from underground sources; however, neither the White House nor Congress championed major legislation in response. Instead, the Minerals Management Service—the federal entity charged with overseeing such drilling operations—was dissolved and reconstituted as the Bureau of Ocean Energy Management, Regulation, and Enforcement within the Department of Interior.

In 2015, leaders from around the world came together to continue work under the United Nations Framework Convention for Climate Change (UNFCCC) in Paris, France. The Paris Climate Agreement was agreed upon with the goal of keeping the increase in global temperature to below 2 degrees Celsius above preindustrial levels to reduce the risks and effects of climate change. Each country who is a signatory to the agreement develops and implements their own plan to meet the goals of the agreement. The Paris agreement is significant because it was adopted by all participating member nations. While there is ample reason to criticize the agreement because of its lack of enforcement mechanisms, the agreement is a huge step in uniting the world to fight climate change together. These efforts, though, met with tepid reception in Congress.

In light of Congress's reluctance to engage in environmental matters and the challenges on the international stage, the Obama administration did seek to achieve its policy goals through nonlegislative means. The

Clean Power Plan is an example of how the Obama administration, like administrations before it, endeavored to use executive actions to pursue a policy agenda. Recognizing that Congress was unlikely to act on climate change, the EPA began action on climate change per Obama's direction. The CPP required that states meet specific reductions of carbon dioxide emissions, using whatever means they choose to address the concerns and conditions of their states. These plans would be submitted to the EPA for review. Different regions of the country would have different goals based on a host of factors, including its electrical grid and existing fossil fuel power plants. The EPA was looking to achieve reductions of 25% by 2030. Besides the results that should help slow climate change, the administration touted expected public health benefits and economic development opportunities. Unsurprisingly, the plan quickly found itself the focus of court challenges as the rulemaking process unfolded, with challengers alleging that the EPA overstepped its legal authority. These challenges were ongoing at the end of Obama's term in office and steps are being taken in the Trump administration to repeal this plan through rulemaking processes.

By the conclusion of Obama's second term in office, his record on the environment was mixed. Legislatively there was little progress on major environmental efforts and even a disaster like the Deepwater Horizon could not compel action. Nor was Congress able to address concerns over the safety of the nation's drinking water after the lead contamination of Flint, Michigan's water supply became widely known. However, administratively, Obama achieved quite a bit through executive action. And his administration was able to make progress on the international level. the administration did pursue executive actions and made progress at the international level. His administration's efforts, though, stand in sharp contrast to the early years of the Trump administration, however.

The Trump Administration: The Undoing of Environmental Policy?

Whenever the political party that controls the White House changes, we can expect changes to the nation's environmental policy agenda and priorities, especially as views on environmental issues are increasingly a litmus test for politicians to affiliate with one party or the other. This was true when Ronald Reagan became president after Jimmy Carter as well as when Barack Obama became president after George W. Bush. However, the first years of the Trump Administration have demonstrated not just a change in priorities but a fundamental undoing of the nation's environmental policy. Time will tell how significant these efforts are as well as how lasting the effects might be, but as these pages are written halfway into the first term of the administration, the changes are stark and unprecedented. Many high-ranking government officials that served in both Republican and Democratic administrations are concerned about the dismantling of environmental protections (Kaufman 2018).

From the beginning, Donald Trump's presidential campaign rhetoric signaled his desire for a dramatic shift in the nation's approach to environmental issues. Regarding climate change, candidate Trump rejected the scientific evidence that climate change is occurring and caused by human activity. Indeed, he went so far as to say that climate change is a hoax perpetrated by China (Wong 2016). In a Fall 2018 *60 Minutes* interview, President Trump changed his rhetoric a bit about climate change, saying "I think something's happening. Something's changing and it'll change back again. I don't think it's a hoax, I think there's probably a difference. But I don't know that it's manmade" (Stahl 2018). He also stated that the EPA was waging a "war on coal" that had to be stopped; and he even donned a miner's hard hat to demonstrate his commitment to the coal industry in campaign stops. Other campaign pledges included approving the Keystone XL pipeline (which is a pipeline bringing tar sands oil from Canada through the US to the Gulf of Mexico that was vehemently debated during the Obama administration and ultimately rejected), "canceling" the Paris Climate Change Agreement, and opening up more government lands to oil and gas development (Beeler 2018).

Upon his election, Trump took the first steps to fulfilling these campaign promises and "Making America Great Again" through his appointments in this policy area, as well as through his federal budget proposal and policy priorities. Among his appointments, two stand out— his appointment of Rick Perry as Secretary of Energy and Scott Pruitt as EPA administrator. Rick Perry was one of the candidates for the Republican nomination for president in 2016. The former governor of Texas thought that his appointment as Energy Secretary meant that "he was taking on a role as a global ambassador for the American oil and gas industry that he had long championed in his home state" (Shelbourne 2017; see also Lewis 2017). To provide a point of comparison, Perry, who had a stint on *Dancing with the Stars* and majored in animal science at Texas A&M University, replaced Ernest Moniz in the role. Moniz, was a professor at MIT and had earned a Ph.D. in theoretical physics from Stanford. As we will discuss in greater detail (particularly in Chapter 9), the Department of Energy, is charged with pursuing the nation's energy interests and security, including research and development, conservation, stewardship of nuclear weapons and oversight of the wastes generated from nuclear energy.

Trump's first administrator of the EPA was Scott Pruitt (see more in Chapter 6). Pruitt had previously served as Oklahoma's attorney general (AG), elected in 2010, running as a member of the Tea Party, and reelected to that role in 2014. During his time as AG, Pruitt directed his office to respond to the "constitutional crisis" being brought on by the Obama administration. Regarding the environment, Pruitt sued the EPA 14 times—collaborating with litigants from industry—and typically had little luck in the court system (Talbot 2018). These attitudes and actions guided his efforts at the EPA.

Upon assuming his role, Pruitt announced that he was taking the EPA "back to basics" in an effort to refocus on the agency's work on its "traditional" priorities, such as cleaning up contaminated sites under Superfund, rather than focusing on current environmental threats, like climate change (Talbot 2018). Many observers were concerned that with his previous efforts, he was fundamentally against the mission of the EPA that he headed. The administration's first federal budget proposal included steep cuts to the EPA of more than 25% and Pruitt supported those cuts. He has overseen more than 30 significant environmental rule rollbacks, has supported the administration's efforts to remove the United States from the Paris Climate Agreement, favored undoing of the Clean Power Plan, and has stood by as the morale and organizational culture of the EPA have plummeted leading to nearly 1000 career civil servants leaving the agency (Roston and Flavelle 2018).

Pruitt has also found himself the subject of much controversy while in his role. He has been criticized for traveling first-class at the expense of taxpayers. He had a soundproof booth in his office built and routinely has his office swept for listening devices. After he faced outrage because he would not release his calendar, he provided sparse details of his day-to-day activities, but did not reveal the organizations he spoke to and the meetings he took, which were almost exclusively with industry representatives and without public health or environmental organizations. Heads of regulatory agencies can and should meet with members of the community that they are tasked with regulating, but they should not meet exclusively with them. Pruitt received flack for renting a house for a ridiculously cheap rate in the D.C. area from the spouse of an energy industry lobbyist, implying some favors may have been done. All of this has contributed Pruitt's disapproval among the general public. According to a Quinnipiac Poll in April 2018, 52% disapprove of the job he is doing as EPA administrator and only a quarter of respondents approving (the remainder were unsure) (Quinnipiac Poll 2018).

In July 2018, Pruitt was compelled to resign as EPA administrator as his tenure with the agency succumbs to scandal. Andrew Wheeler was appointed to replace Pruitt as administrator, and his leadership is already raising questions. Wheeler's government career has included working for the EPA's Office of Pollution Prevention and Toxics during the George H.W. Bush administration as well as working for the Senate Environment and Public Works Committee and serving as an aide to Senator Jim Inhofe, a prominent climate change denier; and Wheeler has been on record as a climate denier too (Kormann 2018). In addition to these roles, Wheeler was also an energy industry lobbyist, representing electric utilities, coal companies, uranium producers, and even Murray Energy (Friedman 2018). More recently, he has acknowledged that humans have some impact on the climate, but says that impact is not completely understood (Kormann 2018).

This context sets the stage for some highlights of what the first years of the Trump administration have meant for environmental policy. At the beginning of a new administration, it is common for an agency like the EPA to put a hold on rulemaking that is in progress; but that hold typically lasts for a month or two to allow the new administration to establish its priorities. Under the Trump administration, these holds have lasted well into the second year of the administration. As already indicated, the EPA has rolled back dozens of major environmental rules. For example, the Clean Power Plan has been repealed and the agency is not only not advancing efforts to combat climate change but it is undoing existing actions regarding the issue. Regulations on heavy-duty trucks— known as gliders—that are trucks with new cabs and chassis built on old engines—have been undone. These regulations, effecting 5% of the truck fleet, were aimed at reducing the more than 300,000 tons of nitrous oxides and 8000 tons of diesel particulate matter a year that resulted in 1600 premature deaths (Talbot 2018). Besides the American Lung Association, Volvo Group North America (manufacturer of Volvo and Mack trucks) and the American Trucking Association were against this repeal. Superfund regulations are being dismantled so that contaminated sites can be redeveloped more quickly. References to climate change and the science concluding that the climate is changing because of human activity are being removed from the EPA's website. The administration has also announced reconsideration of the rules around fuel economy that mandated automakers achieve a fleetwide average of 54.5 miles per gallon by 2025. Time will be the ultimate arbiter of these efforts though. Seventeen states and the District of Columbia have sued the EPA over these efforts (Domonoske 2018).

The EPA is not the only federal agency shifting course on environmental protection. The Bureau of Land Management is taking steps to rescind rules protecting the environment and public health from the harmful effects of hydraulic fracturing, or fracking, for natural gas (see Chapter 9). Rules designed to ensure the integrity of fracking wells on public lands and ensure natural resources are not contaminated require BLM review and approval of them, but those requirements are now up for repeal. And, the Endangered Species Act, which has been protecting species for almost five decades, is now being attacked. While the ESA has often been criticized in the past, even under periods of Republican control, the law has not been attacked the way it is under the Trump administration (Davenport and Friedman 2018). The Departments of Interior and Commerce, at the direction of the administration, announced fundamental changes to the ESA with provisions that would, for the first time, allow economic consequences of protecting species to be considered in deciding whether or not to protect the species. If these proposals are adopted, it would also be much harder to list a new species and much easier to remove species from the list. It is worth noting that the ESA is credited with saving the American alligator, bald eagle, and gray whale from extinction, among many others (Davenport and Friedman 2018).

At this juncture in the administration, we can make some preliminary statements. First, the Trump administration is demonstrating some progress and achievement of its campaign promises about the environment. Rules are being repealed, but it is interesting to note in much of this that the rollbacks do not align with the typical conservative priorities of devolving authority back to the states or curbing environmental protection in an effort to promote economic growth and job creation. Many of these actions appear to be designed to benefit particular industry sectors. Second, these efforts represent a significant departure from the trajectory that the nation has been on for decades regarding environmental issues;

but it is too soon to tell how significant the effects of these changes will be. Perhaps what should be focused on most is the increasing dismissal of science and facts surrounding our natural environment that is being advocated by this administration. Again, it is early in this administration's tenure to make more definitive statements, but what can be concluded is that Trump's presidency signals major changes in the nation's efforts to protect the environment since the modern environmental movement took hold. It remains to be seen if the results of the 2018 midterm elections, which shifted power in the House of Representatives to the Democrats, will result in any significant actions to conduct oversight of the Trump administration's actions regarding the environment. With the Senate firmly in Republican control, however, it is unlikely that there will be any major legislative accomplishments and appointments to federal agencies will still be under the purview of the Republican Senate majority.

Themes in the United States' Experience with Environmental Policy

As we close our discussion of the historical evolution of environmental policy in the United States, several key trends emerge. First, at the end of the second decade of twenty-first century, the American government has had nearly six decades of experience with environmental policy already. Today, most citizens expect the government to be involved with environmental policy, at least insofar as it concerns protecting the population from the ill effects of pollution and hazardous materials. That said, these expectations do not preclude ongoing conversations about the extent to which the government should be engaged in environmental protection.

With decades of experience with modern environmental policy in the United States, it is important to note that how governmental action impacts the environment varies. Put differently, during the first major efforts regarding environmental protection in the 1970s, we saw legislative action to determine environmental outcomes. Over time, however, with the evolving role of Congress, the increasing power of the presidency and its influence on executive branch agencies, and the growing partisan divide, environmental concerns have been crowded out of the legislative agenda of Congress; however, this has compelled the use of nonlegislative pathways for the continued development and execution of environmental policy (cf. Klyza and Sousa 2013). With major environmental legislation unlikely to make its way through Congress, executive agencies are increasingly using powers given to them by Congress and following directives of the White House to ensure ongoing environmental protection.

Recognizing the length of time that the government has been involved in protecting the environment and the legitimacy that time affords leads to another key point about the government's action in this area: governmental response to environmental concerns is largely reactive. Generally speaking, the American government is reactive rather than proactive in its actions. Because we value a democratic system in the United States and we want government to act on behalf of what the people want, there is generally only consensus for governmental action in response to events and circumstances. For example, prior to 9/11, Americans probably would not have voluntarily acquiesced to extensive airport screening; however, after such a horrific attack, Americans consent daily. The same is true with environmental concerns. The government does not proactively regulate or limit behaviors until they are proven to be detrimental to the health of its population and the environment. This reactionary nature is as our Founders intended, and ensures that government represents the will of the people. The flip side, however, is that the government is often seen to be slow to act and only fixes problems after they arise. It is important to keep in mind that truly proactive governments are, generally, those that Americans do not want to resemble—dictatorships, authoritarian regimes, and the like. However, being reactionary does, often, leave pollution and contamination to happen before the government steps in.

With a governmental structure that is reactive, a third theme emerges: the importance of the public's role in demanding governmental action. The influence of the public extends to undoing or weakening environmental regulations and even inaction. As we have seen, modern environmental regulation in the 1960s and 1970s came about because the public demanded it. By the 1980s and the election of Ronald Reagan, the public demanded that government lessen its regulatory burden, and that happened. Then, the public became concerned as environmental disasters occurred and, through Congress, the public pushed back on regulatory retreats. During the Trump administration, there has been mobilization of the public, as evidenced in events like the March for Science on Earth Day 2017 and others. In the coming years we will see what effect the public's response to governmental action regarding the environment might engender, if any. In the realm of policy, inaction is just as important and significant as action. These trends in America's experience with environmental protection are important to note, particularly when considered in conjunction with the public's sentiment regarding environmental issues over time.

PUBLIC OPINION AND THE ENVIRONMENT

Much of our history with environmental matters in the United States is a product of how the public thinks about the issues and whether or not the public wants government to take action. In a country with a democratic tradition, we do ascribe to the ideal of government of the people, by the people, and for the people. Therefore, it is worth exploring, chronologically, how the people have thought about the environment, past and present, and look to the future for signs of what might come before next articulating key trends in public opinion on the environment. Understanding these trends is important as policy scholars, such as Kingdon (2011), emphasize the significance of public opinion in setting the nation's agenda for government action.

Americans have long been obsessed with public opinion data. Nationwide polls began in the mid-nineteenth century, and Alexis de Tocqueville famously noted in his travels in the United States and the resulting tome, *Democracy in America*, just how fixated Americans are with public opinion. With regard to the environment, public opinion and support of environmental issues have swung dramatically over time; however, we do not have much public opinion data before the 1970s because public opinion on this category of issues was neglected (Dunlap 1991). Furthermore, Americans' opinions about the environment are complex and, depending on the question, one might draw very different conclusions about their opinions.

As previously mentioned, public concern over the environment grew dramatically throughout the 1960s and into the 1970s. By the first Earth Day, 53% of Americans believed that reducing pollution was one of the three biggest national problems; nonetheless, after that April event, public sentiment dropped rapidly by June of the same year (Layzer 2012, 80; Vaughn 2007, 18). However, Americans generally thought the United States was making progress in terms of the right balance of environmental laws and regulations. In 1973, 34% of survey respondents said the existing regulations had not gone far enough, whereas 32% said there was the right balance (Dunlap 1987, 9). Moreover, in that same year, only 13% of survey respondents thought the environmental laws went too far (Dunlap 1987, 9). Americans were willing to align government spending with their opinions as well. Throughout the 1970s, survey data reveal that between 48 and 61% thought the government spent too little money on environmental protection (Dunlap 1987, 10). Furthermore, a plurality of Americans thought economic growth should be sacrificed for environmental quality during the 1970s (Dunlap 1987, 11). However, various other challenges and realities in the 1970s often crowded out environmental concerns—in particular, the energy crisis and mounting Cold War tensions often diverted public saliency (Vaughn 2007, 18). Opinions changed, however, by the early 1980s with the Reagan Administration.

Our earlier discussion of environmental policy in the 1980s demonstrates that, by the Reagan administration, we had more experience with environmental protection, and opinions seemed to shift. In 1981, a Roper Poll found that 31% of Americans thought environmental regulations had not gone far enough, 38% thought they had hit the right balance, and 21% thought they went too far (Dunlap 1987, 9). After a few years of Reagan-led challenges to environmental protection, the percentage of Americans who thought more regulations were needed peaked at 48% in 1983 (Dunlap 1987, 9). In addition, during the 1980s, Americans continually expressed concern that the government was spending too little on the environment—as much as 58% of respondents to surveys in 1984, 1985, and 1986 said there was too little spending (Dunlap 1987, 10). For further substantiation that the American public was generally put off by some of the Reagan administration's efforts related to the environment, 58% of survey respondents in 1986 said economic growth should be sacrificed for environmental quality and, in the same year, 66% of respondents said that the environment should be protected regardless of cost (Dunlap 1987, 11, 22). Indeed, by the close of the 1980s, it was apparent that public support for environmental protection had endured the efforts of the Reagan administration to roll it back. However, public support for environmental protection did not then—and does not now—necessarily translate into political action.

Response to the government's environmental policy efforts in the 1980s led to widespread public support for environmental protection in the 1990s. A Gallup Poll in 1990 found that 76% of respondents considered themselves environmentalists, and a Washington Post Poll found that nearly three quarters thought the environment had grown worse since 1970 (Vaughn 2007, 24). In addition, the saliency of environmental concerns is demonstrated in public opinion data in 1990 that found 71% of Americans thought the government was spending too little on the environment—an all-time high (Dunlap 2002, 11). Moreover, in 1992, 63% of people thought the government had not gone far enough to protect the environment—another record (Dunlap 2002, 11). The early 1990s saw the high-water mark in terms of public support for governmental action regarding the environment. Since then, polling reveals steady narrowing of the gap between support for more robust action and keeping things status quo or even weakening existing mandates.

In the twenty-first century, Americans continue to say more is needed in terms of environmental protection, but other major issues and debate over, arguably, the dominant environmental issue—climate change—has caused some significant alternations to the sentiments Americans express about the natural environment. For example, a March 2001 Gallup Poll indicated that 42% worry "a great deal" about the health and quality of the environment, but only 27% thought "immediate and drastic" action is needed (Saad and Dunlap 2001, 6).

By 2008, a decidedly different trend of public opinion and the environment began to emerge. For the first time ever, the percentage of survey respondents who favored economic growth was higher than those who favored environmental protection (Gallup 2013). In 2011, this trend peaked with 54% of Americans saying economic growth should be prioritized over the environment (Gallup 2013). These responses are significant because, even during the 1980s when environmental protection was not a priority of the White House, polls still revealed that Americans ranked environmental protection above economic growth. Data from the Spring of 2018 indicates a shift since then in that more Americans are prioritizing the environment (57%) over economic growth (35%) (Gallup 2018). Other standard questions about environmental protection ask if the government is doing too much or too little regarding the environment. Since 2000, the percentage of Americans who think the environment is doing too much increased from 10 to 17% in 2012, but that number has declined quite a bit as only 9% of respondents in 2018 thought the government was doing too much (Gallup 2018). This coincides with an increase in the percentage of Americans who think the government is doing too little to 62% in 2018, up from 47% in 2013 (Gallup 2018). Americans increasingly appear to think that the government is doing too little for the environment, and these figures have shifted in this direction since Trump took office. Finally, Americans remain pessimistic about the overall state of the environment; a majority of respondents (56%) told pollsters in April 2018 that they think the condition of the environment for the next generation will be worse, while 14% thought it would be better and 29% believed it would remain the same (CBS News Poll 2018). These figures have been fairly steady in the last ten years.

These shifts in public opinion need to be considered along with public sentiment about climate change, as that issue is proving increasingly pivotal. Typically, when a new threat—environmental or otherwise—emerges on the national scene, we observe a period in which the public gains knowledge about the threat and comes to understand it better. With climate change, polling indicates that the public is more knowledgeable, yet increasingly convinced that the concern over climate change is exaggerated. Gallup has been asking for more than 20 years about Americans' assessments of climate change. In 1998, 34% of Americans thought the seriousness of climate change was duly reported in the media, 31% thought it exaggerated, and 27% thought it underestimated. In 2006, 38% of Americans thought the seriousness was underestimated, 30% thought it exaggerated, and 28% thought it was about correct. Then, in 2010, 48% of Americans thought its seriousness exaggerated and the remaining percentages were about evenly split between underestimates and generally correct.

In 2018, a third of Americans think that concern over climate change is exaggerated, while 41% think the seriousness is underestimated. The remaining quarter think it is adequately represented by the media (Gallup 2018). CBS News Polls have tracked Americans' understanding of the causes of climate change—and whether or not it is even a problem. In the Spring of 2018, 54% of Americans reported that human activity mostly causes climate change and 24% said it is caused by natural phenomena (CBS News Poll 2018). The numbers of Americans who think climate change does not exist has been growing since 2014 and in 2018, 13% of Americans do not think climate change is real (CBS News Poll 2018). These trends demonstrate that although the science of climate change has become increasingly certain, additional studies point to the seriousness of the issue and that much of the rest of the world comprehends its magnitude, Americans are increasingly uncertain about climate change (see also Rabe 2010). The Trump administration is undoubtedly spurring some of these trends given its rhetoric and leadership. This is just a snapshot of one particular environmental issue and how public opinion is far from predictable. Subsequent chapters in this text will explore some of the complexities of this particular issue and discuss how various stakeholders are shifting public discourse about this and other issues.

By way of summary of Americans' perceptions about the environment since the first Earth Day, several points are warranted. First, for the most part, Americans consistently say the environment needs to be protected and that more should be done (Dunlap 2002). However, it is easy to abstractly respond to a pollster and say more action is needed and that the environment should be protected. The more significant question is that of salience—or how prominent environmental concern is for the average American and whether that concern translates into political action. This is where things are more muddled. Support for environmental protection is largely contingent on the broader economic realities confronting Americans, as well as reaction to recent and significant environmental events such as major disasters (Daniels et al. 2012). Therefore, just because there is support for environmental concerns, it does not mean that these concerns drive government, as Americans and lawmakers have to prioritize their actions. The environmental concerns in recent years do not drive most voters' decisions about which candidates for office to support. In the 2018 midterm elections, 84% said those issues were not a motivating factor in casting their votes (Siciliano 2018). Public opinion about particular environmental issues is complicated. We touched on the complexities of opinions surrounding climate change as one example. Much of what we think about environmental issues has a lot to do with how we seek out and consume highly scientific and technical information as well.

ROLE OF SCIENCE IN PUBLIC DISCOURSE

The final section of this chapter investigates how Americans talk about and consume scientific and highly technical information. You might be wondering why a chapter focusing on the evolution of environmental policy concludes with a discussion of how science is treated in policy discourse. The answer is simple: scientific and technical knowledge drives complex policy discussions and actions, including in the environmental arena. Keep in mind that biologist Rachel Carson conveyed, in an easy-to-understand manner, the ill effects of pesticides on wildlife, and

she did so in a way that precipitated the modern environmental movement. Fast-forward to today: underlying policy conversations about
climate change is a debate as to whether scientists know what they are
talking about and if the planet's climate is experiencing fundamental
change. To understand part of the reasons why Americans think the way
they do about the environment, we need to examine how Americans
view scientific information and how its reception has changed.

As we delve into this topic, first consider the nature of science and
how the scientific method works. We are taught in school the broad
counters of the scientific method. First, scientists formulate a question
and, then, they do research to generate a hypothesis, or an educated
guess, in answer to that question. Thereafter, scientists figure out a way
to conduct a test to see if they were right or not. After the test, the data
are analyzed and an answer is determined. This method is simple enough
and its essence permeates so many aspects of our lives. However, as with
most things, the scientific method is not that simple.

With the scientific method and its widespread place of veneration, we
strive for rational, orderly studies of phenomena that we do not understand. The scientific method applies rationality and linearity in understanding something and enabling future researchers to build on the work
of those in the past. At the conclusion of an experiment—so frequently
our minds go to laboratories full of individuals with beakers in hand
and white labcoats—we expect a single, uniform answer. After all, that
is what science is to us. Moreover, we await the answers science gives us
because we assume that more scientific knowledge reduces uncertainty.
However, what we desire from science is not always what we get, particularly when we couple science with politics.

Politics and science mix in many policy arenas, but particularly when
we consider protection of our natural environment. President Obama's
second EPA administrator, Gina McCarthy, pledged, in her first speech
to Congress, that her agency would be driven by science, particularly
when it came to the controversial requirements under the Clean Power
Plan to limit carbon pollution (Daley 2013). By contrast, President
Trump's first EPA administrator Scott Pruitt is uncertain if science supports the conclusion that the climate is changing (*The Guardian* 2017).
Utilizing science is not quite so simple. Scientific knowledge provides
us information, but we increasingly find that information is marred in
debates—and even battles—over what that information actually tells
us. Our simplistic notion of the scientific method and the results it

provides gets caught up in debates about whether the science was done correctly or actually answers more questions than it produces. After all, one scientific study often gives us more questions than answers. There are arguments over whether appropriate scientific tests were employed or the "right" data were gathered in the "right" manner—all of which presumes there is one right way to study anything, and there simply is not. There are, indeed, plenty of widely accepted research protocols, but that does not imply universality. Moreover, as we learn more about the world around us and advance technologically, we figure out new ways to study phenomena. Just remember, in the Middle Ages, it was commonly thought that draining the blood of a patient with the help of leeches alleviated many ailments. Today, medical science cringes at the thought of that widely accepted notion. All of this discussion is not to undermine or delegitimize the role and value of science; rather, it is simply important to remember that just because there are methods of studying something does not mean that someone will not find fault with how that study was done.

One additional point about science that is paramount is when we talk about how science intersects politics. Rarely, if ever, will scientists "prove" anything. In fact, proving something is anathema to most scientists. Instead, scientists work at ruling out a causal factor or some other explanatory variable and, then, help us understand what might be a possible explanation. This always leaves a degree of uncertainty, and this is exactly where politics come in.

Politics are often discussed as a struggle over who gets what and, in that struggle, there are vested interests on all sides of whatever issue. As a result, supporters and opponents of a particular policy are going to leap on any uncertainty in the work of scientists—and there is always going to be uncertainty—and exploit it in the pursuit of their policy goals. Small disagreements among scientists over largely procedural issues end up being characterized in public discourse as massive bouts of dissension among scientists, all of which leave the public perplexed and wondering who to believe. This frustration among the public is hard to grapple with because our understanding of science is that scientific study will find us solutions to problems because, well, it generally has.

Think of all the wretched diseases that used to plague young people: mumps, measles, and even chicken pox. Through the hard and diligent work of scientists, most young people have no idea what any of those childhood diseases are like because we have vaccines for them. Parents today never experienced more debilitating diseases such as polio that their parents' generation faced because of advances in science. Parallel arguments to this one can be made in so many facets of life, from portable mp3 devices replacing CD players that replaced record players to automotive safety features such as airbags.

Scientists are, often, unfairly subjected to scrutiny because the public does not fully grasp the work of scientists and how they do what they do. Over time, public perceptions of scientists and whether their study of the environment is to be trusted has seen a significant shift. A *Washington Post*/ABC News Poll, during a three-year span, asked respondents how much they trust what scientists say about the environment. In 2016, Pew Research Center found 21% trusted scientists a great deal, 55% a fair amount, 18% not too much, and 4% hardly trusted them (Funk 2017). In 2009, 40% of respondents hardly trusted scientists (*Washington Post/* ABC Poll 2009). When pollsters ask directly about the work of scientists on climate change, there is less support for the conclusions of scientists. These fluctuations in opinion should be noted and considered. Scientists have the scientific method, but that method does not reduce uncertainty, and the results scientists do provide us have to exist in a broader context that includes behavioral, social, cultural, and economic values. This is where science and politics intersect. On the one hand, just because we have the science, does not mean the government will adopt it and follow its recommendations. On the other hand, just because a law is passed and makes it through the political process does not mean it is based on the best available science and technical knowledge. Chapter 3 will pick up here and help us understand the messy roles that scientists and other policy stakeholders play in crafting and passing laws related to the environment.

CHAPTER WRAP-UP

This chapter has explored the American experience with environmental policy. Over time, we have seen the government go from a minimal level of involvement to significant action. Public support for environmental action has driven much of our broad structure of environmental laws in the United States, with much aid from the scientific advances of the twentieth century. However, the first part of the twenty-first century seems to indicate pretty significant changes to how Americans have traditionally approached environmental issues. Due in part to significant shifts in our nation's focus on global security and the economy, environmental concerns remain largely in the shadows of policy discussions, and even in political campaigns. Major environmental legislation has not been passed in decades, whereas scientific knowledge continues to advance. However, how Americans consume science and view science is changing, in large part due to the increasing tendency to question the work of scientists and exploit the inherent nature of uncertainty that is endemic in science. Accordingly, we turn, in the next chapter, to look at how policy gets made and how policy debates today are largely a function of our country's history with environmental policy, what Americans think about environmental issues, and their levels of salience.

Water Is Safe to Drink, Right?
After reading this chapter, it is appropriate to conclude that substantial progress has been made in the United States addressing major environmental issues; therefore, it should be plausible that seemingly basic issues like clean drinking water should not be a problem anymore. However, the cleanliness of drinking water in the twenty-first century is still an issue in some American communities—just look at Flint, Michigan. A study published in the winter of 2018 in the *Proceedings of the National Academy of Sciences* documented that almost 21 million Americans relied on water from community water systems that violated basic standards in 2015 alone (Rice 2018). The study examines water systems in the US from 1982 through 2015 and found that as many as 45 million Americans—28% of the US population—were subject to systems that do not meet standards (Rice 2018). Just because a water system does not meet minimum standards, though, does not mean people will be sick; rather, this research demonstrates that regular access to safe and clean water is not just an issue in other parts of the world, it is a problem in the United States. Flint is just one example.
   In early 2016, the water crisis in Flint catapulted to national attention when Governor Rick Snyder (Michigan) declared a state of emergency in Genesee County because of the lead in the

water supply of Flint. Lead can cause a host of long-term health problems, many of which are irreversible, particularly in young children. A federal state of emergency came just two weeks later. Nevertheless, the problems began much earlier. Starting in the summer of 2012, the city of Flint began looking for ways to save money by changing the provider of water to its residents as Flint's finances—just like many other communities—were stretched thin. Flint had relied on water from the Detroit Water and Sewerage Department (DWSD) but the city began to explore getting water from the Karegnondi Water Authority (KWD). By the spring of 2013, the decision is made to switch to the KWD, which would require building a pipeline. Therefore, in the interim, in 2014, Flint decides to get water from the Flint River, which had been the city's water source until the 1960s. The water drawn from the Flint River was not immediately treated because there was concern that the chemicals that would be used to treat the water might cause pipe corrosion.

It did not take long before residents to start complaining about the poor quality of the water. Complaints ranged from the smell and color of the water and multiple boil advisories were issued. By October 2014, General Motors stops using water from the Flint River because it is damaging its machines. In January 2015, Flint is found to be in violation of the Safe Drinking Water Act over levels of total trihalomethanes (TTHM), so the state decides to buy bottled water for its government employees. Flint is back in compliance by September 2015.

Concern about the quality of the water is ongoing, however, and testing continues. By the end of 2015, exceptionally high levels of lead were found in the water. Researchers from Virginia Tech documented lead levels in one resident's home at 13,200 parts per billion, whereas 5000 ppb is considered hazardous (Kennedy 2016). Additional research finds high levels of lead in children and lead advisories go into effect. By mid-October 2015, Flint switches back to DWSD—now known as the Great Lakes Water Authority.

Since then, the problems have not gone away because the corrosion of the city's pipes is what allowed lead to leach into the water supply and sicken residents. Efforts are still underway to unpack what went wrong in this situation as well as plans to fix the city's corroded pipes. Even some local government officials have been charged with felonies over misleading other government officials. A court settlement was reached in March of 2017 authorizing $97 million to replace water pipes in Flint with the remaining costs being covered by the state of Michigan. While media coverage has waned, Flint officials and residents are still dealing with the mess and many residents will have a lifetime of effects from the contaminated water.

The takeaway from this case study is that even environmental issues that the nation seemingly addressed in legislation decades ago can still present problems. In the case of our drinking water, the pipes that carry water to us get old and reflect the construction practices of years gone by. By 2020, the average water pipeline will be 45 years old and some may be as old as 150 years (Parks-Ramage 2018). Environmental challenges are far more complicated then they might appear to be and the policy process—which we explore in the next chapter—can and does yield solutions. However, those solutions are only as effective as their implementation allows and may not solve every dimension of the problem.

SUGGESTED RESOURCES

Readings and Websites

Andrews, Richard L. *Managing the Environment, Managing Ourselves: A History of American Environmental Policy*. 2nd edition. New Haven, CT: Yale University Press, 2006.

Brinkley, Douglas. *The Wilderness Warrior: Theodore Roosevelt and the Crusade for America*. New York: Harper Perennial, 2010.

Carson, Rachel. *Silent Spring*. New York: Houghton Mifflin, 1962.

Layzer, Judith. *Open for Business: Conservatives' Opposition to Environmental Regulation*. Cambridge, MA: MIT Press, 2012.

Lepore, Jill. "The Right Way to Remember Rachel Carson." *The New Yorker*, March 26, 2018. https://www.newyorker.com/magazine/2018/03/26/the-right-way-to-remember-rachel-carson.

Milazzo, Paul Charles. *Unlikely Environmentalists: Congress and Clean Water, 1945–1972.* Lawrence, KS: University Press of Kansas, 2016.
Scheberle, Denise L. *Industrial Disasters and Environmental Policy: Stories of Villains, Heroes, and the Rest of Us.* New York: Routledge, 2018.

Films or Video

An Inconvenient Truth. Directed by Davis Guggenheim. 2006. Lawrence Bender Productions, Participant Media. DVD.
An Inconvenient Sequel: Truth to Power. Directed by Jon Shenk and Bonni Cohen. 2017. Actual Films, Participant Media. DVD.
The Roosevelts: An Intimate History. Directed by Ken Burns. 2014. PBS. DVD.
War on the EPA. PBS Frontline. 2017.

References

Andrews, Richard L. *Managing the Environment, Managing Ourselves: A History of American Environmental Policy.* New Haven, CT: Yale University Press, 2006.
Beeler, Carolyn. "Trump and the Environment, One Year into the Presidency." PRI's The World, January 19, 2018. https://www.pri.org/stories/2018-01-19/trump-and-environment-one-year-presidency.
Daley, Beth. "EPA Chief Vows to Develop Carbon Rules Based on Science." *Boston Globe,* July 31, 2013. http://www.bostonglobe.com/.
Daniels, David P., Jon A. Krosnick, Michael P. Tichy, and Trevor Tompson. "Public Opinion on Environmental Policy in the United States." In *The Oxford Handbook of US Environmental Policy,* edited by Sheldon Kamieniecki and Michael Kraft (pp. 461–486). New York: Oxford University Press, 2012.
Dunlap, Riley E. "An Enduring Concern." *Public Perspective* no. 10–14 (September/October 2002): n.p.
———. "Public Opinion on the Environment in the Reagan Era." *Environment* 29, no. 6 (July/August 1987): 7–11, 32–37.
———. "Trends in Public Opinon Toward Environmental Issues." *Society and Natural Resources* 4 (1991): 285–312.
Domonoske, Camila. "States Sue the EPA to Protect Obama-Era Fuel Efficiency Standards." *National Public Radio,* May 1, 2018. https://www.npr.org/sections/thetwo-way/2018/05/01/607447344/states-sue-the-epa-to-protect-obama-era-fuel-efficiency-standards.
"Environment." CBS News Poll. Accessed May 30, 2018. http://www.pollingreport.com/enviro.htm.
"Environment." Gallup Poll. Accessed July 15, 2013. http://www.gallup.com/poll/1615/Environment.aspx?version=print.

"Environment." Gallup Poll. Accessed May 30, 2018. http://www.pollingreport.com/enviro.htm.

"EPA Head Scott Pruitt Denise That Carbon Dioxide Causes Global Warming." *The Guardian*, March 9, 2017. https://www.theguardian.com/environment/2017/mar/09/epa-scott-pruitt-carbon-dioxide-global-warming-climate-change.

Davenport, Coral, and Lisa Friedman. "Lawmakers, Lobbyists and the Administration Join Forces to Overhaul the Endangered Species Act." *The New York Times*, July 22, 2018. https://www.nytimes.com/2018/07/22/climate/endangered-species-act-trump-administration.html.

Friedman, Lisa. "Andrew Wheeler, New EPA Chief, Details His Energy Lobbying Past." *The New York Times*, August 1, 2018. https://www.nytimes.com/2018/08/01/climate/andrew-wheeler-epa-lobbying.html.

Funk, Cary. "Mixed Messages About Public Trust in Science." *Pew Research Center*, December 8, 2017. http://www.pewinternet.org/2017/12/08/mixed-messages-about-public-trust-in-science/.

Kaufman, Alexander C. "Scott Pruitt's First Year Set the EPA Back Anywhere from a Few Years to 3 Decades." *Huffington Post*, January 20, 2018. https://www.huffingtonpost.com/entry/pruitt-one-year_us_5a610a5ce4b074ce7a06beb4.

Kennedy, Merrit. "Lead-Laced Water in Flint: A Step-by-Step Look at the Makings of a Crisis." *National Public Radio*, April 20, 2016. https://www.npr.org/sections/thetwo-way/2016/04/20/465545378/lead-laced-water-in-flint-a-step-by-step-look-at-the-makings-of-a-crisis.

Kingdon, John W. *Agendas, Alternatives and Public Policies*. Updated 2nd edition. New York: Longman, 2011.

Klyza, Christopher McGrory, and David Sousa. *American Environmental Policy: Beyond Gridlock*. Updated and expanded edition. Cambridge: MIT Press, 2013.

Kormann, Carolyn. "In Andrew Wheeler, Trump Gets a Cannier EPA Chief." *The New Yorker*, July 11, 2018. https://www.newyorker.com/news/news-desk/in-andrew-wheeler-trump-gets-a-cannier-epa-chief.

Kraft, Michael E. *Environmental Policy and Politics*. 5th edition. New York: Longman, 2011.

Layzer, Judith. *Open for Business: Conservatives' Opposition to Environmental Regulation*. Cambridge: MIT Press, 2012.

Lewis, Michael. "The 5th Risk." *Vanity Fair*, September 2017, 192–197, 240–246.

Nash, Roderick. *American Environmentalism*. 3rd edition. New York: McGraw-Hill, 1990.

Parks-Ramage, Jonathan. "These US Cities Are Dealing with the Worst Drinking Water Problems Nationwide." *Vice*, February 5, 2018. https://impact.vice.

com/en_us/article/wj4qvx/these-us-cities-are-dealing-with-the-worst-drinking-water-problems-nationwide.

Portney, Paul R. "Air Pollution Policy." *Public Policies for Environmental Protection*. Washington, DC: Resources for the Future, 2000.

Quinnipiac University Poll, April 20–24, 2018. Available at http://www.pollingreport.com/trump_ad.htm.

Rabe, Barry. *Greenhouse Governance: Addressing Climate Change in America*. Washington, DC: The Brookings Institution, 2010.

Rice, Doyle. "Tens of Millions of Americans Exposed to Unsafe Drinking Water Each Year." *USA Today*. February 12, 2018. https://www.usatoday.com/story/news/health/2018/02/12/tens-millions-americans-exposed-unsafe-drinking-water-each-year/330516002/.

Ringquist, Evan J. *Environmental Protection at the State Level: Politics and Progress in Controlling Pollution*. Armonk, NY: M. E. Sharpe, 1993.

Rosenbaum, Walter A. *Environmental Politics and Policy*. Washington, DC: CQ Press, 2011.

Roston, Eric, and Christopher Flavelle. "Shrinking EPA Workforce Has Already Reached Reagan-Era Levels." *Bloomberg*, January 11, 2018. https://www.bloomberg.com/news/articles/2018-01-11/shrinking-epa-workforce-has-already-reached-reagan-era-levels.

Saad, Lydia, and Riley E. Dunlap. "Only One in Four Americans Are Anxious About the Environment." *Gallup Poll Monthly* no. 407 (April 2001): n.p.

Shabecoff, Philip. "Reagan Order on Cost-Benefit Analysis Stirs Economic and Political Debate." *New York Times*, November 7, 1981. http://www.nytimes.com/.

Shabecoff, Philip. "Reagan and Environment: To Many, a Stalemate." *The New York Times*, January 2, 1989. http://www.nytimes.com/.

Shelbourne, Mallory. "Rick Perry Misunderstood Energy Secretary Job: Report." *The Hill*, January 18, 2017. http://thehill.com/policy/energy-environment/315005-rick-perry-misunderstood-energy-secretary-job-report.

Siciliano, John. "Climate Change Has Slipped from Voters' Minds." *The Washington Examiner*, November 6, 2018. https://www.washingtonexaminer.com/policy/energy/climate-change-has-slipped-from-voters-minds.

Stahl, Lesley. "President Trump on Christine Blasey Ford, His Relationships with Vladimir Putin and Kim Jong Un and More." *60 Minutes* Interview Transcript, October 15, 2018. https://www.cbsnews.com/news/donald-trump-interview-60-minutes-full-transcript-lesley-stahl-jamal-khashoggi-james-mattis-brett-kavanaugh-vladimir-putin-2018-10-14/.

Sussman, Glen, Byron W. Daynes, and Jonathan P. West. *American Politics and the Environment*. New York: Longman, 2002.

Talbot, Margaret. "Scott Pruitt's Dirty Politics: How the Environmental Protection Agency Became the Fossil-Fuel Industry's Best Friend." *The New*

Yorker, April 2, 2018. https://www.newyorker.com/magazine/2018/04/02/scott-pruitts-dirty-politics?mbid=nl_Daily%20032618&CNDID=46231412&spMailingID=13196148&spUserID=MTcwMDQ5OTAxNzk5S0&spJobID=1362395989&spReportId=MTM2MjM5NTk4OQS2.

Vaughn, Jacqueline. *Environmental Politics: Domestic and Global Dimensions.* 5th edition. New York: Thomas Wadsworth, 2007.

Vaughn, Jacqueline, and Hanna J Cortner. *George W. Bush's Health Forests: Reframing the Environmental Debate.* Boulder: University Press of Colorado, 2005.

"Washington Post-ABC News Poll." *Washington Post*, December 10–13, 2009. http://www.washingtonpost.com/wp-srv/politics/polls/postpoll_121509.html.

Wong, Edward. "Trump Has Called Climate Change a Chinese Hoax. Beijing Says It Is Anything But." *The New York Times*, November 18, 2016. https://www.nytimes.com/2016/11/19/world/asia/china-trump-climate-change.html.

The Messy Process of Making Environmental Policy

Contents

© The Author(s) 2019
S. R. Rinfret and M. C. Pautz, *US Environmental Policy in Action*,
https://doi.org/10.1007/978-3-030-11316-2_3

67

Governor Moonbeam Fights Climate Change

In the second decade of the twenty-first century, there is much debate among citizens and lawmakers as to what the government should do about myriad environmental challenges, and especially climate change. The Donald J. Trump administration has demonstrated that, at least at the federal level, the government is taking a very different approach to environmental issues than it had in previous administrations. In particular, the incremental progress that had been made under Barack Obama's presidency regarding climate change has been reversed. These actions have upset many, including foreign leaders, mayors, and governors—notably the governor of California.

Governor Jerry Brown (Democrat) is the longest serving governor of California, which includes the 28-year gap between his second and third terms as governor. While first elected governor in 1975 (where he earned the moniker Governor Moonbeam), Brown was elected again in 2011 and 2014 (Whitaker 2017). Indeed, his political career may appear to some as having taken some unexpected turns. After two terms as governor and several unsuccessful bids for president, Brown returned to politics as the mayor of Oakland, California in 1999. He went on to be elected as the state's attorney general, and then returned to the governorship.

As Brown concluded his tenure as California's governor, he became increasingly outspoken against the shift in direction of the federal government's efforts regarding climate change. California is feeling the effects of climate change, and Governor Brown says the time for action is now. The state experienced an unprecedented fire season and scientists indicate that extremes in temperatures are going to become the new normal (Whitaker 2017). He, along with other governors, mayors, and elected officials, is taking steps to combat climate change.

In the Spring of 2017, Brown announced a partnership with China's president Xi Jinping to reduce carbon emissions, and declared a commitment with the Under2 Coalition, which is an alliance of 175 cities, states, and jurisdictions in 35 countries that encompass more than 1.2 billion people (Eggers 2017). Besides work on the international stage, California is weaning itself off of fossil fuels and there is a push to generate 50% of the state's electricity from renewable sources by 2030 (Whitaker 2017). California has also embraced a cap and trade system and a zero emissions vehicle mandate. In September 2018, Gov. Brown signed legislation that would require all of California's energy to come from clean power sources (e.g. solar, wind) by 2045 (Dillon 2018). These efforts stand in contrast to President Trump's statements during the 2016 campaign that climate change is a hoax (Whitaker 2017).

The federal system of government in the United States provides opportunities and challenges, as we have already discussed throughout this textbook. In this story of Governor Brown, a state is able to take actions itself to pursue environmental priorities its citizens have established despite seemingly countervailing efforts at the federal level. From one point of view, a federal system that enables diversity and action in policymaking is exciting as various efforts can be tried and states do not have to wait for the federal government to be in lockstep. But from a contrasting perspective, the federal system of government further complicates making environmental policy as one state out of 50 may be taking these actions (it is worth noting that other states and localities are pursuing their own efforts to combat climate change too). States in a federal structure only have so much power as the federal government retains supremacy. As this chapter reveals, the messy process of environmental policymaking is often driven by the challenges of our federal system of government.

The discussion of major environmental laws that we detailed in our look at the history of environmental policy in the United States may lead one easily to conclude that environmental laws are fairly simple to pass. Although this observation is logical, it is far from accurate. With today's hyper-partisanship in Washington, DC, we are acutely aware of the politics involved in policymaking, but that is only part of the story. Policymaking is often described as akin to sausage making—you never want to know what goes into the process; rather, you should just focus on the end result. Once you get those images out of your mind, we focus our attention to the messy process of making environmental policy. As you will discover, policymaking is, indeed, messy and, on reflection of the process, it is increasingly impressive that we have as many environmental laws as we do, and it is unsurprising that we see so many challenges surrounding environmental policymaking today.

Our examination of the policymaking process in this chapter demonstrates several themes: (1) the complexity exacerbated by numerous steps in the process, (2) the nature of the process will never yield the perfect legislation or solution, and (3) the process ensures that what does become policy has endured an arduous process that, whereas far from perfect, required consensus. These themes echo in our discussions of what policy is, how policy is made, and that the broader the context that policy is made in, it is wrought with competing factors. It would be easy to read this chapter and conclude that policymaking is a mess and nothing good could come of it. However, such a reading misses the point that the system was designed to be messy and if we start there, our study of policymaking will be much more fulfilling.

What Is Environmental Policy?

Frequently, the best place to start with a new concept is at the beginning with a definition. However, before we can define environmental policy, we need to back up and consider what policy is more generally, as environmental policy is but one type. Countless definitions of public policy abound and we make mention of a few of them here. Sara Rinfret et al. (2019) define public policy as "a course of action adopted or created by the government in response to public problems" (20). Michael Kraft and Scott Furlong (2007) define public policy as what is done or not done about public problems (4). Guy Peters (2004) defines public policy as the sum of government activities whether acting directly or through agents that influences the lives of citizens (4–6). Finally, Thomas Birkland (2016) defines policy as "a statement by government—at whatever level, in whatever form—of what it intends to do" (9). From just this handful of policy definitions, we can deduce several important attributes: policy is the action or inaction of government to a particular problem, and the government makes policy even if it is other actors (e.g., private contractors) who carry out the policy.

Public policy itself can take many forms. Policy may be statutes passed by Congress (or another legislative body at the state or local level of government); policy may be regulations written by an administrative agency (such as the Bureau of Land Management); policy may be the decision in a court (such as the Supreme Court's decision in the 1978 *Tennessee Valley Authority v. Hill* case that, because of the paper clip-sized snail darter fish, stopped a dam project that had already seen hundreds of millions of dollars spent); or policy may be a government agency's activities (such as Smokey the Bear's campaign to remind us that only we can prevent forest fires). It is important to understand that references to public policy can be any or all of the aforementioned manifestations of policy. The bulk of this chapter focuses on the actions of a legislative body—Congress—and, to some extent, governmental agencies.

As you might surmise from the previous paragraphs, environmental policy is but one area of public policy that the government is called to address by its citizenry. More specifically, environmental policy is government action related to the natural environment. Under the rubric of environmental policy, we might encounter policies related to natural resources issues, such as forests and endangered species to energy and transportation concerns to pollution. In this text, we use the term "environmental policy" as a broad umbrella term to encompass all these areas of policy, although they are often found to be their own policy subfields.

THE CONTEXT OF POLICYMAKING

At this juncture, note that environmental policy, like any other policy arena, exists in a much broader context, and it is easy to dive deeply into it and forget that environmental policy unfolds alongside many other policy arenas, events, and circumstances. Put differently, environmental policy does not exist in a vacuum. To help examine the various factors that impact environmental policy, we consider four different categories of factors. First, current circumstances and realities, along with public opinion on issues, affect environmental policymaking. "Focusing events" is the term political scientists and policy scholars use to describe major events that galvanize attention on a particular issue such as a crisis or a disaster (Kingdon 2011, 94). For instance, in the spring of 2010 an environmental focusing event was the explosion and subsequent sinking of the drilling platform Deepwater Horizon in the Gulf of Mexico. However, focusing events may or may not result in major policy action, and this one did not. Other notable environmental focusing events that led to policy enactments include the 1989 Exxon Valdez oil spill disaster off the coast of Alaska, which resulted in the Oil Pollution Act of 1990, or the actions of the residents of Love Canal, New York in the late 1970s, which ultimately brought about the Superfund law (more on this in the chapter's case study). Focusing events are defined events, or a series of events, that garner the attention of citizens and lawmakers around a particular issue.

Furthermore, also part of this category of factors that influences policymaking is the mood of the public and public opinion about issues. For example, as we saw in Chapter 2, public opinion and activism in the 1960s and 1970s helped spur the long list of environmental laws that were passed. In a country with a democratic tradition of government of the people, by the people, and for the people, the people ultimately have to want policy change and compel their lawmakers to enact it. The Deepwater Horizon incident surprised many environmental policy observers because it did not lead to significant legislation about the drilling of oil offshore. We can point to the mood of the public as a significant reason such policy was not made. Rightly or wrongly, at the time of the event, the public was mired in an economic downturn and believed low energy prices to be important for economic recovery; therefore, there was no public will to stop, or even slow, offshore.

Finally, this example helps demonstrate another dimension of this factor that influences policymaking—consideration of what else might be going on. What are the other priorities that may compete with a particular policy? Just as you can only take so many classes during a semester, governmental policymakers (and the public, for that matter) can only take on so many policy issues at any given time; therefore, different issuedrillings and policies are always competing for time and attention. Moreover, when crises emerge, some policy issues get crowded out in the environmental realm. Continuing with the example of the Deepwater Horizon explosion and sinking, the public and its lawmakers were consumed with many other competing priorities in 2010, and changes to offshore drilling policies did not make it onto the government's agenda.

A second category of factors that influences the context of environmental policymaking is economic considerations. As is the case in numerous facets of life, money matters. Often policymaking is contingent on the condition of the overall American economy, and even the global economy. Typically, when the economy is doing well, Americans are willing to consider quality of life issues such as the health and condition of the natural environment. When the economy is not doing well, moreover, Americans are usually more concerned with immediate financial considerations than environmental ones. In other words, if a policy might adversely impact the job market—or even just give the appearance of negatively influencing job prospects—many Americans will not support environmental policies for fear of further damaging a fragile economy.

Related to the overall condition of the economy are concerns about the cost of a particular policy proposal. Nearly all policies come with a price tag and, in the creation and passage of policy, these costs become a significant factor. How policies might be paid for garner significant debate. Perhaps, other programs or policies will be cut to pay for the new environmental policy or, maybe, new revenues will have to be raised, and either scenario begets debate. New revenues in the environmental realm might include increases in fees for permits or grazing cattle, or utilization of tax changes to reward environmentally friendly technology at firms and punish those with older, more antiquated technology.

A third category of factors that impacts environmental policymaking has to do with politics. Political timing is essential in almost all facets of governmental action. In particular, proximity to elections matter. For instance, if the next congressional election is just around the corner and a member of Congress is from a district that is overwhelmingly supportive of a new environmental law, then it behooves her to support the legislation as she seeks reelection, and vice versa. Furthermore, many policy issues get tabled if the next election is upon lawmakers because they may not want to take a stand on a particular issue and would rather focus their time on campaigning. For example, climate change legislation introduced in Congress in 2010 stalled in large part because of the upcoming midterm elections (cf. Hulse and Herszenhorn 2010; Stromberg 2010). However, if the election is a long way off, a lawmaker may act differently. Additionally, political calculations enter into play here. If a lawmaker is looking for support from a particular interest group or constituency, he might be more or less willing to support a particular policy if it aligns with his efforts to secure support (such as from the coal industry if his district's largest industry is coal mining). Finally, the actions and positions of the two major political parties influence which policies gain traction in government or go nowhere. Each political party chooses which issues it will emphasize and the positions that it endorses. Because of the role of parties in campaigns, and also in how elected bodies function and are organized, if a party does not endorse action, then action is unlikely to happen.

A final category of factors that impacts environmental policymaking has to do with the broader culture and values in the United States. The values Americans hold (such as liberty, equality, property rights, etc.) set the broad parameters for what is possible when it comes to policymaking. In other words, how the American populace feels on the whole about what the government should and should not do sets the tone for all governmental action. For example, an argument might be made that, in order to combat pollution from mobile sources (e.g., cars), everyone should drive a Toyota Prius or a plug-in electric car. Would such a policy ever stand a chance of passing Congress? Absolutely not! The reason for this is that Americans value a free market economy that emphasizes consumer choice. This may be an extreme example, but it demonstrates the broad values—and not those values that are typically ascribed to particular political ideologies—that set the outer bounds for policymaking. It is important to point out, particularly as environmental issues seem increasingly polarized politically, that the government is involved in environmental protection because the citizens want it to do so. In our form of government, and under the auspices of the social contract, government acts when it is directed to do so by the governed. Public opinion routinely demonstrates that the government has a role in environmental protection, but it is the extent of that role that is debated (Dunlap 2002; Sussman et al. 2002, 58). In March 2018, a Gallup Poll reported 28% of Americans said the government is doing about the right amount in terms of protecting the environment, 62% said it was doing too little, and only nine percent said it was doing too little (Gallup Poll 2018).

So far, through the lens of environmental policy, we have defined the major influences driving policymaking. It is easy to grow frustrated with elected lawmakers for the slow speed at which they pass policies (or do not pass them), but it is essential to remember that citizens demand much from their lawmakers across a variety of policy arenas, not just in the environmental realm. This is not to say that lawmakers could not strive to be more efficient and effective, but rather it is a reminder that policymaking is a messy business in an often busy context. The next section of this chapter explains the policy process, and demonstrates that process is far more complicated in light of this context. Although this chapter focuses on the process, Chapters 4 and 5 investigate the role of all the actors in the policy process.

THE POLICY PROCESS

After acknowledging the context of the policy process, we now look to demystifying that process. We focus on the stages model to policymaking, which is the policy model that dominates the academic study of the policy process. Before we get into the stages approach to policymaking, a few comments about policy models are necessary. As in so many areas of study, models are sought in policy studies in an effort to derive some order and pattern to the policy process. It is hoped that this order might help provide some predictability to policy. In addition, policy models help provide us a common vocabulary to talk about how policy is or is not made.

Although these attributes of policy models are beneficial, it is also important to note that policy models do not always fulfill our aspirations for them. For instance, there is far from one universally accepted policy model. We are going to spend the bulk of our time working through the stages model because it is the most detailed and commonly used policy model (cf. deLeon 1999; Nakamura 1987). However, this model and many others are far from predictive and do not always (or even generally) explain every policy that is enacted. The stages model assumes that the steps happen sequentially and in a linear fashion; again, as we will see, this may or may not describe policymaking in reality. You might be wondering why we are bringing up all of these issues with a model before we even discuss the model. The reason for these caveats is it is important to know from the outset that policymaking is difficult and it is, perhaps, a Sisyphean task to derive a policy model that explains it all. However, to understand this messy process, we must begin somewhere.

STAGES MODEL OF POLICYMAKING

The stages model to policymaking (sometimes also referred to as the textbook model or the stages heuristic model) continues to endure in policy studies and textbooks (cf. deLeon 1999; Nakamura 1987). The model articulates six steps to policymaking: (1) problem identification and definition, (2) agenda setting, (3) policy formulation, (4) policy legitimation, (5) policy implementation, and (6) policy evaluation (see Table 3.1).

Table 3.1 Steps of the policymaking process

1.	Problem identification and definition
2.	Agenda setting
3.	Policy formulation
4.	Policy legitimation
5.	Policy implementation
6.	Policy evaluation

Each of these six steps in the policymaking process comprises many dimensions, and each merits individual consideration.

Problem Identification and Definition

Before policy can be crafted, there has to be a problem. We often hear that the first step to solving a problem is articulating that problem, and the same is true in policymaking. This initial stage of the policy process requires that a problem be identified and defined. Although this step might seem obvious and clear, it is far more involved than initially indicated. First, consider how a problem is even acknowledged. All sorts of circumstances lead to the identification of a problem. In some instances, a singular event might focus citizens' and lawmakers' attention on a particular issue; an investigative journalist might call attention to a problem; scientists might publish a report indicating a major issue in need of a solution; or citizens might organize at the grassroots level and lobby for action to address an issue. Just because an issue is thought to be a problem by some people does not mean it is a problem to everyone. In addition, there may be a major problem, but few recognize the threat of the problem. For example, escalating carbon dioxide emissions have been an issue for decades, yet it has only been since the 1990s that there has been a concerted discussion of how carbon dioxide is a greenhouse gas. We can only guess what environmental issues that are already present today are going to be major issues 30 years from now.

Complicating problem identification in environmental policy is the tension between individual and societal values and the health and protection of the environment. Americans value their individual freedoms, such as their right to choose the kind of car they drive, but collectively the nation might prefer to see fuel efficient and low emissions vehicles for the sake of the planet. Reconciling these competing values can be difficult in the best of circumstances and downright impossible in others.

At this juncture, let us consider an example of problem identification related to the environment: gas prices. What might spur the notice of citizens and lawmakers about high gas prices? Perhaps, a rapid jump in gas prices over a short period of time might focus attention. Or, maybe, an environmental disaster at an oil refinery might threaten to bring about a major spike in gas prices as the refinery, which produces significant quantities of gasoline, will be shutdown indefinitely. Or, maybe, consumer groups get together and advocate for action regarding gas prices because of the struggling economy. Just because gas prices are high might not be a sufficient impetus to get lawmakers thinking about policy action because their attention could be focused elsewhere.

Simply uncovering a problem is only part of this step; the second half of problem identification encompasses defining that problem. This might seem simple enough—from our example, gas prices are high—but it is not quite that simple. Why is something a problem? Who says it is a problem? What is the cause of the problem? Answers to these questions are vital in policy discussions because these answers drive the rest of the policymaking process. As you might imagine, defining a problem becomes political; even with issues that you might consider to be highly technical and belonging to the realm of experts and scientists, those definitions can become highly charged. Consider the current discussions about climate change. Nearly all scientists conclude that carbon dioxide emissions are increasing globally and that human activity is the cause of those emissions, which is raising average temperatures across the planet. However, naysayers maintain that the scientists are wrong and that carbon dioxide levels are cyclical and caused by nature (Mann 2012; Powell 2011). The politics of the issue—and the implications that politicians will face if they acknowledge the problem—are trumping the science of the issue.

Much of how you define problems has to do with your vantage point and assessment of the situation, along with society's take on the matter. Put differently, problem definition is largely a social construction. Helen Ingram et al. (2007) point out that there is no single view of reality, as people understand and interpret reality differently. According to Deborah Stone (2002) "[p]roblem definition is a matter of representation because every description of a situation is a portrayal from only one of many points of view" (133). Accordingly, problem definitions are not correct or incorrect; rather, the definition is a function of the information, data, and sources to understand that problem and the social context of that problem definition. Just as your conception of a study session in college may include loud music and various beverages and your parent's view might not, the same is true in any policy arena, especially with regard to environmental issues.

A lot of the consternation over environmental issues has to do with how the various actors conceive of a problem. For some, saving a population of sea turtles might be a major issue that should command whatever resources are necessary, whereas, to others, saving sea turtles is great, but not at the expense of feeding the poor. Moreover, others may say that populations of sea turtles elsewhere will survive; therefore, we should not be too concerned with a few sea turtles in one geographic area. This example is rather stark and presents some false choices; nevertheless, it does demonstrate how different perceptions come into play when defining a problem. The social construction of issues is evident when we talk about saving polar bears—after all, society thinks they are cute and cuddly, as compared with saving a reptile or an insect. Society collectively places values on animals, and this value determination affects our problem identification and definition. How society comes to understand problems is a function of past policies, our institutions, culture, and the populations involved, according to Ingram et al. (2007, 3).

Let us return to our example of gas prices. Working from the recognition of high gas prices, how might you explain them? Why are gas prices high? Is it because there are not enough oil refineries to produce gasoline? Is it because we simply need more petroleum extraction than we currently have? Is it because our cars need more gas? Is it because more people have cars that are fuel inefficient? As you can see, answers to these questions go a long way in determining how the problem of high gas prices is conceptualized. If you think gas prices are high because there is not enough refining capacity or enough petroleum to refine into gasoline, then we have a supply issue. If you think gas prices are high because cars need to be more fuel efficient or people should drive less, then we have a demand issue. One's understanding of the problem will dramatically affect the rest of the policy process because an understanding of the problem coincides with possible solutions to it and how those solutions might receive adequate attention to facilitate action.

Agenda Setting

Step two in the policy process, after figuring out that there is a problem, is how to get the problem on the agenda of the government. Thomas Birkland (2011) defines the agenda as "the list of things that are being discussed and sometimes acted upon by an institution, the news media, or the public at large" (168). Simply having a problem defined may not be enough to compel it onto the radar of government. That problem has to become part of the government's agenda. "Agenda setting is the process by which problems and alternative solutions gain or lose public and elite attention, or the activities of various actors and groups that cause issues to gain greater attention or prevent them from gaining attention" (Birkland 2016, 200). Put differently, there are many identified public problems, but that does not mean that all those problems are being worked on by lawmakers or that solutions are being formulated. Only so many environmental issues, for instance, may find themselves scheduled on the calendars of lawmakers or the subject of committee hearings, or talked about in the public sphere. Accordingly, the obvious follow-up question is what does it take to get something on the government's agenda?

Getting a problem onto the agenda of government is difficult and unpredictable. Much of the progress from step one to step two in the policy process has to do with the actions of individuals and significant events, often referred to as focusing events. Let us take each factor in turn. First, individuals and organized groups do much to galvanize the government's attention and action on public problems. For example, much is being made of the process of hydraulic fracturing to extract natural gas from the shale beneath the earth's surface. Some groups are opposed to the process because of environmental concerns and are actively lobbying lawmakers to slowdown or thwart permits allowing this process to occur. Many groups were mobilized in the 1980s and 1990s to protect specific types of animals such as whales and polar bears. In these circumstances, groups committed to a particular issue work to get lawmakers to act on the issue.

A second factor is the influence of focusing events. A focusing event is "a sudden event that can generate attention to public problems or issues, particularly, issues and problems that are actually or potentially harmful" (Birkland 2016, 215). Put more succinctly, a focusing event draws the public's attention to a problem (Kingdon 2011). The terrorist attacks on September 11, 2001 have become a ubiquitous example of a focusing event that reshaped the nation's agenda. Furthermore, there are examples of focusing events, as we mentioned earlier, in the environmental realm that led to passage of environmental policy such as the Exxon Valdez spill off the coast of Alaska that led to the 1990 Oil Pollution Act, and examples of events that did not result in major legislation such as the Deepwater Horizon incident in 2010.

A third factor in bringing public problems to the agenda of government is the activities of key individuals, sometimes referred to as policy entrepreneurs. These individuals—many of whom might hold key government positions such as a legislative director for a member of

Congress or similar positions in interest groups—often do much to advance a particular policy issue by having the ability to access key decision-makers. According to John Kingdon (2011), the defining characteristic of policy entrepreneurs "is their willingness to invest their resources ... in the hope of a future return. That return might come to them in the form of policies" (122–123). In addition, researchers might put forth significant new work that demonstrates the emergence or discovery of a new problem or the increased severity of an existing problem. Such efforts can lead to an issue being propelled onto the government's agenda. A historical example is biologist Rachel Carson's publication of *Silent Spring* in 1962 that did much to raise alarm about the dangers of pesticides. Moreover, an elected official may fixate on a particular problem and do much to champion a policy solution for it. This individual's loud and persistent calls for action may galvanize support from fellow lawmakers.

Finally, the mood and focus of the general public might do much to catapult an issue onto the policymaking agenda. If enough members of the public get worked up over a particular issue and speak out about it, then the government may be inclined to appease its constituents and take action on that issue. Furthermore, if lawmakers are fixated on an issue, but the general public seems apathetic about it, there is a good chance that such a policy proposal might not gain the requisite traction in government to bring about policy change. The American Clean Energy and Security Act of 2009 might be an example. The bill, introduced during the 111th Congress, was approved by the House, but defeated in the Senate due, in part, to the lack of public interest.

Nonetheless, it is important to mention that environmental issues faced a couple of significant challenges, in recent years, in jettisoning them onto the government's agenda. In particular, the complexity of many environmental issues often stands in the way of them making it through this stage of the policy process. Put differently, many environmental issues—such as the loss of species biodiversity—are so complex and so many factors contribute to the problem, it can be difficult for government to take up the issue because tackling it is anything but straightforward. Moreover, issues like biodiversity are difficult to reduce to political rhetoric or slogans. What is the catchphrase for ensuring adequate biodiversity? It is not as easy as "Save the whales!"

A related issue is the increasingly political polarization surrounding environmental concerns. Much like marriage equality and abortion are litmus tests for a politician's political ideology, environmental concerns are more frequently becoming part of this calculus. Environmental issues are increasingly seen as issues important to liberals or progressives, even though that was not always the case. Finally, recalling the discussion in Chapter 2 about the role of science in public discourse, environmental issues frequently fail to get on the government's agenda as a result of how society thinks and consumes scientific information.

As we have done throughout our discussion of the policy process thus far, let us bring back the example of gas prices. We have already detailed how problem identification and definition is important in this example; therefore, we will pick up where we left off and consider how high gas prices might make it onto the agenda of government. From our discussion of the factors that often compel a problem onto the agenda, one way that gas prices might make it onto the agenda is that different organized groups might mobilize and protest what they believe to be arbitrary price hikes. Or a major fire at a refinery and the subsequent halting of gasoline production might be enough of a focusing event for lawmakers to fret over gas prices increasing. Or a new economic forecast might be released that projects gas prices will double in the next 12 months. Or a report from an organization such as the American Automobile Association (AAA) may indicate that only half the number of Americans took to the nation's roadways for the Fourth of July holiday because of high prices. Any of these scenarios might make gas prices a focus for policymakers. But it is essential to remember that just because prices may be high at the gas pump is not enough to get the issue on the agenda; other factors come into play.

Policy Formulation

After an issue is identified, defined, and put on the agenda of the government, policy formulation occurs. In terms of a definition, this is the stage of the policy process that comes when government is actively considering action on a particular issue and works to figure out what should be done, and also what should and should not be included as part of the policy solution. Birkland (2016) reminds us that this part of the process necessitates both technical analysis and politics (299). In other words, a technically devised and rational solution to a problem has to be balanced with political calculations to secure passage. This balance is why policies often get passed that may not be the best solution to a problem, as political expediency has to come into consideration at this stage. Furthermore, because of different conceptions of problem definition, the best solution is likely to be as elusive as a unicorn.

Before we can get into the various steps a government can and cannot take to solve a public problem, there are a number of policy design elements that Thomas Birkland (2016) articulates: goals, causes, tools, targets, and implementation that merit consideration. With government actively considering action on a particular problem, we first have to understand the goals or the intentions of that action. Is the intention to eliminate the problem altogether or simply make things better in the short term? Are efforts supposed to stop the problem from getting worse or make conditions better than what they are currently? Consider climate change as an example of something that policymakers might tackle. In evaluating climate change policy options, are the goals to stop it from happening? Or is the goal to slow the pace of climate change? Is the emphasis on diminishing the rates of carbon dioxide released into the atmosphere or is it to reduce the total levels of carbon dioxide in the atmosphere? Answers to these questions dictate which tools or actions the government may take to address a policy problem. Questions about goals, moreover, beget a discussion of competing goals. In American society, numerous goals are espoused, including: liberty, security, and efficiency (Birkland 2016; see also Stone 2012). The conceptual implication is that these goals can all be achieved simultaneously, whereas, in reality, that is often not the case.

Consider liberty and efficiency. Perhaps, the most efficient way for government to limit the emissions of carbon dioxide is for the government to mandate that all Americans take public transportation or carpool to any destination. Maybe such a policy approach is, by far, the most "scientific" and "rational" solution to the problem, along with the most efficient. Think for a moment, is this a policy solution that is ever going to be considered? The answer is emphatically no. Why? Because we value personal freedoms in this country and believe that we should not be constrained in the manner in which we get from one place to another. We want choice. Therefore, in this example, tensions between liberty and efficiency dominate.

Answering questions about the goals of a policy further necessitates a consideration of causation. Policymaking depends heavily on the causes of problems because, without understanding those causes, how can a solution be devised (cf. Stone 2012)? For instance, is the climate changing because of significant growth in carbon dioxide emissions due to human sources? If so, then the policy tools that might be employed will be directed at human behavior. If, by contrast, the cause of climate change is the simple cycle of the natural environment, then the array of policy tools before policymakers will be radically different. As Deborah Stone (2012) reminds us, however, causal stories often "have a political life independent of the evidence for them" (207). In other words, science and research may tell us one thing about causation, whereas political rhetoric—in an effort to reduce problems to their most simplistic language for political motives—might tell us another story. Accordingly, different political forces might come up with competing stories, thereby complicating policy formulation. Even if causes can be determined, those causes must be readily linked to the ability of the government to address the matter.

A third element of policy design that Birkland (2011) discusses is the target of a particular policy. More specifically, Birkland is referring to whose behavior and whose actions a policy is intended to affect, and how those populations are viewed by society. Different populations that may or may not be affected by a particular policy solution are likely to garner more support and interest from policymakers than others (Schneider and Ingram 1997). For instance, there are certain groups of people in society that policymakers are likely to defend and seek to help, almost regardless of political party affiliation; such groups include small business owners and members of the military. These groups are considered more advantaged in our society than, say, individuals we consider deviants such as criminals, and even the poor and those on welfare (Schneider and Ingram 1997, 102–145).

Think for a moment, how often do you hear politicians talk about protecting small business owners versus protecting those individuals collecting welfare? Have you ever stopped to think about why? The reason is that we, as a society, think of small business owners as the epitome of the American dream—pursuing an endeavor and giving it all they have—whereas we often collectively think of those on welfare as lazy and needing to take more responsibility in life. Of course, these are gross over-generalizations, but they are indicative of how we view different groups in society. The views of groups in society affect how policymakers approach any possible policy solution that may impact these groups. As we have seen in recent years, this is why aid to small business owners is easier and more politically palatable for politicians to support, whereas additional aid for those collecting unemployment benefits, is much harder to get behind and accomplish politically.

In the realm of environmental issues, efforts to curb the effects of climate change may, indeed, have adverse effects on the manufacturing sector in the United States and may bring about additional costs to employers.[1] As a result, such policies are proceeded with in a tepid fashion because of how we view the companies that create jobs. By contrast, some fringe environmental groups advocate eco-terrorism (see Chapter 5's case study for further discussion) such as torching vehicles that are not fuel efficient or burning ski resorts or neighborhoods that are perceived as flagrantly wasting resources and, as such, are not viewed nearly as positively in society, regardless of one's opinions about the points these organizations may be endeavoring to make.

The final element of policy design that has to be considered is how a policy is going to be implemented. Here, Birkland (2011) is referring to the practical aspects of policy design. Who is going to carry out the policy and how are they going to do it? These dimensions are critical because if policymakers are going to invest the time and energy in a policy solution, then, they want to be sure that the policy has a good chance of succeeding in achieving its desired ends. Particular issues here refer to what government agency at what level of government (i.e., federal, state, or local) is going to be responsible for implementation. Moreover, is it the policymakers themselves who are going to write all the particular rules or is a government agency going to do that and might those affected by new rules be part of the rulemaking process (more on this subject in Chapter 7)? In deciding what to do about a particular problem, policymakers consider these important questions at this juncture of policy formulation. This discussion of implementation leads us into a conversation about the more tangible policy tools at the disposal of government.

When policymakers are actively working on a policy solution to a given problem, they have a lot of different options or tools for how to address the issue. Simply put, policy tools are the various methods at the disposal of policymakers to achieve their goal. Policymakers have lots

---

[1] Such a claim, however, is contentious in the realm of environmental regulation as there are countless examples of where environmental goals do not jeopardize economic goals, even though society oftentimes views these aims as mutually exclusive. The use of this debate here is more for example purposes rather than advocacy of one view over another.

of different ways of getting individuals or organizations to do things or stop from doing things. James Anderson (2002) discusses policy tools as "techniques of control" whereas Anne Schneider and Helen Ingram (1997) discuss tools as the aspects of policy "that cause agents or targets to do something they would not do otherwise with the intention of modifying behavior to solve public problems" (Schneider and Ingram 1997, 93). At this juncture, stop and think about all the different ways government achieves its goals; government collects money, gives out money, tells us only we can stop a forest fire, mandates safety features on cars, and ensures that the foods we eat have labels to tell us what is in them and their nutritional values. These are just a handful of many examples of the methods in government's policy toolbox.

To help us organize our discussion of policy tools, there are numerous typologies devised by policy scholars. Here, we look to B. Guy Peters's (2004) categorization scheme that includes six broad categories of policy tools: laws, services, money, taxes, other economic instruments, and suasion. Consider each of these categories in turn. Laws refer to the regulations that tell people and organizations what they can and cannot do. They tell us that you must be 21 to purchase and consume alcohol and they tell facilities that, if they are going to emit air pollution, they must have a permit to do so. Laws directly dictate particular behaviors. Services comprise another category of policy tools. These include the direct provision of goods and services by government. For example, the government provides postal service to Americans and provides weather information and forecasts through the Department of Commerce's National Oceanographic and Atmospheric Administration (NOAA) and the National Weather Service.

A third category of tools is money. The government conveys funds, often through grants for all sorts of projects, from academic research on the causes of problems and possible solutions to creating and maintaining government corporations such as the Federal Deposit and Insurance Corporation and Amtrak, ensuring our money in banks is secure and providing passenger rail service, respectively. Taxation is another category of policy tools. The government collects taxes to spend money on everything from national security and snow removal to research into new alternative energies. Furthermore, the government provides tax credits for using energy efficient products in homes or buying hybrid vehicles. Other economic instruments are another category that includes loans and subsidies to achieve policy goals. A prime example is student loans.

The government helps its citizens access higher education by providing loans to help pay for it. In addition, the government employs various subsidies to farmers and insurance programs for those individuals who live in areas highly likely to flood. Finally, the government employs various methods of suasion to solve public problems. These are less direct ways that the government aims to encourage or discourage particular behaviors. For instance, the campaign of Smokey the Bear to prevent forest fires is an example, just as there are public service announcements about the ill effects of drug use or warnings on tobacco products.

In light of our discussion of the elements of policy design, we begin to get a sense of what this stage of the policy process entails. With these considerations, policymakers in this part of the process figure out what to do about a problem and how it might be solved, or at least ameliorated. It is important to point out that this step of the process has a multitude of actors (which will be discussed more thoroughly in Chapters 4 and 5) that impact the design of a policy solution and articulate—often competing—views on a problem and its proposed policy's goals, causation, targets, and means of implementation. All of which compounds the difficulties of this stage.

As we have with the preceding discussion of each step in the policy process, let us return to our example of high gas prices. Policy formulation surrounding this issue stems from how the problem was defined and what compelled the issue onto the agenda. Presume that the issue has been defined in such a way that stipulates that high demand is the cause of high gas prices and that the latest consumer craze among cars is a vehicle that is chic and stylish, but gets 8 miles per gallon because it is massive and easily transports 10 people. What might some policy solutions be? An option might be to stop the sale of vehicles with fuel efficiency less than 10 miles per gallon, but, as discussed previously, how would competing goals and values of society respond to such a proposition? Moreover, regulation might achieve this end, but would a campaign of suasion be more effective in getting consumers to want to buy vehicles that are more fuel-efficient? Another option might be to encourage more citizens to take part in public transportation and to carpool. Think about what kinds of incentive programs—perhaps, tax credits or programs such as discounted fares—might make this policy solution more approachable. Any policy solution advocated must then take heed of the political forces in play and consider how the politics of the time might advance or impede such efforts. And this takes us to the fourth stage of the policy process.

Policy Legitimation

After policy formulation comes the fourth stage of the process, policy legitimation. This is the part of the policy process with which you are likely most familiar. In a nutshell, this is how a bill becomes a law. Indeed, many of us may remember the classic segment "I'm Just a Bill" from *Schoolhouse Rock* (and if you do not, find it on YouTube). More formally, policy legitimation is the stage of the policy process when a proposed policy becomes law. This might happen in Congress for federal policymaking, or it may occur in state legislatures, or maybe even at the local level in entities like a city council. For our purposes, we are largely focused at the federal level. Therefore, let us briefly review how a bill makes it through Congress to become law.

After a policy solution has been advocated and the language drafted in the form of a bill, or proposed law, it is introduced in one chamber of Congress, either the House of Representatives or the Senate. We often think that all bills must start in the House, but that is only true of bills that raise revenues. A member of Congress must introduce the bill to a particular chamber, but that does not mean that a member has to write the bill. In fact, many bills are written by congressional staffers, members of interest groups, or other individuals rather than by a member of Congress. This wide range of authors allows for greater diversity in the authorship of a bill and greater democratic access to the process of crafting policy solutions.

When the bill is introduced, it may be referred to a particular committee, or very likely, may not go beyond simple introduction to a chamber of Congress. The process of committee referral in each chamber varies and is beyond our scope here, but it is important to note that the committee a bill is referred to makes all the difference in a bill's chances for passage. Bills are sent to committees for closer examination and revisions. Which committee a bill gets referred to depends on politics—which leaders in the chamber are doing the referring and whether or not those leaders want the bill to survive committee review or not. To start with, there are a multitude of committees with competing jurisdictions; therefore, it is not as simple as referring anything related to the environment to one committee; moreover, within committees, there are subcommittees to contend with. Table 3.2 lists the 115th (January 2017–January 2019) Congress' Committees and Subcommittees that have a connection with environmental and natural resource issues.

Table 3.2   Congressional committees and subcommittees pertaining to environmental and natural resource issues

House

- Agriculture
  - Commodity Exchanges, Energy, and Credit
  - Conservation and Forestry
  - Nutrition
  - General Farm Commodities and Risk Management
  - Biotechnology, Horticulture, and Research
  - Livestock and Foreign Agriculture
- Appropriations
  - Agriculture, Rural Development, Food and Drug Administration, and Related Agencies
  - Commerce, Justice, Science, and Related Agencies
  - Energy and Water Development, and Related Agencies
  - Interior, Environment, and Related Agencies
  - Labor, Health and Human Services, Education, and Related Agencies
- Energy and Commerce
  - Energy
  - Environment
  - Health
  - Oversight and Investigations
- Natural Resources
  - Energy and Mineral Resources
  - Federal Lands
  - Oversight and Investigations
  - Water, Power, and Oceans
- Science, Space, and Technology
  - Energy
  - Environment
- Transportation and Infrastructure
  - Coast Guard and Maritime Transportation
  - Highways and Transit
  - Railroads, Pipelines, and Hazardous Materials
  - Water Resources and Environment

Senate

- Agriculture, Nutrition, and Forestry
  - Commodities, Risk Management, and Trade
  - Rural Development and Energy
  - Conservation, Forestry, and Natural Resources
  - Nutrition, Specialty Crops, and Agricultural Research
  - Livestock, Marketing, and Agricultural Security

(continued)

Table 3.2 (continued)

House

- Appropriations
  - –Agriculture, Rural Development, Food and Drug Administration, and Related Agencies
  - –Commerce, Justice, Science, and Related Agencies
  - –Energy and Water Development
  - –Interior, Environment, and Related Agencies
  - –Transportation, Housing and Urban Development, and Related Agencies
- Commerce, Science, and Transportation
  - –Aviation Operations, Safety, and Security
  - –Consumer Protection, Product Safety, Insurance, and Data Security
  - –Oceans, Atmosphere, Fisheries, and Coast Guard
  - –Surface Transportation and Merchant Marine Infrastructure, Safety, and Security
- Energy and Natural Resources
  - –Energy
  - –National Parks
  - –Public Lands, Forests, and Mining
  - –Water and Power
- Environment and Public Works
  - –Clean Air and Nuclear Safety
  - –Fisheries, Water, and Wildlife
  - –Superfund, Waste Management, and Regulatory Oversight
  - –Transportation and Infrastructure

Sources Available from http://www.house.gov/committees/ and https://www.senate.gov/committees/committees_home.htm

The use of committees is well-intentioned in terms of contending with the scale and scope of the work before Congress at any given time; however, this same structure designed to ease the workload can also encumber the process of lawmaking. Indeed, most bills never make it out of committee. Multiple committees may have jurisdiction over an issue, such as gas prices, and the committee chairpersons might fight over getting a bill referred to their committee. Or a bill could face multiple committee assignments.

After a bill makes it to committee, the committees and subcommittees begin studying the problem, the proposed bill, and alternative solutions. Hearings are often held in which experts are called to testify before the committee, and revisions to the bill take place. If a bill has survived all these steps, it may then be subjected to a committee vote. If the committee votes in favor of the bill, it will be referred to the entire chamber for consideration. Then, a bill may be scheduled for a floor debate before the entire membership of the chamber and, perhaps, even a vote. Only if a bill successfully survives this entire process might the bill pass one chamber of Congress and, then, go on to the other chamber to repeat the entire process.

If a bill survives the same process in the other chamber, only then does the bill go on to the White House for the president to consider. However, Congress cannot send the president two different versions of a bill. Although the bills before each chamber might start off similarly to each other, they frequently get different revisions in the two chambers; therefore, those differences have to be worked out in a conference committee before heading to the president. Then, the president can sign the bill or veto it. More conversation about the actors involved in this process, particularly at this stage, follows in Chapters 4 and 5.

Let us return to our example of high gas prices. Based on a problem definition that there is not enough gas, so the price per gallon has dramatically risen, a policy solution might be to increase offshore drilling such that there will be more oil extracted that can be refined into gasoline. Perhaps, a member of the House drafts a bill in consultation with her staffers and with some input from the American Petroleum Institute to help dictate which areas should be more easily drilled. Now, the Let's Get More Oil Bill has been drafted and introduced to the House. A fight invariably ensues over which committee the bill should be referred to. On the one hand, the bill's sponsor wants to see her bill go before the House Energy and Commerce committee because she sits on the committee and she knows her committee chairperson is like-minded in what should be done about reducing the burden of high gas prices for Americans. On the other hand, other members of the House want to see the bill referred to the Natural Resources committee because that committee may be inclined to take a careful look at the threat to marine life that may be impacted if another drilling rig offshore suffers a catastrophic event such as Deepwater Horizon did. This committee could potentially rewrite significant portions of the Let's Get More Oil Bill so the bill effectively becomes the Let's Get More Oil as Long as We Don't Hurt the Fish Bill. Without taking this example too much further, it is already evident how political this process might become, even without the Congress considering other issues and worrying about the broader context (as we discussed earlier in this chapter) of the legislative environment.

It is understandable to decry the speed at which Congress legislates; however, a couple of important points should be mentioned. First, our founders intentionally set up Congress to function slowly because they feared the possible outcomes if the legislative process was too easy or too quick. This slower, more deliberative process ensures that the bills that are passed are truly what the majority want, what the people want.

Second, the issues before Congress are frequently complex—just recall our discussion of how we define problems. Therefore, it can be advantageous that Congress takes its time considering how a proposed bill might solve—or at least ameliorate—a public problem. Complicated problems take time to understand and figure out solutions and rushing action is likely to cause more problems.

Third, as a result of the lawmaking process, compromise and consensus building are a must. As a result, the law that eventually passes may be quite different—or at least contain some rather unexpected provisions—simply because of what needed doing to get the bill passed. Reviewing the process in which a bill becomes a law reminds us how involved and slow lawmaking often is, but remember this is just the fourth of six steps in the policymaking process. At times, it is easy to wonder how any policy gets passed.

Policy Implementation

The passage of a bill and its signing into law—complete with a presidential signing ceremony with lots of ceremonial pens at the White House or some other picturesque location—is often where our attention to policies stop. After all, creation of the policy is the cantankerous part of the process, where anything can happen. After a bill becomes law, how interesting can things be? The simple answer is quite interesting. Policy implementation is the fifth step of the policy process and this step is frequently removed from the public spotlight as it is presumed to be merely carrying out a law. Birkland (2011) defines policy implementation as the "process by which policies enacted by government are put into effect by the relevant agencies" (263). This is where the rubber meets the road; however, it is not quite that simple.

It is commonly thought that "implementation should be easy" and people are "upset when expected events do not occur or turn out badly"

(Pressman and Wildavsky 1973, xi–xvii). Implementation can easily go awry when we stop to think about the actual language of a law that Congress gives the multitude of government agencies to work with to implement. For example, the 1972 Clean Water Act discusses the aims of the law to ensure the nation's waterways are "swimmable" and "fishable." Pause for a moment and consider this language. How would you define swimmable? Is swimmable simply a body of water that is liquid, one that you can paddle around in that is not radioactive? Or do you prefer a water body that is free of debris floating in it? But what about the pollution you cannot see in the water? So, perhaps, you would rather swim in a water body that is crystal clear and seemingly untouched by humans? Clearly, there are many interpretations of this vague statutory language, and herein lies the challenge of policy implementation.

To make the nation's waterways swimmable and fishable, standards need to be determined along with what is an acceptable level of pollution and what is unacceptable. Here is where scientists and other experts step into figure out these standards based on evidence and modeling. Accordingly, policy implementation brings together lots of people and lots of organizations, frequently all over the country, in an effort to figure out what policymakers actually meant by the language in a newly created piece of legislation and how lofty goals can be given concrete action steps. It would be much simpler if laws were clear and specific regarding what the elected leaders of the country wanted done and how they wanted it done. However, laws are far from clear. Think back to the process of how a bill becomes a law. There is a lot of political wrangling and there is much compromise to even get that vague statutory language in the first place. Furthermore, a lot of the details are left to experts in the field. For example, Congress saved many of the details associated with the Clean Water Act to be worked out by the US Environmental Protection Agency (EPA) because that is where the scientists are, not (necessarily) in the halls of Congress. Given the significance of this often-negated step of the policy process, Chapters 6 and 7 will devote far more detail to this part of the process and examine the actors involved in this step.

When we last discussed high gas prices, the Let's Get More Oil Bill was working its way through a maze of congressional committees. When our fictional bill was passed by Congress and signed by the president, it contained provisions to allow more drilling offshore in the United States, but only in selected areas. It might make sense for those areas to be determined by study of the reserves of oil under the seabed, for example, but Congress decided that to appease its members and ensure those members of Congress who did not want more drilling could go back to their districts and say they stopped drilling in certain areas; thus, the bill contains a list of areas where drilling is permitted. Some of those areas include Lake Michigan, the Cuyahoga River in Cleveland and the East River in New York City. Consider for a moment how these designations fit with what even the average person knows about offshore drilling. Can you picture huge drilling rigs in these areas? Is it even worth drilling in these areas? This is an extreme example, of course, but it conveys that the provisions in bills may or may not make the most scientific sense, much less commercial. To implement this bill, Congress delegated responsibility to the Department of the Interior—more specifically, to the US Geological Survey and the Bureau of Ocean Energy Management, Regulation and Enforcement. These subunits of the Interior Department then have the onerous task of figuring where, in the specified waterways, drilling can commence, what the parameters for drilling in those areas must be, especially taking into consideration that those waterways are used for lots of other purposes, including transportation and recreation. It is increasingly evident that there are numerous challenges ahead for this Department in implementing the Let's Get More Oil Bill, and it will invariably take a good bit of time. Again, we will return to the challenges of implementation in subsequent chapters.

Policy Evaluation

We have finally made it to the last stage of the policymaking process: policy evaluation. Formally, policy evaluation is the "measurement and assessment of policy and program effects, including successes and failures" (Kraft and Furlong 2007, 71). This description seems straightforward enough; evaluation is about figuring out if the policy is working or not. However, as we have seen in each of the steps of the process so far, the process is much more complicated than it appears. For starters, a simple determination of whether a policy is working is far from a decisive conclusion. Rarely, if ever, is the answer a yes or a no. The answer usually lies somewhere between those two conclusions. Moreover, this does not even consider the difficulty in getting to a conclusion. Let us unpack some of the challenges associated with policy evaluation and the varying motivations behind policy, keeping in mind that a more robust conversation about these issues will come later in Chapter 8.

First, to figure out if a policy is working, you have to have a definition of what constitutes working. This may seem simple enough, but think about the challenges policies are supposed to overcome—cleaning the air, protecting the water, preventing contamination. What is clean air? Does that mean the air is clean enough that it is pure oxygen? Is it clean enough not to make people sick? Well, what is clean enough? The significance of this conversation is that, if we do not have a clear understanding of what the goal of a policy is, it is difficult to assess the effects of that policy.

This leads us to a second issue in policy evaluation—determining causality. One must measure that if there is an observed change such as cleaner air, is it the result of a particular policy or something else? Herein lies the difficulty associated with determining causation in the social sciences. Does X cause Y? Does the Clean Air Act lead to improved air quality? Ultimately, it is difficult to make such conclusions because there are too many factors that might be influencing outcomes. Consider the classic social science causation scenario: as the number of churches in a town increases, so does the number of bars. Does this mean that churches incite more bars? No, not at all. So what is going on here? As a town grows in size, there are usually more places of religious worship, as well as more of everything else, including bars. Air quality may improve for a multitude of reasons that may or may not be attributable to a particular policy.

Third, the effects of a policy may be diffuse and difficult to measure. In other words, a policy may, indeed, be helping improve a particular condition or even having its intended effects, but there are a lot of other effects; therefore, it is difficult to attribute those positive effects to the policy. Returning to the Let's Get More Oil Law, let us say that drilling is occurring in the East River and maybe gas prices are falling, but they are only falling by 5 cents a gallon. The drilling may actually be having a more profound effect on gas prices, but geopolitical tensions in other parts of the world are driving up the cost of gas; therefore, the effects of the Let's Get More Oil Law are not demonstrating the true nature of its impact.

All of the aforementioned challenges of policy evaluation presume that the data needed to study if a policy is working are obtainable. Data acquisition issues plague policy evaluation. How do we measure improvements in public health, for example? Associated with challenges in gathering data is also the issue of resistance. Oftentimes, the data sought to figure out if a policy is working has to come from the people and the agencies responsible for implementing that policy. Sometimes, they are freely willing to provide whatever data they can and, at other times, they are not. At first glance, you might be taken aback by resistance from these officials, but on closer consideration it makes sense. Government agencies are much maligned in society; therefore, the releasing of data is often construed in a way to make an agency look bad and full of lazy, incompetent bureaucrats who are wasting time and money. Given the resource challenges of government agencies, they may have difficulty even collecting or managing the data.

Our brief discussion of the challenges associated with policy evaluation enable us to see that this step is far from simple, and it is increasingly evident how some individuals may read the evaluation of a policy one way, whereas others may perceive it differently. Again, a more robust conversation about policy evaluation emerges in Chapter 8.

Policy Failure

The outcome of policy evaluation may be that a policy is not working as intended or perhaps is creating problems that were not anticipated when the policy was created and implemented. These findings may lead to conclusions that the policy is a failure. It is important to note that a policy can be labeled a failure for any number of reasons that may or may not be substantiated by systematic research and evidence through policy evaluation. It may instead be based on political ideology, or even a lack of complete information. Just like problem definition can vary based on different understandings of an issue, policy failure can be a result of contrasting views on a policy and how the objectives of that policy were operationalized and assessed. Therefore, to one stakeholder a policy may have failed while to another stakeholder a policy might be successful.

The reasons that policies fail are as varied as the policies themselves. Thomas Birkland (2016) summarizes existing policy research into a handful of explanations, including:

1. other policy alternatives may have been more or less successful;
2. circumstances changed effecting the success or failure of the policy in question;

3. political institutions may have impeded the implementation of the policy;
4. there were implementation problems associated with the policy;
5. the understanding of the cause of the public problem was flawed; and
6. the expectations for the ability of the policy to solve the problem were simply too grandiose.

Of course these explanations are simplistic, but they illustrate that even well-designed policy can fail and objective assessments of well-crafted policy can also conclude failure. But even in failure, lessons can and should be learned. Just as doing poorly on a particular exam or paper should encourage reflection and study as to what went wrong (e.g., a thorough understanding of a topic was erroneously presumed), policy failure should result in learning and improvements in the future. The use of high occupancy vehicle (HOV) lanes could be argued to be an example of policy failure. These lanes were conceived as a way to provide cars with multiple people the advantage of their own dedicated highway lanes on particularly congested stretches of road. The intent with these lanes was threefold: (1) gasoline usage and emissions would decrease, (2) carpooling would increase, and (3) vehicle traffic would decrease. These goals have not been achieved, and according to some studies, the use of these lanes has actually decreased (Ganos 2011)! It is worth mentioning that different regions have had varying experiences with these lands, but widespread reductions in vehicle traffic, gasoline usage, and emissions have not been realized with this policy.

FLAWS OF THE STAGES MODEL AND ALTERNATIVE POLICY MODELS

Many pages have been spent discussing the process of policymaking in an effort to organize the seemingly chaotic nature of making policy. In addition, we have to look at different policy theories or policy models beyond the stages model to help us make sense of the messy nature of the process. At this juncture, we may have ended up someplace far different than you were expecting when we began our look at the policymaking process. As in many areas of study, you might have imagined the process would be nice, neat, and easy to understand. After only this brief review of the process, you are likely to conclude that policymaking is messy and, seemingly, without much order. Now we are going to add to that frustration. The policy process that we have detailed is arguably the most common model for policymaking, but it is far from perfect; therefore, we need to consider the flaws associated with this model (cf. deLeon 1999).

The six-step policymaking process we have just covered is often referred to as the textbook approach or the stages model. These labels come from the model's ease of understanding and its, seemingly, orderly progression. However, these descriptors are also indicative of the model's flaws. First, this model assumes that policymaking happens in an orderly or linear way. Step one happens before step three, for example. The reality is, this may or may not be the case depending on the particular policy issue. For example, a policy solution may already be developing when a crisis happens, catapulting the issue onto the national agenda. Often in a crisis, there are already ideas or options to solve or even prevent that crisis in the first place that have been discussed prior. For example, prior to the Exxon Valdez oil spill, there were already recommendations and policy options about mandating double-hulls for oil tanker ships. Policy solutions are always being crafted, regardless of whether or not a problem is clearly identified and defined.

Second, the stages model does not do a good job taking into account external forces that may impact policymaking at any step along the way. As we discussed earlier, policymaking does not happen in a vacuum—other forces and factors are likely to impact the success of a particular policy option—but where are those forces accounted for in this model? The simple answer is they are not, beyond a consideration of how a policy idea comes to the agenda of government. The stages model isolates a particular policy issue so the broader policymaking context is neglected.

Third, little about this model is predictable. Just because agenda setting is occurring, this does not mean that the policy will move to policy formulation, and this model provides no indication of how long a policy may stay in one part of the process. Therefore, this model has little to no predictive capabilities. The stages model does not help us understand how long any of the stages of the model will take.

If there are so many flaws associated with it, you are probably wondering why we spent pages explaining this model to you? To begin, when we broach the subject of policymaking in the United States, we have to start somewhere, and this model provides us with a good, concrete overview for individuals new to the policy process. In addition, this model affords us the ability to talk about key aspects of policymaking and gives us relevant vocabulary to build our understanding of the process.

Accordingly, this discussion demonstrates that there is not one clear model to follow when it comes to policymaking, and that is acceptable. In fact, that is part of what keeps the study of policymaking interesting. Numerous other policy models exist and are discussed in policy studies, but none more so than the stages model. The stages model, although far from perfect, achieves our introductory goals: first, it provides us some basics of policymaking and gives us a language to talk about the dimensions of the process and, second, it helps us understand the messy and unpredictable nature of the process.

In response to some of the shortcomings of the stages model, other policy models endeavor to represent more accurately the policymaking process. It is worth mentioning a couple of those models, particularly as they respond to the issues we have identified in the stages model. John Kingdon (2011), after studying policymaking in the health and transportation sectors, articulated the Multiple Streams Framework (MSF). This approach to policymaking demonstrates that it is not necessarily a neat, linear process and much happens simultaneously. There are three "streams" of activity that exist alongside one another: the politics stream, the problem stream, and the policy stream. Only when these three streams come together does policymaking happen. While Kingdon's MSF responds to critiques of the stages model being too linear as compared with reality, the Advocacy Coalition Framework (ACF), developed by Paul Sabatier and Hank Jenkins-Smith (1993), strives to contend with complicated policy matters and accounting for the array of actors at multiple levels of government and the public sector who exert influence on the policy process in different ways and at different times of the process. The ACF also takes into account the external factors that might affect policymaking as well. Yet another policymaking theory is Punctuated Equilibrium that looks to explain policymaking in periods of relative stability, or "equilibria," and policymaking in times of instability, or "punctuations." Frank Baumgartner and Bryan Jones (1993) seek to explain how policy is often made incrementally but, on occasion, can be made dramatically during times of crises. While these three models of policymaking—in addition to many other policy theories—endeavor to accurately represent policymaking in the real world and overcome the shortcomings of the stages model. In the end, though, all of the models are imperfect, yet they do help advance our understanding of the messy nature of policymaking in the United States.

Structural Factors and Influences on Policymaking

The final section of this chapter discusses various structural factors and other influences on the policymaking process that roil policy scholars as they endeavor to devise an accurate policymaking model. First, we consider structural influences of our governmental system and their effect on policymaking, and, then, we turn to broader tendencies and conditions in our society that impact this messy process.

Checks and Balances

Several structural factors in the American government and society serve to influence how policy is made. First among these factors is the notion of checks and balances. In an effort to ensure that the three branches of government—the legislative, the executive, and the judicial—would stay in balance with one another, the founders put forth a variety of ways in which one branch of government can exercise control over the other branches. James Madison, in *Federalist 51*, spoke of a need to ensure that ambition must counteract ambition. Thus, these checks thwart the ability of one branch to dominate another. For instance, Congress checks executive power by approving the appointments a president makes to executive agencies and by overriding a presidential veto. The Congress checks judicial power by confirming federal judicial appointments, making the laws that may be considered by the courts, and being a key part of the process to amending the Constitution. The executive branch can veto laws passed by the Congress and is responsible for implementing the laws the legislature passes. In addition, the executive branch selects the members of the federal courts (with Senate confirmation). The courts are responsible for determining the constitutionality of laws made and the actions of the executive branch. These checks serve to complicate the policy process in that their considerations of the other branches of government and their probable actions could slow or stymie action. For example, much political wrangling over a piece of environmental legislation may come about because of what the White House may or may not do in response to a particular law, or Congress may decide that with the threat of a presidential veto, the already tepid support for a piece of environmental policy is not worth the trouble.

Federalism

The federal system of government employed in the United States is another structural factor to consider. Federalism is a system of government in which there is a national level of government with various subnational governmental units. Several other countries besides the United States employ this sort of system, including Germany and India, but it is far from a common system. Here, we have a national government (often referred to as the federal government), we have 50 state governments, and we have more than 89,000 local units of government (based on the last Census Bureau Census of Governments), which include counties, towns, and school districts (US Census Bureau 2012). Simply put, a federal system of government has a lot of different governmental units that have to be coordinated and may have to work collaboratively to accomplish the work of government. The effects of this factor are particularly apparent in environmental policy when you think about the fact that most major environmental laws were passed at the national level and then contain provisions for the involvement of the US EPA along with the relevant state agencies. For instance, consider the Clean Air Act. Congress passed this law, as discussed in the last chapter, then dictated to the US EPA to figure out the specifics, and then told the 50 states to implement the law. Part of the provisions of this law, along with many others, is that the federal government establishes the minimum standards or requirements for states to enforce. States can—and sometimes do—go beyond those requirements. We saw with the chapter's opening story about California's Governor Jerry Brown an instance where the state is trying to do more than the federal government on climate change. These additional actions can complicate already action on complex policy issues and a case can be made that additional standards or different ways of dealing with environmental issues can be both positive and negative. These structural realities tie into fragmentation.

Fragmentation

A final influence on policymaking that results from our governmental structure is fragmentation. Fragmentation also encompasses the separation of powers among the branches of government. In a way, our discussion of checks and balances and federalism feed into this third influence on policymaking. In our system of government, three branches of government (and not just at the national level) play a role in policymaking. The legislative branch makes laws, the executive implements and enforces them, and the judicial interprets them. And this power distribution is mimicked at the state level too.

There are lots of government entities around the country, and, in addition to those units, there are many non-profit organizations that work with government entities or even on behalf of government to accomplish environmental policy goals. Accordingly, there are thousands and thousands of organizations working on environmental issues. Sometimes these organizations and their people work well and in coordination with others, but sometimes the work can be in tension with the efforts of others.

As a nation, we contend with fragmentation because of our federal system of government and our fears over too much power being consolidated within one branch of government or one entity, so we inevitably end up with lots of different governmental entities all involved in the same thing, including environmental issues. Fragmentation is not just the number of governmental units, and non-profits, either; it also includes the mechanisms within organizations for dealing with environmental issues. For instance, many different congressional committees, as we saw earlier, are involved in environmental issues, so there can be overlapping jurisdiction and guidance. Decentralization in the public sector ends up complicating matters.

The resulting fragmentation can have upsides and it can have downsides. On the one hand, fragmentation ensures that there are many people and organizations who can put their time and resources into achieving goals and networks to enable effective implementation. Fragmentation also fosters lots of opportunities for all sorts of people and interests to impact the policymaking process and to provide input about a potential government action. After all, in a democracy, access is vital. On the other hand, fragmentation results in many instances where policy efforts are duplicated; the process invariably becomes slower, and there are many more people and agencies that have to be coordinated to accomplish a particular task.

GOVERNMENTAL TENDENCIES THAT INFLUENCE POLICYMAKING

The final grouping of factors that influence policymaking include governmental conditions and realities. Here, we discuss the propensity for incrementalism, reactionary politics, and our pluralist traditions. First, let us consider incrementalism. This is the idea that government does not generally engage in massive, abrupt change. Instead, government takes small steps—incremental steps—and steadily pursues goals. The notion of incrementalism originates from Charles Lindblom in the late 1950s. Although rational decision-making is sought after, Lindblom argued that the realities of decision-making in the public sphere do not lend themselves to a methodical, careful consideration of every option for as long as is needed. Instead, public decision-makers endeavor to make decisions and pursue courses of action in the most rational manner feasible, but the broader political environment stymies efforts at rational decision-making; therefore, we end up "muddling through" (Lindblom 1959). Stated differently, incrementalism and the idea of "muddling through" is the notion that governmental action is slow and rarely dramatic or drastic because making decisions methodically and with all the time in the world to consider possible alternatives is not the environment government finds itself in. As a result, the decisions that government does make are usually incremental changes to the existing structures, and change happens over time. Sweeping changes in government are generally rare and this is true in the context of environmental policy.

Along these lines, our government behaves in a reactionary manner rather than a proactive one, generally speaking. Our government is set up to respond to identified problems and deal with matters only after they become an issue. Rarely do you see the government taking action to solve a problem that has not yet presented itself as a problem. Therefore, it may seem that government cannot anticipate problems and address issues before they happen; this is because our government is not set up to be proactive, in fact, a proactive government would largely be anathema to our broad ideals of the role of government.

Finally, as articulated by James Madison in *Federalist 10*, we have a pluralist tradition in the United States. Pluralism is the notion that competition among different groups ensures that no single group will dominate government because there will be so many different groups competing with each other. To accomplish anything in government, some of these competing groups will have to work together. It is important to keep these different factors in mind as they are an important component of the broader context in which policymaking occurs in the United States, which is addressed in Chapter 5.

CHAPTER WRAP-UP

The focus of this chapter has been the process of how policy is made, and more specifically, on the six steps of the process: (1) problem identification and definition, (2) agenda setting, (3) policy formulation, (4) policy legitimation, (5) policy implementation, and (6) policy evaluation. Although this process appears to be simple and logical, we discovered that the process is far from simple. Moreover, our look at this process might leave us amazed that any policy makes it through the process to become law and achieve its goals. Although the policy model helps us understand the messy process, we found that the model is far from an accurate depiction of the process; nevertheless, the model helps us organize conversation around policymaking and provides us a much-needed vocabulary to study and discuss policy.

Much of the messiness of the process has to do with structural and societal influences in policymaking. And this messiness reflects the complexity of these policy issues and the reality that rarely, if ever, is there a "perfect" solution to the problem. As a result, it is easy to view the process as debilitating and painfully slow. However, this process ensures that the policies that are passed have ample time for consideration by our elected leaders and multiple points at which the public can influence the process—conditions that are essential in a democracy. The speed of policymaking also reflects the consensus that is required. Our system of government relies on consensus, but achieving it can be slow and have implications for policy implementation.

The next two chapters will more fully investigate the individuals involved in the policy process, but, here, we can already identify numerous career paths that you can pursue related to the making of public policy. More specifically, possible career paths include working with an elected government official, in an environmental agency, for a group that lobbies for environmental policy, or in a research institution that studies environmental issues.

Love Canal, Holding EPA Inspectors "hostage," and Superfund
For the case study in this chapter, we turn to a disaster that was many decades in the making and resulted in the Comprehensive Environmental Response, Compensation, and Liability Act (CERCLA), better known as "Superfund." Even though this law is decades old, its origins are helpful in understanding and applying the policy process. Plus, this law continues to be the foundation of how the nation handles environmental messes.

Love Canal is an area in the city of Niagara Falls, New York. The area got its name from an executive with Western Railroad Company, William T. Love, who in the late nineteenth century actioned plans to build a neighborhood with homes and parks. Part of the plans included a canal for shipping and possibly even hydroelectric power. The project was eventually abandoned and the already dug canal became a dump site by the 1920s. Hooker Chemical Company used the site to dispose of lots of chemical wastes. The dump site was closed in the 1950s and the canal was covered with clay to prevent seepage and vegetation began to grow on the site.

In 1953 the Niagara Falls School Board bought the dump site for $1 to build a new school for the growing community. The 99th Street School was built and it opened in 1955. Homes and the infrastructure of a growing community were built on land adjacent to the site. Over time, residents began noticing odors and mysterious substances oozing out of the ground and tests revealed the presence of numerous chemicals and other contaminants. Residents complained of myriad health issues and high rates of unusual illnesses, prompting investigations. By the late 1970s, the situation was garnering national media attention.

A local resident, Lois Gibbs, organized homeowners in 1978 after her son developed epilepsy, in addition to many other health problems. In one notable event, Lois Gibbs refused to allow two US EPA officials to leave her home while to galvanize attention and action. In the summer of 1978, President Jimmy Carter announced a federal health emergency, enabling federal resources to respond to the disaster. This was the first time such a declaration and allocation of resources was used for circumstances other than a natural disaster.

The federal government worked with state and local officials to begin clean-up of the area and relocate some of the residents, as property values plummeted and homeowners were not able to sell their homes and move. Congress responded to these events by passing CERCLA in 1980.

To help us better understand the stages model to policymaking, we apply the six steps of the process to CERCLA.

Problem identification and definition: Love Canal residents were not the only citizens coming to grips with the hazards of waste disposal practices from the past. As the nation began to deal with these sites, it became increasingly clear that there was a problem. But, the question became, how to define the problem and spur action. In many instances companies like Hooker Chemical Company were following protocol for disposing of wastes at the time they were doing so and many of the companies were no longer in business, so the questions that followed were how should clean-up be orchestrated and who should pay for it? In the case of Love Canal and the legislation that it spawned, it was decided that this was a public health problem and it was ultimately up to the government to clean it up and deal with figuring out who was to blame and making them pay for it later. There are other ways to think about defining the problem of old, hazardous waste dump sites, including developing a registry of facilities that use hazardous materials or banning the use of anything hazardous outright. Or when dump sites are discovered, the decision could be made to simply move everyone away from the affected area and leave the mess alone.

Agenda setting: Getting the national government to pay attention to the problems in Love Canal took persistent local reporters, especially David Pollak and David Russell, from the *Niagara Falls Gazette*, and local residents, like Lois Gibbs and the neighbors she organized, to demand action. The activism eventually resulted in a presidential emergency declaration and efforts to clean up the mess and put a structure in place to deal with other messes that were likely around the country, such as the "Valley of the Drums" in Kentucky.

Policy formulation: As members of Congress began debating action, they had many policy tools or options to think about.

Should the federal government be responsible for cleaning up these sites? Should they all be done at once? Should they be prioritized given finite resources? Should sites be cleaned up by the responsible party? These are complicated questions especially when tracking down who did the dumping and figuring out what was dumped is hard when a company or entity no longer exists and any records of what was dumped are long since gone.

Policy legitimation: Congress ultimately decided that the federal government would establish an initial "super fund" of $1.6 billion dollars to pay for clean-up. And when responsible parties could be identified and held accountable, those fines would go back into the fund to support future clean-ups. The law that ultimately became CERCLA was introduced in the House on April 2, 1980, was passed by the House on September 23, 1980 and was passed by the Senate on November 24, 1980. President Jimmy Carter signed the bill into law on December 11, 1980.

Policy implementation: The US EPA was delegated authority under Superfund to implement the law and get environmental messes cleaned-up. The agency created the National Priorities List (NPL) to rank and prioritize sites for clean-up. During the first years of CERCLA, under the Reagan administration, only 16 of the 799 identified sites were cleaned-up and only $40 million of the estimated $700 million was recovered from responsible parties.

Policy evaluation: During the first years of Superfund's implementation, challenges were identified, as briefly noted above. In 1986 the Superfund Amendments and Reauthorization Act (SARA) were passed that established minimum clean-up standards and authorized more money for the Superfund. More recently, the federal government has decreased the amount of money in the fund, since the George W. Bush administration. Initial budgets under the Trump administration see the fund cut by about 30%. At the time of writing, there are 1,341 sites on the NPL, with an additional 55 proposed (US EPA 2018). About the same number of sites have been cleaned up in the nearly forty years since the passage of the law, but new sites are identified and added regularly.

As a postscript to this story, the site was taken off the National Priorities List in 2004 and lawsuits are still in progress about exposure to hazards more than four decades later.

If you are interested in Superfund sites near you, search the US EPA's listings at https://www.epa.gov/superfund/search-superfund-sites-where-you-live.

SUGGESTED RESOURCES

Readings and Websites

Birkland, Thomas A. *An Introduction to the Policy Process: Theories, Concepts, and Models of Public Policy Making*. New York: Routledge, 2016.

Gibbs, Lois Marie. *Love Canal and the Birth of the Environmental Health Movement*. Washington, DC: Island Press, 2010.

Kingdon, John W. *Agendas, Alternatives and Public Policies*. 2nd edition. New York: Longman, 2011.

Kraft, Michael E., and Scott R. Furlong. *Public Policy: Politics, Analysis and Alternatives*. 2nd edition. Washington, DC: CQ Press, 2007.

Rinfret, Sara R., Denise Scheberle, and Michelle C. Pautz. *Public Policy: A Concise Introduction*. Thousand Oaks, CA: Sage/CQ Press, 2019.

Schneider, Anne L., and Helen Ingram. *Policy Design for Democracy*. Lawrence: University Press of Kansas, 1997.

Stone, Deborah. *Policy Paradox: The Art of Political Decision Making*. 3rd edition. New York: W. W. Norton, 2012.

Films or Videos

Schoolhouse Rock: America Rock. 1973. American Broadcasting Company. DVD.
War on the EPA. 2017. PBS Frontline. DVD.

REFERENCES

Anderson, James E. *Public Policymaking*. 5th edition. Boston, MA: Houghton Mifflin, 2002.

Baumgartner, Frank R., and Bryan D. Jones. *Agendas and Instability in American Politics*. Chicago, IL: University of Chicago Press, 1993.

Birkland, Thomas A. *An Introduction to the Policy Process: Theories, Concepts, and Models of Public Policy Making*. Armonk, NY: M. E. Sharpe, 2011.

Birkland, Thomas A. *An Introduction to the Policy Process: Theories, Concepts, and Models of Public Policy Making*. New York: Routledge, 2016.

deLeon, Peter. "The Stages Approach to the Policy Process: What Has It Done? Where Is It Going?" In *Theories of the Policy Process*, edited by Paul A. Sabatier. Boulder, CO: Westview Press, 1999.

Dillon, Liam. "California to Rely on 100% Clean Electricity by 2045 Under Bill Signed by Gov. Jerry Brown." *Los Angeles Times*, September 10, 2018. Available at http://www.latimes.com/politics/la-pol-ca-renewable-energy-law-signed-20180910-story.html#.

Dunlap, Riley E. "An Enduring Concern." *Public Perspective* 13, no. 10–14 (September/October 2002): n.p.

Eggers, Dave. "'Jerry Brown Is Too Busy with Climate Change to Worry About His Legacy." *Vanity Fair*, July 7, 2017. Available at https://www.vanityfair.com/news/2017/07/jerry-brown-climate-change.

Gallup Poll. 2018, March 1–8. Available at http://www.pollingreport.com/enviro.htm.

Ganos, Todd. 2011. "Diamond Lanes: Another Failed Energy/Environmental Policy." *Forbes*. https://www.forbes.com/sites/toddganos/2011/07/18/diamond-lanes-another-failed-energy-environmental-policy/#7b1e731744c4.

Hulse, Carl, and David M. Herszenhorn. "Democrats Call Off Climate Bill Effort." *The New York Times*, 2010.

Ingram, Helen, Anne L. Schneider, and Peter deLeon. "Social Construction and Policy Design." In *Theories of the Policy Process*, edited by Paul A. Sabatier, 93–128. Cambridge, MA: Westview Press, 2007.

Kingdon, John W. *Agendas, Alternatives and Public Policies*. 2nd edition. New York: Longman, 2011.

Kraft, Michael E., and Scott R. Furlong. *Public Policy: Politics, Analysis and Alternatives*. 2nd edition. Washington, DC: CQ Press, 2007.

Lindblom, Charles E. "The Science of 'Muddling Through'." *Public Administration Review* 19, no. 2 (Spring 1959): 79–88.

Mann, Michael E. *The Hockey Stick and the Climate Wars: Dispatches from the Front Lines*. New York: Columbia University Press, 2012.

Nakamura, Robert T. "The Textbook Policy Process and Implementation Research." *Policy Studies Review* 7, no. 1 (Autumn 1987): 142–154.

Peters, B. Guy. *American Public Policy: Promise and Performance*. Washington, DC: CQ Press, 2004.

Powell, James Lawrence. *The Inquisition of Climate Science*. New York: Columbia University Press, 2011.

Pressman, J.L., and Aaron Wildavsky. *Implementation: How Great Expectations in Washington Are Dashed in Oakland; or, Why It's Amazing That Federal Programs Work at All*. Oakland: University of California Press, 1973.

Rinfret, Sara R., Denise Scheberle, and Michelle C. Pautz. *Public Policy: A Concise Introduction*. Thousand Oaks, CA: Sage/CQ Press, 2019.

Sabatier, Paul A., and Hank C. Jenkins-Smith. *Policy Change and Learning: An Advocacy Coalition Approach*. New York: Routledge, 1993.

Schneider, Anne L., and Helen Ingram. *Policy Design for Democracy*. Lawrence: University Press of Kansas, 1997.

Stone, Deborah. *Policy Paradox: The Art of Political Decision Making.* Revised edition. New York: W. W. Norton, 2002.

———. *Policy Paradox: The Art of Political Decision Making.* 3rd edition. New York: W. W. Norton, 2012.

Stromberg, Stephen. "What Sank the Senate's Climate Bill." *Washington Post,* July 29, 2010. A23.

Sussman, Glen, Byron W. Daynes, and Jonathan P. West. *American Politics and the Environment.* New York: Longman, 2002.

US Census Bureau. "Census Bureau Reports There Are 89,004 Local Governments in the United States." US Census Bureau, 2012. https://www.census.gov/newsroom/releases/archives/governments/cb12-161.html.

US Congress. "Resource Conservation and Recovery Act." US Environmental Protection Agency. Update/Modified/Accessed Date 2013. https://www.epa.gov/rcra/resource-conservation-and-recovery-act-rcra-overview.

US EPA. "Superfund: National Priorities List." 2018. Accessed April 27, 2018. Available at https://www.epa.gov/superfund/superfund-national-priorities-list-npl.

Whitaker, Bill. "The Governor Who's Castigating the President on Climate Change." *CBS News,* December 10, 2017. Available at https://www.cbsnews.com/news/the-governor-whos-castigating-the-president-on-climate-change/.

CHAPTER 4

Official Actors in the Policy Process

Contents

© The Author(s) 2019   111
S. R. Rinfret and M. C. Pautz, *US Environmental Policy in Action*,
https://doi.org/10.1007/978-3-030-11316-2_4

The Snowball in the Senate

The United States—along with the rest of the planet—has experienced severe weather fluctuations due to climate change (Global Change 2018). This has caused colder and warmer days, causing melting of polar ice caps, rising sea level rise, and intense summer forest fires in the Western United States (Meyers 2017). On October 8, 2018, the Intergovernmental Panel on Climate Change (IPCC) released a report written by over ninety scientists from forty countries. The report stated that addressing global climate change would require rapid and far-reaching policy responses now and if not we should be prepared to confront extreme consequences by 2030 (e.g., sea level rise, food shortage) (IPCC Press Release 2018). However, the United States has not passed federal legislation to address climate change and the story of Senator Inhofe (R-Okla.) illustrates some of the reasons why.

Before joining the US Senate in 1994, Inhofe was a member of the US Army and was an executive for Quaker Life Insurance. His career in politics began at the state level, serving in Oklahoma's House of Representatives and Senate, which led to becoming mayor of Tulsa and eventually the US House of Representatives (1987–1992). In 1994, these experiences eventually led to Inhofe's election to the US Senate where he remains today (James Inhofe 1998).

Inhofe, a lifetime member of the Republican Party, defines himself as an "unabashed conservative," because he is not afraid to speak his mind. Most notably, he is one of the leading policymakers ardently against climate policy. He describes in his book, *The Greatest Hoax: How the Global Warming Conspiracy Threatens Your Future* that climate change has been falsified by scientists and Hollywood elite (James M. Inhofe 1998). Simply put, Inhofe believes that climate change is a result of the natural cooling and warming of the planet, debunking the expertise of scientific reports that it is manmade.

To thwart congressional action on climate policy, on February 26, 2015, Senator Jim Inhofe (R-Okla.) stood on the Senate floor with a real-life snowball, lamenting to his colleagues that global warming was a hoax. As previously indicated, his rationale is that the Earth naturally heats and cools itself so climate change is not a result of human activity. Therefore, we should not move forward with climate legislation.

Whether you agree or disagree with Inhofe's sentiments, he is one of the highest-ranking senators on the Environment and Public Works Committee. Since the political party in power determines key-level positions on committees, his voice can continue to affect what legislation makes it to the congressional floor for debate and consideration. This is because the Republican Party retained control of the US Senate in the 2018 mid-term elections. This Committee focuses on legislative matters concerning air quality, pollution, endangered species, natural disasters, to name a few, and it determines what legislation transitions from the committee to the Senate floor for deliberation and voting. The majority party determines who oversees each US Senate and House of Representative Committee. Senator Inhofe has served as the ranking chairperson for this committee.

Although Senator Inhofe is not alone in his viewpoints, governance in the US operates within a system of checks and balances. Senator Inhofe's is just one piece of the puzzle to understanding the role institutional actors (e.g., president, court, congress, bureaucracy) play in shaping environmental policy. Making environmental policy, as noted previously, is often described as a tug of war between institutional actors. To comprehend the broader implications of Inhofe's perspectives, the following chapter outlines just how difficult it is for institutional actors to make environmental policy in the United States.

The Official Actors

This chapter lays out the role that the official actors within our three branches of the federal government (Congress, the President, and the US Supreme Court) play in relationship to US environmental policy-making. More specifically, the US Constitution provides in Article I that Congress is the lawmaking body, in Article II that the President serves as the executive, and in Article III that the courts resolve legal disputes. Although the official actors (elected officials, the president, and federal judges and Supreme Court justices) are important to our understanding of how environmental policy is made, we often forget about the significant amount of work that the bureaucracy undertakes. As such, we suggest, that the so-called fourth branch of government—the bureaucracy—needs to also be considered because of its extensive role in implementing environmental policy in the United States. Put differently, this chapter documents that the bureaucracy also needs to be included in discussions about environmental policymaking because career civil servants, the individuals who work for the bureaucracy, such as police officers and environmental inspectors are charged by Congress with implementation of the major environmental laws described in Chapters 2 and 3. Accordingly, the intent of this chapter is to understand how the official, institutional policy actors play an essential role in US environmental policymaking.

First, we begin the chapter with an overview of how Congress has shifted from enacting a great deal of environmental legislation to an era of gridlock. Second, we examine the "environmental presidency" through an examination of presidential State of the Union addresses from Presidents Nixon through Trump. By focusing on these presidential speeches, we can investigate how a president can influence the environmental agenda. Then, we shift our focus to the federal bureaucracy by defining it and exploring how agencies, such as the Environmental Protection Agency (EPA) and the U.S. Fish and Wildlife Service (USFWS), affect environmental policy. Lastly, we end the chapter with a discussion about the federal courts in the United States, with a particular focus on the US Supreme Court.

Upon completion of this chapter a few themes will emerge. First, institutional actors in the US will continue to shape environmental policymaking well into the future. Yet, the role institutional actors' play varies. For instance, there are growing concerns that Congress is so entrenched in political squabbles that legislative action might never occur again to address growing environmental concerns. We suggest that gridlock is not something new and will continue to ebb and flow. As Congress is in a state of gridlock, we argue that we must pay attention to how policies can be made within the US bureaucracy. Second, we suggest that presidential State of the Union addresses serve as a guidepost for a president's platform to inform Congress on his policy priorities. This often includes policy directives for the environment. Quite simply, in Article II, Section 3 of the US Constitution, the President must inform "from time to time" information about the state of our union. Lastly, we provide caution that the US Supreme Court is determining the outcome of extremely technical scientific cases without any specific expertise in such areas.

CONGRESS: THE MAKING OF POLICY

In US Government and Politics 101 courses, we are taught how a bill becomes a law, with many professors remarking that it is messy. However, to briefly review the process (see also the discussion in Chapter 3), a member of Congress sponsors a bill, and then a bill is introduced and assigned to a committee. Within a committee, members of Congress (US House or US Senate) analyze the bill and make revisions. The committee decides whether to approve or reject the bill. Remember that if a policy is not popular with the public, it is not likely to move forward. Members of Congress are reelection maximizers and will do what they can to get reelected (Mayhew 2004). If approved, the bill is debated on the floor of the House of Representatives or the US Senate. Then, the bill is voted on. If agreed upon by the majority of both the House of Representatives and the US Senate, it is sent to the president's desk to be considered and signed into law.

The aforementioned description of how a bill becomes a law, however, does not truly capture the messy nature of policymaking. After all, "Congress is still largely an institution of fragmented powers and divided geographical loyalties" (Rosenbaum 2013, 87). Our point here is not to rehash the linear *Schoolhouse Rocks* version of the stages of lawmaking because this is not how it generally occurs. Rather, we need to remember that environmental legislation is often crisis inspired and reactionary, not proactive (Rosenbaum 2013). More specifically, Christopher McGrory Klyza and David Sousa (2013) have argued that Congress is gridlocked when it regards environmental policymaking. Michael Kraft (2011) articulates six elements that explain this congressional gridlock: (1) divergent policy perspectives of political parties; (2) separation of powers; (3) difficulties of environmental issues; (4) deficient public support; (5) role of interest groups; and (6) lack of political leadership. We briefly explain each in turn.

The divergence, or political polarization, between the dominant political parties, Republicans,and Democrats, has grown over time. According to Kraft (2011), "On average they have differed nearly 25 points on a 100-point scale, and the differences grew wider during the 1980s and 1990s" (129). This growing polarization between the two parties exists in the environmental policy arena because politicians have strong viewpoints when it comes to issues such as climate change because these seemingly discrete environmental issues reach far beyond the environmental arena to include farm subsidies and even thornier questions about taxation of carbon (cf. Rabe 2010).

The realities of constitutionally mandated separation of powers further complicate matters. For example, when politicians are confronted with issues of species protection or toxic chemicals, members of both chambers of Congress and the president all have to agree on a policy. For example, in 2009, the House of Representatives secured the necessary 219 votes out of 435 needed for climate change legislation, but the US Senate did not adopt the legislation (Rabe 2010). The lack of acceptance for a policy like the one on climate change can also be explained by Kraft's sixth criteria—political leadership. The Speaker of the House and Senate majority leader, regardless of what party they are from, must forge consensus between both parties. If this is not achievable, then getting the rest of the members of Congress to support legislation will be difficult.

Inextricably linked to political leadership is the support of various public interest groups. As elected officials want to get reelected, it is difficult for them to justify policy decisions to protect the environment that may increase costs for their constituents when domestic issues (e.g., the economy and healthcare) are a pressing concern for the American public. In addition, linked to a congressional member's reelection quest is the financial support of interest groups. In summary, although Congress supported the environment during the 1970s, its attention has shifted elsewhere, namely, to today's economy. To continue our conversation about the complexities of environmental policy within the legislative arena, we turn next to our chapter's case study about climate change, where we focus on one of the most essential stages of lawmaking in the United States—the congressional committee.

The Role of the Select Committee: Why Climate Policy Continues to Stall

Before jumping into our case study, it is pertinent to begin with the historical context of congressional committees. Congress has used the committee system to structure its operations since the beginning of the Republic (Aldrich and Rohde 2009). Typically, congressional legislation travels through the common process where a member of Congress introduces a bill, it is referred to a committee, the committee reports out a bill, the bill goes up for a vote in both houses of Congress, and is signed by the president (Lipinski 2009). However, few bills ever make it out of committee, let alone are passed by Congress. For instance, in 2017, only two percent of bills introduced in Congress became law (Sunlight Foundation 2014). This is due, in part, to the power of committee chairs, historically, in determining what bills are reported out of committee (Aldrich and Rohde 2009). Committee chairpersons in the past were typically selected through a seniority system, with little incentive to act upon party leadership policy goals (Aldrich and Rohde 2009). Furthermore, Lipinski (2009) notes that some committees may be more enthusiastic about a particular piece of legislation than others; therefore, the committee in which the legislation is referred may determine whether the legislation becomes law.

After 1975, committee chairpersons from both parties began to see their power erode due to changes that stripped power from chairs and generally shifted it toward party leadership (Aldrich and Rohde 2009; Evans and Grandy 2009). Party leaders have, since, exerted greater power over the committee system by influencing the language of bills in committee, bypassing committees altogether, controlling the floor agenda, and, often, more unorthodox lawmaking (Aldrich and Rohde 2009; Sinclair 2007). Although our case may seem dated, it serves a purpose. This case illustrates as a key moment in our environmental policy history—it is the last time Congress considered climate policy.

In 2006, the Democrats controlled both the House of Representatives and the Senate. As a result, Congress began to take a more active approach in discussing the importance of climate change as a national issue (Klyza and Sousa 2013). At the time, Speaker of the House, Nancy Pelosi (D-CA), created the select committee on Energy Independence and Global Warming to find a solution to address climate change and coordinate the actions of several committees to produce legislation on this issue (Lipinski 2009; Smallen 2007). Here, we evaluate the role of this select committee and its relevance in the legislative process.

During the 110th Congress, Speaker Pelosi selected Representative Edward Markey (D-Massachusetts), a strong advocate for the environment as chair of the select committee on

Energy Independence and Global Warming. She also appointed the remaining eight Democratic members, whereas Republican Minority Leader John Boehner (R-Ohio) appointed the six Republican members (Cleaver 2007; Kriz 2007b; Pelosi 2007). Representative Markey and Chief Counsel David Moulton suggested that the premise of the committee was to provide the best political climate in the House of Representatives to produce climate change legislation (Kriz 2007a, b).

Representative Markey argued that the goal of the committee was to promote the need for a bill on climate change and advocate for its passage in the 110th Congress (Kriz 2007a). The committee held 50 hearings investigating issues driving climate change; the first hearing held by the committee was entitled *Geopolitical Implications of Rising Oil Dependence and Global Warming* (Select Committee 2007). Representative Markey called the inaugural hearing to illustrate the connection between energy consumption and climate change and to illustrate the need for swift action (Select Committee 2007). This hearing, along with others such as the *Dangerous Global Warming, Green Collar Jobs*, and *Voluntary Carbon Offsets*, represented the first congressional hearings ever held discussing these issues specifically (Select Committee 2008; Sensenbrenner 2009).

During the term, the House passed two major pieces of energy legislation that dealt with both energy dependence and climate change. The legislation included the Energy Independence and Security Act (EISA) of 2007 and the Energy Improvement and Extension Act (EIEA) of 2008 as a part of the Emergency Economic Stabilization Act of 2008 (Select Committee 2008).

First, the EISA contained several main provisions, including an increased fuel economy standard, a renewable fuel standard, energy-efficient appliance standards, a green jobs training program, and accelerated research and development for renewable energy. The development of this bill took the better part of a year, with President George W. Bush signing it into law in December 2007. Prior to its passage in the Senate and confirmation in the House, the select committee held hearings discussing several aspects of the final bill. These included hearings regarding the development of a green jobs program, the economic impacts of high energy prices, the future of biofuels, pathways to higher energy efficiency standards, and the overall impacts of climate change on the economy (Select Committee 2009). The final version of the EISA included policy proposals that in some way addressed many of the points brought up in these hearings, with legislative language addressing the new corporate average fuel economy (CAFE) standard for cars and trucks, renewable fuel standards, and green job training programs (Select Committee 2009).

Throughout the next year, House leadership worked on developing another piece of legislation to deal with a host of issues that ultimately were not a part of the final EISA. This included developing a response to the need for increased investments in renewable energy technologies, hybrid vehicles, smart grid technology, and biofuels. Again, the Select Committee held hearings regarding virtually all of these policy topics throughout the 110th Congress (Select Committee 2009). Ultimately, within H.R. 1424, the Emergency Economic Stabilization Act of 2008, Congress included the language of the previous EIEA (H.R. 1424–110th Congress 2008). This act incorporated an extensive set of tax credits to increase the development and implementation of renewable electricity, carbon capture and sequestration research, biofuel production, and smart grid investments (Select Committee 2008; H.R. 6049–110th Congress 2008).

Finally, by the end of the 110th Congress, the select committee produced a report that illustrated the efforts of the committee and the 110th Congress to develop legislation to address the policy area of energy and climate change. Within this report, the committee included a set of recommendations for the following congressional session to pick up where this committee had left off. The committee recommended that the next Congress enact a cap and invest program for greenhouse gases (GHGs), boost efficiency of the power sector and residential buildings, expand renewable energy development, foster green job development, and transform the US transportation system (Select Committee 2008).

After Democratic majorities took control of both the legislative and executive branches of government, it appeared that the

time was ripe for the development of a national response to climate change under the 111th Congress (Klyza and Sousa 2008).
This is, in part, affirmed by the vote of the Democratic Caucus to
remove Representative John Dingell (D-Michigan) as the chair of
the Energy and Commerce Committee, in favor of Representative
Henry Waxman (D-California). Waxman suggested that he would
move more aggressively to produce a host of legislation, including comprehensive climate change legislation. Moreover, Speaker
Pelosi reauthorized the Select Committee to continue its work
during the 111th Congress to produce feasible energy and climate
change legislation (Sensenbrenner 2000).

Due to the severity of the economic recession inherited by the
111th Congress, both chambers moved quickly to spur economic
growth and to avoid a catastrophic economic failure. Within the
American Recovery and Reinvestment Act (also referred to as the
Stimulus or Recovery Act) legislation, Congress included more
than $80 billion to promote clean energy and energy efficiency,
with investments directed toward weatherization and retrofit-
ting of residential homes and federal buildings, energy efficiency
and renewable energy research, renewable energy loan guaran-
tees, state and local energy efficiency, smart grid development,
smart appliances, and public transit improvements (Brost 2009).
However, the stimulus bill did not address the primary recommendation from the Select Committee that encouraged Congress
to develop a cap and trade program for carbon emissions (Select
Committee 2008). As such, during the 111th Congress, the select
committee began to focus its hearings toward the negative effects
of climate change and the measures in which the United States can
mitigate these impacts (Select Committee 2010). Many of these
hearings revolved around a discussion that the science behind climate change was valuable, and that the technologies available
should be used to address the issues driving climate change, illus-
trating the need for a cap and trade approach (Select Committee
2010).

As a result, the House passed the landmark legislation H.R.
2454: American Clean Energy and Security Act of 2009 that introduced a cap and trade program to reduce carbon dioxide and other
GHG emissions. After the passage of this momentous legislation,

a companion bill was never brought for a vote in the Senate due to partisan disagreement (Rabe 2010). Nevertheless, the select committee continued to hold hearings discussing the importance of energy security, renewable energy development, and climate change throughout the remainder of the 111th Congress (Select Committee 2010). However, after the Republican victories in the 2010 elections, the new majority dissolved the select committee and it now remains a moment in history or the one attempt by members of Congress to address climate policy (Steinhauer 2010).

With the absence of the select committee focused on climate policy in the 112th, 113th, 114th, and 115th Congress, the overall number of hearings discussing climate change as a national policy issue precipitously dropped, thereby reducing the number of viable policy proposals. More notably, under the Trump presidency, climate policy is not a top priority. Despite the lack of federal climate policy, this did not prevent California from adopting their own statewide cap and trade in 2013 to lower its emissions levels. Post-2018 mid-term elections, the Democratic Party regained control of the House of Representatives and is likely to refocus its efforts on climate policy. It remains to be seen if a Democratic-controlled House of Representatives and a Republican US Senate can negotiate climate legislation.

Regardless, this case documents the important role that committees have in shaping environmental policy in Congress and how changes in political parties shape the policymaking agenda. As our introductory story reminds us, the party in power determines who oversees committees and the fate of policies like climate policy.

As we conclude our discussion of Congress, we would be remiss not to mention a few other facets of Congress. In addition to the legislative process and the integral role of committees, environmental policy is affected through other functions of Congress, notably oversight and constituent services. A major function of Congress is overseeing the work of government agencies, including the EPA and USFWS. For example, in the wake of the Deepwater Horizon incident, the House Committee on Natural Resources and the House Committee on Energy and Commerce conducted extensive hearings into the disaster in an effort to assign responsibility and to make recommendations on preventing future incidents. Furthermore, members of Congress are also committed to serving their constituents. In this capacity, members' offices field inquiries and complaints from their districts and states in order to address concerns from voters such as the Deepwater Horizon incident.

THE PRESIDENT, THE ENVIRONMENT, AND SETTING THE AGENDA

Our understanding of the congressional role in environmental policymaking is important; however, we cannot overlook the powerful presence of the president. As the nation's chief executive, the president affects environmental policymaking in a variety of ways. Starting with constitutionally expressed or enumerated powers, the president can propose or veto legislation, propose policy priorities to Congress, issue executive orders, and appoint federal judges and heads of agencies. These powers can affect environmental policy.

Appointment powers, for example, allow a president to shape an agency's actions by selecting its leadership. Although the US Senate must confirm these appointments, the president is influential and generally gets his chosen leaders. In Chapter 6, we discuss President Trump's presidential appointee to oversee the US EPA. Trump's first US EPA political appointee, Scott Pruitt took a drastically different approach than Obama's agency head, Lisa Jackson. Pruitt's approach was to rollback all of the environmental regulations surrounding climate policy that Jackson lead under President Obama. Additionally, presidents also shape the makeup of federal courts, and most notably, the US Supreme Court. Again, the president nominates justices and the US Senate confirms such appointments. President Trump's Supreme Court nomination process for Judge Brett Kavanaugh was by far one of the most controversial to date. It remains to be seen what implications this particular appointment will have on the environment. However, the decisions of the Supreme Court have far-reaching policy implications for environmental policy, which we discuss later on in this chapter.

The president also has inherent or implied powers by which he can infer power from the Constitution. These powers are not explicitly stated, but are powers that the president has garnered over time.

For instance, the president cannot declare war—Congress does— yet, Congress has not declared war since World War II. Therefore, "[i]n practice, presidential ability to capitalize on the presidency's political resources for environmental purposes has varied greatly.

One explanation for this variability is the many ways in which circumstances can alter the political climate surrounding the White House—events such as economic recessions, changing congressional majorities, and the changes in the political 'seasons'" (Rosenbaum 2013, 82).

Despite presidential influence on policymaking more broadly, there is still limited research on the environmental presidency to date. As Norman Vig (2013) succinctly notes, "Few presidential scholars have devoted much attention to environmental policy, and conversely, environmental policy scholars have been slow to integrate the increasingly sophisticated literature on the presidency into their analyses. When the first academic conference on the 'environmental presidency was held in 2000, only a handful of political scientists had published in the field'" (307). However, we offer a few examples of what we do know about the environmental presidency.

One example that explores the role of the president and the environment originates from Norman Vig and Michael Kraft (2013). These scholars extensively examine the impact that President Ronald Reagan had on environmental policy in the United States. The idea is that popular presidents, President Reagan in this instance, pushed for deregulatory efforts during his presidency because he had the public's support. However, we need to remember that this public support eventually subsided, and Americans found Reagan's policy perspectives on the environment unfavorable.

Another example is Dennis Soden's (1999) *The Environmental Presidency* that develops the administrative presidency model to document that a president can impact environmental policy through his or her role as commander-in-chief (head of the military), chief diplomat (negotiations with other countries), chief executive (oversight of federal agencies), legislative leader (policy suggestions to Congress), and party leader (head of his party). More specifically, as commander-in-chief, the president can order the national guard to implement public policies, such as Presidents Kennedy and Johnson did during the desegregation of the South.

As the chief diplomat, a president can enter into discussions with countries abroad about climate change, just as President Clinton did. As the legislative leader, the president can set the policymaking agenda, promoting to Congress and the American people his policy initiatives. For instance, President Obama in June 2013 addressed the nation with regard to climate change, stating, "The question is not whether we need to act. The question is whether we will have the courage to act before it's too late" (Graves 2013). With this said, our focus here is the role of the president in setting the environmental agenda as the legislative leader, as Soden (1999) suggests. We argue that this emphasis is significant because many large-scale pieces of environmental legislation have not been updated since the 1970s.

We focus our attention on presidential speeches, specifically State of the Union addresses from presidents Nixon through Trump, to document how US presidents set the policy making agenda for the environment. State of the Union addresses, arguably, are important indicators of a president's environmental stances or preferences. For instance, Mathew Moen (1988) notes, "scholars long have understood that the clearest expression of an administration's priorities may be found in the president's annual State of the Union message" (775). Moreover, as Vig (2013) suggests, "the 'bully pulpit" can be used to rally public support behind these proposals, especially during the president's first year in office" (311). It is important to look past the rhetoric to determine if presidential speeches add up to a strong environmental record.

ENVIRONMENTAL PRESIDENCY: DOES IT EXIST?

Perhaps most notable about the Golden Age of environmental policy is that a Republican president, Richard Nixon, signed into law most of the major policies. Today, this would seem unbelievable. Accordingly, the question becomes what role a president plays in promoting or shaping environmental policy.

To address this question, we review environmental statements made at the beginning of their terms during State of the Union addresses for each president, from Nixon through Trump. Then, these statements are compared to each president's overall environmental record (i.e., legislation). The goal is to determine if an Environmental President has ever existed, and if so, who deserves the title.

Richard Nixon (1969–1974)

The great question of the seventies is, shall we surrender to our surroundings, or shall we make our peace with nature and begin to make reparations for the damage we have done to our air, to our land, and to our water?

(Nixon 1970)

President Nixon certainly used the most forceful language to promote environmental policy during his first State of the Union address, making it a cornerstone of his legislative agenda. In fact, Nixon (1970) called for "the most comprehensive and costly program in this field in America's history." Outside of promoting plans to clean up the air, Nixon also called for the development of wastewater treatment plants nationwide, new funding for parks, preserving open space, and for improvements in automotive fuel efficiency.

Despite the costs, Nixon argued that his environmental policies would actually help the economy by not abandoning growth but redirecting it. He suggested that "For example we should turn toward ending congestion and eliminating smog the same reservoir of inventive genius that created them in the first place" (Nixon 1970). He then called on Americans to "make some minimal demands on themselves" to leave the environment "a little cleaner, a little better, a little more pleasant for [themselves] and those around [them]" (Nixon 1970).

Ultimately, Nixon was successful in seeing his legislative agenda carried out (see Chapter 2) because he helped shepherd the Clean Air and Water Acts into law, and created the EPA to implement these laws. Riding the wave of his previous success, Nixon used the State of the Union address in his short-lived second term to promote a new energy policy for the United States. He set the goal of being energy independent by 1980, arguing that the "United States will not be dependent on any other country for the energy we need" (Nixon 1974). He proposed new funding for energy research and development and increased funding for mass transit to help achieve this goal. However, he was unable to push these policies through Congress because he later resigned amid the Watergate scandal.

Gerald Ford (1974–1977)

We depend on others for essential energy.

(Ford 1975)

President Ford built upon President Nixon's arguments to direct a new energy policy program for the United States. However, his policies were far more focused on the exploration of fossil fuels and deregulation for the coal industry under the Clean Air Act (CAA) because he wanted the economy to improve. In fact, he argued that "voluntary conservation continues to be essential" in his first State of the Union address.

Much of his focus was on exploiting existing resources, especially oil, both on and offshore, calling for drilling at Elk Hills Naval Petroleum Reserve in California. Moreover, he promoted increased coal mining, submitting amendments for the CAA to "allow greater coal use without sacrificing clean air goals" (Ford 1975). In addition, he vetoed strip mining legislation passed by Congress because it was too stringent on coal. His vision for the future included "200 major nuclear power plants; 250 major new coal mines; 150 major coal-fired power plants; 30 major new [oil] refineries; 20 major new synthetic fuel plants; the drilling of many thousands of new oil wells; the insulation of 18 million homes; and the manufacturing and the sale of millions of new automobiles, trucks, and buses that use much less fuel" (Ford 1975).

Ultimately, Ford did see the opening of Elk Hills to drilling, and Congress did pass amendments to the CAA, but not until after President Ford left office. He was unsuccessful in implementing the majority of his energy program and, in particular, his energy tax due to lack of congressional support.

Jimmy Carter (1977–1981)

Almost 5 years after the oil embargo dramatized the problem for us all, we still do not have a national energy program.

(Carter 1977)

President Carter used the State of the Union address to comment on energy priorities. He suggested that it was time for the United States to develop a national energy program to "use more of those fuels which are plentiful and more permanent" (Carter 1978). Carter was a major proponent of incorporating cleaner alternative energies such as solar and wind into the US energy mix. These priorities culminated with his effort to install a solar water-heating system on top of the White House (it was then removed by President Reagan, but President Obama had it reinstalled in August 2013).

Legislatively, he oversaw the passage of the National Energy Act of 1978, which provided new tax incentives for renewable energy development, and required utilities to purchase this energy when it came online. Thus, President Carter was successful in pushing national energy policy forward. However, he was largely unsuccessful in achieving his other environmental initiatives, which did not even make it into his speech.

Ronald Reagan (1981–1989)

Now, we have no intention of dismantling the regulatory agencies, espe-cially those necessary to protect environment and assure the public health and safety.

(Reagan 1981)

President Reagan paid lip service to protecting the environment in his first State of the Union address; however, his record speaks to the exact opposite. More specifically, much of the environmental regulation and the agencies responsible for that regulation were subject to substan-tial budget and staffing cuts to achieve his objective of smaller govern-ment. He did openly suggest in his first address that he wanted to repeal the Department of Energy's synthetic fuel program, which illustrates just one of the many efforts of the Reagan administration to walk back efforts to move toward promoting cleaner burning fuels and stronger environmental policies. In fact, many of the gains made by Carter in regard to energy policy were undone, unfunded, or ignored by the Reagan administration.

However, by Reagan's second term, he was somewhat humbled by the backlash from the American public to his environmental rollback efforts. In his first address to Congress after becoming reelected in 1984, he called for the "reauthorization and expanded funding for the Superfund pro-gram to continue cleaning up hazardous waste sites which threaten human health and the environment" (Reagan 1985). He did oversee the efforts of Congress to reauthorize this law in 1986; however, he attempted to veto efforts to amend and strengthen the Clean Water Act (CWA).

George H.W. Bush (1989–1993)

If we're to protect our future, we need a new attitude about the environment.

(Bush 1989)

President George H.W. Bush distanced himself from his predecessor's environmental record and used his first address to the nation as a plat-form to outline his environmental agenda. President Bush argued for a new and stronger CAA. In addition, he called for a program to reduce sulfur dioxide emissions, which cause acid rain, and advocated for more funding for national parks. Moreover, he placed a strong emphasis on enforcing laws against toxic waste dumping and he proposed doubling the government's efforts to clean up existing sites, arguing that America needs to "clean up the old mess that's left behind" (Bush 1989).

President Bush, however, took his own approach to pushing for new environmental policy by suggesting that the United States needed to "respect the environment." In effect, this messaging indicates that economic development can occur as long as it takes the environment into account. In this fashion, he opened the door for further energy development, particularly in the Arctic National Wildlife Refuge (ANWR), arguing that it can and should be done, but in a way that respects the environment.

President Bush was quite successful in implementing his environmental agenda, particularly by steering the passage of the 1990 CAA Amendments, which provided regulation of more than 100 chemicals, and a cap and trade program to reduce sulfur dioxide emissions. He nearly achieved his directive to drill in the ANWR, but that effectively died after the Exxon Valdez Oil spill in 1989. Despite this setback, he did sign into law the Energy Policy Act of 1992, which promoted more energy development of both traditional fossil fuels and clean energy sources.

Bill Clinton (1993–2001)

I recommend that we adopt a Btu tax on the heat content of energy as the best way to provide us with revenue to lower the deficit because it also combats pollution, promotes energy efficiency, promotes the independence, economically, of this country as well as helping to reduce the debt ... and it is environmentally responsible.

(Clinton 1993)

President Clinton used his first State of the Union to call for a new direction for the United States that focused on building the economy, healthcare reform, and reducing the debt. In this speech, Clinton showcased his top environmental policy proposal—a tax on energy sources based on the sources' heat content in order to achieve deficit reductions. However, much like most of the initiatives in Clinton's first term, this policy fell flat after the 1996 Republican takeover of the House of Representatives. As a result, Clinton's efforts to achieve a new environmental policy in his first term were lackluster. However, he did manage to oversee the passage of the Safe Drinking Water Act Amendments of

1996 that set new goals for drinking water and methods to achieve those goals.

In comparison, Clinton's address in 1997 called for a much stronger role for environmental policy for his second term. Clinton used this speech to highlight the fact that his administration had already cleaned up 250 toxic waste sites, with a goal to clean up 500 more. In order to achieve this goal, he called for Congress to approve his proposal to "make big polluters live by a simple rule: if you pollute our environment, you should pay to clean it up." Moreover, Clinton argued for the revitalization of America's rivers, suggesting his River Heritage program would prove "once again that we can grow the economy as we protect the environment" (Clinton 1997). Finally, Clinton used this speech to highlight his global initiatives and, in particular, his efforts to reduce GHG emissions at the international level through the Kyoto Protocol.

Ultimately, Clinton's speech was far more focused on promoting environmental protection but, again, Clinton's legislative initiatives largely failed. His effort to make polluters pay, in effect reauthorizing the Superfund program, died in Congress. In addition, he never brought up for ratification in the Senate the Kyoto Protocol on Climate Change, requiring mandatory GHG emission cuts because it would have certainly failed. Thus, despite Clinton's rhetoric shift, his success rate remained low, especially for his major initiatives. However, one important or essential aspect of Clinton's administration was the work of his Vice President, Al Gore, who was, and still is, an ardent supporter of combatting climate change.

George W. Bush (2001–2009)

> Excellent schools, quality health care, a secure retirement, a cleaner environment, a stronger defense, these are all important needs, and we fund them.
>
> (Bush 2001)

In his first term address, President George W. Bush called for an accelerated cleanup of toxic waste sites, full funding for the Land and Water Conservation Fund, and more funding for the upkeep of national parks. The cornerstone of his environmental and energy goals revolved around his call for a renewed push on energy policy, suggesting that "we can produce more energy at home while protecting our environment" through promoting "alternative energy sources and conservation" (Bush 2001).

Despite President Bush's commitments to the environment as noted in his speech, his policy record follows a similar track to that of President Reagan. Ultimately, the taskforce he created to develop the new energy program, headed by Vice President Dick Cheney, was focused almost exclusively on fossil fuel energy. Because of the backlash he received from Congress and the public regarding the secrecy of the proceedings and the lack of significant alternative energy components, Bush was unable to get his energy policy enacted in his first term.

After his second inauguration, President Bush again promoted the need for a new national energy policy. However, in this speech he focused on the national security concerns of imported energy, urging "Congress to pass legislation that makes America more secure and less dependent on foreign energy" (Bush 2005). More specifically, Bush promoted the plan developed by Vice President Cheney in his first term, suggesting that his plan "encourages conservation, alternative sources, a modernized electricity grid, and more production here at home" (Bush 2005). In addition, he used this speech to promote his Clear Skies initiative that would "cut power plant pollution and improve the health of our citizens" (Bush 2005).

Ultimately, Bush got his wish regarding energy policy, as Congress passed the Energy Policy Act of 2005. However, Bush's Clear Skies initiative was widely panned, with some observers suggesting the term Clear Skies was exactly the opposite of what would occur if the policy was enacted (the idea was to reduce power plant emissions, namely sulfur dioxide).

Barack Obama (2009–2017)

> But to truly transform our economy, protect our security, and save our planet from the ravages of climate change, we need to ultimately make clean, renewable energy the profitable kind of energy.
>
> (Obama 2009)

President Barack Obama, suggested "our survival depends on finding new sources of energy," has, perhaps, been the most vocal proponent of clean energy sources since President Carter (Obama 2009). Similar to Clinton, Obama argued that investing in energy would spur economic growth while also reducing the deficit. Moreover, Obama touted the passage of the American Recovery and Reinvestment Act (ARRA) of 2009, which provided funding for this energy research as well as funding for "constructing wind turbines and solar panels … [that] will double this nation's supply of renewable energy in the next three years" (Obama 2009). Moreover, Obama argued for a new market-based cap and trade program to reduce carbon pollution to drive "the production of more renewable energy in America" (Obama 2009). Finally, to meet this new demand for renewable energy, he called for investments of "fifteen billion dollars a year to develop technologies like wind power and solar power, advanced biofuels, clean coal, and more fuel-efficient cars and trucks built right here in America" (Obama 2009).

Obama's push for ARRA did have the intended effect of doubling renewable energy production in the United States. In addition, the bill included funding for research and development for renewable energy, and he was successful in increasing renewable energy investment, although this success waned after the Republican takeover of the House in 2010. The most notable failure in Obama's presidency was his call for a cap and trade program for carbon emissions. Although it passed the Democrat-controlled House, it failed in the Senate.

After Obama's second inauguration, he renewed his call for action to reduce the effects of climate change, noting GHG emissions had slightly decreased, but "we must do more to combat climate change" (Obama 2013). Again, he called for a cap and trade program from Congress. He suggested, "We can make meaningful progress on this issue while driving strong economic growth" (Obama 2013). However, in this State of the Union address, he suggested that if Congress did not act on climate change he would by issuing executive orders and using the EPA to create rules based upon existing legislation. As noted in Chapter 2, Obama kept this promise and instructed the EPA to promulgate a rule on GHG emissions from coal-burning power plants. This rule was not finalized by the end of his term and, therefore, a target for President Trump to rollback.

Donald J. Trump (2016–)

We have ended the war on American energy, and we have ended the war on beautiful clean coal. We are now very proudly an exporter of energy to the world.

(Trump 2018)

To the casual observer, President Trump's approaches to the environment are similar to that of Senator Inhofe in our opening vignette. In his first few years in office, he has touted efforts to undo climate policy efforts from the Obama administration. For example, he has withdrawn the United States from the Paris Climate Accord, approved the permit to construct the controversial Keystone XL Pipeline, rolled back greenhouse gas emissions regulations, and opened the Arctic National Wildlife Refuge area for oil and gas drilling. Unlike many other world leaders, Trump suggests climate change is a hoax or simply, a con job by the scientific experts much like Senator Inhofe in our introductory story (Biesecker 2016).

President Trump's approach to environmental policy is in direct contrast to public opinion. In 2018, the Pew Research Center reported that 67% of Americans believe that the U.S. is not doing enough to reduce the impacts of climate change (Funk 2018). Typically, presidents promote public policy reflective of the populace. This has not been the case for President Trump, but it could with a new Democratic-controlled House of Representatives in 2018.

To keep pace with the flurry of rollbacks for US environmental policy, National Geographic has pledged to keep a running list of how President Trump is changing the environment. This way we can objectively observe and determine if President Trump is a friend or foe to US environmental policy (Gushenko 2018).

This brief review of some of the language used to tackle environmental concerns by presidents in their State of the Union addresses and then comparing it with their environmental initiatives provides an indication of where presidents stand regarding their commitment to the environment. With this examination, we can better define if any president truly is the environmental president.

Is There an Environmental President?

In order to determine if any president has abided by his State of the Union statements to become a stand-alone presidential leader in environmental protection, we first turn to a few themes presidents have used to aid them in their legislative agendas. First, each president attempts to justify environmental actions in regard to the economy. President Nixon (1970) argued that environmental policy would drive the economy; Presidents Clinton (1997) and Obama (2013) used similar arguments. President

George H. Bush (1989) suggested that the economy could grow, while also "respecting the environment." Finally, President George W. Bush (2005) used a less forceful argument, but did suggest that the economy required new affordable and environmentally responsible energy sources (i.e., exploration of oil and gas resources on public lands in the West).

Another prominent method used by presidents to promote their environmental goals is through a moral argument. Nixon (1970) was the first to do this, suggesting "those who make massive demands on society … need to make some minimal demands on themselves." President George H. Bush (1989) promoted his environmental initiatives as a necessary effort to "care for our future." Similarly, Clinton (1997) argued that his environmental policies were necessary "so that our children grow up next to parks, not poison." Finally, Obama (2013) used similar arguments, commenting on the need to implement his environmental policies "for the sake of our children and our future."

Several presidents have used a national security argument to promote environmental and energy goals. Presidents Nixon (1974), Ford (1975), and Carter (1978) all argued for a new energy program to reduce the impact of foreign sources of fuel, with Nixon indicating, "our growing dependence upon foreign sources has been adding to our vulnerability for years and years." More recently, President George H. Bush (1989) argued more succinctly that "our national security depends on it" and his policy would make America "more secure." Finally, Obama (2013) touted his initiatives that have reduced oil imports to levels not seen in the past 20 years.

Thus, presidents have used the State of the Union address to highlight emerging environmental issues and methods to solve them. Climate change has become an increasingly debated topic and both Democratic Presidents Clinton and Obama made combating climate change an important component of their legislative agendas. Clinton (1997) argued that the United States should take a leadership position to meet challenges to the global environment. Obama suggested that embracing climate change policy could spur economic growth (Obama 2008; 2013). However, Clinton was unsuccessful in his legislative efforts, and Obama had a similar fate. How future presidents frame this policy issue and other emerging concerns may help explain whether they achieve legislative success. Ultimately, both Presidents Nixon and George H. Bush had the strongest environmental records based upon initiatives proposed and subsequently carried out.

However, Ford's imported oil tax, Carter's support of renewable energy (i.e., solar panels on the White House), Clinton's Btu tax, and Obama's carbon cap and trade program could have had significant impacts on improving the condition of the environment, putting each of them on the same level as Nixon and George H. Bush, if such legislation had been successful in Congress. In this regard, with Nixon's Watergate scandal, it would seem that President George H. Bush may have been a more viable candidate than Clinton to assume the title of environmental president.

George H. Bush and Nixon, however, had something that Obama and Clinton did not, and that is a public consensus for the need to act on environmental issues. In the 1970s, public opinion was so much in favor of environmental policy that Nixon suggested that "restoring nature to its natural state is a cause beyond party and beyond factions. It has become a common cause of all the people of this country." Thus, many of the environmental policies advocated by Nixon were supported by both political parties, making their passage easier. President George H. Bush's policies found a similarly warm reception in Congress. That reception has dramatically changed since the Clinton administration. Environmental protection has become a highly partisan issue, with the poster child being climate change policy, and disregard for scientific evidence by many members of Congress such as Senator Inhofe Moreover, the United States has had a divided government during much of the past 25 years, making environmental policy increasingly difficult to produce. Finally, the American public has not been as vocal about environmental protection as it has been in the past; indeed, public opinion polls show that citizens are more concerned with the economy and other policy issues rather than the environment (see Chapters 2 and 3).

During the 2008 presidential campaign, however, one topic for discussion was climate change policy. As a result, Senator McCain and then-Senator Obama made climate change policy an important component of their election campaign platforms. However, with the onset of the Great Recession, this support waned and so too was the will of policymakers to act. Public opinion may be the most important component in determining presidential priorities and the best measure to determine presidential priorities, provided they can break through the legislative gridlock in this policy area.

Although presidents assert their legislative priorities in their State of the Union addresses, President Obama and Trump opted for the use of the administrative state. If presidents can no longer be successful in pushing environmental agendas through Congress, presidents can use their role as the chief executive to bypass congressional gridlock and use existing environmental laws to make policy in the federal bureaucracy (cf. Klyza and Sousa 2013). Obama and Trump are not the first presidents to take this approach. As our discussions of Congress and the presidency indicate, environmental policymaking is not an easy endeavor. As such, we now turn to an important, yet overshadowed, piece of the environmental policymaking puzzle–the US bureaucracy.

THE ENVIRONMENTAL BUREAUCRACY

Recall that our underlying argument here is that understanding the bureaucracy is essential for students of environmental policy. Chapter 2 provided a list of environmental policies created within the last several decades, and we cannot help but notice that not much is happening legislatively (cf. Klyza and Sousa 2013). However, if we examine the *Federal Register* (website/portal—www.federalregister.gov for federal bureaucratic policymaking, which will be discussed further in Chapter 6), a great deal is happening. This suggests that policymaking is occurring within the federal bureaucracy. The bureaucracy plays a significant role in environmental policy for the future. In Chapter 6, we will focus on how rulemaking is particularly important for environmental policy, but the focus in this section is on defining the bureaucracy and providing examples of what environmental agencies do.

It is, first, important to begin with general assumptions about the bureaucracy and its bureaucrats. For some, when we think about the bureaucracy, we think of red tape and inefficiency. When we think of a bureaucrat, what comes to mind is a lazy, incompetent, career civil servant. However, we argue otherwise. As Anthony Downs' *Inside Bureaucracy* (1964) reminds us:

> It is ironic that the bureaucracy is still primarily a term of scorn, even though bureaus are among the most important institutions in every nation in the world. Not only do bureaus provide employment for a very significant fraction of the world's population, but also they make critical decisions which shape the economic, political, social, and even moral lives of nearly everyone on earth. (130)

The bureaucracy and a bureaucrat's role in society are much more than the common stereotypes.

There are a variety of ways scholars have defined "bureaucracy." According to William Niskanen (1971), "the original use of the term, I understand, referred to cloth covering the desk (bureau) of eighteenth century French officials" (23). More recently, the bureaucracy, as defined by James Q. Wilson (1991), is "a complex and varied phenomenon, not a simple category or political epithet" (10). Armies, schools, and prisons, as Wilson (1991) notes, are all bureaucracies. Moreover, the seminal approach to define the bureaucracy originates from the work of Max Weber (1947). For Weber, the bureaucracy is synonymous for defining all large organizations. However, the underlying idea is that the bureaucracy was created by Congress to translate vague congressional statues and to implement the policies. It is the people within the bureaucracy, the bureaucrats or civil servants—police officers, teachers, or environmental inspectors—who carry out legislation on a daily basis (Niskanen 1971). More succinctly, "The term bureaucrat will sometimes be used in the more general sense to define any full-time employee of a bureau" (23). Thus, the question becomes why Congress would delegate its power to allow bureaucrats to carry out public policy?

Delegation of Authority

As Table 4.1 suggests, there are a variety of federal agencies in the United States created by Congress to carry out environmental policy. Each of the agencies listed in Table 4.1 receives its authority from Congress, which is known as delegation of authority—when Congress provides policymaking power to the executive branch (i.e., the

Table 4.1 Sample list of federal environmental agencies

- Bureau of Land Management (BLM)
- National Park Service (NPS)
- U.S. Fish & Wildlife Service (USFWS)
- Environmental Protection Agency (EPA)
- US Geologic Service (USGS)
- Bureau of Safety & Environmental Enforcement (BSEE)
- Bureau of Ocean Energy Management (BSEE)
- Office of Surface Mining Reclamation & Enforcement (OSMRE)
- U.S. Forest Service (USFS)

bureaucracy or federal agencies). We discuss this in greater detail in Chapter 6, but a few details are worth noting here.

Delegation occurs because programs are necessary and no one (meaning Congress or the president) is willing to set specific guidelines. Congress may prefer delegation for a number of reasons. First, the bureaucracy has more expertise in these policy areas and more flexibility to make changes if necessary. Take the CAA for instance; with the 1990 amendments, the EPA had to carryout out more than 300 rules to meet the requirements set forth by Congress. Second, Morris Fiorina (1982) argues that Congress delegates its authority in order to "shift the responsibility" of decision-making to the agencies; this way Congress can avoid the controversy and criticism associated with such policies by leaving open the possibility of blaming the bureaucracy.

One of the overriding questions about this delegation of authority is the role of accountability. Put differently, members of Congress are held accountable through elections by the people. Members of the federal bureaucracy, or those individuals who work for an agency, are not elected, so accountability is less obvious and direct. Civil servants are selected for their positions based upon their expertise and hired through a merit process. For instance, a biologist may be hired by the U.S. Forest Service to oversee forest management in the Coconino National Forest in Flagstaff, Arizona. Although expertise is important to carry out congressional statutes, members of elected institutions can influence agency policy and limit discretion through a variety of oversight techniques by Congress and the President. As Sara Rinfret and Scott Furlong (2012) note, "This dual political oversight demonstrates the interesting situation of an agency having multiple principals or, in other words, needing to respond to two different 'bosses.' On the one hand, Congress provides statutory and budget authority to the agencies; on the other hand, the president is the head of the executive branch and ultimately sits at the top of the bureaucratic hierarchy" (374).

To demonstrate the far-reaching impact that the federal bureaucracy has on environmental policymaking, we offer a brief examination of two environmental agencies—the EPA and USFWS. We focus on the EPA and the USFWS for a couple of reasons. First, the EPA is the largest environmental agency in the United States and one of the oldest environmental protection agencies in the world. More specifically, the focus of the EPA is to protect "human health and the environment." In turn, we also offer an analysis of the USFWS—an agency designed to protect and restore our nation's plants and animals. This protection is done through the Endangered Species Act of 1973 (ESA), which is legislation crafted to protect species, and something that many countries do not have.

One of the Oldest Environmental Agencies in the World

The creation of the EPA dates back to the so-called environmental decade when people became more concerned with the nation's deteriorating air, water, and land resources. According to Dunlap and Mertig (1992), "In the terminology of public opinion analysts, environmental protection had become a consensual issue by 1970, as surveys found a majority of the public expressing pro-environmental opinions and typically only a small minority expressing anti-environment opinions" (93). With growing public sentiment for environmental protection, the United States embarked on a dramatic outpouring of federal legislation to protect the environment, from the National Environmental Policy Act of 1969 to the Resource Conservation and Recovery Act of 1976 (see Chapter 2).

On December 2, 1970, President Nixon issued an Executive Order (an order by the president that carries the same weight as a congressional statute) to create the EPA. With one pen stroke, the EPA became an agency with 5000 employees from a variety of existing organizations: the National Air Pollution Control Administration; the Public Health Service Bureaus of solid waste, water hygiene, radiological hygiene, and pesticide research; the Federal Water Quality Administration; pesticide regulation for the Department of Agriculture; pesticide research programs from the Department of Interior; and radiation regulation from the Atomic Energy Commission. The EPA converted several agencies into one, creating an amalgam of existing programs and cultures without an overall mission or framework (Andrews 2006).

To transform the internal structure of the EPA, the first administrator, William Ruckelshaus, used an aggressive managerial approach. The creation of ten regional offices helped to enforce and carry out massive 1970s federal environmental initiatives—the CAA, CWA, Federal Environmental Pesticides and Control Act, Safe Drinking Water Act, Toxic Substances Control Act, Resource Conservation and Recovery Act, and the Comprehensive Environmental Response, Compensation, and Liability Act (CERCLA or the Superfund Act). But most important, as Jack Lewis (1985) stated, "The EPA has developed into the most competent agency in the federal government, and morale is still very high among our extremely talented and dedicated staff" (npn). The EPA is dominated by its top-down bureaucratic organizational structure, with its sole purpose being environmental protection (Andrews 2006). More specifically, the organizational structure of the EPA contains an administrator who is appointed by the president and confirmed by the Senate. The headquarters are located in Washington, DC and ten regional offices are located around the country. The primary duties of EPA offices are to regulate and protect air quality, water quality, hazardous waste, chemicals (i.e., pesticides), and, sometimes, the transportation of equipment.

Protecting Species for the Future

The origin of the USFWS dates back to the early nineteenth century when it was tasked with overseeing the nation's fish and wildlife supplies, respectively. The Commission of Fish and Fisheries studied the supply of coastal and lake fisheries, which later become the Bureau of Fisheries in the Department of Commerce. In 1905, the Bureau of Biological Survey in the Department of Agriculture was established, with the stated mission of studying birds and mammals in the United States (Loomis 1993).

By 1939, as Richard Andrews (2006) notes, one of Franklin Roosevelt's New Deal policies was to consolidate these two agencies (the Bureau of Fisheries and the Bureau of Biological Survey) under one umbrella within the Department of Interior; this consolidation created the USFWS. According to Bird Loomis (1993), the primary responsibilities of USFWS are to manage migratory birds, develop hunting regulations, acquire/protect habitats, and enforce international treaties that protect migratory birds. To provide financial support for the agency, the first administrator of USFWS, Jay "Ding" Darling, used monies from the Duck Stamp Act of 1934 and the Pittman–Robertson Act of 1937 (licensing fees from hunting and taxes on sporting goods or ammunition) to create a funding source outside the annual federal budget. Beyond finding monetary support, a few of the USFWS' first acts included the establishment of a River Basin Study to prevent damage to fish and wildlife from water projects and improving the management of migratory waterfowl hunting. Then, in 1956, the Fish and Wildlife Act created two new bureaus: the Bureau of Commercial Fisheries and the Bureau of Sports Fisheries and Wildlife. The Bureau of Fisheries, in turn, became the National Marine Fisheries Service in 1970 and transferred its jurisdiction to the Department of Commerce (Andrews 2006). The broadest sources of statutory authority for the USFWS are the Fish and Wildlife Act of 1956, the National Environmental Policy Act (NEPA) of 1969, and the Endangered Species Act of 1973. The Fish and Wildlife Act of 1956 is important because, as Loomis (1993) stated, "Under this act, the agency is instructed to take steps required for the protection, conservation, and advancement of fish and wildlife resources" (60). Then, in 1969, NEPA served as a formal vehicle for USFWS to analyze the impact of projects on all types of fish and wildlife through environmental assessments.

The other key directive for USFWS came in 1973 with the passage of the ESA to protect endangered or threatened plants and animals. Under the ESA, USFWS, along with the Department of Commerce, is responsible for carrying out this law through rulemaking processes. The language of the ESA directs USFWS to use only the best scientific data to list a species, develop a recovery plan, and designate critical habitats once a species goes through the rulemaking process and is listed as endangered or threatened. Thus, the sole mission of USFWS is to work with others to conserve, protect, and enhance fish, wildlife, plants and their habitats for the continuing benefit of the American people.

By way of comparison, the organizational structure is somewhat similar to that of the EPA. The director's office and the major program areas are located in Washington, DC. In addition to deputy staff, the USFWS has regional offices across the United States too. Again, this is helpful in carrying out national policies such as the ESA and managing our nation's wildlife refuges.

In order to protect our nation's wildlife, air, and water, both agencies offer a wide range of expertise varying from science to policy. This is not a small task, and without these agencies species such as the Salt Creek Tiger Beetle in Nebraska would no longer exist, nor would some of the nation's Great Lakes be swimmable or drinkable.

Environmental Bureaucracies

In summary, the bureaucracy plays a definitive role in implementing environmental policy in the United States. First, the bureaucracy was created to implement public policy in the United States because members of Congress do not have the time or expertise to carry out the laws they pass. Thus, environmental agencies, including the EPA and the USFWS, fulfill an essential role in ensuring that landmark legislation such as the CAA or the ESA is carried out and implemented. This section on the bureaucracy provides a basic understanding about the federal bureaucracy so that we can explore the processes of bureaucratic decision-making in Chapter 6 and the role of the states in environmental protection in Chapter 7.

THE NINE—THE FINAL DECIDERS

Even if a policy is passed by Congress, promoted by the president, and implemented by the bureaucracy, we have not reached the end of the story. The Supreme Court may enter into decision-making and change the course of how environmental policy is implemented. We end this chapter explaining how the US Supreme Court has affected US environmental policy in the twenty-first century.

When we think about the US Supreme Court and its impact on environmental policy in the United States, we frequently turn to *Massachusetts v. Environmental Protection Agency* (2007). In this landmark decision, the Supreme Court ruled that carbon dioxide could be regulated by the EPA under the CAA. The Supreme Court noted that the EPA had to determine if carbon dioxide emissions were, indeed, a threat to human health and the environment, and if so, the agency needed to write regulations to curb these emissions under the CAA. In 2009, the EPA, for the first time, promulgated a rule (more in Chapter 6 about this process) to address GHG emissions.

This case is extremely noteworthy; however, we need to consider the broader role that the US court system plays in environmental policy. To begin with a basic understanding of the US court system, we turn to Fig. 4.1. As Figure 4.1 indicates, we have a dual court system in the United States. For instance, there are three types of law in the United States: public, criminal, and civil. Public law often deals with constitutional and administrative questions related to government actions. Criminal law regulates the conduct of individuals and civil law deals with disputes between individuals or organizations. Moreover, there are differences between federal and state courts. For instance, the entry point for all federal criminal cases (such as robbing a bank) or civil cases (disputes between states or individuals, such as divorce) is the US district court. If convicted at the US district court level, the accused have the

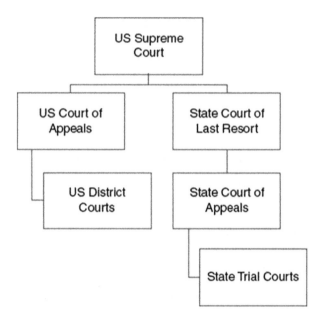

Fig. 4.1 US court system

right to appeal your case. If the appeal is heard, this would take place at the US Court of Appeals (13 total, 11 geographically located and two specialty circuits for bankruptcy and patents). If again convicted, cases can be appealed to the US Supreme Court. However, keep in mind that, on average, the US Supreme Court hears about 70–80 cases per year, representing approximately 1–5% of all cases appealed to the court.

The state process is somewhat similar, with the entry point being the state trial court for civil, criminal, and public cases. If convicted, individuals can appeal their cases and, if granted, be heard at the state appellate level. The state supreme court, or the court of last resort, is where individuals can appeal cases from the state appellate level. In order for a state case to make it to the US Supreme Court (federal), the case must have reached the state court of last resort and ask a constitutional question (Ginsberg et al. 2013).

For our purposes here, we focus on the federal court system, and, specifically, how the US Supreme Court affects environmental decisions. The US Supreme Court includes nine justices who are appointed by the president and confirmed by the Senate. The justices can serve for life, providing "good behavior." The common assumption is that a Supreme Court justice decides a case from either the so-called perspective of activist or one who advocates constraint. More specifically, an activist justice views the law or the Constitution as a living document, with an interpretation that changes over time. In contrast, a justice who embraces judicial constraint values the way in which the Constitution was written in 1787, and tries to stick to the original language and meaning of the framers (Ginsberg et al. 2013). In particular, one will be able to determine if a specific justice is pro- or anti-environment in using an activist or constraint approach. For instance, justices who use an activist approach can rule in favor of environmental protection, whereas judicial constraint could be viewed as anti-environmental.

Recognizing that these different interpretations of the Constitution are important; however, Rosemary O'Leary (2013) succinctly argues that there are a few ways that the court can shape environmental policy. First, the courts determine who has the right to sue. If standing to sue is established, the second way that the courts can shape policy is by determining the ripeness of a case, or in other words, if a case is ready for review. Put differently, standing to sue means that, in order to file a lawsuit in court, the individual must have to be directly affected by the legal dispute you are suing about. For instance, if the company that you work for caused health defects because of a chemical it was using, you could sue your employer because you suffered adverse health effects, whereas someone who was not affected directly could not sue.

Furthermore, the courts impact policy by how they choose to interpret the law. If a business decides to sue the government because the business believes that the CAA placed unwarranted economic burdens, then, the court would need to interpret the intent of the law.

One concern here is that many environmental laws require a great deal of scientific expertise. For instance, the backgrounds of many Supreme Court justices originate from previous experiences as lawyers or lower level judges rather than backgrounds in the natural sciences or engineering. The question becomes whether the legal backgrounds of justices are adequate to decipher highly technical scientific jargon. For example, in 2009, the Court had to determine if the US Navy's high-powered sonar off the California coast was endangering dolphins and whales (Savage 2008). Arguably, the technical wherewithal of the justices is important to recognize because, "A more recent study predicts

Table 4.2   Sample of US Supreme Court environmental cases from 2000 to 2015

Year	Case	Decision
2000	*Palazzolo v. Rhode Island*	5 (Rehnquist, O'Connor, Scalia, Kennedy, Thomas)-4 (Stevens, Souter, Ginsburg, Breyer)
2003	*Alaska Department of Environmental Conservation v. EPA*	5 (Stevens, O'Connor, Souter, Ginsberg, Breyer)-4 (Rehnquist, Scalia, Kennedy, Thomas)
2006	*Environmental Defense v. Duke Energy Corp.*	9 (Roberts, Stevens, Souter, Scalia, Kennedy, Thomas, Ginsburg, Breyer, Alito)-0
2009	*Burlington Northern v. United States*	8 (Roberts, Stevens, Scalia, Kennedy, Souter, Thomas, Breyer, Alito)-1 (Ginsburg)
2013	*American Trucking Associations v. City of Los Angeles*	9 (Roberts, Scalia, Kennedy, Thomas, Ginsburg, Breyer, Alito, Sotomayr, Kagan)-0
2015	*Michigan v. EPA*	5 (Scalia, Roberts, Kenney, Thomas, Alito, Ginsburg, Breyer, Sotomayor, Kagan)-4

that the courts will become an increasingly important pathway for revising policies since Congress has been legislatively gridlocked since 1990" (O'Leary 2013, 153). As such, Table 4.2 examines five recent cases that deal with environmental issues, allowing the reader to decide if an individual with a legal background has the best judgment to determine the outcome of scientifically driven environmental cases.

Courts and Environmental Policy

To understand the role that the Supreme Court has played in environmental issues during the last decade, we have put together a brief list of environmental cases for review (see Table 4.2). The six cases represent a 15-year time span. The goal is to understand the cases, the actors, and the decisions made by the court. We argue that having a better understanding of how Supreme Court justices determine environmental cases over time provides a benchmark for how future cases will be decided or if an environmental background is, indeed, needed.

Our first case for consideration, *Palazzolo v. Rhode Island* resulted in a
5–4 decision by the US Supreme Court. The facts of the case surround a
waterfront property in Rhode Island owned by Anthony Palazzolo. This
parcel of land was brought into question by the Rhode Island Resources
Management Council's Coastal Resources Management Program
because Palazzolo's property is considered a salt marsh. Palazzolo tried
to develop this land, which is restricted due to its salt marsh designation;
thus, he argued that Rhode Island's wetlands regulations were a violation of the Fifth Amendment's takings clause because he was deprived
compensation. In the 5–4 decision, the court ruled that Palazzolo was
allowed to challenge the state's wetland regulations under the Fifth
Amendment.

The second case, *Alaska Department of Environmental Conservation
v. EPA*, examines the "best available technology" clause within the CAA.
Simply put, under the CAA, federal and state agencies are required to
implement the law. In this case, state agencies try to prevent air pollution by requiring that companies use the best technology available to limit pollution. However, in 1998, a mining company in Alaska,
Teck Cominco Alaska, requested from the Alaska Department of
Environmental Conservation (ADEC) a permit to build an additional
generator at one of its mining facilities. The US EPA stated that the
ADEC did not issue a permit with the best available technology in mind.
Thus, the ADEC responded that the US EPA did not have the right to
interfere with its decision-making when issuing permits. In a 5–4 decision, the Supreme Court determined that the US EPA does have the
authority to tell the ADEC what constitutes best available technology.

Our third, fourth, and fifth cases for consideration, *Environmental
Defense v. Duke Energy Corp, Burlington Northern v. United States*, and
American Trucking Associations v. City of Los Angeles, represent more
decisive decisions by the court. *Environmental Defense v. Duke Energy
Corp* centers on the definition of the CAA's Prevention of Significant
Deterioration Program (PSD), in which the EPA requires that power
companies must apply for permits to modify emissions increases. In this
case, the Environmental Defense Fund, along with other environmental groups and the EPA, sued Duke Energy Corporation because it did
not obtain PSD permits for 29 improvements for power plants. The
Duke Energy Corporation argument was that the EPA modification process was unclear; thus, they did not need to comply. Nevertheless, the

Supreme Court ruled otherwise in a unanimous decision, noting that EPA requirements needed to be followed.

In *Burlington Northern v. United States*, there was one dissention in the court, Justice Ruth Bader Ginsburg, but this is explainable. In this case, the EPA and California's Department of Toxic Substances Control (DTSC) sued responsible parties (Burlington Northern Railroad, Santa Fe Railway, and Shell Oil Company) for the cleanup of contaminated land. However, the US Court of Appeals noted that the companies were only responsible for a portion of the cleanup due to statutory language specified within CERCLA. The major issue at hand is who is the arranger for the contamination of the site in question. The Court argued that the companies did not intend or arrange for their products to be disposed of in an improper fashion. Justice Ginsburg dissented from her colleagues because she argued that Shell Oil should qualify as the arranger of the contaminated site.

Our fifth case, also a unanimous decision by the Court, centers on *American Trucking Associations v. City of Los Angeles*. The focus in this case is the expansion of cargo terminals in the port of Los Angeles. The driving concern was that this expansion would increase air pollution and, as a result, the Board of Harbor Commissioners CAA, to reduce emissions in the port area, focusing on drayage trucks. The American Trucking Association (ATA) sued the city of Los Angeles for this plan. In the end, the court unanimously decided that a city government cannot limit federally licensed motor carriers from a port.

The final case for consideration, *Michigan v. EPA* resulted in a 5–4 decision. The CAA is the focus here and costs for electric utility steam generating units (EGUs). Simply put, in writing the majority opinion, Scalia argued that he EPA must examine costs when determining a regulation and in this case, power plants. This determination should be made prior to the EPA's decision that a regulation is appropriate and necessary.

Although many of these cases did not make national news like *Massachusetts v. EPA*, the point here is to demonstrate that environmental cases are far-reaching, often dealing with highly technical information. Coupled with this is how the justices made their decisions from the perspectives of judicial activism or constraint. Take, for example, the 2000–2003 cases—each had four dissenters. In comparing the two cases, Justices William Rehnquist, Antonin Scalia, Clarence Thomas, and Anthony Kennedy agreed with the person or organization bringing suit against environmental perspectives. According to Jeffrey Toobin

(2007), this would make sense because their approach to understanding the constitution is from the strict constructionist perspective, or rather, the conservative ideology. In comparison, Souter, Breyer, and Ginsburg are known for their activist perspective, viewing the Constitution as a living document (Toobin 2007). However, Stevens and O'Connor varied in their approaches in the 2000 and 2003 decisions, indicating that the approach used depends on the case (Toobin 2007).

In short, the courts do play a role in environmental policymaking—after all; they do have the final say. Therefore, it is important to take the time to pay attention to the cases reviewed by the Court, why they are decided, and whether justices do have the expertise to understand highly technical cases. One case to watch carefully is *Juliana v. US* where 21 plaintiffs within the ages of 11–22 filed suit against the federal government for not curbing greenhouse gas emissions (Spinelli 2018). As we finish writing the final pages of this textbook, the outcome of this case remains.

CHAPTER WRAP-UP

This chapter has presented a whirlwind tour of the institutional actors—Congress, the President, the bureaucracy, and the Courts—that shape environmental policy in the United States. When it comes to Congress and environmental policy, not much has changed since the 1990s in terms of reauthorizing the major laws of the 1970s. For some, this is alarming, but explainable, because of gridlock.

Next, we suggest that, although scholars spend a significant amount of time deciphering who the environmental president is, we contend that it might be rhetoric. In examining brief excerpts from State of the Union addresses from presidents Nixon through Obama, the conclusion can be made that presidents can make statements in their inaugural addresses to Congress, but, without public support, congressional action will be problematic. However, as we have learned, presidents such as Nixon and George H. Bush were successful in turning words into action.

In our examination of the bureaucracy, or the fourth branch of government, we argue that understanding it is essential to understanding the future of environmental policy. In this section of the chapter, we offer a snapshot of the mission and structure of two environmental agencies, the EPA and the USFWS. It is clear expertise is important in both of these agencies in order to effectively carry out congressional law. In our final section of the chapter, our discussion about the US Supreme Court offers a brief review of six cases during the course of 15 years. The goal of this investigation of cases was to explain the actors involved, how justices make decisions, and whether the court has the background to determine the outcomes of often highly technical environmental cases. Expertise matters and we should be paying attention. As students of public policy, we can participate and inform institutional policymaking (e.g., internships, submitting public comments), which we cover throughout this book.

SUGGESTED RESOURCES

Readings and Websites

Durant, Robert, and Daniel Fiorino. *Environmental Governance Reconsidered*. MIT Press. https://books.google.com/books?hl=en&lr=&id=oGYyDwAAQBA-J&oi=fnd&pg=PR9&ots=y0mpr0_1ay&sig=3HBrNtbt34qNvgXiMzvXA-CiEMa0#v=onepage&q&f=false.

Graham, Ottis. *Presidents and American Environment*. University of Kansas Press, 2015.

Huffington Post. 2013. Retrieved from http://www.huffingtonpost.com/2013/02/17/forward-on-climate-rally_n_2702575.html.

Lipsky, Michael. *Street Level Bureaucracy: Dilemmas of the Individual in Public Service*. Russell Sage Foundation Publications, 1983.

Films or Videos

PBS. "Frontline: Climate of Doubt." 2012. Retrieved from http://www.pbs.org/wgbh/pages/frontline/climate-of-doubt/.

PBS. "Decoding the Weather Machine." 2018. Retrieved from www.pbs.org/wnet/peril-and-promise/2018/04/watch-now-decoding-weather-machine/.

REFERENCES

Alaska Department of Environmental Conservation v. EPA.

Aldrich and Rohde. "Congressional Committees in a Continuing Partisan Era." In *Congress Reconsidered*, edited by Dodd and Oppenheimer. 9th edition, 337–360. Washington, DC: Sage, 2009.

American Trucking Associations v. City of Los Angeles.

Andrews, Richard N. L. *Managing the Environment, Managing Ourselves: A History of American Environmental Policy*. 2nd edition. New Haven, CT: Yale University Press, 2006.

Biesecker, Michael. 2016. Retrieved from https://apnews.com/9f61f5a9f8b242
bc8eb12a9b36449b54.
Brost, K. *Summary: American Recovery and Reinvestment Conference Agreement*
[Press Release]. February 13, 2009. Retrieved from Committee on
Appropriations website http://democrats.appropriations.house.gov/images/
stories/pdf/PressSummary02–13–09.pdf.
Burlington Northern v. United States.
Bush, George W. "Address Before a Joint Session of the Congress on Administration
Goals." In *Speech*. Washington, DC: The American Presidency Project. February
27, 2001. http://www.presidency.ucsb.edu/ws/index.php?pid=29643.
———. "Address Before a Joint Session of the Congress on the State of the
Union." In *Speech*. Washington, DC: The American Presidency Project.
February 2, 2005. http://www.presidency.ucsb.edu/ws/index.php?pid=58746.
Bush, Herbert Walker. "Address on Administration Goals Before a Joint
Session of Congress." In *Speech*. Washington, DC: The American Presidency
Project. February 9, 1989. http://www.presidency.ucsb.edu/ws/index.
php?pid=16660.
Carter, Jimmy. 1977. https://history.house.gov/Institution/SOTU/List/.
Carter, Jimmy. 1978. "The State of the Union Address Delivered Before a
Joint Session of The Congress." In *Speech*. Washington, DC: The American
Presidency. http://www.presidency.ucsb.edu/ws/index.php?pid=30856.
Cleaver, E. *Press Release: Speaker Pelosi Announces the Appointment of
Congressman Cleaver to New Select Committee On Global Warming*. March 9,
2007. Retrieved from House of Representative website at http://www.house.
gov/list/press/mo05_cleaver/SelectCommitteeEstablishment.html.
———. "Address Before a Joint Session of the Congress on the State of the
Union." In *Speech*. Washington, DC: The American Presidency Project.
February 4, 1997. http://www.presidency.ucsb.edu/ws/index.php?pid=
53358.
Clinton, William J. "Address Before a Joint Session of Congress on Goals." In
Speech. Washington, DC: The American Presidency Project. February 17,
1993. http://www.presidency.ucsb.edu/ws/index.php?pid=47232.
Downs, Anthony. *Inside Bureaucracy*. Long Grove, IL: Waveland Press, 1964.
Dunlap, Riley E., and Mertig, Angela G. 1992. https://www.researchgate.net-
publication/249015332_The_evolution_of_the_US_environmental_move-
ment_from_1970_to_1990_An_overview.
Environmental Defense v. Duke Energy Corp.
Evans, C. Lawrence, and Claire E. Grandy. "The Whip Systems of Congress." In
Congress Reconsidered, edited by B.I. Oppenheimer and L.C Dodd. 9th edi-
tion, 189–215. Washington, DC: CQ Press, 2009.
Fiorina, Morris. 1982. https://link.springer.com/article/10.1007/BF00242147.

Ford, Gerald. "Address Before a Joint Session of the Congress Reporting on the State of the Union." Washington, DC: The American Presidency Project. January 15, 1975. http://www.presidency.ucsb.edu/ws/index.php?pid=4938.

Funk. 2018. Accessed October 19, 2018. http://www.pewinternet.org/2018/05/14/majorities-see-government-efforts-to-protect-the-environment-as-insufficient/.

Ginsberg, Lowi, Weir, and Tolbert. *We the People: An Introduction to American Politics.* New York, NY: W. W. Norton, 2013.

Global Change. 2018. https://wun.ac.uk/wun/globalchallenges/view/responding-to-climate-change.

Graves, Lucia. "Obama Climate Change Policy." *Huffington Post.* 2013. Accessed January 21, 2014. http://www.huffingtonpost.com/2013/06/25/obama-climate-change-2013_n_3497151.html.

Gushenko. 2018. Accessed October 19, 2018. https://news.nationalgeographic.com/2017/03/how-trump-is-changing-science-environment/?user.testname=none.

Inhofe, James M. 1998. https://www.inhofe.senate.gov/.

IPCC Press Release. Accessed October 18, 2018. http://www.ipcc.ch/pdf/session48/pr_181008_P48_spm_en.pdf.

Klyza, Christopher McGrory, and David Sousa. 2008. https://escholarship.org/uc/item/0h19v9hk.

Klyza, Christopher McGrory, and David Sousa. *American Environmental Policy 1990–2012: Beyond the Gridlock.* Cambridge: The MIT Press, 2013.

Kraft, Michael E. *Environmental Policy and Politics.* 5th edition. New York: Longman, 2011. https://books.google.com/books/about/Environmental_Policy_and_Politics.html?id=tIVIQgAACAAJ.

Kriz, M. "On the Hot Seat." *National Journal* 43–44 (May 19, 2007a). Retrieved from Academic Search Complete.

———. "House Select Energy Independence and Global Warming Committee." *National Journal* 96 (June 23, 2007b). Retrieved from Academic Search Complete.

Lewis, Jack. "The Birth of the EPA." 1985. Accessed June 23, 2008. Available at http://www.epa.gov/history/topics/epa/15c.htm.

Lipinski, D. "Navigating Congressional Policy Processes: The Inside Perspective on How Laws Are Made." In *Congress Reconsidered*, edited by Dodd and Oppenheimer. 9th edition, 217–240. Washington, DC: Sage, 2009.

Loomis, John. *Integrated Public Lands Management.* New York: Columbia University Press, 1993.

Mayhew, David. *Congress: The Electoral Connection.* New Haven: Yale University Press, 2004.

Moen, Mathew. "The Political Agenda or Ronald Regan: A Content Analysis of State of the Union Addresses." *Presidential Studies Quarterly* 18, no. 4 (1988): 775–785.

Nixon, Richard. "Annual message to the Congress on the State of the Union." In *Speech*. Washington, DC: The American Presidency Project. January 22, 1970. http://www.presidency.ucsb.edu/ws/index.php?pid=2921.

———. "Address on the State of the Union Delivered Before a Joint Session of the Congress." In *Speech*. Washington, DC: The American Presidency Project. January 30, 1974. http://www.presidency.ucsb.edu/ws/index.php?pid=4327.

Niskanen, William. *Bureaucracy and Representative Government*. London: Aldine Transaction, 1971.

Obama, Barack. 2008. https://history.house.gov/Institution/SOTU/List/.

Obama, Barack. "Address Before a Joint Session of the Congress." In *Speech*. Washington, DC: The American Presidency Project. February 24, 2009. http://www.presidency.ucsb.edu/ws/index.php?pid = 85753.

———."Address Before a Joint Session of Congress on the State of the Union." In *Speech*. Washington, DC: The American Presidency Project. February 12, 2013. http://www.presidency.ucsb.edu/ws/index.php?pid=102826.

O'Leary, Rosemary. "Environmental Policy in the Courts." In *Environmental Policy: New Directions for the 21st Century*, edited by Norman J. Vig and Michael E. Kraft, 135–137. Washington, DC: CQ Press, 2013.

Palazzolo v. Rhode Island.

Pelosi, N. "Pelosi Announces Members of Select Committee on Energy Independence and Global Warming." In *FDCH Press Releases*. 2007. Retrieved from Newspaper Source Plus.

Rabe, B. (ed.). *Greenhouse Governance: Addressing Climate Change in America*, 1–20. Washington, DC: The Brookings Institution, 2010.

Reagan, Ronald. "Address Before a Joint Session of the Congress on the Program for Economic Recovery." In *Speech*. Washington, DC: The American Presidency Project. February 18, 1981. http://www.presidency.ucsb.edu/ws/index.php?pid=43425.

———. "Address Before a Joint Session of the Congress on the State of the Union." In *Speech*. Washington, DC: The American Presidency Project. February 6, 1985. http://www.presidency.ucsb.edu/ws/index.php?pid=38069.

Rinfret, Sara R., and Scott Furlong. "Defining Environmental Rulemaking." In *Oxford Handbook of U.S. Environmental Policy*, edited by Michael E. Kraft and Sheldon Kamieniecki, 372–383. New York: Oxford University Press, 2012.

Rosenbaum, Walter A. *Environmental Politics and Policy*. 9th edition. Washington, DC: CQ Press, 2013.

Sandall, Clayton, and Jennifer Duck. *Al Gore Brings Global Warming Crusade to Congress*. 2007. Retrieved from http://abcnews.go.com/Politics/story?id=2970093&page=1.

Savage, David. 2008. Retrieved from http://www.latimes.com/news/nation-world/lana-scotus24–2008jun24,0,3345943.story.

Select Committee on Energy Independence and Global Warming. *Geopolitical Implications of Rising Oil Dependence and Global Warming*. April 18, 2007. Retrieved from Select Committee website at http://globalwarming.house.gov/files/HRG/FullTranscripts/110–1_2007–04–18.pdf.

———. *110th Congress Final Staff Report*. November 21, 2008. Retrieved from Select Committee website at http://globalwarming.house.gov/pubs/archives_110?id=0059#main_content.

———. *Hearings from the House and Senate (including the Select Committee) Regarding Energy Independence and Global Warming*. 2009. Retrieved from Select Committee website at http://globalwarming.house.gov/files/WEB/EIGWHearings/110_EIGW_hearings.pdf.

———. *Select committee Hearing Testimony*. 2010. Retrieved from Select Committee website at http://globalwarming.house.gov/pubs/testimony.

Sensenbrenner, J. "Sensenbrenner Looks Forward to Extending Congressional Record on Energy Security and Climate Change." In *FDCH Press Releases*. December 8, 2000. Retrieved from Newspaper Source Plus.

———. "Sensenbrenner Reappointed as Select Committee Ranking Republican." In *FDCH Press Releases*. January 15, 2009. Retrieved from Newspaper Source Plus.

Sinclair, Barbara. *Unorthodox Lawmaking: New Legislative Processes in the U.S. Congress*. Washington, DC: CQ Press, 2007.

Smallen, J. "Pelosi Creates Global-Warming Panel." *National Journal* 47 (January 20, 2007). Retrieved from Academic Search Complete.

Soden, Dennis. *The Environmental Presidency*. Albany, NY: SUNY Press, 1999.

Spinelli, Dan. "Landmark Children's Lawsuit hits Roadblock." Accessed November 11, 2018. https://grist.org/article/landmark-childrens-climate-lawsuit-hits-new-roadblock/.

Steinhauer, J. "Republicans Killing Climate Committee." *New York Times* 26. December 2, 2010. Retrieved from Academic Search Complete at www.ebscohost.com.

Sunlight Foundation. "Only Four Percent of Bills Become Law." *Huffington Post*, 2014. Accessed January 21, 2014. http://www.huffingtonpost.com/wires/2009/08/25/the-vast-majority-of-bill_ws_268630.html.

Toobin, Jeffrey. *The Nine*. New York: Anchor Publishers, 2007.

Trump, Donald. 2018. https://history.house.gov/Institution/SOTU/List/.

Vig, Norman J. "Presidential Powers and Environmental Policy." In *Environmental Policy: New Directions for the 21st Century*, edited by Norman J. Vig and Michael E. Kraft. Washington, DC: CQ Press, 2013.

Vig, Norman J., and Michael E. Kraft. *Environmental Policy: New Directions for the 21st Century*. Washington, DC: CQ Press, 2013.

Weber, Max. *Capitalism, Bureaucracy, and Religion*. New York: Routledge, 1947.

Wilson, James, Q. *Bureaucracy: What Government Agencies Do and Why They Do It*. New York: Basic Books, 1991.

Unofficial Actors in the Policy Process

Contents

"Detox the Box"

We are consumers of products in our everyday lives. As consumers, we might not consider the broader effects that products have on the environment and our own health. Founded in 1995, Women's Voices

© The Author(s) 2019   155
S. R. Rinfret and M. C. Pautz, *US Environmental Policy in Action*,
https://doi.org/10.1007/978-3-030-11316-2_5

for the Earth (WVE) was created to reduce toxic exposure for women and families. Detox the Box is just one of WVE's campaigns to reduce toxic chemicals in feminine care products. In their *Chem Fatale Report*,[1] WVE found, to name a few (Scranton 2013):

• Feminine care products is a $3 billion dollar industry in the United States.
• Tampons include hazardous materials, including chlorine bleach from the processes to maintain the bright white color.
• Pads contain unknown fragrance chemicals, which can cause allergic rashes.
• Feminine wipes can use hazardous ingredients such as iodopropynyl butylcarbamate where exposure can lead to cancer or endocrine disruption.

The chemicals used in feminine care products are often unregulated by the Food and Drug Administration (FDA) because they are classified as cosmetics (Scranton 2013). More specifically, products such as tampons and pads are categorized as medical devices and therefore, do not have to disclose the ingredients. Accordingly, WVE has used their scientific research to inform conversations at the federal level and lobied members of Congress and companies for the passage of The Safe Cosmetics and Personal Care Products Act (2013), which is still pending as we write this chapter.

Due to their small budget, WVE has adapted its approaches to engender discussion through social media (e.g., Twitter hashtags and YouTube videos) to educate the public about the intricacies of feminine products. On one of their YouTube videos, for example, they attempt to educate and caution women about the drawbacks of using feminine care products. This approach is intended to create visibility online for offline action.

Although you might see a disconnect between WVE and the environment, consider that the products we consume end up in the landfill (see Chapter 1); harmful toxins can and are found in our food, as described in Chapter 10; and all of this suggests a broader connection between or consumerism behaviors and our impact on the environment.

---

[1] https://www.womensvoices.org/feminine-care-products/detox-the-box/

In the following pages, we demonstrate how the WVE is just one example of an unofficial policy actor, attempting to invoke policy change. Such efforts can and do find resistance. As we show in this chapter, groups challenge each other in the public policymaking arena to influence the actions of official policy actors and have even been classified as eco-terrorists.

In contrast to the last chapter, this one turns to understanding organizations such as WVE who are unofficial actors within environmental policy. Unofficial actors are those individuals and organizations—be it a political party or interest groups—that try to influence the actions of official actors (Congress, the president, the courts, and the bureaucracy) and the outcomes of elections. Accordingly, we survey the different types of unofficial actors. First, we discuss political parties and interest groups because both try to influence the decision-making of government. "Political parties and interest groups serve as linkage institutions tying citizens to their representatives in government. Political parties control the institutional arrangement of the government, [and] interest groups mobilize in a variety of ways to influence the behavior of politicians who control the apparatus of government" (Sussman et al. 2001, 88). More specifically, to truly understand how organized interests exert their influence, we offer two examples. The first example considers how interest groups try to influence the US Congress in its role overseeing oil subsidies. The second example examines how interest groups try to influence the bureaucracy.

The second section of this chapter focuses on how unofficial actors use the media to mobilize public opinion. Interest groups try to use traditional media (television advertising), and increasingly social media (Facebook, Twitter), to reach the public regarding environmental issues. More specifically, groups use a variety of approaches to garner media attention to make their voice heard. The final section of the chapter provides a peculiar case study that unpacks the story of Daniel McGowan, who was involved with the environmental organization Earth Liberation Front (ELF) and convicted for conspiracy and arson. The point of this chapter is to demonstrate the multitude of actors outside government who affect the decisions of official policy actors within the environmental realm and how they do it.

Upon completion of this chapter, several themes will materialize. First, influence matters; however, how unofficial actors try to influence official policy actors has changed over time because of adaptation to new uses of technology. In addition, there are different approaches that these actors can and do use to influence policymaking. Nevertheless, the question we pose in this chapter is if certain tactics such as writing a policy report (e.g., Chem Fatale) head or setting a building on fire should be classified as eco-terrorism. Put differently, are the efforts used by unofficial actors enough to breakthrough congressional gridlock?

Unofficial Policy Actors

Unofficial policy actors are those individuals who try to shape policy outcomes. As an introduction, we focus on defining two unofficial actors: political parties and interest groups. The purpose of a political party is to represent the policy preferences of the American people and put forward candidates to win elections. In comparison, the goal of an interest group is to influence the actions of official policy actors to gain favorable outcomes for their particular group. The following discussion provides a brief overview of the role of political parties in environmental policy, before turning to interest groups.

Political Parties

In the United States, elections are dominated by a two-party system, meaning that two political parties vie for winning elections at the local, state, and federal level. Historically, the two parties that have maintained a strong presence are the Republicans and Democrats. As Amy Below (2012) notes, "Republican ideology argues for individual liberty as opposed to government interference. Its preference for small government coincides with a pro-business, free-market attitude and thus an aversion to government control" (527). In comparison, "Democratic ideology is more commonly associated with liberalism and an acceptance of government involvement in the political, economic, and social lives of people" (Below 2012, 527). These perspectives affect who the American people believe is the best candidate to protect the environment.

To distinguish how a party affects the electoral decisions of the populace, a party has a platform. This platform is used to inform citizens about the party's perspectives or attitudes about a particular topic. For instance, in the 2016 presidential election, the Democratic Party was identified as pro-environment and the Republican Party as anti-environment. However, as Chapter 2 noted, the environment is not necessarily *the* focal point of US elections due to conversations regarding the environment. According to Below, "The majority of political discussions around the environment are among specialists rather than among the general electorate" (531). More specifically, environmental issues have become low salience—meaning they are not a pressing issue for many Americans. As a result, national parties do not make environmental issues their primary target during campaigns. Instead, candidates running for office focus on issues like jobs or healthcare—topics that resonate with voters within their districts and help to get them elected. For instance, during President Obama's reelection campaign, efforts centered on healthcare, affordable college education, and reductions in greenhouse gas (GHG) emissions. The 2016 presidential campaign of Donald J. Trump primarily focused on "making America Great Again," by rolling back policies enacted during the Obama administration (e.g., health policy, fuel efficiency standards for cars, and increasing energy exploration in the United States).

Interest Groups

Interest groups, which are organized groups of individuals who fight for a cause, are another type of unofficial actor. When we think about environmental policy, interest groups are usually broken down into business and environmental organizations. These groups are far-reaching, from protecting whales in the Pacific Ocean to coal miners' rights in West Virginia, for example. Robert Duffy (2003) argues, "Today there are perhaps tens of thousands of organized interests active in environmental and natural resource policymaking across all levels of government" (506). Thus, interest groups invest their time and resources to impact policies in the United States.

More specifically, interest groups are "[i]ndividuals who organize to influence the government's programs and policies" (Ginsberg et al. 2013, 435). There are several types of interest groups in the United States, ranging from businesses and professional associations to public interest and ideological interest groups. As we examine a few of these types to provide a broader overview, keep in mind that this list (see Table 5.1) is not exhaustive. The goal for the remainder of the chapter

Table 5.1   Understanding interest groups

Type of interest group	Purpose or goal	Examples
Business interest group	To promote economic interests	Chamber of Commerce, American Farm Bureau Federation, American Coal Council
Professional interest group	To represent the interest of a professional field or expertise	American Bar Association, American Medical Association, American Political Science Association, Association of Energy Engineers
Public interest group	To promote the protection of a particular issue	Sierra Club, Greenpeace, Natural Resources Defense Council, National Audubon Society
Ideological interest group	To address extreme political currents	Christian Coalition, National Organization for Women, National Association for the Advancement of Colored People

is to evaluate how business and environmental groups try to affect US environmental policy.

As Table 5.1 indicates, there are three broad ways we can categorize interest groups in the United States. For instance, a *business interest group* wants to protect economic interests and includes groups such as chambers of commerce or the American Farm Bureau Federation, which represents farm and ranching individuals in the United States. In turn, *professional interest groups* include organizations such as the American Bar Association (which represents lawyers), the American Medical Association (which includes medical professionals such as physicians), and the American Political Science Association (which is largely an academic organization for those individuals researching in the field of political science).

In addition to these basic descriptions, business and professional interest groups do play a role in environmental policymaking. The US Chamber of Commerce and the American Farm Bureau Federation, for example, have been pivotal in questioning whether or not the EPA has the authority to regulate GHG emissions under the Clean Air Act

(CAA). In particular, these groups have sued the EPA, maintaining that Congress never intended the EPA to regulate GHG emissions; thus, the EPA does not have the authority to move forward with such regulations. The Supreme Court has yet to determine the outcome of this case (US Chamber of Commerce 2013).

Public interest groups include those organizations that advocate for causes such as consumer or environmental protection. One of the oldest and largest environmental interest groups in the United States is the Sierra Club, founded in 1892, whose mission is "to explore, enjoy, and protect the wild places of the earth; to practice and promote the responsible use of the earth's ecosystems and resources; to educate and enlist humanity to protect and restore the quality of the natural and human environment; and to use all lawful means to carry out these objectives." One of the major issues that the Sierra Club is currently working on is thwarting the development of oil and gas drilling in Bears Ears National Monument.

The final type of interest group, *ideological groups*, provides individuals an organization to promote their broader political perspectives and government ideologies. For instance, individuals from a more conservative, religious perspective might be attracted to the Christian Coalition (CC). The purpose of the CC is to "offer people of faith the vehicle to be actively involved in impacting the issues they care about—from the county courthouse to the halls of Congress." When it comes to environmental issues, the CC believes that the exploration of drilling should increase domestically in order to lessen the reliance by the United States to use foreign sources of fuel.

Beyond the descriptions of the aforementioned types of interest groups, each group does advocate for specific causes. Recall that the Sierra Club is advocating for the United States not to build a pipeline from Canada to the Gulf of Mexico. Or that the US Chamber of Commerce is fighting the EPA's efforts to regulate GHGs under the CAA. Further, we offer additional examples of how specific groups, such as the National Audubon Society, Greenpeace, the National Wetlands Association, and Americans for Balanced Energy Choices approach environmental issues.

Albatrosses, Petrels, and Whales

Indeed, the goal of an interest group is to promote a particular cause by garnering public support, which, in turn, is likely to pressure lawmakers to act in a particular way. We consider examples from the National Audubon Society and Greenpeace. The National Audubon Society, which focuses on the conservation of birds and wildlife, asked its members to write letters to Congress to protect albatrosses and petrels. The concern is that these are two of the most endangered birds across the globe, and the National Audubon Society wanted its members to ask Congress to ratify an international agreement—the Agreement on the Conservation of Albatrosses and Petrels—so they are not entangled by fishing lines, which can cause death (National Audubon Society 2013). The assumption is that if the National Audubon Society's 600,000 members wrote letters to Congress, their voices could make a difference (Guber and Bosso 2013). The question becomes whether these efforts are sufficient to convince members of Congress to do something to save these imperiled birds.

By way of comparison, some environmental organizations such as Greenpeace do not necessarily believe conventional letter writing campaigns make an impact. Instead, environmental activism, in their opinion, should use unconventional efforts (e.g., Diane Wilson poured syrup on her head as a proxy for arguments against oil during a congressional hearing). Greenpeace tries to be the, "leading independent campaigning organization that uses peaceful protest and creative communication to expose global environmental problems and to promote solutions that are essential to a green and peaceful future" (Greenpeace 2013). The Rainbow Warrior is a ship used by Greenpeace to travel the ocean and challenge those they oppose. For instance, in their campaign to protect whales, Greenpeace used the Rainbow Warrior ship to board a Russian oil rig to protect the species. Although this may have halted the oil rig's production for the day, it did not stop extraction altogether; rather, Greenpeace used this approach to demonstrate a global message that oceanic oil extraction hinders the migration patterns of whales (Greenpeace 2013).

Our first two examples were about environmental organizations, but business groups are also effective in trying to impact policymaking and public perceptions about the environment. Business groups, more broadly, are successful in running public relations campaigns to support their endeavors, or what some might classify as greenwashing—the idea is that a company will spend money on advertising, claiming that it is working on green technology or providing a green product, but this is only a small fraction of what the company does overall (Vaughn 2007).

As Glenn Sussman et al. (2001) note, "The National Wetlands Coalition is not concerned with protecting the nation's wetlands but rather is committed to reducing the burden of wetlands regulations on real estate from oil and gas interests" (114). In 2012, the group Americans for Balanced Energy Choices produced several commercials noting their investment in clean coal technology for the future. However, is coal an environmentally clean energy source for consumption? Some individuals may question why groups would use a term (clean coal) that could mislead the public. The goal, as previously mentioned, is for business organizations to serve their own best interests.

In short, there are several different types of interest groups, and each impacts environmental policy through a variety of approaches. These groups are composed of American people, and their tactics attempt to encourage lawmakers to act on behalf of their group.

THE ADVENTURES OF A LOBBYIST

Most Americans belong to many interest groups without even thinking about it (such as parent–teacher associations, the American Automobile Association, etc.). There is, typically, an annual membership fee to be involved in an interest group. The idea is that, by becoming a "dues paying member" of an interest group, you receive benefits. These benefits could include a monthly newsletter that keeps citizens informed about issues to discounts on nature hikes or a cute stuffed animal. However, one of the most notable benefits is that this organization will fight for causes that you believe in. This often occurs through lobbying members of Congress. Each of the aforementioned types of interest groups generally uses membership dues to employ lobbyists.

Lobbyists often have degrees in political science or law and perhaps were a congressional staffer or even a former member of Congress. A lobbyist uses the power of persuasion when meeting with members of Congress. As Nick Naylor, a tobacco lobbyist in the film *Thank You for Smoking*, notes, "I get paid for talking." The goal of a lobbyist is to persuade members of Congress by presenting research and evidence that supports his or her cause in the hope that Congress will pass legislation in the group's favor. For instance, a lobbyist from the Sierra Club may urge members of Congress to support legislation to curb emissions that cause climate change. In turn, a business interest group, such as the American Petroleum Institute, might counter the Sierra Club's lobbying efforts with its own lobbyist, arguing that legislation to curb climate change in the United States could be devastating for the economy. As a result, these lobbyists compete with each other to persuade members of Congress.

Rebranding

One underlying concern with a professional career in lobbying is that it can carry a negative stereotype due to historical cases of corruption or money laundering scandals. A former lobbyist, Jack Abramoff, was recently convicted of illegally providing gifts to members of Congress in exchange for votes on pieces of legislation. The Lobbying Disclosure Act of 1995 (2 U.S.C.§ 1601) is supposed to prevent illegal activity such as this, and requires every lobbyist in the United States to register with the US House of Representatives.

Because of the negative perceptions about the profession, Clines (2013) argues that the term "lobbying" needs rebranding. The traditional view is that lobbyists meet with members of Congress to impact the outcome of legislation. Instead, the contemporary lobbyist has transcended into other venues, such as political strategy and campaign fundraising. The idea, based upon a survey conducted by the American League of Lobbyists (an organized group to represent lobbyists in the United States), suggests a new name for lobbyists: government relations professionals (Clines 2013). It still remains to be seen if the name change will endure, but lobbyists continue to have an impact on the outcome of public policy in the United States.

Moreover, many interest groups have their own Political Action Committee (PAC). The purpose of an interest group's PAC is to influence electoral politics through candidate selection and election outcomes. A PAC provides financial support to a candidate running for office. As of 2012, there are approximately 5000 PACs in the United States that contribute to federal-level elections (i.e., running for the US Congress; Center for Responsive Politics 2013a). According to the Center for Responsive Politics (CFRP) (2013), the American Farm Bureau PAC spent approximately $28,622 supporting Democratic and Republican candidates running for office. The idea is that these members will then support farm-friendly legislation if elected into office.

The natural concern becomes that interest groups, through their various activities, can exert too much power into the policymaking process.

"The framers of the US Constitution feared the power that could be wielded by organized interests. Yet they believed that interest groups thrived because of liberty–the freedom that all Americans enjoy to organize and to express their views" (Ginsberg et al. 2013, 435). Nevertheless, the idea is that if one group of organized interests forms to address a particular issue, another group will form to challenge. Therefore, competing groups balance one another when competing for access to influence congressional decision-making. To make this point clearer, we turn to an example of how interest groups do try to influence congressional policymaking.

INFLUENCE

Interest group influence on national policy has been a closely watched and well-documented phenomenon by scholars. Some argue that only a few, the *political elite*, have the power to influence policymaking in a democratic society Mills 1956). However, David Truman (1951) and Robert Dahl (1961) contend that all people in the United States have equal power to influence decision-making because we live in a pluralistic society. However, Mancur Olson (1965) and Charles Lindblom (1977) criticize the pluralist framework, asserting that business-oriented groups possessed a significant advantage due to their greater access to resources.

Nevertheless, while how much interest groups influence policy is still up for debate, it is abundantly clear that they at least try to do so (Baumgartner and Leech 2001; Baumgartner et al. 2009; Kingdon 2003; Lowi 1972). This is especially evident within the environmental arena, and we use the example of energy tax policy, and, more specifically, fossil fuel subsidies, to provide some insight into how interest groups can influence congressional policy. After our examination of how interest groups try to influence congressional policymaking, we then note that students of public policy and environmental policy cannot forget that interest group influence also occurs within the bureaucratic realm.

Oil or Clean Energy?

Energy tax policy in the United States for much of the twentieth century has favored oil and gas development, as economic growth is championed (Sherlock 2010). More specifically, the intangible drilling costs (IDCs) tax credit introduced in 1916 and the depletion tax credit introduced in 1926 are two of the longest standing fossil fuel subsidies. More specifically, the IDC tax credit allows developers to fully deduct expenses that may be incurred at a well site during the first year, as opposed to paying taxes on its depreciated value over time. In comparison, the depletion credit allows developers to deduct a fixed percentage from their tax bill, as opposed to a percentage based upon price, as they extract more of the resource from the well. Although these subsidies were reduced in the 1970s and again in the 1980s, on balance, these and other energy tax provisions continued to favor fossil fuels over the emerging clean energy industry for more than a century. However, the American Recovery and Reinvestment Act of 2009 (ARRA), clean energy surpassed oil and gas in terms of total tax incentives (Sherlock 2010).

Nevertheless, fossil fuel subsidies continue to amount to nearly $4 billion every year (Weeks 2011). As a result, since the 1970s when gas prices increased, policymakers discussed reforming the energy tax code. During the 2012 election, President Obama called on Congress to hold a vote on repealing oil subsidies in favor of clean energy spending. Obama argued "You can either stand up for the oil companies or you can stand up for the American people" (Cooper and Weisman 2012). In fact, this comment may be more substantive than just rhetoric, as public opinion polls have shown broad support for repealing oil and gas subsidies. A 2011 *NBC News/Wall Street Journal* poll found that 74% of Americans opposed federal subsidies for oil and gas. The Yale Project on Climate Change and Communication (2013) found a lower level of support, but still a significant majority (59%) opposed the subsidies. At the same time, the Yale poll found that 70% supported increased investment and research in renewable resources (Yale Project on Climate Change and Communications 2013). A poll conducted by the Pew Research in 2017 echoed the results from the Yale study—over 65% of Americans want investment in clean, renewable energy sources (Kennedy 2017).

Despite the public's support for clean energy sources over fossil fuels, Congress has created a new policy. Efforts to repeal fossil fuel subsidies have faltered over the several legislative sessions. Yet, why would Congress not use public opinion to inform a new legislative agenda for energy? To address this question, we examine interest group influence through an evaluation of congressional lobbying expenditures to provide one potential explanation.

The CFRP documents interest-group campaign and lobbying expenditures on an annual basis. In 2012, the top five oil industry lobbyists included Royal Dutch Shell, Exxon Mobil, Koch Industries, Chevron Corporation, and British Petroleum (BP), who spent a combined total of more than $56 million (CFRP 2013a). In addition, the top five natural gas industry lobbyists included the Williams Corporation, America's Natural Gas Alliance, Spectra Energy, Interstate Natural Gas Association of America, and Cheniere Energy, which spent a combined total over $8 million to lobby members of Congress (CFRP 2013b).

In comparison, the top five alternative energy lobbyists include the American Wind Energy Association, Growth Energy, Clean Energy Group, the National Biodiesel Board, and Clean Energy Fuels Corp, all of which spent a combined total of more than $7 million (CFRP 2013c). Finally, the top environmental lobbying firms include the BlueGreen Alliance, Environmental Defense Fund, the Nature Conservancy, Earthjustice Legal Defense Fund, and the National Wildlife Federation, and spent just under $7 million collectively (CFRP 2013d).

Clearly, the fossil fuel interests have a resource advantage over that of the clean energy supporters, with just the top ten players in the oil and gas industry spending more than four and a half times the amount of money on lobbying for their interests than their counterparts. In addition, it is unlikely that the environmental and alternative energy lobbyists are focusing all of their resources trying to repeal oil and gas subsidies alone, making the spending disparity even larger. More specifically, research organizations, like the CFRP, allow members of the public to track the involvement of interest groups in national policy. Thus, as this example shows, regardless of the extent of a given interest group's resources, groups certainly spend a lot of money trying to impact policymakers' decisions.

It is not just within the halls of Congress that interest groups are influential, however. Groups are increasingly involved across the stages of the rulemaking process (Kerwin and Furlong 2011). Unfortunately, assessing influence within the regulatory or bureaucratic realm is difficult to track because most of the interactions between agencies and interest groups occur off the record and out of the public eye (Cook and Rinfret 2013). Therefore, although scholars have a better understanding of what interest groups do at the congressional level, as noted in the aforementioned example, it is far less certain how they impact administrative rulemaking, which is of growing importance in the environmental arena

(Klyza and Sousa 2013). As a result, we offer a brief overview in the next section of how interest groups can and are influential during agency policymaking.

AGENCYMAKERS

Chapter 4 explained that the bureaucracy plays a major role in environmental policymaking because agencies translate vague congressional law into policy. Interest group involvement with the bureaucracy and Congress varies.

One way that interest groups can influence the bureaucracy is by working with Congress (Baumgartner and Leech 1998; McCubbins et al. 1987). This occurs when Congress pressures agency personnel to favor interest groups during policy implementation. The issue of climate change is an example of how congressional members, such as Representative Edward Markey (D-Michigan), sided with environmental groups to exert pressure for policy change utilizing rulemaking processes instead of through congressional legislation. For example, Representative Markey agreed with the Sierra Club that the United States needed to regulate climate change-causing agents such as carbon dioxide. Due to congressional gridlock on climate change, Representative Markey worked with the EPA on ways to move forward with the regulation of carbon dioxide under the CAA (Morris 2009). Representative Markey is bypassing the gridlock by using the EPA and its regulatory processes to enact policy change.

Our second example examines ways organized interests have tried to influence agency policymaking, known as rulemaking. Rulemaking is the process by which every federal agency—such as the National Park Service (NPS) or the EPA—writes, a rule based upon congressional legislation. As previously discussed, Congress creates laws that are vague; therefore, agencies have to make sense of this vague language to carry out the law's implementation. Rules offer clearer specifications for the implementation of a law passed by Congress. For instance, Congress created the Endangered Species Act of 1973 in which agencies, including the U.S. Fish and Wildlife Service (USFWS), must ensure the protection of species from becoming endangered or extinct. In order to interpret the law, Agencies, such as the USFWS, must first propose a rule in the *Federal Register*.

This announcement of draft rules asks for the public to submit comments about the proposed rules. Usually, comments range from someone angry about a given rule to a scientist who provides technical expertise about the pros and cons of the rule. Often, agencies receive thousands of comments, which is a concern because generally only one or two staff members examine the comments. However, one approach that agencies use when examining public comments is a computer software program, Discover Text, which detects for duplicative comments. Therefore, when environmental organizations such as the National Audubon Society have their membership send a mass letter to an agency as described earlier, the agency will count this as one substantive comment. Thus, submitting public comments to an agency is not like lobbying your member of Congress. The agency is seeking substantive comments about the rule. Thus, submitting public comments is one way for organized interests or the general public to influence agency decision-making (Magat et al. 1986; Golden 1998; West 2004; Chapter 6 explores this area of research in much greater detail).

Ultimately, there are a variety of pathways—congressional and bureaucratic—for interest groups to influence environmental policymaking in the United States, and this chapter presented two ways in which this can occur. Agenda setting is often achieved through acts of lobbying, but another important piece of the puzzle for unofficial policy actors is how best to use the media to persuade not only members of Congress or the bureaucracy, but also the American public. Accordingly, we turn to how the media can set or lessen the agenda for particular interest groups to influence environmental policymaking.

The Media and Interest Groups

There are several useful functions of the media that are utilized by interest groups to set the policymaking agenda. We focus our attention in this final section of the chapter on: how different types of media are utilized by a group, who controls media coverage, and how social media applications (apps) are changing the contemporary landscape for driving political participation for environmental issues.

First, in the United States, there are three ways to classify the different types of media—*broadcast, print,* and *the Internet.* Put simply, broadcast media includes radio and television, print encompasses newspapers and magazines, and the Internet is an online resource that incorporates cyber versions of the more traditional media sources. Interest groups use all types of the media to market their message to the public, trying to garner support for their stances on particular issues. Nevertheless, the usage of these types of media has varied throughout history (Ginsberg et al. 2013).

Historically, print (notably, newspapers) has been one of the dominant sources for groups to convey to the public that they should support or be against a certain issue. Benjamin Franklin, for example, used the *Pennsylvania Gazette* to try to persuade politicians to address water pollution in Philadelphia (Sussman et al. 2001). Although this example is from a prominent official policy actor, it helped to lead the way for environmental interests to gain traction in garnering public support for pollution prevention. For instance, print media has been able to use images such as the Cuyahoga River on fire in the 1960s or the satellite images of the ozone depletion in the Earth's atmosphere to demonstrate the need for action. However, using print media as a way to attract the public's support for groups has become more difficult in the twenty-first century, as we will see in our further discussion.

The political elite (elected officials) continue to rely upon print media to examine information about a particular issue (Ginsberg et al. 2013); however, a shift in the 1960s to television became a popular approach for groups to promote environmental protection to entice the American public. After all, this is about the time that television became a prominent fixture in the majority of American households. More recently, California's Proposition 37 attempted to place labels on foods indicating if an item was a genetically modified organism (GMO). However, major industry organizations, such as Monsanto, spent approximately $45 million in television advertisements to defeat the measure in November 2013 (*The Guardian* 2013). In New York, where the decision to allow hydraulic fracturing is still to be determined, natural gas interest groups such as Friends of Natural Gas NY have run advertisements maintaining that, if the state does not allow fracking, it will be detrimental not only to the state's economy, but also to the US economy (Friends of Natural Gas NY 2013).[2]

[2] https://www.womensvoices.org/feminine-care-products/detox-the-box/.

Due to the lack of financial resources for advertisements, many environmental organizations alternatively use the popular site YouTube to reach a broader audience. In particular, the Natural Resources Defense Council (NRDC) gained thousands of viewers with its "Great Plastic Purge" YouTube clip, explaining that major companies that produce plastic need to curb their practices because of the detrimental impacts that plastic has on nearby oceans (NRDC 2013). Although interest groups use these sources or approaches, the question is: what effect do these have?

Who Gets Air Time?

In addition to the types of media in the United States, we also need to consider that coverage plays a large role in shaping Americans' perceptions about the environment. After all, "News coverage of the environment has a significant impact on public opinion, policymaking, and whether we, as a society, expand and deepen our stewardship ethic" (Miller and Pollak 2012, 3). Journalists—those individuals who report stories to an audience—play an important role in news coverage because these are the people who are interpreting or framing the story to the public. Framing is a powerful mechanism, as Christen and Huberty (2007) argue, because it shapes a person's preferences regarding policy priorities. Headlines of news stories such as "Artic Drilling Would Set Bad Precedent" or "Bush: Cut Trees to Save Forests" impact an individual's perspective on an issue (Christen and Huberty 2007).

Moreover, framing has added to an overarching argument that environmental activism is anti-jobs or anti-worker (Guber and Bosso 2013). This particular argument can be expanded through the analysis of how climate change is framed in US Environmental organizations such as the Sierra Club, National Wildlife Federation, and the National Audubon Society, all of which argued that climate change is the result of human activities, and legislation needs to pass to further prevent further warming of the Earth. In fact, the United Nations International Panel on Climate Change released a 6-year study that demonstrated research from more than 800 scientists who are 95% confident that climate change is caused by humans (Hennen et al. 2013). However, the counter-perspective from business lobbyists has been strong in creating an atmosphere in which many Americans believe that climate change is not the result of humans. The climate-deniers like Senator Inhofe maintain that climate change is a ploy by environmental groups to create legislation that would inhibit the US economy (Vig and Kraft 2013). Therefore, framing of either side of the climate change debate is playing out in television advertisement.

Closely linked to framing and shaping someone's perception about a topic is the role of priming. When a journalist or presidents use images (e.g., photos, videos, or Tweets), priming occurs. For instance, think about the images of seagulls and other ocean life covered in oil after the Exxon Valdez oil spill, or in the 1960s when the Cuyahoga River in Cleveland, Ohio caught fire. These images stick in the minds of the American public, and groups use them to support their causes. Social media is another form of framing—consider President Donald Trump's tweets[3]—these images are retweeted by millions of followers. GIFs or memes also used in Instagram, Snapchat, or Twitter can go viral, impacting Americans perceptions about environmental issues. However, these issues only garner the public's attention for a short period of time.

One explanation for lack of coverage is that many environmental problems are inherently difficult for journalists to cover because they do not understand the science or data. Moreover, if a person cannot visualize the problem or results, covering environmental problems becomes problematic. For example, take smog in the 1970s; the sea of smog covering many of our US cities drove action because people could see that it was a problem. However, carbon monoxide, one of the leading drivers of climate change, is not visibly apparent to the public in the same way as dirty skies. Thus, if we cannot see something happening in front of our own eyes, it is hard to press for change.

Second, inextricably linked to media coverage is also understanding who owns many of the news outlets in the United States. For instance, CNN is owned by Ted Turner, and Fox News is owned by Rupert Murdoch. The idea here is that these individuals also affect the portrayal or coverage of a story. After all, the media's goal is to make money; therefore, the question becomes how covering environmental stories lends itself to making money. According to a study conducted by the *Pew Project for Excellence in Journalism*, only 1.2% of news headlines in the United States focus on the environment. Even more startling, as Media Matters found "between January 1, 2011 and June 26, 2012, prominent newspapers and television news from major networks and

---

[3] https://www.vox.com/policy-and-politics/2017/6/1/15726472/trump-tweets-global-warming-paris-climate-agreement.

cable stations mentioned reality TV stars the Kardashians a combined 2,133 times while ocean acidification was only mentioned 45 times in the same period" (Environmental Coverage 2013, 3). We use climate change as an example because, whatever the subject, media coverage does shape public perception.

In the 1950s, the *Christian Science Monitor* published an article written by Robert Cohen (1957) that questioned whether humans were changing the climate. However, media coverage of climate change was sparse throughout the 1960s and 1970s, not returning to the front pages until 1988 when James Hansen, a government scientist, testified in the United States. Congress that he was 99% certain that warming temperatures were due to the burning of fossil fuels. His statements fueled a great deal of public interest, but the US media then began to scrutinize science. This is partly because of efforts spearheaded by Senator James Inhofe (R-OK) who argued that climate change is a hoax (see Chapter 4). Moreover, Michael Crichton's fictional *State of Fear* challenged the conclusion that climate change is caused by humans. However, he was invited by President George W. Bush to discuss climate policy (Boykoff and Rajan 2007). Thus, in examining several major newspapers (*The Los Angeles Times, The New York Times, The Wall Street Journal, The Washington Post*) since 1998, the efforts of Inhofe and Crichton have been successful; coverage has resulted in approximately 250 stories in 1988 to 750 in 2006 (Boykoff and Rajan 2007). At first glance, one might assume that coverage has increased, but this is a relatively small number for almost a decade's worth of news stories.

While there is a lack of overall coverage by mainstream media about the environment; however, there are news sources that continue to investigate environmental issues such as Columbia Law School's Sabin Center for Climate Change Law, *The Huffington Post* and the state of Washington's *The Daily Herald* (Environmental Coverage). Moreover, we are seeing a growing trend of providing information to viewers through alternative sources of media. This is often referred to as the "alternative movement" where retired experts from agencies such as the NPS or Environmental Protection Agency have created AltNPS or AltEPA for followers on Tweeter to receive information. Arguably, this is out of resistance to President Trump's, rollback of the Obama administration's environmental policies, and formulated alternative websites (e.g., silencing science tracker) to provide information.

Alternative Media

Clickivism or Activism

Due to the lack of attention and coverage by the mainstream media, interest groups are becoming more creative in using technological advancements for their benefit. For those individuals wanting quick information, blogs, Facebook, or Twitter might be a way to go. This allows individuals to like or share information about specific causes with the friends or family or create a hashtag movement to promote information (e.g., #DetoxtheBox video). *The New York Times* has a section—Dot Earth—that provides readers a venue to convey their opinions about environmental policy. The Environmentalblog.org covers a variety of aspects of green living in order for readers to get involved in the community. One blog entry—"6 Powerful Tips to Save Energy and the Environment around your House" (June 26, 2018)—explains simple household tips on ways to reduce energy consumption. The US EPA even has its own blog! The EPA's blog, "It's our Environment, EPA's Blog About our World" is written by EPA employees to explain to the public what they do in their daily work lives and also provide the public with up-to-date information. Although these examples might not be from specific, organized interests groups, they highlight how individuals consume environmental information. This information could lead to action (e.g., protesting, pressuring lawmakers to act).

There is concern that the online–offline environmental engagement is not quite like sinking a boat in the Gulf of Mexico or participating in a sit-in on Capitol Hill. Quite simply have we become clickivists or activists? Braun (2013) argues that we should be optimistic about this new wave of eco-activism. For example, a student from Arizona State University was able to persuade her gym to recycle plastic bottles, have letters to the editor published in the *Arizona Republic* on hydropower, and recycle her old washing machine. The argument can be made that a new wave of environmental activism is transpiring, which brings together online–offline communities.

In short, when news coverage dissipates across mainstream media, different types of technology are being used to engage individuals to address environmental issues. Social media is just one mechanism to promote action.

CHAPTER WRAP-UP

Unofficial policy actors do matter in the environmental policymaking arena. Political parties help shape the viewpoints of the electorate, but have not played as large of a role in recent history. Alternatively, this chapter describes that there are a sufficient number of interest groups in the United States for anyone to become involved, whatever the issue of the day. Nevertheless, for the purposes of environmental policy, interest groups are usually delineated as either environmental organizations or business organizations.

One of the most effective ways a group can exert influence is through lobbying. Lobbying, as we suggest in this chapter, usually occurs when a lobbyist from an organization tries to influence a member of Congress. However, due to congressional gridlock, we argue that more attention should be paid to how interest groups influence bureaucratic decision-making or rulemaking. In our description of how individuals or groups can submit comments on agency rules, the general argument is that business groups dominate the submission of public comments.

In our last section of the chapter, we observe that the media's waning coverage of environmental issues might cause concern; however, we note that there are additional social networking venues in which organizations are trying to engender a new wave of environmental interest.

Unofficial policy actors are just one piece of the larger puzzle that helps us to understand and investigate environmental policymaking. The mechanisms in which organized interests attempt to influence decision-making is not easy, but, in terms of environmental protection, we need to be mindful of tracing who gets what, when, and how. One environmental expert reminds us, "Industry and environmental groups can lobby all they want, but we have to keep the environment safe." The question becomes what measures individuals or groups are willing to take to protect or to fight for the environment? Creating an alternative website for information may be one outlet, but we end this chapter with a thought-provoking case—the case of Daniel McGowan and the ELF. His actions to protect the environment are classified as too extreme, or eco-terrorism.

Environmentalist or Terrorist? Daniel McGowan and the Earth Liberation Front

In 2007, Daniel McGowan was convicted of arson, labeled an eco-terrorist, and given a terrorist enhancement sentence (Cascadia 2007). This meant he was sentenced to 7 years in federal prison, and spent most of his time in a Communicating Management Unit (CMU), which, following the 9/11 attacks, is a special federal prison designed specifically for terrorists (McGowan 2013). How McGowan met this fate highlights two pressing debates in regard to environmental policy and activism: how environmentalists should achieve their priorities and whether actions associated with those priorities can be labeled terrorism.

McGowan's story dates back to events in 1997 in Eugene, Oregon. At the time, 11 environmental activists attempted to protect 40 large trees in downtown Eugene from being removed for a new parking lot (Mercado 2013). The activists climbed the trees, and the police used pepper spray to remove the activists; one activist endured a dozen canisters of pepper spray before giving in (Mercado 2013). The activists failed in their attempt, and the trees were removed. In response to the nonviolent protests, McGowan said "what's the point why bother, it's not getting us anywhere … I like a lot of people I knew at the time experienced a massive loss of faith that systemic change could happen through the system regulating itself or reforming itself" (McGowan 2011). Therefore, McGowan decided to take a different approach and joined an environmental organization called the ELF, which focused on inflicting property damage on those who harm the environment (Harden 2006).

That same year, McGowan started his violent activism by protesting against a Brooklyn, New York Macy's for selling furs by breaking windows and spray painting ALF, or Animal Liberation Front (a sister organization of ELF), on the building (Cascadia 2007). In 2000, McGowan participated in the Black Bloc protest in Seattle. After his protests in Seattle, McGowan became an important member of the ELF "Family." He traveled to the Midwest and participated in an ELF attack on a U.S. Forest Service's Biotechnology Facility in Rhinelander, Wisconsin, which was developing genetically modified timber products.

Subsequently, McGowan returned to the West Coast where he participated in his two most notorious acts of arson against Superior Lumber and the Jefferson Poplar Farm (Cascadia 2007). McGowan noted that Superior Lumber was targeted because it was a timber company and Jefferson Poplar Farm because ELF suspected that the facility was growing genetically modified trees (McGowan 2011).

However, when McGowan found out that the Jefferson Poplar Farm was not growing genetically modified trees, he began to rethink his work with ELF. McGowan commented that, at the time, "I thought it was effective [when] you're in the thick of it, it's hard to look at all the consequences and the real repercussions of that. Did this action push them in a better direction? Did it scare them? Did it help the movement in any capacity? ... There are a lot of questions but I don't think at the time I was asking those questions too much" (McGowan 2011) Upon reflection, McGowan came to the conclusion that "this is futile, there has to be better ways of addressing what's going on in the world than just burning things down" (McGowan 2011).

As a result, McGowan returned to New York City in 2002 and continued his advocacy work, but, this time, through conventional means. In New York, he worked on a number of causes including rainforest preservation, national forest protection, and biodiversity (Support for Daniel McGowan 2013). In 2005, he entered a graduate program at the Tri-State College of Acupuncture, with interests in providing medical care for those who cannot afford it (Support for Daniel McGowan 2013). However, the law caught up to him, and he was arrested in 2005 as a part of the Federal Bureau of Investigation's Operation Backfire in which 11 members of ELF were indicted (Harden 2006).

Then US Attorney General Alberto Gonzales praised the arrests, arguing "today's indictment proves that we will not tolerate any group that terrorizes the American people, no matter its intentions or objectives" (Harden 2006). McGowan was released from prison in December 2012 (Woodhouse 2012). However, he was briefly jailed again in April 2013 for allegedly violating his terms of release when he published an article in *The Huffington Post* that was critical of the government (McGowan 2013). However, he was released shortly thereafter, when his lawyers found that the regulation allowing this arrest was found unconstitutional (Sledge 2013). Post-release, McGowan attempted to file a class action lawsuit for his first amendment rights (free speech) for being violated while in prison. This case was unsuccessful.

McGowan's story raises an important question—what type of approaches impact policy outcomes? Is it the unconventional approaches of McGowan, or is it letter-writing campaigns to members of Congress? Further, if you use unconventional approaches, should these mechanisms be classified as eco-terrorism? McGowan is highly critical of the use of the term "eco-terrorist" in relation to his actions because he argues that it is a buzzword or: "a boogeyman word. It's, like, whoever I really disagree with is a terrorist" (McGowan 2011). Lauren Regan (2007), a member of his legal team agreed, arguing that labeling McGowan and the other plaintiffs as terrorists was a mistake because these individuals were "charged with property crimes that didn't cause any harm to human life." However, Assistant US Attorney Stephen Peifer (2011) argued that the terrorist label was justified because "terrorist acts, under the definition of the law, can vary all over the board. There's no requirement for purposes of terrorism that you physically endanger another person's life." The Federal Bureau of Investigation also defines eco-terrorism as "the use or threatened use of violence of a criminal nature against innocent victims or property by an environmentally-oriented, subnational group for environmental-political reasons, or aimed at an audience beyond the target, often of a symbolic nature" (Jarboe 2002). As a result, although McGowan's actions led to no physical human harm, under the law, he was labeled a terrorist and sent to prison (Stewart 2011).

Since McGowan was convicted of terrorism, the definition of eco-terrorism has expanded to include "setting mink free at fur farms, campaigns to financially bankrupt animal testing firms and protests in front of the homes of some of those firms' executives" (Eilperin 2012). Nevertheless, it remains to be seen if this is the end of the movement toward violent environmental activism, or if it is simply dormant, waiting for the next generation of McGowans.

SUGGESTED RESOURCES

Readings and Websites

Braun, Ashley. "Facebook App Translates Online Efforts into Real-World Environmental Change." *Grist*, 2013. http://grist.org/article/2009–05–12-facebook-efforts-real-change/.

Discover Text. *Collobarative Text Analytics Soluction*. June 14, 2014. http://www.discover-text.com/.

"Is Using Social Media Bad for the Environment?" October 15, 2018. https://www.vice.com/en_uk/article/d3wa7a/is-using-social-media-bad-for-the-environment.

Sledge, Matt. "I Got Snatched." *Huffington Post*. Accessed January 22, 2014. http://www.huffingtonpost.com/2013/09/12/daniel-mcgowan-prison_n_3860426.html.

Wilson, Diane. *An Unreasonable Woman: A True Story of Shrimpers, Politicos, Polluters, and the Fight for Seadrift, Texas*. White River Junction, VT: Chelsea Green Publishing, 2005.

———. *Diary of an Eco-outlaw: An Unreasonable Woman Breaks the Law for Mother Earth*. White River Junction, VT: Chelsea Green Publishing, 2011.

Films or Video

If a Tree Falls: A Story of the Earth Liberation Front. Directed by Marshall Curry. 2012.

Independent Television Service, Corporation for Public Brodcasting. DVD.

Thank You for Smoking. Directed by Jason Reitman. 2005. Fox Searchlight. DVD.

Miss Sloane. Directed by Jonathan Perera. 2016.

REFERENCES

About Us: National Audubon Society. Accessed June 13, 2013. http://www.audubon.org/about-us.

Baumgartner, Frank, and Beth Leech. *Basic Interests: The Importance of Groups in Politics in Political Science*. Princeton, NJ: Princeton University Press, 1998.

Baumgartner, Frank, and Beth Leech. "Interest Niches and Policy Bandwagons: Patterns of Interest Group Involvement in National Politics." *The Journal of Politics* 63, no. 4 (2001): 1191–1213.

Baumgartner, Frank R., Jeffrey M. Berry, Marie Hojnacki, David C. Kimball, and Beth Leech. *Lobbying and Policy Change: Who Wins, Who Loses, and Why*. Chicago: University of Chicago Press, 2009.

Below, Amy. "Parties, Campaigns, and Elections: Their Influence on Environmental Politics and Policymaking." In *Oxford Handbook of U.S. Environmental Policy*, edited by Michael E. Kraft and Sheldon Kamiencki, 525–553. New York: Oxford University Press, 2012.

Boykoff, Maxwell, and S. Ravi Rajan. "U.S. Library of Medicine." March 2007. http://www.ncbi.nlm.nih.gov/pmc/articles/PMC1808044/.

Braun, Ashley. "Facebook App Translates Online Efforts into Real-World Environmental Change." *Grist*, June 13, 2013. http://grist.org/article/2009–05–12-facebook-efforts-real-change/.

Cascadia, Gumby. "Daniel McGowan's Sentencing Report." *Portland Independent Media Center*, June 4, 2007. http://portland.indymedia.org/en/2007/06/360572.shtml.

Center for Responsive Politics (CFRP). *Oil & Gas: Lobbying*, 2012. Accessed August 23, 2013. http://www.opensecrets.org/industries/lobbying.php?cycle=2012&ind=E01.

Center for Responsive Politics (CFRP). *Alternative Energy Production & Services: Lobbying*, 2012. Accessed August 23, 2013. http://www.opensecrets.org/industries/lobbying.php?cycle=2012&ind=E1500.

Center for Responsive Politics (CFRP). *Natural Gas Pipelines: Lobbying*, 2012. Accessed August 23, 2013. http://www.opensecrets.org/industries/lobbying.php?cycle=2012&ind=E1140.

Center for Responsive Politics (CFRP). *Environment: Lobbying*, 2012. Accessed August 23, 2013. http://www.opensecrets.org/industries/lobbying.php?cycle=2012&ind=Q11.

Christen, Cindy T., and Kelli E. Huberty. "Media Reach, Media Influence? The Effects of Local, National and Internet News on Public Opinion Inferences." *Journalism & Mass Communication Quarterly* 84, no. 2 (2007): 315–334.

Clines, Francis X. "Lobbyist Look for Euphemism." *New York Times*, September 21, 2013. http://www.nytimes.com/.

Cook, Jeffrey, and Sara R. Rinfret. "A Revised Look: EPA Rulemaking Processes." *Journal of Environmental Studies and Sciences* 3, no. 3 (2013): 279–289.

Cooper, Helene, and Jonathan Weisman. "Obama Seeks to End Subsidies for Oil and Gas Companies." *New York Times*, August 23, 2012. http://www.nytimes.com/.

Cohen, Robert C. "Are Men Changing Earth's Weather?" *Christian Science Monitor*, December 4, 1957, p. 13.

Dahl, Robert A. *Who Governs? Democracy and Power in an American City*. New Haven, CT: Yale University Press, 1961.

Duffy, Robert J. *The Green Agenda in American Politics: New Strategies for the Twenty-First Century*. Lawrence: University Press of Kansas, 2003.

Eilperin, Juliet. "As Eco-Terrorism Wanes, Governments Still Target Activist Groups Seen as Threat." *Washington Post*, August 8, 2012. http://articles. washingtonpost.com/.

Environmental Coverage. 2013. http://www.earthisland.org/journal/index. php/articles/entry/mainstream_environmental_coverage_the_sound_of_ silence/.

Friends of Natural Gas. August 2, 2013. http://www.friendsofnaturalgasny.com/.

Ginsberg, Benjamin, Theodore J. Lowi, Margaret Weir, and Caroline J. Tolbert. *We the People: An Introduction to American Politics*. New York: W. W. Norton, 2013.

Greenpeace. "About Us." August 23, 2013. http://www.greenpeace.org/usa/en/.

Golden, Marissa Martino. "Interest Groups in the Rule-Making Process: Who Participates? Whose Voices Get Heard?" *Journal of Public Administration Research and Theory* 8, no. 2 (1998): 245–270.

Guber, Deborah Lynn, and Christopher J. Bosso. "High Hopes and Bitter Disappointment." In *Environmental Policy: New Directions for the 21st Century*, edited by Michael E. Kraft and Norman J. Vig, 525–553. Washington, DC: CQ Press, 2013.

Harden, Blaine. "11 Indicted in 'Eco-Terrorism' Case." *Washington Post*, 2006. Accessed August 8, 2013. http://www.washingtonpost.com/.

Hennen, Dave, Brandon Miller, and Eliott McLauglin. "U.N. Climate Change Report Points Blame at Humans." *CNN*. Accessed August 8, 2013. http:// www.cnn.com/2013/09/27/world/climate-change-5-things/index. html?hpt=hp_t1.

Jarboe, James F. "Testimony Before the House Resources Committee, Subcommittee on Forests and Forest Health." Federal Bureau of Investigation, 2002. http://www.fbi.gov/news/testimony/the-threat-of-eco-terrorism.

Kennedy, Brian. 2017. Assessed at http://www.pewresearch.org/fact-tank/2017/01/23/two-thirds-of-americans-give-priority-to-developing-al-ternative-energy-over-fossil-fuels/.

Kerwin, Cornelious M., and Scott R. Furlong. *Rulemaking: How Government Agencies Write Law and Make Policy*. Washington, DC: CQ Press, 2011.

Kingdon, John W. *Agendas, Alternatives and Public Policies*. 2nd edition. New York: Longman, 2003.

Klyza, Christopher McGrory, and David Sousa. *American Environmental Policy, 1990–2006: Beyond Gridlock*. Cambridge: MIT Press, 2013.

Lindblom, Charles. *Politics and Markets*. New York: Basic Books, 1977.

Lowi, Theodore. "Four Systems of Policy, Politics and Choice." *Public Administration Review* 32, no. 4 (1972): 298–310.

Magat, Wesley, Alan Krupnick, and Winston Harrington. *Rules in the Making: A Statistical of Regulatory Agency Behavior*. Washington, DC: Resources for the Future Press, 1986.

McCubbins, Matthew D., Roger G. Noll, and Barry R. Weingast. "Administrative Procedures as Instruments of Political Control." *Journal of Law, Economics, and Organization* 3 (1987): 243–277.

McGowan, Daniel. *If a Tree Falls: A Story of the Earth Liberation Front.* Directed by Marshall Curry and Sam Cullman. Oscilloscope Pictures, 2011. DVD.

———. "Court Documents Prove I Was Sent to Communication Management Units (CMU) for My Political Speech." *Huffington Post*, August 8, 2013. http://www.huffingtonpost.com/.

Mercado, Jeffrey. "In Defense of Trees." *Envision Environmental Journalism.* August 7, 2013. http://envision.uoregon.edu/archives/1697.

Miller, Tyler, and Todd Pollak. 2012. "Environmental Coverage in Mainstream News: We Need More." Accessed July 13, 2014. http://greeningthemedia.org/wp-content/uploads/Environmental-Coverage-in-the-Mainstream-News.pdf.

Mills, C.W. *The Power Elite.* London: Oxford University Press, 1956.

Morris, David. 2009. Accessed August 26, 2014. http://grist.org/article/2009-10-05-new-roposed-climate-change-bill-in-washington-is-simpler-and-mor/.

Natural Resources Defense Council (NRDC). Accessed February 13, 2013. http://www.nrdc.org/globalwarming/.

NBC News/Wall Street Journal. *Study #11091. Wall Street Journal*, 2011. Accessed August 23, 2013. http://online.wsj.com/article/SB10001424052748704005404576176981643217882.html.

Olson, Mancur. *The Logic of Collective Action: Public Goods and the Theory of Groups.* Cambridge, MA: Harvard University Press, 1965.

Peifer, Stephen. *If a Tree Falls: A Story of the Earth Liberation Front.* Directed by Marshall Curry and Sam Cullman. City of Production: Oscilloscope Pictures, 2011. DVD.

Regan, Lauren. Interview by Amy Goodman and Juan Gonzalez. *Democracy Now a Daily Independent Global News House with Amy Goodman & Juan Gonzalez*, 2007. Accessed August 9, 2013. http://www.democracynow.org/2007/6/11/exclusive_facing_seven_years_in_jail.

Scranton, Alexandra. 2013. Accessed October 15, 2018. https://www.womensvoices.org/wp-content/uploads/2013/11/Chem-Fatale-Report.pdf.

Sherlock, Molly F. "Energy Tax Policy: Historical Perspectives on and Current Status of Energy Tax Expenditures." 2010. Accessed August 23, 2013. http://www.national-aglawcenter.org/assets/crs/R41227.pdf.

Sledge, Matt. "Daniel McGowan Released After Lawyers Confirm He Was Jailed for HuffPost Blog." *Huffington Post*, August 8, 2013. http://www.huffingtonpost.com/.

Stewart, Christopher S. "Little Gitmo." *New York Magazine*, 2011. Accessed August 8, 2013. http://nymag.com/news/features/yassin-aref-2011-7/.

"Support for Daniel McGowan." Accessed 9, 2013. http://www.supportdaniel.org/whois/bio.php.

Sussman, Glen, Byron W. Daynes, and Jonathan P. West. *American Politics and the Environment*. New York: Longman, 2001.

The Guardian. "Prop 37: Food Companies Spend $45 Million to Defeat California GM Bill." Accessed August 9, 2013. http://www.theguardian. com/environment/2012/nov/05/prop-37-food-gm-bill.

Truman, David. *The Governmental Process*. New York: Alfred A. Knopf, 1951.

US Chamber of Commerce, American Farm Bureau Federation, and the State of Alaska v. Environmental Protection Agency (EPA). Accessed February 12, 2013. http://www.chamberlitigation.com/us-chamber-commerce-american-farm-bureau-federation-and-state-alaska-v-environmental-protection-agen.

US EPA. "The Toxics Release Inventory: A National Perspective." *A Report on the First Year of Data Collected Under Section 313 of the Emergency Planning and Community Right-to-Know Act of 1986*. Washington, DC: GPO, 1987.

Vaughn, Jacqueline. *Environmental Politics: Domestic and Global Dimensions*. 5th edition. New York: Thomas Wadsworth, 2007.

Vig, Norman, and Michael E. Kraft. *Environmental Policy: A New Direction for the 21st Century*. 5th edition. Washington, DC: CQ Press, 2013.

Weeks, Jennifer. "Energy Policy Should the U.S. Use More Clean-Energy Sources?" *CQ Research* 21, no. 20 (2011): 457–480.

West, William. "Formal Procedures, Informal Procedures, Accountability, and Responsiveness in Bureaucratic Policymaking: An Institutional Policy Analysis." *Public Administration Review* 46, no. 2 (2004): 66–80.

Woodhouse, Leighton. "Earth Liberation Front Activist Released After 7 Years in 'Little Guantanamo.'" *Huffington Post*, 2012. Accessed August 8, 2013. http://www.huffing-tonpost.com/.leighton-woodhouse/earth-liberation-front-ac_b_2295064.html.

Yale Project on Climate Change and Communication. 2013. Accessed August 23, 2013. http://environment.yale.edu/climate-communication/files/Climate-Policy-Report-April-2013-Revised.pdf.

Translating Vague Statutes into Rules and Regulations

Contents

A Political Appointee, the Environmental Protection Agency, and Rulemaking Rollbacks

If you were walking down the street one afternoon and a news reporter asked for your candid thoughts on environmental rulemaking, you would probably respond with a blank stare or you might say the act of rulemaking included a bureaucrat sitting behind a computer all day, filling out forms. As you will learn in this chapter,

© The Author(s) 2019
S. R. Rinfret and M. C. Pautz, *US Environmental Policy in Action*,
https://doi.org/10.1007/978-3-030-11316-2_6

185

186 S. R. RINFRET AND M. C. PAUTZ

rulemaking is an essential component to a thorough understanding of how environmental policy works. While this aspect of the policymaking processes is not normally covered in your American government textbook, that might change due to lessons learned from President Trump's former EPA administrator, Scott Pruitt.

Rulemaking comprises the agency process of translating congressional legislation into specific, actionable rules. Rule-writers, or regulatory analysts, within agencies like the EPA are charged with this task. There is far more to the process than simply having a bureaucrat sit behind a computer, filling out forms. How an agency constructs a rule, what policy options it selects to carry out that rule, and the methods used to invite stakeholder input are all components of the rule-writing process, which make it particularly complicated. These complexities often lead to disgruntled members of both the regulated communities and the interest groups because they might find it challenging to comply with requirements such as emissions trading standards (e.g., trying to determine tradable credits to cut pollution) under the Clean Air Act (CAA) of 1970.

Yet, what happens when the head of the EPA becomes an individual that has spent an entire career fighting to prevent the creation of environmental regulations—one of those disgruntled parties? In 2017, President Trump nominated Scott Pruitt, the former Attorney General for Oklahoma to become the EPA administrator. As Oklahoma's Attorney General, Mr. Pruitt represented oil and gas interests, suing the agency for overreaching and damaging economic interests.

EPA administrators are responsible for setting policy directives for the agency. From 2017 to 2018, Mr. Pruitt, removed climate change data from the agency's website, proposed 30% budget cuts to his own agency, and was firmly committed to rolling regulations aimed at reducing greenhouse gas emissions (Keneally and Ebbs 2018). Despite these swift changes, Mr. Pruitt's stint as EPA administrator was short-lived. He resigned from his position on July 5, 2018 due to questionable and excessive spending habits.

Although Pruitt's tenure only lasted a little over one year, his perspectives on environmental regulatory processes have had an impact. As noted in Chapter 5, the EPA administrator can affect policy implementation in addition to the president. In particular, the EPA administrator impacted the agency's federal regulatory process—rulemaking. The following pages uncover the importance of environmental rulemaking and our understanding of its stages.

Federal agencies, on average, can spend $800 billion per year to create rules (Shapiro 2006). Undoubtedly, this is a heavy price tag; therefore, we should pay attention to how an agency writes rules. Remember, many of the environmental laws of the 1970s are still used today by government agencies to implement policy. However, translating vague environmental statutes (legislation) into environmental rules and regulations is not an easy task, as Fiorino's story suggests. This chapter is unusual because it offers a perspective of environmental policy that other textbooks do not—the role of administrative rulemaking, what it entails, and how groups try to influence the process.

More specifically, the goal of this chapter is to explain what happens after Congress passes a law. It is easy to argue that after a law is passed it falls into a bureaucratic "black hole" and is magically implemented, but this tendency to gloss over this part of the process is a mistake. Within the environmental arena, rulemaking is the way policy creation beyond the gridlock in Congress (Klyza and Sousa 2013). Agencies such as the National Park Service (NPS) or the U.S. Fish and Wildlife Service (USFWS) create environmental rules that range from protecting the habitat of the polar bear to determining how amount of snowmobiles allowed each winter in Yellowstone National Park.

Accordingly, this chapter starts with an explanation of how bureaucrats have the authority to make rules, which are laws. Then, we explain the stages of rulemaking and how particular groups try to influence rulemaking. After our discussion of the stages of rulemaking, our chapter case study puts the rulemaking process into practice through the lens of Corporate Average Fuel Economy (CAFE) standards rule and the impact political appointees like Pruitt can make. The final pages of the chapter also suggest attention be paid to state rulemaking processes. States are making important decisions regarding issues such as hydraulic fracturing and creating myriad rules of their own. Most importantly, we argue throughout this chapter that the work of a rule-writer is ever changing and provides a significant opportunity to shape the direction of environmental policy.

Upon completion of this chapter, a few themes become apparent. We have noted repeatedly throughout this text environmental rulemaking matters. As the following pages demonstrate, environmental rulemaking matters because it is where environmental policy is translated into concrete action. Federal and state rule-writers across the United States have a significant amount of discretion to interpret federal and state legislation to create rules that affect the future of the environment. However, most people have never heard of the *Federal Register*. We demonstrate the *Federal Register* is an important tool in a democracy for individuals to participate in policymaking.

Why Would Congress Delegate Its Authority?

The bureaucracy, or the fourth branch of government, is not described in the US Constitution, but it has a lot of power to make rules. Because of the significant amount of time it takes to carry out or implement congressional legislation, Congress delegates its authority to agencies for a variety of reasons. Put succinctly, the process by which Congress shifts responsibilities to the bureaucracy is more commonly known as the delegation of authority. There are a variety of reasons why members of Congress choose to delegate their power. One reason why members of Congress delegate is because of their lack of time and expertise. Put differently, to implement public policy, they delegate their authority to the experts in the bureaucracy because the technical expertise required about every issue before them is not something members of Congress have—nor could anyone. In addition, the time—months, if not years—required to promulgate (or write) a rule is beyond the time any member of Congress has to devote to one specific issue. For example, the CAFE standards program was established by Congress as a method to reduce oil consumption from vehicles in response to the 1973 Oil Embargo. After passing the Energy Policy and Conservation Act (EPCA) of 1975 (42 U.S.C. §6201), Congress directed the National Highway Traffic and Safety Administration (NHTSA) to establish higher fuel economy standards for cars and light trucks. Congress delegated its authority because the NHTSA is composed of trained experts in the technical aspects of fuel economy standards.

The second and, arguably, the most important reason why Congress delegates its authority is what Morris Fiorina (1982) argues is a "shift the responsibility" rationale. More specifically, Congress can avoid the controversy and criticism associated with policies it created, but still have the ability to oversee agency actions and complain if an agency's actions do not work out. Here, a member of Congress can use the agency and its rulemaking as a scapegoat. Therefore, although some may scratch their heads and question the constitutionality of Congress' actions of shifting its responsibility to unelected members of the bureaucracy to make decisions about the law, it becomes clearer with the Supreme Court's interpretation.

The Supreme Court's interpretation of "Legislative power vested in Congress of the United States" (Article I, Section I, US Constitution) changed with the shifts in the makeup of the Court, and with the passage of the Administrative Procedure Act (which will be discussed later), and a variety of laws enacted in the 1960s and 1970s (Rinfret and Furlong 2013). In more recent cases, the Supreme Court has upheld a broader interpretation of delegation authority and has allowed Congress to provide significant policymaking power to executive agencies (see *Industrial Union Department, AFL-CIO v. American Petroleum Institute* (1980), *American Textile Manufacturers Institute v. Donovan* (1981), and *Whitman v. American Trucking Associations* (2001)).

As a result, agencies have a significant amount of discretion. However, before exploring some of the ways agency decisions are checked by other branches of government, we must first expand our understanding of delegation with a discussion of discretion. As the aforementioned CAFE standards example suggests, when the Energy Policy Act (EPCA) of 1975 mandated a CAFE standard of 27.5 miles per gallon for cars and a 20.7 miles per gallon (mpg) standard for light trucks, the NHTSA was given discretion (or the authority) to set standards for Model Year (MY) 1978 vehicles. Thus, since the NHTSA was delegated authority by Congress, it had the discretion to determine how these standards should be met and how much to increase the standards year to year.

MECHANISMS OF ACCOUNTABILITY

Agency discretion is limited by several accountability mechanisms— Congress and the president have different means to check the bureaucracy's work. As Sara Rinfret and Scott Furlong (2013) note:

> This relationship between elected leaders and the bureaucratic agencies is described by the principal-agent model, which refers to the ongoing relationship between the political principal and the bureaucratic agent and how each tries to achieve its sometimes inconsistent goals (see Kerwin and Furlong 2011). Gary Bryner (1987) characterizes the tools that political principals use as falling into three categories: administrative procedures, economic and scientific decision rules, and political oversight. (375)

Thus, there are a number of ways to check the power of the bureaucracy to make decisions, ranging from congressional to presidential oversight, which set standards for agency decision-making.

Congressional and Presidential Oversight: Congress and the President can exercise oversight to ensure the accountability of agency actions. Congress can write legislation stating what limits an agency has in writing a rule and can even change the course of previous actions of an agency. Consider our example on the NHTSA and CAFE standards. During the 1990s, there was significant debate regarding whether the CAFE standards were effective; automobile manufacturers contended that Americans demanded bigger vehicles and higher efficiency standards would not accommodate this demand. To an extent, manufacturers were correct because as sport utility vehicles (SUVs) became popular in the 1990s, public relations campaigns by the industry to thwart CAFE standard increases were successful (Plungis 2000). In fact, for much of the 1990s, Congress made it impossible to increase the CAFE standards. From 1995 to 1999, Congress attached an amendment to an appropriations bill to stop the NHTSA from studying the need for increased standards (McCutcheon 2001). Moreover, from 1997 to 2001, Congress instituted a freeze on the CAFE standards for light trucks (Lorenzetti 2014). However, as oil prices continued to climb during the early 2000s, industry began to lose momentum and the NHTSA was then again able to slowly increase fuel economy standards for light trucks (Lorenzetti 2014). This example shows that, although an agency such as NHTSA has been created to carry out CAFE standards, there are limits set by Congress.

Moreover, agencies need monetary resources to carry out policy. Congress authorizes agency budgets and how much money can be spent on particular programs. More specifically, the Appropriations Committees in the House of Representatives and the Senate distribute available funds among all federal agencies. Thus, if Congress does not like a specific program or agency, money can be cut from an agency or redirected. Congress can also approve the presidential nomination of a political appointee to set policy directives favorable to that of their own. This was the case with the appointment of former EPA administrator Scott Pruitt.

Another oversight function that Congress can use is something called hammers. A hammer is a provision in a piece of legislation that states if an agency fails to finalize a rule by a certain date, then Congress will force action. Often, the regulated community does not appreciate hammers. This is because, if the EPA is supposed to create a rule by a certain date and it does not, Congress could state within the legislation that certain chemicals used by the regulated community are then banned from use until the EPA can finalize the rule. Thus, it is up to the agency to examine a particular product by the deadline and, if it does not, it could impact the business that produces it.

A final example of congressional oversight can be classified as either police patrol or fire alarms. The police patrol approach is the notion that Congress examines every rule or action taken by an agency that is seen as costly and inefficient. The other approach is the fire alarm, in which Congress conducts oversight hearings of problem areas to ensure the processes that agencies use are effective (Kerwin and Furlong 2011). Nevertheless, there are a variety of ways that Congress can check the bureaucracy and the actions it takes.

Congressional forms of oversight are important, but presidents also perform oversight functions. These mechanisms include appointments, executive orders, and even reorganization. The president has the authority to appoint an individual to oversee an agency. These appointments have to be confirmed by the US Senate, but presidential appointment can and do impact the direction of an agency. For instance, President Obama's last EPA administrator Gina McCarthy aggressively tried to combat climate change. Comparatively, Trump's EPA first administrator, Pruitt attempted to rollback his predecessor's work.

Another form of presidential oversight of the federal bureaucracy is the use of executive orders. Executive orders are mandates by the president that carry the same weight as a law passed by Congress. In 2009, President Obama issued Executive Order 13514, which instructed all federal agencies to set sustainability goals. More specifically, within 90 days of the issuance of the order, each agency had to create and submit a 2020 greenhouse gas pollution reduction target, explaining how its agency would become more environmentally friendly (Council on Environmental Quality 2014). President Trump's Executive Order 13783 stresses that the United States will become energy independent by opening federal lands to oil and gas leasing (see Chapter 9). Trump's executive order also rolls back President Obama's rule to regulate coal-burning power plants.

The last example of presidential oversight is the authority of the president to reorganize the federal bureaucracy. This rarely occurs, but it is a way for a president to combine agencies to either reward or punish them or perhaps focus on a particular issue. One recent example of presidential reorganization was in 2011 after the Deepwater Horizon oil spill. One of the primary agencies responsible for overseeing this offshore drilling was the Minerals Management Service (MMS); however, due to its poor industrial oversight of offshore drilling procedures, the Obama administration created two new agencies (the Bureau of Safety and Environmental Enforcement and the Bureau of Ocean, Energy Management, Regulation and Enforcement) to reorganize the efforts of MMS. In 2018, President Trump announced plans to reorganize the Department of Interior and it remains uncertain as this book goes to press.

In short, although there are concerns that the bureaucracy runs amuck when making public policy, Congress and the president have a number of ways to oversee its processes. More importantly, we need to remember that Congress delegates its authority for a variety of reasons, namely, to shift its responsibility to those who have more time and expertise. However, the idea is that members of Congress can also shift the blame to the bureaucracy if the policy goes awry. The notion of delegating congressional power might seem questionable; oversight mechanisms are in place to ensure that unelected officials do not abuse their power. We turn to one of the most essential duties of the federal bureaucracy—rulemaking, or as the title of the chapter describes, how members of the bureaucracy turn vague congressional statutes into law.

RULES IN THE MAKING

As noted, rulemaking is the process used by government employees to translate vague congressional statues into rules of law. The administrative rulemaking process includes many stages and access points for both stakeholders and the public to participate. This section begins with a brief historical overview of the Administrative Procedures Act (APA) and how this act helps define the stages of the rulemaking process (also referred to as the promulgation process). Then, we discuss how groups try to influence different stages of this process.

The Administrative Procedures Act

From 1933 to 1945, there was significant growth in the size of the federal government in order to implement President Franklin D. Roosevelt's New Deal policies and programs to help bring the nation out of the economic depression and to address the nation's war efforts. With this growth came the creation of a multitude of federal agencies such as the Civilian Conservation Corps (CCC). In response, the APA was adopted in 1946 as an oversight and accountability tool for the rapidly expanding government under the New Deal.

The APA requires agencies to follow administrative rulemaking guidelines to ensure that government entities carry out congressional statutes in a uniform, prescribed manner. According to the APA, a rule "means the whole or part of an agency statement of general or particular applicability and future effect designed to implement, interpret, or prescribe law or policy." A rule created by an agency then carries the same legal force as a law. Administrative rulemaking is comprised of various stages by which an agency creates and implements a rule. The description of the rulemaking stages, in the following, demonstrates that the APA requirement of public participation during the notice and comment portion of the rulemaking processes allows for significant public involvement.

There are many forms of administrative rulemaking: formal, informal, negotiated, and hybrid. Formal rulemaking demands official hearings that resemble the proceedings of a courtroom. Informal rulemaking, also known as "notice and comment," requires that agencies encourage the public to participate in the process by submitting comments once a draft or final rule is published in the *Federal Register*. Over the last decade, the *Federal Register* has become available online (https://www.federalregister.gov/) and a resource for the public to search when an agency publishes a rule and to provide feedback. An additional resource for the public is also Regulations.gov, which describes to the public, by agency, the rulemaking actions that agencies are taking. Negotiated rulemaking (sometimes informally referred to as "reg neg," as noted in the introduction of this chapter) occurs when agency officials organize and participate in negotiations with stakeholders to develop a rule. Hybrid rulemaking, in comparison, happens relatively infrequently, and involves agencies using aspects of both informal and formal processes (Cooper 2007). With a working understanding of rulemaking and different approaches, we focus on notice and comment rulemaking because it is the most common process.

DIFFERENT THAN CONGRESSIONAL LAWMAKING

Figure 6.1 illustrates the common stages of the process for formal or notice and comment rulemaking. Typically, these stages occur across 11 detailed stages; however, for the purposes of brevity, we have condensed our explanation into three stages.

Fig. 6.1   Stages of rulemaking

Stage 1: Rule development is the first stage and it includes an agency's efforts to gather technical, scientific, and economic information regarding why a rule is necessary, as well as how a rule should be developed. For example, the EPA creates rules associated with the CAA. Therefore, at this stage, EPA agency personnel often work with stakeholders from a variety of perspectives (e.g., public health, environmental, and industry) to produce a draft rule. However, the way in which the agency and stakeholders discuss information at this stage is via informal communication and is not subject to legal restrictions from the APA, but is simply a way for agencies to collect information (Rinfret and Furlong 2013). Although this might seem alarming, the rule development stage is also a way for an agency to uncover any issues that might arise regarding controversial rules. For instance, the USFWS designation of critical habitats for the polar bear in parts of Alaska created a great deal of concern—notably, about issues surrounding land preservation and oil production—from a variety of industry and environmental groups.

As a result, there are other approaches that an agency can use during the rule development phase, which can range from an Advanced Notice of Proposed Rulemaking (ANPRM), Notice of Intent (NOI), or outreach meetings. The ANPRM and NOI are published in the *Federal Register* (more details will be provided in our explanation of stage 2) and the agency can solicit comments about particular ideas (e.g., certain sections of land to be set aside for the polar bear's habitat). Furthermore, an agency can offer stakeholder outreach sessions by inviting groups to meet with an agency to discuss topics pertaining to a particular rule.

As the agency finalizes information within the first stage, agencies must also conduct economic and scientific analyses (Kerwin and Furlong 2011).

President Reagan issued Executive Order 12291 that required agencies to conduct regulatory impact analyses showing that the potential costs to society would outweigh the benefits when moving forward with a rule, and the Office of Management and Budget (OMB) oversees this process. Then, in 1993, President Clinton replaced Reagan's Executive Order 12291 with Executive Order 12866, which continues the use of cost–benefit analysis and encourages agencies to conduct risk assessments or performance-based standards (see Chapter 8 for more details). Executive Order 12866 delegated that the Office of Information and Regulatory Affairs (OIRA, which is within OMB) to coordinate rulemakings to encourage these aforementioned priorities. After OIRA signs off on a draft rule, an agency is then able to move into the next phase of the process.

Shapiro (2006) argues that these added layers of the rulemaking process create "paralysis analysis." Put differently, this means that the additional analysis that an agency is required to conduct can inhibit its efforts to move forward quickly. However, an extensive analysis could also lead to a better outcome. For example, consider the rule surrounding a "dangerous dust," also known as silica, which are tiny stone particles produced when a worker blasts material such as sandstone, brick, or concrete (Verchick 2013). The Occupational Safety and Health Administration (OSHA) wants to create a new rule that would lessen the amount of silica that a person could inhale on the job. The idea is that this would save a great number of lives, but it took OSHA more than 9 years to propose this rule. In the time it took to write this rule, 1400 lives could have been saved (Verchick 2013). Nevertheless, during stage 1 of the process, an agency conducts a great deal of research in order to move forward.

Stage 2: The second stage, notice and comment, is where the agency publishes a Notice of Proposed Rulemaking (NPRM) in the *Federal Register*, which is a daily publication of all federal rules. This required stage in the process ensures that an agency provides notice and a way for the public to participate in the process. When an agency publishes an NPRM, it typically grants the public 30–60 days to submit a public comment about the rule.

Before 2002, if a person or group wanted to submit a public comment to the *Federal Register* it had to be mailed. Then, if someone wanted to read the public comments submitted by others, this information needed to be requested from either the *Federal Register* or the agency issuing the rule. This might be a difficult endeavor as, across all federal agencies in the United States, approximately 8000 rules are proposed each year (Kerwin and Furlong 2011). However, within the last decade, agencies are required to allow the public to electronically submit comments on Regulations.gov. This online resource has provided a timelier way of following a rule's development. In 2003, Regulations. gov made our lives even easier by creating a search engine in which one can search by agency and rule. After you have found a rule of interest, the public can submit comments electronically and see other comments that have been submitted. If someone is extremely interested in what is going on, anyone can subscribe to an RSS feed that will notify you via email if a particular agency posts new regulations.

Stage 3: When the comment period ends, the agency moves to stage 3, the final publication stage, and examines the comments to determine the language of the final rule. Once a rule is final, it is published in the *Federal Register*. However, during this final phase, the agency must sometimes prepare for litigation in the form of petitions for reconsideration of a rule from stakeholder groups. For instance, in 2013, several meat industry organizations sued the US Department of Agriculture over the country-of-origin labeling rule. The argument made by these manufacturers was that this particular rule places an undue burden on their respective companies to place an origin label on each meat and poultry package, which ultimately increases prices for the consumer (Supermarket News 2013). In 2016, the rule was finalized. The court concluded it did not place an unfair burden on manufacturers.

Now that we have a basic understanding of the process used by all federal agencies to create a rule and why Congress delegates its authority, it is helpful to contextualize this process with a more thorough example—one that may even help to explain why it would take an agency 9 years to write a rule.

Stalled: Achieving the Unthinkable, Raising the CAFE Standards
In order to truly understand how contemporary environmental policy is made, we turn back to the example of the CAFE standards program administered by the National Highway Traffic Safety Administration (NHTSA). This case illustrates how a rule transitions through the stages of the process, interest group participation, and post-rulemaking activities.

Stage 1: President Obama issued a Presidential Memorandum in May 2010. This memorandum noted that the NHTSA and the EPA should conduct a rulemaking setting standards from MY 2017 to MY 2025. This encouraged the participation with stakeholder groups and California (Obama 2010). The NHTSA and the EPA conducted stakeholder outreach meetings with manufacturers, labor unions, and environmental groups to gather information regarding emerging technologies to improve fuel economy and capabilities to commercialize these and other existing technologies. The agencies, in conjunction with the California Air Resources Board (CARB), produced a Technical Assessment Report (TAR) that compiled this information into one document.

The EPA and NHTSA published an NOI in the *Federal Register* in September 2010. The NOI outlined the agencies' findings from TAR and provided a listing of potential stringency levels for the new standards. The agencies used this document to set the rulemaking timetable, with a proposed rule planned for September 30, 2011 and a final rule published by July 31, 2012 (EPA 2010). The agencies offered a 30-day comment period on this document and the two agencies received comments from 30 organizations and 100,000 people.

The agencies produced a supplementary NOI in November that outlined responses to comments from the first NOI. It was noted that there was significant support from commenters to set a 6-percent annual reduction in GHG emissions, resulting in a 60-mpg standard by 2025. However, industry commenters were concerned about the costs associated with technologies that would be required to implement this standard.

During the course of the next six months, the agencies continued to negotiate with automobile manufacturers, which included three weeks of intensive negotiations between the agencies, CARB, members of the Executive Office of the President, and manufacturers. After these negotiations, the agency submitted another supplementary NOI in July 2011. However, the agencies had secured Letters of Commitment from 13 major car companies, representing almost 90% of the market, including Ford, GM, Toyota, Honda, and Chrysler (NHTSA 2011).

This supplementary NOI was, however, significantly different from the first two because the agencies took a strong position promoting a five percent annual reduction in GHG emissions level, which would result in a 54.5 mpg CAFE standard. In addition, the agency included several new incentives and methods to achieve these standards, including a new incentive multiplier for electric vehicles and plug-in hybrids, an incentive credit for game-changing technology on full-size trucks, and credits for air conditioner efficiency improvements, among others. Finally, the agencies also included a midterm review requirement to assess the ability of manufacturers to achieve the standards from MY 2022 to MY 2025. With the publication of this supplementary NOI, President Obama gave a speech promoting the policy, suggesting that it would save consumers nearly $2 trillion in fuel costs, and reduce oil consumption by 2.2 million barrels per day (Obama 2011).

Stages 2 and 3: The agency reviewed the comments on this NOI and published a Notice of Proposed Rulemaking (NPRM) in the *Federal Register* in December 2011 (EPA and NHTSA 2011b). The agency held three public hearings—one each in Detroit, Philadelphia, and San Francisco. The agencies received 300,000 comments from the general public, with 400 additional comments from the three public hearings, and 140 comments from various organizations (EPA and NHTSA 2012).

After reviewing the comments, the agencies published the final rule in the *Federal Register* in October 2012. In this rule, the agencies made many minor changes that focused on definitions and minor analytical adjustments. In terms of substance, the agencies did clarify that a future rulemaking after the midterm review would determine the mandatory requirements for the MY 2022 to MY 2025. Furthermore, the agencies modified market penetration requirements for some existing incentives (EPA and NHTSA 2012). Nevertheless, the major tenants of the rulemaking remained unchanged from the NPRM to the final rule. What once was impossible—getting not just some vehicle manufacturers, but nearly 90% of them to accept CAFE standard increases—became a reality.

Some question the auto industry's acceptance of this rulemaking. A likely explanation is because the Obama administration granted California the CAA waiver. If the federal government did not act, California might have. Therefore, the manufacturers would have had an incentive to see the federal government produce a rule as opposed to producing two types of cars to comply with different standards.

Post Rulemaking Activity: Rulemaking is one plausible pathway around congressional gridlock. It allows an agency to use existing policy (CAA in this case) to create rules. As this chapter discusses, there are checks on an agency's ability to make policy. Presidents can issue executive orders and their appointments drive policy directives. The successes of the revised CAFÉ standards were short-lived and the Trump administration on August 2018 announced that the EPA and NHTSA would abandon long-term fuel economy standards for passenger cars and light trucks. The Trump administration plan is to freeze standards at the 2021 levels and not to pursue the goal of 54 miles per gallon by 2025. What is even more interesting is the Trump administration also revoked California's CAA waiver. This means that California cannot exceed federal standards. As a result, California and 16 other states have sued the EPA for not moving forward, without citing scientific evidence for the change (Roberts 2018). A divided government in 2018 (e.g., the US House is controlled by the Democratic Party and US Senate by the Republican Party) could determine the fate of CAFÉ standards in the United States.

Inevitably, this case provides an interesting look into how agencies produce policy through rulemaking. As noted, administrative rulemaking is structured by the APA, which requires a notice of the proposed rulemaking and a public comment period. However, as this case illustrates, there is so much more to the process than meets the eye.

INFLUENCE: WHERE IT OCCURS

As our case study indicates, influence can and does occur in rulemaking processes. Yet, at what stage in the process of rulemaking can a group be influential? For instance, being involved during the pre-proposal phase enables groups to speak with agency rule-writers about potential language or provide important information that the agency may not have due to lack of resources or expertise. For instance, one rule-writer was writing the language of proposed critical habitat for the Holmgren Milkvetch (a type of plant in parts of Arizona and Utah) for the USFWS but did not necessarily have the appropriate background to write such a rule, so reaching out to others in the scientific community was necessary (Rinfret 2011a). Remember that neither is participating in this stage of the process required by the APA, nor does the APA require that an agency disclose this information. However, submitting a public comment via the *Federal Register* can also be influential, again providing important information to the agency that it might not have considered. Next, we examine influence during the stages of the rulemaking process.

Behind the Scenes: As our case illustrated, stakeholders are heavily involved during the first stage of rulemaking (rule development/pre-proposal phase; see West 2009; Hoefer and Ferguson 2007; Naughton et al. 2009; Rinfret 2011a, b; Rinfret and Furlong 2013; Yackee 2012; Cook and Rinfret 2013a). For example, interest groups can use their resources (i.e., studies or reports) to give agency decision-makers advice during the pre-proposal stage in exchange for gaining a better idea of what actions an agency is considering taking (Hoefer and Ferguson 2007). Moreover, Sara Rinfret (2011a) even suggests that these groups are working behind the scenes because they are exchanging information with an agency via ex parte communication, or off the record. Put differently, the APA does not require the agency to provide information about the exchanges going on during this stage.

But, what if your organization is not part of the groups that are asked by the agency to help with rule development processes? Susan Webb Yackee (2012) tried to quantify this stage by examining the pre-rule classification of the Unified Agenda. The Unified Agenda is a semiannual publication listed in the *Federal Register* that describes all the actions that any federal agency has taken on a given rule. Here you are able to search the Unified Agenda by the stage in the process.

Another approach to determine who is involved is to ask the agency for a list of participants and, then, talk with these individuals to confirm. The presumption is that influence can indeed occur at this stage. However, we also suggest that these findings are alarming because only certain groups are invited to the table to participate during the first stage of the process, shutting others out. Thus, we encourage additional research surrounding this stage of the process.

Put it on the Record: Another approach used by scholars is to examine the comments submitted during the publication of an NPRM to determine influence. For example, one argument is that business groups dominate the phase in which participants can submit comments to an agency in regard to a particular rule (see Fritschler 1989; Golden 1998; Kerwin and Furlong 2011; Magat et al. 1986; West 2004). In examining the EPA's regulatory standards for water pollution, Wesley Magat (1986) concluded that industry interest groups participated far more often than any other group in agency rulemaking. The reason for industry's heavy participation is because of the implications for its individual businesses if regulations would increase.

More alarming about this stage is the use of "bots" by outside global actors to influence US decision-making. A 2018 Wall Street Journal investigation disclosed that for the Federal Communication Commission's net neutrality rule thousands of fraudulent public comments. These comments were from fake accounts, attempting to influence the outcome of the final rule (Grimaldi and Overberg 2017).

Regardless of the stage, it is apparent that groups are involved often throughout the process to impact agency decision-making. Moreover, it is important for students to realize that interest groups are not only involved in congressional decision-making, but also agency decision-making. Do note, however, that the purpose of the aforementioned discussion is to provide clarity in the way in which stakeholders or interest groups try to approach a member of Congress is much different than an agency rule-writer.

Expanding Our Understanding of Environmental Rulemaking

We have only skimmed the surface with just a few examples of how agency decision-making is shaping the future of environmental policy. To expand the breadth of how far-reaching rulemaking is, we end this chapter with additional examples for consideration. We use examples from the EPA, New York, and the Department of Energy (DOE) to stress why rulemaking will continue to be important for decades to come in the environmental arena.

Reg Neg or Reg Neg Lite?

The EPA has employed different approaches to create environmental rules in order to bring a variety of groups (e.g., environmental organizations and industry groups) to the table to discuss a particular rulemaking. As noted, throughout the 1980s and 1990s, the EPA used reg neg. Remember, reg neg is a voluntary approach adopted by agencies such as the EPA to develop the terms of a rule prior to publishing an NPRM in the *Federal Register*. During reg neg, with a formal mediator presiding over the conversations with a variety of groups, an agency convenes negotiations to achieve consensus (Harter 1982). Over time, the use of reg neg decreased because it could be a time-intensive process, thereby increasing costs for an agency (Harter 1982; Susskind and McMahon 1985); thus, the decline of its use (Harter 1982; Kerwin and Langbein 2000).

This is not to say that rulemaking innovation is dead, however. The EPA has sought alternatives, trying to salvage some of ideas of reg neg (Kerwin and Furlong 2011). In 2007, the Council for Excellence in Government stated that the Office of Transportation and Air Quality (OTAQ), a division within the EPA, was using a new method—shuttle diplomacy—to create rules. Basically, shuttle diplomacy is a way for an agency to bring groups together informally to discuss a rule—it is not a formal process with an official mediator such as reg neg, but a way for groups to explain their perspectives on a given rulemaking (Rinfret and Cook 2013).

States Matter

Federal rulemaking processes are important, but state rulemaking also matters. Recall in Chapter 3, we discuss how our system of governance is driven by federalism. After all, we have seen many policy arenas where states arrive at quite different policies, such as climate change, same-sex marriage, or marijuana use when there is a lack of federal policy available. As a result, we see a policy patchwork throughout the country (Rinfret et al. 2018). This often allows for trial and error at the state level before a major policy is adopted at the federal level. Federalism endures because it offers a useful way to bring state governments together to achieve larger goals, while at the same time offering many points of access into the policy process.

Because hydraulic fracturing or fracking is one of the top environmental issues of the twenty-first century, we use it as an example to touch upon state rulemaking and its importance. With fracking, states find themselves overseeing this policy area because the 2005 Energy

Policy Act's so-called "Halliburton Loophole" exempted fracking oversight from the US EPA (42 U.S.C. §15801). Congress, since 2017, has attempted to provide a law for guidance—the Fracturing Responsibility and Awareness Chemicals Act (a.k.a FracAct), but approval is still pending. The argument could be made that this federal legislation will not be adopted due to President Trump's energy independence rhetoric (see Chapter 5).

Consider New York as an example. Rulemaking must follow the State Administrative Procedure Act (SAPA) and the process unfolds over three stages. The process begins with an internal agency review to determine if rulemaking is the best or most appropriate action to address a particular problem. At this stage, agency staff often will reach out to stakeholder groups to receive input on the issue. Stage 2 of the process unfolds when the agency submits a formal proposed rulemaking in the *New York State Register*. After the agency publishes the notice of proposed rulemaking, the public comment period begins. The agency has 180 days to review and respond to public comments, as well as to determine what action to take on a rule. Stage 3 of the rulemaking process begins when the agency provides a complete text of the rule to notify the Governor, the President of the Senate, the Speaker of the Assembly, and the Administrative Regulations Reviews Commission (within the New York State Senate) that a rule is being finalized. Therefore, at this stage, the filing of the final terms of the rule is published in the *New York State Register* (Rinfret et al. 2014).

Thus, states use their own form of rulemaking processes to implement state law (Rinfret et al. 2014). State rulemaking is of additional importance when there is a lack of federal policy. For instance, due to the lack of federal policy for fracking, it is up to states to use rulemaking processes to come up with their own policies. In their examination of fracking rules in Colorado, New York, and Ohio, Rinfret et al. (2014) found that states are offering unique frameworks to solve the fracking debate. However, the question still remains whether the federal government will adopt one of these approaches on a national scale. We do know that states have taken steps, using rulemaking to provide policy when there is a lack of federal law. New York, Vermont, and Maryland have decided to ban fracking within their states altogether due to public health concerns (e.g., contamination of water due to extraction processes).

Microwaves and Carbon

Although state rulemaking processes are important, we offer another example, about the DOE's approach to making our household microwaves more energy efficient. There was something notably different about the DOE's rulemaking to improve the energy efficiency of microwave ovens: the agency changed the Social Cost of Carbon (SCC) metric to determine the benefits of reducing greenhouse gases.

As Jeffrey Cook and Sara Rinfret (2013b) note, "The SCC was first developed in 2010 by a task force of twelve U.S. agencies including the Environmental Protection Agency (EPA), DOE, and the National Economic Council, among others. These agencies developed the SCC metric to standardize how federal agencies quantify the benefits of reduced carbon pollution." This new approach to rulemaking engendered a great deal of discussion, and possibly outright controversy, because when the DOE was creating the microwave oven rule, the agency reported a new SCC, $36 per ton, versus the previous value of $22 per ton. Critics suggested that this change in cost favored environmental interests. However, as Cook and Rinfret (2013b) concluded, "In its microwave oven rule, the DOE argued that the 2013 White House Economic Report called for agencies to revise the SCC in order to reflect new scientific information on the impacts of climate change on the environment and public health. Thus, the agency argued that it was only following necessary procedures when it updated the SCC to reflect new information."

The carbon cost sparked by the microwave oven might seem alarming; however, it is explainable. We cannot ignore that federal agencies have not updated the SCC in nearly 4 years. Put differently, without the change, federal agencies like the DOE would be using outdated information to determine climate impacts, calling into question the accuracy of the cost–benefit analyses that accompany regulatory actions (Cook and Rinfret 2013b).

CHAPTER WRAP-UP

In short, this chapter has documented not only the stages of the federal rulemaking process, but also how groups can and changing presidential administrations can shape this process. The CAFÉ rule is exemplary of understanding how groups vying for access shape agency policy.

Arguably, being involved early and often in rulemaking is important, but not most Americans do not vote, let alone understand the intricacies of the *Federal Register*. Thus, increasing our knowledge about rulemaking is essential.

Beyond process and influence, there are a variety of future pathways for rulemaking—particularly at the state level. More specifically, there is a lack of research at the state level, and it is important to expand our understanding when there is limited federal direction on tackling issues such as fracking. Furthermore, in order for us to be informed participants about regulatory affairs, receiving a weekly email from the University of Pennsylvania's Regulatory Review may spark your interests to become more involved in regulatory affairs.

Our discussion about rulemaking provides a nice transition into our next chapter on implementing environmental policy, which focuses on what occurs after a rule becomes law. It is up to individuals such as environmental inspectors to ensure that the rules written are carried out. To this end, we offer an important lesson from Neil Kerwin and Scott Furlong (2011)

> We must convince those with little or no direct stake in the outcome of rulemaking that they too should be concerned with the result. This is a very tough sell when people are able to keep up with only a fraction of the issues that profoundly affect their daily lives and become involved in only a few of them. In a nation where so many fail to vote, is it reasonable to expect an outpouring of interest in rulemaking from average citizens with comparatively little to win or lose? Perhaps not, but lowering our expectations is a dangerous choice. (293)

SUGGESTED RESOURCES

Readings and Websites

Deadly Dust. YouTube. Accessed June 13, 2014. http://www.youtube.com/watch?v=eXsGJ1C4Xcw.

Federal Register. Accessed June 13, 2014. https://www.federalregister.gov/.

Penn Program on Regulation: Regulatory Review. Accessed October 19, 2018. https://www.theregreview.org/.

Regulations.gov: The Voice of Federal Decision-Making. Accessed October 19, 2018. http://www.regulations.gov/#!home.

Unified Agenda. Accessed October 19, 2018. http://www.reginfo.gov/public/do/eAgendaMain.

Films or Videos

If a Tree Falls: A Story of the Earth Liberation Front. Directed by Marshall Curry. 2012. Independent Television Service, Corporation for Public Brodcasting. DVD.

The Cove. Directed Louie Psihoyos. 2009. Lions Gate. DVD.

Food, Inc. Director Robert Kenner. 2009. Magnolia Home Entertainment. DVD.

REFERENCES

Bryner, Gary. *Bureaucratic Discretion: Law and Policy in Federal Regulatory Agencies.* New York: Pergamon Press, 1987.

Cook, Jeffrey J., and Sara R. Rinfret. "The EPA Regulates GHG Emissions: Is Anyone Paying Attention?" *Review of Policy Research* 30, no. 3 (2013a): 263–280.

———. "Adjusting the Social Cost of Carbon: A Commonsense Revision." University of Pennsylvania Law School's Regulatory Blog. August 20, 2013b. www.regblog.org/2013/08/20-cook-rinfret-scc.htm.

Cooper, Phillip. *Public Law and Public Administration.* Belmont, CA: Thomson Wadsworth, 2007.

Council for Excellence in Government. *Working with Stakeholders: The Nonroad Diesel Rule.* Washington, DC: GPO, 2007.

Council on Environmental Quality. "Federal Leadership in Environmental Energy and Economic Performance—Executive Order 13514." Accessed January 27, 2014. http://www.whitehouse.gov/administration/eop/ceq/sustainability.

EPA. "2017 and Later Model Year Light-Duty Vehicle GHG Emissions and CAFE Standards: Notice of Intent." *Federal Register*, 2010.

"EPA and NHTSA 2017–2025 Model Year Light-Duty Vehicle GHG Emissions and CAFE Standards: Supplemental Notice of Intent." *Federal Register*, 2011a.

"EPA and NHTSA 2017–2025 Model Year Light-Duty Vehicle GHG Emissions and CAFE Standards: Supplemental Notice of Intent." *Federal Register*, 2011b.

"EPA and NHTSA 2012. 2017 and Later Model Year Light-Duty Vehicle Greenhouse Gas Emissions and Corporate Average Fuel Economy Standards; Final Rule." *Federal Register 77 199 (62623–63200).* Washington, DC: GPO, 2012.

Fiorina, Morris. "Legislative Choice of Regulatory Forms: Legal Process or Administrative Process." *Public Choice* 39 (1982): 33–66.

Fritschler, Lee A. *Smoking and Politics.* Upper Saddle River, NJ: Prentice Hall, 1989.

Golden, Marissa Martino. "Interest Groups in the Rule-Making Process: Who Participates? Whose Voices Get Heard?" *Journal of Public Administration Research and Theory* 8 no. 2 (1998): 245–270.

Grimaldi, Jamves V., and Paul Overberg. 2017. https://www.wsj.com/articles/millions-of-people-post-comments-on-federal-regulations-many-are-fake-1513099188.

Harter, Phil. "Negotiating Regulations: A Cure for Malaise." *Georgetown Law Journal* 71 (1982): 1–116.

Hoefer, R., and K. Ferguson. "Controlling the Levers of Power: How Advocacy Organizations Affect the Regulation Writing Process." *Journal of Sociology and Social Welfaree* 34, no. 2 (2007): 83–108.

Keneally, Meghan, and Stephanie Ebbs. 2018. https://abcnews.go.com/Politics/timeline-scott-pruitts-bumpy-time-epa/story?id=56394470.

Kerwin, Cornelius, and Laura Langbein. "Regulatory Negotiation: Claims, Counter Claims, and Empirical Evidence." *Journal of Public Administration Research and Theory* 10 (2000): 599–632.

Kerwin, Cornelius, and Scott R. Furlong. *Rulemaking: How Government Agencies Write Law and Make Policy.* Washingston, DC: Island Press, 2011.

Klyza, Christopher McGrory, and David Sousa. *American Environmental Policy, 1990–2006: Beyond Gridlock.* Cambridge: MIT Press, 2013.

Lorenzetti, Maureen. "Revised CAFE Standards Gaining Wider Support." 2005. Accessed January 3, 2014. http://www.cqweekly.com.

Magat, W., A. Krupnick, and W. Harrington. *Rules in the Making: A Statistical Analysis of Regulatory Agency Behavior.* Washington, DC: Resources for the Future Press, 1986.

McCutcheon, Chuck. "Bush Urged to Shift Emphasis to Fuel Efficiency Standards." *CQ Weekly*, 2001. Accessed January 3, 2014. http://www.cqweekly.com.

Naughton, Keith, Celeste Schmid, Susan Webb Yackee, and Xueyong Zhan. "Understanding Commenter Influence During Rule Development." *Journal of Policy Analysis and Management* 28, no. 2 (2009): 258–277.

NHTSA and EPA. "2017 and Later Model Year Light-Duty Vehicle GHG Emissions and CAFE Standards: Supplemental Notice of Intent." *Federal Register*, 2010.

NHTSA. *Letters of Commitment from Stakeholders Supporting the MYs 2017–2025 Rulemaking Process,* 2011. Accessed August 7, 2013. http://www.nhtsa.gov/Laws+&+Regulations/CAFE+-+Fuel+Economy/Letters+of+Commitment+from+Stakeholders+Supporting+the+MYs+2017–2025+Rulemaking+Process.

Obama, Barack. *Presidential Memorandum Regarding Fuel Efficiency Standards,* 2010. Accessed August 7, 2013. http://www.whitehouse.gov/the-press-office/presidential-memorandum-regarding-fuel-efficiency-standards.

———. "Remarks by the President on Fuel Efficiency Standards." 2011. Accessed August 7, 2013. http://www.whitehouse.gov/the-press-office/2011/07/29/remarks-president-fuel-efficiency-standards.

Plungis, Jeff. "GOP Again Blocks Changes in Fuel Efficiency Standard." *CQ Weekly*, 2000. Accessed January 3, 2014. http://www.cqweekly.com.

Rinfret, Sara R. "Behind the Shadows: Interest Groups and the U.S. Fish and Wildlife Service." *Human Dimensions of Wildlife: An International Journal* 16, no. 1 (2011a): 1–14.

———. "Frames of Influence: U.S. Environmental Rulemaking Case Studies." *Review of Policy Research* 28, no. 3 (2011b): 231–246.

Rinfret, Sara R., and Jeffrey J. Cook. "Environmental Policy Can Happen: Shuttle Diplomacy and the Reality of Reg Neg Lite." *Environmental Policy and Governance* 24, no. 2 (2013): 122–133.

Rinfret, Sara R., and Scott Furlong. "Defining Environmental Rulemaking." In *Oxford Handbook of U.S. Environmental Policy*, edited by Michael E. Kraft and Sheldon Kamieniecki, 372–394. New York: Oxford University Press, 2013. http://www.oxfordhandbooks.com/view/10.1093/oxfordhb/9780199744671.001.0001/oxfordhb-9780199744671-e-17.

Rinfret, Sara, Denise Scheberle, and Michelle Pautz. 2018. *Public Policy: A Concise Introduction*. Washington, DC: CQ Press. https://us.sagepub.com/en-us/nam/public-policy/book249415.

Rinfret, Sara R., Jeffrey J. Cook, and Michelle C. Pautz. "Understanding State Rulemaking Processes: Developing Fracking Rules in Colorado, New York, and Ohio." *Review of Policy Research* 31, no. 2 2014: 88–104.

Roberts, David. 2018. https://www.vox.com/energy-and-environment/2018/5/3/17314000/trump-epa-cars-trucks-fuel-economy-cafe-standards.

Shapiro, Stuart. "Political and Regulatory Policy Analysis." Rutgers University, 2006. Accessed January 27, 2014. http://policy.rutgers.edu/faculty/shapiro/regulation%20article.pdf.

Supermarket News. "Industry Groups Sue USDA Over COOL Rule." Accessed January 4, 2013. http://supermarketnews.com/laws-amp-regulations/industry-groups-sueusda-over-final-cool-rule.

Susskind, Lawrence, and Gerard McMahon. "The Theory and Practice of Negotiated Rulemaking." *Yale Journal on Regulation* 3 (1985): 133–165.

Verchick, Robert. "Dangerous Dust and Deadly Delay: OSHA's Proposed Silica Rule." University of Pennsylvania Reg Blog, 2013. Accessed January 3, 2014. http://www.regblog.org/2013/11/26-verchick-silica.html.

West, William. "Formal Procedures, Informal procedures, Accountability, and Responsiveness in Bureaucratic Policymaking: An Institutional Policy Analysis." *Public Administration Review* 46, no. 2 (2004): 66–80.

———. "Inside the Black Box: The Development of Proposed Rules and the Limits of Procedural Controls." *Administration and Society* 41, no. 5 (2009): 576–599.

Yackee, Susan W. "The Politics of Ex Parte Lobbying: Pre-proposal Agenda Building and Blocking During Agency Rulemaking." *Journal of Public Administration Research and Theory* 22 (2012): 373–393.

Implementing Environmental Policy and Regulations: Where the Rubber Meets the Road

Contents

© The Author(s) 2019
S. R. Rinfret and M. C. Pautz, *US Environmental Policy in Action*,
https://doi.org/10.1007/978-3-030-11316-2_7

Dodging Tomatoes and Being an Oreo Cookie as a Hazardous Waste Inspector

Given the widely held negative perceptions about government bureaucrats, you might cringe at the outset of a story about a government regulator at a state environmental agency. Despite the disdain afforded most government regulators, Brandon's story is worth telling. We should note first, however, that given the negative attitudes about regulators and the polarization of our politics, we have opted to keep Brandon's identity confidential (both his name and which state environmental agency he works for). Nevertheless, Brandon's experiences encapsulate those of many of his colleagues across the 50 states.

Brandon has worked for a state environmental protection agency for more than two decades and he has spent the bulk of that time working in hazardous waste. He began his career as a Resource Conservation and Recovery Act (RCRA) inspector and, over time, became a supervisor for RCRA inspectors. His primary job duties include ensuring that facilities in his assigned geographic region are properly permitted and that they comply with applicable state and federal law regarding the treatment, storage, and disposal of hazardous wastes. He and his colleagues spend a good deal of time—although they generally wish it was more time—out in the field checking on facilities such as landfills to see environmental regulation in action. For the most part, Brandon finds he has a good working relationship with the regulated community he oversees, and he thinks these positive interactions are vital to ensuring compliance. Brandon describes his work as being the cream in an Oreo cookie—he is caught in the middle between industry and citizens and helps hold it all together. Moreover, he believes it takes everyone to ensure adequate protection of the environment.

Although Brandon would rather think of Oreos, he has also come face to face—literally—with tomatoes. Part of Brandon's role with the RCRA is participating in public hearings when operating permits, which allow facilities to deal with hazardous wastes, are being issued. One of Brandon's assigned facilities sought a modification to its permit so it could accept another type of hazardous waste, and part of the process for amending a permit (as we will discuss further in this chapter) often involves a public hearing to facilitate discussion with the public about any concerns it might have with the facility modifying its operations. Brandon showed up at the public hearing to represent his agency and explain that the facility had appropriately requested to take a different type of waste and had properly filed a permit modification and, upon review, his agency found the modifications within the parameters of the hazardous waste regulations in the state. This particular facility, however, did not have the best relationship with its neighbors—especially a number of citizens whose homes share the same road with the facility.

By the number of people at the meeting, Brandon quickly got a sense that things might get heated. Many residents who disliked the facility and its operations were irate that the government would allow the facility to take more types of wastes, but these residents did not understand that the regulations from the RCRA mostly provide processes for dealing with waste and, as long as processes are followed, the facility can take on more. However, instead of taking their frustrations out on the policymakers who created the RCRA decades ago or state legislators who could make modifications to relevant state laws and procedures, Brandon bore the brunt of their frustrations in the form of flying fruit. Tomatoes were thrown at Brandon during the course of the public hearing. Fortunately, Brandon has quick reflexes—all those years of outdoor activities gave him that—so he managed to dodge most of the tomatoes. Brandon still laughs about the story today as he retells it because, to him, it clearly demonstrates his role in environmental protection as the cream of an Oreo cookie. Government regulators are stuck between industry and citizens, and that is where they should be in his estimation. After all, he and his fellow regulators are the ones who do environmental policy—not the activists, not the industry representatives, and not the politicians in Washington, DC and state capitals. Therefore, these front-line regulators are the Oreo cream that holds the cookie together.

The "doing" of environmental policy is, arguably, the most crucial component of governmental efforts regarding environmental protection, and it is often neglected in traditional study. In Chapter 6, we began our exploration of how policy language gets translated into practice, and this chapter continues in a similar fashion by focusing on the implementation of policy, notably through the work of those on the front-lines. As you might guess at this point, policy implementation is difficult, and the way policies are carried out may not be at all what you expected. Recall from Chapter 3 that policy implementation is the "process by which policies enacted by government are put into effect by the relevant agencies" (Birkland 2011, 263). This is where the rubber meets the road; yet, it is not quite that simple. In many ways, policy implementation is replete with all the challenges of creating policy in the first place (Smith and Larimer 2013).

Implementation is challenging because it encompasses the "interaction between the setting of goals and actions geared to achieving them" (Pressman and Wildavsky 1984, 341). Think for a moment about your own goals for the semester. Perhaps, you want to earn "all A's" this term to give a boost to your overall GPA, but you know you have a tough science class, and while you want an A, you are expecting a B. Those are your goals. Now, how will you implement these goals? You have been down this path before in other semesters. How did your goals match up with the end result? Presumably, you have had a few of those moments where you recalled your overly optimistic goals and how they may not have aligned with the results at the end of the semester. This analogy helps us understand the implementation of environmental policy.

If policy implementation is so important, it is natural to wonder why such a crucial topic is frequently overlooked in environmental policy discussions and even textbooks. There are many reasons for this neglect. First, policy implementation is not, often, as riveting to observers as the politics and the wrangling associated with passing laws. After all, stories of political deals and intrigue—such as the veto of the Clean Water Act (CWA) and congressional action to override the veto—tend to be more exciting than the process of translating the CWA into concrete action. Furthermore, passing laws usually happens in a much narrower time horizon, whereas the process of implementation unfolds over many years. Media coverage of implementation is much harder and would require lots of detailed explanations that may not be suited to the rapid pace of the news these days. Finally, as Jeffrey Pressman and Aaron Wildavsky (1984) discuss, it is presumed that "implementation should be easy" (340). As we have come to understand in this text—and particularly through Chapter 2—as time progresses, fewer and fewer major laws are passed by Congress; however, this does not mean that environmental policy is not happening. In light of congressional gridlock, Christopher McGrory Klyza and David Sousa (2008, 2013), remind us that environmental policy is increasingly happening through the work of government agencies—or put differently, in the stage of policy implementation.

This chapter explores the often-neglected area of policy implementation by beginning with a discussion of the process associated with implementation and picking up where Chapter 6 concluded. We will focus on the dominant tool of environmental policy—command and control regulations. Then, we will investigate the use of command and control regulations and endeavor to assess whether they work. Afterward, the specifics of this regulatory tool will be outlined, before we turn our attention to the day-to-day realities of implementing and monitoring environmental regulations. Finally, we will consider the actors involved in implementation—actors just like Brandon. A case study about an industrial wastewater processor is presented, which demonstrates some of the many complexities associated with implementing environmental regulations. The chapter concludes by discussing what factors affect implementation and what the future might look like for command and control regulations in the future.

As we proceed, several themes emerge as we focus on implementing environmental policy. First, it is important—if not, arguably, more important—to pay attention to policy implementation rather than just policy formulation in the environmental context. Just because a piece of legislation makes it through Congress does not mean it is going to be implemented as prescribed, nor does it mean it will achieve its goals. After all, it is a lot easier to devise goals than it is to achieve them. Second, as the nation works toward protecting the environment, implementing environmental policy, which happens most often through the use of command and control regulations, requires the coordination of many individuals who are rarely, if ever, considered. Understanding their jobs—and contemplating if they embody the role of the Oreo, as

Brandon describes—is essential to understanding how environmental protection works in the United States, and how it sometimes does not. Third, although command and control regulations have been the dominant policy tool employed for achieving environmental goals, the future is likely to evolve and employ a different regulatory tool; we are going to have to change how we think about environmental regulation and who should do what to protect the nation's environment.

Overview of Environmental Policy Implementation

From our discussion of the policy process (refer to Chapter 3), we know that implementation comes after a policy has passed both chambers of Congress and has been approved by the president. It is worth reiterating that lawmakers have many types of policy tools at their disposal in environmental policy, including taxes, subsidies, financial incentives, or even suasion campaigns, such as Smokey the Bear in U.S. Forest Service commercials. When most of our major environmental laws were passed, however, the focus was on stopping and cleaning up pollution and it was thought that command and control regulations would be the most effective policy tool to utilize. The previous chapter (Chapter 6) expanded our understanding of the policy process by detailing how vague environmental statutes get translated from laudable goals such as "clean water" to language that is actionable: so that clean water, as a goal, becomes many components such as total maximum daily load permits and classifications of the nation's waterways. These actions are usually taken by government agencies such as the Environmental Protection Agency (EPA) or the Department of Energy, because policymakers leave the specifics to the agencies, and their rule-writers, that are delegated authority. This chapter picks up by focusing on how those rules get translated into action and various government agencies ensure that those rules are monitored for compliance. We begin, though, with an overview of this dominant policy tool.

Command and Control Regulations

Although command and control regulations are employed in a range of policy areas beyond the environmental realm, this type of regulation is, frequently, the first tool that comes to mind when we think about environmental issues. Indeed, efforts at protecting the environment usually conjure images of telling a firm to stop doing something, like releasing pollutants into a nearby river. Of the more than 15,000 pages of federal environmental regulations that govern the more than 40,000 stationary air sources, 90,000 facilities that discharge effluent into waterways, the more than 425,000 hazardous waste facilities, and the 173,000 drinking water systems, the majority of those regulations can be characterized as "command and control" (Fiorino 2006, 1, 83; Kraft et al. 2011, 3).

As the name might suggest, command and control regulations direct individuals and/or organizations to comply with particular standards, achieve predetermined controls, and/or follow process and technology requirements (e.g., emission limits or a particular type of pollution control equipment to be employed). These regulations are established by government officials, or rule-writers, through the rulemaking process.

> Under command and control, government agencies develop a set of rules or standards. These determine technologies to be used or avoided; amounts of pollutants that can be emitted from a particular waste pipe, smokestack, or factor; and/or the amounts or kinds of resources that may be extracted from a common pool such as a fishery or a forest. These agencies issue commands in the form of regulations and permits to control the behavior of private firms, other government agencies, and/or individuals. (Dietz and Stern 2002, 3)

Stated differently, command and control regulations are the policy tool most often thought of for protecting the environment because they set specific limits on pollutants, such as nitrous oxides, that may be released from a facility, or they mandate the particular type of pollution abatement technology that another facility must use.

With this explanation of command and control regulations, the next obvious question is: do they work? Generally speaking, this form of regulation in the environmental arena works and produces results (cf. Press and Mazmanian 2013; Davies and Mazurek 1997). According to data from the US EPA in 2017, the emissions from the major air pollutants regulated by the Clean Air Act have decreased from 1970 to 2016. Concentrations of the following air pollutants have dropped significantly since 1990: lead is down 99%, nitrogen dioxide 56%, sulfur dioxide 85%, and particular matter (10 microns) 39%—all while the economy grew, the population climbed, vehicle travel increased, and energy consumption rose (US EPA 2017). Additionally, there has been a virtual elimination of some harmful pollutants (such as polychlorinated biphenyls

(PCBs) and mercury), and there have been significant reductions in emissions and concentrations of common water pollutants (Fiorino 2006, 66). The nation's waterways have also benefited from the CWA as of the more than 3.5 million miles of waterways only about half a million continue to be assessed as "impaired" (US EPA 2015). The traditional approach to environmental regulation "has by no means been a failure. In fact, in many respects it has been a major success" (Fiorino 2006, 27).

Indeed, the United States' regulatory structure boasts expertise, comprises an impressive legal framework that numerous other countries endeavor to replicate, and has built an intimidating set of institutions tasked with environmental protection. However, this regulatory approach has been less effective in some areas, including pollution from nonpoint sources, the amount of waste generated domestically, emissions of carbon dioxide and other greenhouse gases (GHGs), and the volume of toxic wastes accumulating in the environment.

These accomplishments and ongoing challenges naturally give rise to questions about costs and other burdens this approach to environmental regulation has imposed. As you might imagine, arriving at those cost estimates can be difficult given the variation in how estimates are derived and what factors comprise the statistics. Therefore, let us consider a variety of figures. According to the White House Office of Management and Budget (OMB), the cost of environmental regulations from 2005 to 2015 about $47 billion (in 2014 dollars) while the benefits amounted to $427 billion (OMB 2016). And each year, about one percent of all federal government spending is on environmental programs—this is far less than spending for housing, transportation, education, and much less than entitlement programs, including Medicare, social security, and unemployment benefits.

It can be difficult to truly grasp this amount of money, much less make assessments as to whether the costs outweigh the benefits of environmental regulation. Much of this challenge lies in the difficulty in reducing intangibles, like clean air, to dollar figures. Suffice it to say, to date, command and control regulations have generated improvements in the condition of the natural environment and have brought with them costs borne by government, industry, and citizens alike.

Developing and Implementing Command and Control Regulations

Command and control regulations are not, typically, the statutory language Congress enacts; rather, the process of creating these regulations is simply started by the passage of legislation. Chapter 6 detailed this process at a macrolevel, as part of the focus on federal rulemaking. Here, we continue that conversation as it concerns promulgating command and control regulations. The process comprises several stages of setting and enforcing command and control regulations: (1) goal setting, (2) criteria determination, (3) standard setting, and (4) enforcement of the standards (see Table 7.1).

The first stage in establishing command control regulation is the process of setting goals. For example, in the CWA of 1972, one of the law's goals includes eliminating high amounts of toxic pollutants to make the nation's water "swimmable," "fishable," and "navigable." Without being specific, Congress (or another legislative body, like a state general assembly) often establishes broad goals that a law is designed to achieve. In the lead up to the CWA, Congress pursued a national standard of "swimmable" because there was no way it would be implemented the same way everywhere, thereby allowing for regional variation, which was important to getting the bill passed (Milazzo 2006, 201). Numerous political and institutional reasons explain the level of generality in legislation. Elected lawmakers recognize that the expertise for setting specific rules falls to the civil servants in the federal bureaucracy who have the wherewithal to turn broad goals into actionable steps. Moreover, for reasons of consensus building and political expediency, legislators focus on articulating goals and employing politically palatable language to articulate those goals. At this stage, broad goals are defined and weighed against myriad social and economic considerations. These considerations often explain why statutory language may be unclear, confusing, or even contradictory. Once lawmakers, as the people's representatives, come to agreement about those goals, they then delegate authority to various administrative agencies (see Chapter 4 for more detail about the work of administrative agencies).

Next, criteria must be determined during the second stage. For instance, what is meant by "clean water" or "clean air?" Such goal language is laudable, but its meaning is elusive. With the delegation of

Table 7.1 Stages of command and control regulation	• Goal setting
	• Criteria determination
	• Standard setting
	• Enforcement of standards

authority, Congress acknowledges it does not have the technical prowess or the political capacity to determine which pollutants are most harmful to waterways and to establish what the limits on releases of those pollutants should be. Congress leaves those determinations to agencies such as the US EPA. Establishing criteria can be difficult because extensive research and data collection are needed on pollutants and their effects, and much of that information may not be readily available and may take a lot of time. With these data and research, agencies start putting specifics around lofty goals of clean air and clean water. The connections between the ill effects of pollution are considered during this stage of the process, along with their relationship to public health and other ecological risk assessments. These determinations are still quite general in nature, but they are far more specific than statutory language.

After determining the criteria, agencies move into the third stage of command and control regulations: setting standards. After the criteria have determined the broad aims of the regulations, standards are established to describe the specific means of achieving those broad aims. For example, to reduce the presence of 189 hazardous air pollutants (HAPs) identified by the CAA, the standards determine how much a facility may be allowed to emit of HAPs, depending on the facility's size and industrial type. These are the standards that polluting facilities must comply with and that environmental inspectors assess compliance against during inspections. These standards reflect determinations about the level of pollution that is acceptable when weighed against health and other ecological considerations, as well as risk assessments such as the maximum level of a pollutant that is allowed to be discharged in a wastewater stream, or the standards may establish a particular type of technology or a process that must be employed to mitigate the adverse effects of an operation on the environment.

The final stage of command and control regulations has to do with enforcement. This is the part where facilities that are subjected to these regulations are monitored to see if they are complying with applicable regulations. Environmental inspectors conduct inspections as part of this stage which can include the review of required reports with logs of emissions data and other such compliance-monitoring activities. It is up to these inspectors, or environmental regulators, to assess compliance with the established standards. To determine compliance, these inspectors routinely visit facilities—generally, through unannounced inspections—that generate pollution, and gauge their compliance with applicable standards.

If a regulator finds a facility out of compliance with a particular standard, the regulator will begin the enforcement process to see that the facility returns to compliance and that the nation's environmental goals are being met. More on this part of the process comes later in this chapter.

Fundamental Assumptions of Command and Control Regulation

So far, we have broadly outlined the process of establishing command and control regulations. At this juncture, let us pause and consider a few fundamental attributes of this kind of regulation. First, these regulations are top-down, derived by the government. Government dictates these rules, and everyone must comply or else face enforcement proceedings. Although we learned in our discussion of rulemaking in the last chapter that various stakeholders are, often, part of the process of crafting these regulations, the burden still rests on the government to determine the regulations. As a result, the rules come not from those individuals at facilities that generate pollution, but from the civil servants in governmental agencies.

A second important assumption—and one related to the first—is that these regulations presume that government is in the position to know best. Put differently, it is assumed that government has all the information from the best science and technology about what the appropriate standards are and what are the best technologies to mandate. Devising these regulations requires extensive research and modeling about potential effects of one environmental harm or another; therefore, the government must be the one who has all this information in order to craft the best regulations. This reality, coupled with the challenge for devising the regulations, puts a significant burden on government.

Third, these regulations employ a "one-size-fits-all" approach to compliance. All organizations are subject to these regulations, with little differentiation for size and scope of a facility's operations. Therefore, a local dry cleaner has to deal with the same kinds of requirements regarding the use of various chemicals in the dry cleaning process that a huge chain of dry cleaners has to contend with; that large chain, presumably, has a few people whose jobs are devoted to compliance with environmental regulations, whereas the local, single storefront operation has to manage compliance by itself with its smaller staff. This is not to say that there are not some considerations for different kinds of facilities, but, generally speaking, the regulations apply across the board.

Fourth, compliance with these regulations is ensured through a deterrence strategy. A deterrence strategy means that facilities must comply or else they face the consequences set forth by government (these consequences include a range of enforcement options including court-ordered compliance). The presumption of this regulatory approach is that those organizations subjected to regulation have no wish to comply with the rules and would rather pollute the environment. This may have been a more accurate statement decades ago when the environmental regulatory state was being crafted, and this may even still be true for a handful of nefarious operations that could care less about the environment; however, such a sweeping statement is not true for the majority of regulated facilities today (cf. Hoffman 2001; Pautz and Rinfret 2013). Just as deterrence may be an effective strategy for a parent, other strategies may also prove equally, if not more, effective as well. Sometimes, incentives and other similar tools might encourage good environmental stewardship rather than just a looming threat of getting in trouble with government regulators.

A final, and related point about these regulations is that there is little incentive for firms to improve their environmental performance if they are meeting established standards. For example, if a facility is environmentally conscientious and is abiding by all the applicable environmental regulations and producing ten units of pollution annually, where is the incentive for it to work at reducing that impact? There is little about command and control regulations that encourage the firm to strive to generate only nine units of pollution the following year. This is not to say that the firm would not do that on its own, but there may be little regulatory benefit for the firm that might have to purchase new technologies or equipment to reduce its environmental impact.

COMMAND AND CONTROL REGULATIONS IN ACTION

After the overview of command and control regulations, along with a consideration of some of their fundamental assumptions, consider how these regulations work daily, on the front-lines of environmental protection. It is important to point out that this topic is often missing in discussions of environmental policy, and this is unsettling because we have to understand how these regulations work in practice to fully comprehend how environmental policy operates today and how it might in the future. Instrumental to the daily implementation of these regulations are the actors involved and the permitting and compliance-monitoring components of these regulations.

Regulatory Structure

Given our focus on environmental policy in practice, we continue to emphasize those individuals on the front-lines of environmental policy day in and day out. Command and control regulations require a variety of regulators at the federal, state, and, sometimes, even the local level. Typically, federal regulators (notably those with the US EPA) are tasked with promulgating regulations, as detailed in Chapter 6, through rule-making processes. States can impose additional requirements beyond federal ones, but they are not required to do so. Some states choose to impose more stringent regulations, such as California with its air quality laws.

After the regulations have been promulgated, much of the work is delegated to the states for implementation; and typically, state environmental protection agencies assume primary responsibility for the implementation of these laws. Table 7.2 lists the state environmental protection agencies.

This delegation of authority to the state level is a function of our federal structure of government. The agencies listed in Table 7.2 are, for the most part, delegated the responsibility of taking federal environmental laws and regulations and implementing them within their state. The majority of states issue most of the environmental permits and complete most of the environmental enforcement actions rather than the federal government. However, there are some cases in which the federal government has not granted such authority. For example, four states (Idaho, Massachusetts, New Hampshire, and New Mexico) have not been granted program authority to administer the National Pollutant Discharge Elimination System (NPDES) permits under the CWA (US EPA 2018). Notwithstanding these few exceptions, the states have a tremendous role in implementing environmental policy. Barry Rabe (2006) cites the Environmental Council of the States (ECOS), which says the states

Table 7.2   State environmental protection agencies

Alabama Department of Environmental Management
Alaska Department of Environmental Conservation
Arizona Department of Environmental Quality
Arkansas Department of Environmental Quality
California Environmental Protection Agency
Colorado Department of Public Health and Environment
Connecticut Department of Energy and Environmental Protection
Delaware Department of Natural Resources and Environmental Control
Florida Department of Environmental Protection
Georgia Department of Natural Resources
Hawaii State Department of Health
Idaho Department of Environmental Quality
Illinois Environmental Protection Agency
Indiana Department of Environmental Management
Iowa Department of Natural Resources
Kansas Department of Health and Environment
Kentucky Department for Environmental Protection
Louisiana Department of Environmental Quality
Maine Department of Environmental Protection
Maryland Department of the Environment
Massachusetts Department of Environmental Protection
Michigan Department of Environmental Quality
Minnesota Pollution Control Agency
Mississippi Department of Environmental Quality
Missouri Department of Natural Resources
Montana Department of Environmental Quality
Nebraska Department of Environmental Quality
Nevada Division of Environmental Protection
New Hampshire Department of Environmental Services
New Jersey Department of Environmental Protection
New Mexico Environment Department
New York Department of Environmental Conservation
North Carolina Department of Environmental Quality
North Dakota Department of Health
Ohio Environmental Protection Agency
Oklahoma Department of Environmental Quality
Oregon Department of Environmental Quality
Pennsylvania Department of Environmental Protection
Rhode Island Department of Environmental Management
South Carolina Department of Health and Environmental Control

(continued)

Table 7.2 (continued)

South Dakota Department of Environment and Natural Resources
Tennessee Department of Environment and Conservation
Texas Commission on Environmental Quality
Vermont Department of Environmental Conservation
Virginia Department of Environmental Quality
Washington Department of Ecology
West Virginia Department of Environmental Protection
Wisconsin Department of Natural Resources
Wyoming Department of Environmental Quality

collectively issue more than 90 percent of all environmental permits, complete more than 75 percent of all environmental enforcement actions, and rely on the federal government for less than 25 percent of their total funding on environmental and natural resource concerns. (35–36)

These agencies fund this work through a combination of money from their state and from the federal government. According to ECOS, these agencies receive about a quarter of their funds from the federal government and that support has been decreasing in recent years (ECOS 2017). This means that states increasingly have to fund their work to implement federal environmental programs, along with their own agency's initiatives. It is the states and their front-line regulators that are primarily tasked with overseeing implementation of environmental regulations nationwide. The federal government's regulators can and do oversee these programs too, but it is the state regulators who are on the front-lines of ensuring environmental protection. In terms of the doing, states permit and monitor facilities throughout their state for compliance with environmental regulations. The following section explores these activities and examines both sides of regulatory interaction: the regulator and the members of the regulated community.

Permitting and Compliance Monitoring

Carrying out environmental regulations requires permitting and monitoring. When a firm (regulated company) is beginning its operation and constructing a new facility (or when it is making major modifications to its existing facility and/or operations), it is required to apply for a permit to operate and generate pollution. As previously discussed, the federal government's regulations set forth the minimum environmental standards, such as the amount of discharge or the kind of process to use in the firm's operations, and states may choose to go beyond these and have additional requirements. A firm would comply with the requirements and complete the application process which varies state to state. These permit applications can be fairly brief or constitute hundreds of pages of technical information and descriptions of a facility's operation. A front-line regulator then reviews the permit application, seeks any additional information or clarification, and ensures that all conditions are met. In some cases, a public hearing is held to seek input from citizens. Finally, a permit is issued to the facility to begin operations. It is important to note that, if a facility undergoes major modifications or renovations to its facility or changes its production process, it typically has to apply for a permit modification—just like in our introductory story. Permits are issued for a fixed period of time, and then a renewal process occurs. This is not unlike the processes many of us are familiar with regarding driver's licenses.

The permit to operate outlines various conditions that a firm must meet. These conditions are stipulated by the command and control regulations we discussed earlier. They typically include an array of monitoring data that must be collected and reviewed, and frequently incorporate the use of particular pollution control equipment and production process requirements. To guarantee that the requisite monitoring is being done and other requirements complied with, firms are subjected to compliance inspections from their regulatory counterparts: regulators.

Inspection Process

Inspections vary greatly in their frequency, length, and involvement of key actors. They can be brief or they can last for days, depending on why a facility is regulated and the size of the facility and its operations. These inspections are typically done by a single regulator. A regulator begins the inspection process by arriving at a facility, generally unannounced. Regulators conduct the vast majority of their inspections unannounced so they can observe the facility operating normally, rather than when the facility is prepared for a regulator's visit.[1] A brief meeting usually occurs between the regulator and facility contact, reviewing the facility's compliance history and any pertinent issues or concerns. Afterward, the physical site inspection commences where the regulator reviews the production process, walks the operations floor, sees product being made, and records his findings while talking with the facility contact.

Regulators examine pollution abatement technologies and monitoring equipment. They also review various paperwork and data that must be maintained on site. The most frequent activity that regulators report is explaining regulations to members of the regulated community (Pautz and Rinfret 2013, 24). Upon conclusion of the physical inspection, there is, generally, a debriefing between the regulator and the facility contact to go over anything significant and to give the facility a preliminary assessment of the facility's compliance status. Furthermore, it is during this meeting that any additional reports, monitoring data, or questions are addressed. After the closing meeting is conducted, the regulator returns to his office to begin his formal write-up of the inspection and to discuss with his supervisor any issues.

Inspections occur with varying frequency and level of scrutiny. For example, small firms, such as a printing operation may only discharge a small amount of air pollutants, so they would find themselves being inspected every three to five years. By contrast a large power generation might expect annual inspections since they are a major source of pollution. Inspections may not always be a physical site inspection either. In some cases, the review of monitoring logs and other paperwork may constitute the inspection.

Noncompliance During Inspections

If, after a physical site inspection or a paperwork inspection, a regulator finds a problem, there are multiple avenues to resolve the issue. These avenues vary state to state, as each agency has its own policies and procedures. Most regulators aim to facilitate the resolution of the issue as

---

[1]There are, of course, exceptions to the general policy of unannounced inspections. Facilities with extensive security measures in place frequently require advanced notice of an inspection. For example, many U.S. Department of Defense facilities require security clearances to be on site, so inspectors have little choice but to notify the facility in advance of their arrivals.

quickly and painlessly as possible and without utilizing formal mechanisms (cf. Pautz and Rinfret 2013). It is important to note that decisions about how to resolve issues that arise during inspections (or during any other point in compliance monitoring) do not occur in isolation; in other words, inspectors and their superiors make these decisions in a broader organizational and even political context. Here we chart some of the paths toward resolution and then will explore this broader context.

A regulator can informally have the firm address the issue on site and, hopefully, resolve the issue then and there. For instance, if, during the inspection, improperly labeled chemical containers are found, a regulator is likely to point out the issue—and permit violation—to the facility. Ideally, the facility representative ensures the problem is remedied immediately by getting labels corrected. If the matter was resolved as soon as it was pointed out, the regulator might only note the issue in his inspection write-up, rather than pursue any formal means of corrective action. If, however, the facility representative is not cooperative and the labeling is not addressed, then a regulator begins the process of correcting a violation. If the matter cannot be resolved immediately, then a regulator may issue a Request for Corrective Action (RCA). Although an RCA is a formal document that becomes part of a facility's file, as long as the issue is resolved within the timeframe specified by the regulator (e.g., 30 days), there are no significant ramifications for the facility. The regulator will follow up with the facility in the timeframe established to ensure the issue has been corrected and that will, typically, be the end of the matter.

If the regulator, guided by the agency's policies, determines the violation is severe, an RCA may not be appropriate or severe enough given the violation. Violations run the gamut from a container of solvent-soaked rags that is left uncovered on a production floor to printing inks with volatile organic compound (VOC) emissions beyond permitted levels to the improper dumping of chemicals. After consultation with the regulator's supervisor, a formal warning letter may be drafted and issued to the facility.

If the formal warning letter is not sufficient to compel compliance, the state will pursue a formal Notice of Violation (NOV). NOVs are, typically, the next step in the enforcement process and, as might be expected, facility representatives do not relish receipt of a NOV. Issuance of a NOV, typically, involves not only the regulator and his/her supervisor, but also an attorney housed within the regulatory agency or with the states' attorneys general office. Beyond this step, in a typical enforcement proceeding, state attorneys become involved because the environmental agency is unable to get a recalcitrant facility to come back into compliance. In some instances, civil suits or even criminal suits are pursued. Although criminal charges are not commonly pursued in environmental cases, there are some notable exceptions. Donald Blankenship, CEO of Massey Energy Company, was sentenced to one year in prison and fined $250,000 following a conviction for conspiracy to violate federal mine safety standards. The violations were part of the investigation into the 2010 explosion of the Upper Big Branch mine explosion in West Virginia that killed 29 miners (Blinder 2016). It is worth noting that Blankenship announced his campaign for Senate from West Virginia in 2018 (he lost the Republican Party primary but stood for election in the general election as a third-party candidate). With the introduction of attorneys, regulators play a less prominent role in pursuing compliance.

Major findings of noncompliance often elicit the involvement of federal regulators as well. Recall that while state environmental agencies are likely the entities that uncover the noncompliance, major problems usually trigger a collaborative approach to rectify the situation from both state and federal regulators. After all, the federal government typically has the ultimate authority as they have delegated authority to the states to implement federal statutes and regulations.

Findings of noncompliance are not typically viewed positively as they indicate that environmental standards are not being met, and there is a significant chance that harm is being done to the environment. That said, how regulators and their agencies respond to those findings can vary for a host of reasons, from organizational reasons, such as staffing challenges that reduce frequencies of inspections and organizational emphases on particular industrial sectors, to political reasons, such as the priorities of a governor or president. The Trump administration, for example, has opted not to pursue enforcement actions at similar rates from previous administrations of both political parties (Lipton and Ivory 2017). Investigative reporting from *The New York Times* and other media outlets concludes that significant decreases in enforcement efforts have defined the early years of the US EPA under the Trump administration, which align with EPA Administrator Scott Pruitt's orders to back off enforcement of environmental laws per the request of oil and gas industry executives (Lipton and Ivory 2017).

The intermingling of federal and state roles in permitting and monitoring compliance with environmental regulations helps us understand the multitude of actors who are involved in environmental protection. Of particular interest are the populations of actors whose day-to-day job is environmental compliance—the front-line regulators and their counterparts at the firms, subject to environmental regulations.

FRONT-LINE REGULATORS

The front-line regulators work for the aforementioned state agencies and they permit, inspect, and, generally, oversee the environmental activities of facilities in the state. More specifically, they have an array of responsibilities, which keeps their jobs anything but dull because they are the ones who most frequently and consistently are the bridge between environmental policymakers and the regulated community. In many instances, these individuals have backgrounds in the natural sciences and/or engineering and are often toward the bottom of their agencies' hierarchy. Accordingly, their work constitutes what Michael Lipsky (1980) and others define as street-level bureaucrats or front-line workers (cf. Maynard-Moody and Musheno 2003; Riccucci 2005) because they interact daily with the public, and their actions comprise the implementation of environmental policy. As Stephen Fineman (1998) summarizes, "like other street-level bureaucrats environmental inspectors deal with people who may not voluntarily desire their services and who experience some ambiguity in exercising appropriate control" (953). To explore the work and impact of regulators, we begin by understanding their organizational context.

Mirroring the organization of the US EPA, discussed in Chapter 4, most state environmental agencies are structured around the major environmental issues, or environmental "media," and their corresponding statutes.[2] For instance, the 1970 Clean Air Act and its subsequent amendments have compelled federal and state environmental agencies

---

[2] It is worth noting that states vary in their organizational responses to environmental protection. Some states have multiple agencies that are responsible for environmental concerns (e.g., a Department of Environmental Quality and a Department of Natural Resources), whereas other states have one comprehensive agency. The majority of states that participated in our study have multiple agencies and a few (e.g., Wisconsin and New York) have a single comprehensive agency.

to establish divisions or bureaus dedicated to implementing and enforcing the mandates of clean air legislation. The same holds for water and waste, although most waste programs are segregated into solid waste and hazardous waste, and there are frequently delineations in water programs between drinking water and other facets of water laws (Andrews 2006; Kraft 2011). Accordingly, environmental regulators specialize in air, water (sometimes delineated between drinking water and groundwater), solid waste, or hazardous waste.

These media-specific delineations may create problems for both the enforcement of environmental laws and for the facilities themselves (cf. Rosenbaum 2011; US EPA Office of Inspector General 2006; US Government Accountability Office 2003; Rabe 2002). Because regulators focus on a specific environmental media, they learn the intricacies of the environmental laws surrounding their appointed media, and may not be as conversant in the regulations for another media. This specialization is potentially problematic because, for example, modifying a production process at a regulated facility to improve air quality may adversely impact water quality (Rosenbaum 2011).

As is the case with other front-line workers, environmental regulators contend with competing agency goals (cf. Lipsky 1980; Maynard-Moody and Musheno 2003). The stated goals of most environmental agencies include the protection of human health and the environment without impeding development. For instance, the US EPA's mission statement is "to protect human health and the environment" (US EPA 2011). However, following its mission statement, the US EPA's purpose states that "environmental protection is an integral consideration in US policies concerning natural resources, human health, economic growth ... and these factors are similarly considered in establishing environmental policy" (US EPA 2011). Thus, protecting health and the natural environment is the goal of the agency, its stated purpose is that those objectives are achieved with considerations for economic concerns. Although these objectives can work in concert with one another, they can be wrought with tension. For instance, additional requirements on facilities will likely lessen their environmental impact, but they may require the installation of pollution abatement technology, which could be a substantial investment up front before any environmental impact can be realized.

At the state level, for example, new governors—through their appointees—can alter the direction of state environmental agencies, as we have seen in recent years, presenting even more challenges for regulators,

who often serve in their capacity as regulators under numerous administrations. For example, Ohio Governor John Kasich and Wisconsin
Governor Scott Walker, both elected in 2010, have insisted that their
state environmental agencies be more "business friendly."

Within this organizational structure, the day-to-day tasks of regulators are quite similar, although they work in different environmental
media. Given the term regulator, one may rightly assume that a regulator engages in "routine inspections and check visits," but there are
many other aspects of a regulator's job duties (Hutter 1997, 107). In the
course of any workday, a regulator may or may not be in the office, but
rarely does a day go by in which a regulator does not deal directly with a
regulated facility.

Generally, regulators spend their time in the office preparing to be out
of the office and in the field. In the field is where pollution control happens (Hawkins 1984, 47). However, regulators spend, on average, more
than 70% of their time in the office, much to their dismay (Pautz and
Rinfret 2013, 22). Being in the field brings with it a variety of experiences. A regulator is responsible for anywhere from a handful of facilities
to hundreds of facilities. The number depends upon the types of facilities
she oversees and how they are regulated; for example, are the facilities
major sources, as defined by US EPA, or are the facilities that are shut
down, but have ongoing monitoring? The number of facilities a regulator is responsible for varies considerably, depending on the nature of
the regulation. One study reports that the typical workload for a regulator is 50 facilities, with water and waste regulators generally responsible
for more facilities than their regulatory counterparts in air (Pautz and
Rinfret 2013, 23).

To prepare for a visit to assess compliance, a regulator begins by
reviewing a facility's permit, compliance history, and other documents
related to a facility's operation. Keep in mind that regulators are, often,
responsible for a host of facilities with various operations, which can
prove challenging for regulators. For example, an air regulator could be
responsible for nearly 200 facilities that range from a cigarette producing plant to several printing operations, from a power plant to a plastic
injection molding facility. Needless to say, keeping up with such diverse
facility operations can prove taxing for a regulator, but this is simply part
of the job.

The requirements and frequency of physical site inspections vary
depending on many different factors. The size of a facility's operation

and the reasons it is regulated determine how often a regulator must visit the facility and how involved the inspection is while the regulator is there. For example, minor sources of air pollution, such as a dry cleaner, only require physical site inspections once every 3–5 years (cf. US EPA 2011). The same is true for facilities that have boilers—such as older school buildings. However, large facilities, such as power-generating stations, may see their regulators quarterly. The frequency and extent of the physical site inspections are determined by the conditions of a facility's permit, which may vary state to state, as discussed earlier in the chapter.

Physical site inspections are not the only type of inspections. Many inspections are conducted based on paperwork and other reports that a facility submits to the agency, as required by permit conditions and other regulations. Regulators have to keep up with voluminous reports such as stack testing reports, opacity readings, and other data provided by pollution abatement technology and various other monitors. Verifying the reports and then reviewing them for any problems can be time-consuming, particularly when some reports are hundreds of pages each and submitted quarterly.

Misperceptions About Regulators

This discussion of regulators may seem rather unsatisfying because it does not substantiate a lot of perceptions about this group of actors. For starters, environmental regulators cannot shut down facilities regardless of environmental harms—that is something that courts may do only in extreme, rare cases.[3] Moreover, as subsequent discussion will demonstrate, the interactions between regulators and members of the regulated community are generally productive and cooperative, defying images conveyed to us from seemingly innocuous sources (such as movies) that the regulator and the regulated cannot get along (cf. Pautz and Rinfret 2013). Indeed, the confrontational interaction portrayed in the original *Ghostbusters* film, where the EPA inspector, Walter Peck, wants to shut down the Ghostbusters' valiant efforts at ridding the world of meddlesome supernatural beings, is far from the norm; however, these are the

---

[3] It is often thought that environmental regulators can act like Occupational Safety and Health Administration (OSHA) inspectors, who do retain some powers—again in extreme circumstances—to shut down a facility if violations are found. This is not the case with environmental inspectors.

images that can dominate our perceptions about regulators. Moreover, perceptions about environmental regulators may stem from other types of government regulators, such as workplace safety inspectors or even police officers—as both sets of actors have more authority to act with immediate ramifications, such as forcing a facility to stop operations. Environmental regulators do not have this kind of authority.

MEMBERS OF THE REGULATED COMMUNITY

Regulators could not implement environmental policy without the regulated community. This term is used to refer to the individuals at regulated facilities who interact with the regulators in an effort to ensure compliance with environmental regulations. Employed by an array of organizations—from pharmaceutical companies and water treatment facilities to dry cleaners and quarries—members of the regulated community are responsible for dealing with environmental matters on a routine basis. In large, well-established facilities, these individuals are, often, full-time environmental managers who may have an entire staff devoted to achieving compliance with environmental regulations, and they are likely to be well trained in environmental engineering, science, or related fields. At the other end of the spectrum are facility personnel who are responsible for environmental matters as just one of many job duties. Frequently, these individuals do not have extensive backgrounds in environmental matters and may even be the small business owners who shoulder the responsibility for everything the business does. As such, it is difficult to succinctly characterize this diverse group. Generally speaking, these members of the regulated community are committed to their jobs and their companies, and are not intentionally out to harm the environment. Violations of environmental regulations are, frequently, the result of ignorance or confusion over requirements rather than malicious attempts to endanger the environment (cf. Pautz 2009; Pautz and Rinfret 2013).

Despite the importance of these actors, little is known about them or their interactions with regulators. Eugene Bardach and Robert Kagan (1982/2002) simply talk, with little elaboration, about the "good apples" and the "bad apples" that environmental regulators encounter. They do conclude, however, that most of the time regulators encounter "good apples," but the experiences with the "bad apples" tend to sour the experiences for everyone involved. Keith Hawkins (1984) focuses somewhat more on the people with whom inspectors interact, but only insofar as to assert four categories of "images of polluters": socially responsible, unfortunate, careless, and malicious (110–113). According to Hawkins, most of the time, inspectors encounter facility personnel who are socially responsible and are endeavoring to comply with regulations as a matter of principle. Bridget Hutter (1997) builds on existing literature (notably Bardach and Kagan's good and bad apples) by arguing that there are finer distinctions among facilities: poor, reasonable, fairly good, responsible, very good, and exemplary. It is evident from this discussion of the regulated community that misperceptions can, and do, persist about this group of actors.

Misperceptions of the Regulated Community

With the stories of rampant pollution and nefarious companies that are out to harm the environment in the name of profit, it is easy to presume that the regulated community is a malicious group of individuals representing industries that could care less about the environment. From tales of Hooker Chemical Company in Love Canal, New York to Exxon and the Valdez spill to the BP disaster in the Gulf of Mexico, it might seem that these incidents are representative of the regulated community. Indeed, the silver screen is no stranger to such depictions in films like *A Civil Action* or *Erin Brockovich*. However, these portraits of industry are simplistic and, although there are some companies that intentionally harm the environment and defy environmental regulations, they are far from the majority. Indeed, research into the regulated community portrays a far different picture than common perceptions or Hollywood might have us believe. Most members of the regulated community recognize that environmental regulations are important and being good stewards of the environment is good for business (cf. Coglianese and Nash 2001; Hoffman 2001; Kamieniecki 2006).

The persistence of the misperceptions of both regulators and the regulated community can be attributed, in part, to the prevailing narratives about good and bad. Regulation of any kind is rarely popular, yet it prevails because the people want government to protect something or do something. And in such scenarios, there are "good guys" and "bad guys." Depending on your political perspective, the actors that are good and the actors who are bad may vary. But, as we have seen already, reality is never quite that simple. You should be getting a sense from this chapter (and, indeed, the entire text) that environmental protection requires the collaboration and diligence of many groups of people that may seem adversarial on the surface but have to work together to achieve common goals.

REGULATORY INTERACTIONS

Ian Ayers and John Braithwaite (1992) are widely credited with helping shift the conversation about regulations and their implementation with their notion of "responsive regulation." Critical to the implementation of environmental regulations, and contributing to the narratives of good and bad, are the front-line workers and their interactions with each other. Their seminal work, *Responsive Regulation*, helped change the conversation about regulatory enforcement and advance the notion that regulatory encounters are not all the same and often vary—and this is not a bad thing. While such conclusions may seem logical today, the notion that regulatory interactions would be anything other than an authority figure (e.g., the regulator) telling someone (e.g., the regulated community) what to do in a tense situation since it was only through force, or the threat of force, that would compel compliance often dominated. These perceptions, however, still exist about regulation today.

These regulatory encounters are significant in environmental regulation as it is during these encounters and repeated interactions that the actual work of environmental protection happens. At the most basic level, regulators and members of the regulated community are tasked with implementing environmental regulations and ensuring compliance with them, and neither party can do this alone. Individuals at regulated facilities routinely depend on regulators to help interpret regulations and give guidance on new methods for achieving compliance, and regulators rely on the facilities for environmental impact reports and education about the industry, operations of the facility, and the latest technologies and best practices. This interdependence leads Keith Hawkins (1984) to call this relationship "symbiotic" (45). Ultimately, a "substantial amount" of a regulator's time is "spent creating and preserving good relations" with members of the regulated community (Hawkins 1984, 42; see also Pautz and Rinfret 2013). Bridget Hutter (1997) also notes that inspectors and facility personnel "often build up quite a close working relationship" (167).

Exploring the interactions of regulators and members of the regulated community helps us better understand the day-to-day realities of implementing environmental regulations. Typically, the study of these interactions centers on the regulatory style a particular regulator may use, and we can think of these styles as forming the ends of an enforcement spectrum. On one side of the spectrum, a regulator may opt for a compliance-oriented (cf. Hawkins 1984; Reiss 1984) or accommodative approach (cf. Hutter 1988, 1989; Richardson et al. 1983) in which securing compliance with regulations is sought through cooperative or more conciliatory means. In contrast to this approach, the deterrence (cf. Reiss 1984) or sanctioning approach (cf. Hawkins 1984) emphasizes coercion or other more punitive means of achieving compliance. Table 7.3 highlights these different regulatory approaches.

Instead of regulators adopting one of the two approaches in their work implementing environmental regulation, research has demonstrated that regulators employ both approaches in varying combinations, depending on the circumstances, settings, and policy arenas (cf. Braithwaite et al. 1987; Gormley 1998; Hutter 1988, 1989; May and Burby 1998; May and Winter 2000; Scholz and Feng 1986). The different regulatory approaches are determined by a host of factors at the individual, agency, and societal levels (cf. Gormley 1997; Hutter 1989).

This focus on a regulator's enforcement approach does not offer insight into the behavior of the regulated community. Historically, regulatory action (or inaction) was generally explained by individuals pursuing their own self-interests. The interests of the regulatory community are diverse, and their actions may be guided by a plethora of

Table 7.3 Regulatory enforcement approaches

Formal, rule-oriented	*Flexible, results-oriented*
Enforcement approach	*Enforcement approach*
• Focuses on rules	• Understands the perspective of the regulated community
• Emphasis on consistency, regardless of circumstances	• Gives the regulated community the benefit of the doubt
• Tough enforcement	• Uses persuasion instead of threats
• Deterrence as motivation for compliance	• Is flexible as appropriate
• Adversarial posture	• Cooperative

motives, including monetary considerations, job retention or future employment aspirations (the "revolving door" effect), self-gratification, or the desire for tranquility between entities (cf. Gormley 1997; Laffont and Tirole 1991; Levine and Forrence 1990). In contrast to the self-interest perspective, the public interest theory of regulation posits that the ultimate goal of compliance is some measure of public good and, therefore, regulatory actors act to benefit citizens and/or the environment (cf. Joskow and Noll 1981; Viscusi et al. 2005).

More recent research focuses on the factors that compel firms to comply with regulations (cf. Arora and Carson 1996; Haines 1997; Kagan et al. 2003; Prakash 2000). As Peter May (2005) summarizes, the motivations for compliance with regulations generally fit into one of three categories: (1) deterrence or fear of consequences for being found out of compliance, (2) a sense of civic duty and responsibility to be in compliance, and (3) social motivation or pressure to achieve compliance.

These insights are undoubtedly useful; however, they focus on the regulatory actors in isolation and are unable to describe how regulators and the regulated community interact with each other. Eugene Bardach and Robert Kagan (1982/2002) were among the first to explore interactions between actors, but their focus was largely on the nature of the regulations and the approaches the regulators took (e.g., deterrent or accommodative) nearly four decades ago. Their acknowledgment of interactions is more of a digression rather than a focused study, and there is little else to draw on regarding these interactions. Nevertheless, in a variety of settings, from banking and securities to construction and pharmaceuticals, it has been shown that interdependence develops between the regulators and the regulated community (cf. Braithwaite 1984; Hawthorne 2005; May and Wood 2003). In particular, this interdependence breeds strong ties between the regulator and the regulated community (McCaffrey et al. 2007). And some research has shown that environmental regulators do note the collaborative nature of their work and the need to employ varying combinations of both regulatory enforcement approaches depending on the situation and the regulated firm (Pautz and Rinfret 2013). Moreover, with repeated interactions, expectations develop and the relationships between the parties grow, sometimes, into mutual cooperation.

Indeed, some researchers have concluded that cooperation can increase regulatory effectiveness for a host of reasons, including conflict reduction, improved communication, and an increased willingness of parties to work together to achieve a common goal (cf. Bardach and Kagan 1982/2002; Potoski and Prakash 2004; Scholz 1991). However, there are other researchers who maintain that, although cooperation is laudable, it does not necessarily produce better regulatory outcomes (cf. Harrison 1995). The debate over the role of cooperation in regulatory outcomes is far from decided; however, we maintain that cooperation enhances regulatory interactions, which can lead to improved regulatory outcomes.

The takeaway of this section is twofold. First, by considering the interactions of the two parties largely responsible for the day-to-day work of environmental regulation, we understand what environmental protection looks like on the front-lines. And second, we recognize that perceptions of these regulatory interactions may be simplistic and perhaps even wrought with confrontational attitudes, rather than the often collaborative nature of those interactions in reality.

Challenges of Implementing Command and Control Regulations

After unpacking the nature of regulatory interactions, which are at the core of implementing command and control regulations, we explore a number of challenges associated with implementing these regulations, including: (1) politics and competing priorities, (2) federalism, (3) resource constraints, (4) administrative structures and discretion, and (5) concerns of regulatory capture.

Politics and Competing Priorities

As we have seen, environmental policy is both highly technical and highly political. Therefore, political pressures and priorities have a tremendous effect on this policy area, just as they do in many others. Elected leaders set the agenda for legislation and the work of government agencies, so if a president or governor wants to achieve particular objectives, then she will advance those efforts. For example, a governor who wants to rekindle industry in his state may encourage a state environmental agency to deprioritize rigorous inspections to give industry the space to innovate and reinvest in their operations. Or a newly elected president may champion efforts to curb the harmful effects of climate change and direct the US EPA to focus all its activities on achieving those goals. The point is the priorities established through politics can dramatically impact the work of environmental regulations. It is also worth noting that the priorities may be at odds with others, thereby confusing or complicating implementation.

Along these lines, there are less tangible but equally significant factors including the goals and policy objectives of the nation. Recall that the US EPA's mission statement is "to protect human health and the environment" (US EPA About EPA 2011). On the most basic level, there are inherent tensions in such a statement because humans are ultimately responsible for many kinds of environmental damage. Furthermore, environmental concerns are just one of countless areas of focus for the government, and all of those different issues vie for the nation's attention. Quite simply, not all these priorities can be focused on simultaneously and, sometimes, certain priorities—for example, economic recovery or fighting terrorism—crowd out others.

Federalism

Competing priorities and the agendas of politicians can complicate implementation, and that is often exacerbated by the federal structure of government in the United States. Most environmental regulations, as we discussed earlier, are promulgated at the federal level and then delegated to states and, sometimes, even local governments for implementation. The rationale for such an approach is as old as the United States and its desire to keep government close to the people; nevertheless, such a structure can compound difficulties in implementation because multiple organizations have to coordinate among themselves the implementation of environmental protections. Multiple, overlapping agencies become involved in carrying out the same regulations, leading to coordination challenges. As we have discussed elsewhere, the Trump administration has directed the US EPA to cease its efforts related to mitigating the effects of climate change but this has not stopped state, and in some cases local, governments from advancing programs and initiatives to combat climate change in their state or locality. These differing approaches can add to the challenges for the regulated community in trying to abide by an even more complex regulatory thicket. For example, the Regional Greenhouse Gas Initiative (RGGI) is the first cap-and-trade program to reduce carbon dioxide emissions from the power generation sector. The RGGI currently includes states in the northeast and the RGGI has set a cap on carbon dioxide emissions from power plants in the region.

Resource Constraints

It takes a significant amount of resources—both in terms of sheer dollars from government and industry as well as in people and expertise—to implement environmental regulations. At the federal level, those resources are generally under the control of Congress and the White House, as the EPA's budget and personnel have seen periods of significant growth and contraction (see Table 7.4). Trends in agency budgets and personnel help us understand the overall prioritization of the agency's work and reflect the political priorities of elected officials. In federal fiscal year 2017—the first of the Trump administration—the US EPA's enacted budget was about eight billion dollars. In the first budget year that the Trump administration could effect (since the 2017 budget was put into place prior to Trump taking office), the value of the agency has changed dramatically as evidenced by the fact that the president's budget request for the agency is $5.655 billion dollars, representing about a 30% cut from one year to the next (ECOS 2017).

It is important, moreover, to note that the federal government provides much in the way of grants and other resources to state and local agencies; therefore, if the federal government is contracting spending, then, those effects are going to be felt at the subnational level as well. Moreover, state and local governments experience periods of government expansion and contraction.

Administrative Structures and Discretion

There are many factors internal to governmental agencies that affect the implementation of regulations, including bureaucratic processes and structures and the exercise of administrative discretion. Bureaucratic organizations have rigid organizational schemes that can prove less flexible and slower to change than might be ideal for the particular issues the organization confronts. For example, the US EPA and most state environmental protection agencies are still organized largely around pollution areas—air, water (drinking and surface), and waste (hazardous

Table 7.4 US EPA's budget and workforce

Federal fiscal year	Enacted budget	Workforce
FY 2017	$8,058,488,000	15,408
FY 2016	$8,139,887,000	14,779
FY 2015	$8,139,887,000	14,725
FY 2014	$8,200,000,000	15,408
FY 2013	$7,901,104,000	15,913
FY 2012	$8,449,385,000	17,106
FY 2011	$8,682,117,000	17,359
FY 2010	$10,297,864,000	17,278
FY 2009	$7,643,674,000	17,049
FY 2008	$7,472,324,000	16,916
FY 2007	$7,725,130,000	17,072
FY 2006	$7,617,416,000	17,355
FY 2005	$8,023,483,000	17,495
FY 2004	$8,365,420,000	17,611
FY 2003	$8,078,703,000	17,741
FY 2002	$8,078,813,000	17,590
FY 2001	$7,832,211,000	17,558
FY 2000	$7,562,811,000	17,726
FY 1999	$7,590,352,000	18,110
FY 1998	$7,363,046,000	17,739
FY 1997	$6,799,393,000	17,152
FY 1996	$6,522,953,000	17,082
FY 1995	$7,248,412,000	17,508
FY 1994	$6,578,927,000	17,106
FY 1993	$6,861,199,000	17,280
FY 1992	$6,668,853,000	17,010
FY 1991	$6,094,287,000	16,415
FY 1990	$5,461,808,000	16,318
FY 1989	$5,155,125,000	14,370
FY 1988	$5,027,442,000	14,442
FY 1987	$5,364,092,000	13,442
FY 1986	$3,663,841,000	12,892
FY 1985	$4,353,655,000	12,410
FY 1984	$4,067,000,000	11,420
FY 1983	$3,688,688,000	10,832
FY 1982	$3,676,013,000	11,402
FY 1981	$3,030,669,000	12,667
FY 1980	$4,669,415,000	13,078
FY 1979	$5,402,561,000	12,160
FY 1978	$5,498,635,000	11,986
FY 1977	$2,763,745,000	11,315
FY 1976	$771,695,000	9481
FY 1975	$698,835,000	10,438
FY 1974	$518,348,000	9743

(continued)

Table 7.4 (continued)

Federal fiscal year	Enacted budget	Workforce
FY 1973	$2,377,226,000	9077
FY 1972	$2,447,565,000	8358
FY 1971	$1,288,784,000	5744
FY 1970	$1,003,984,000	4084

Source http://www2.epa.gov/planandbudget/budget

and solid). This organizational scheme coincides with the regulatory regime that is built around major pieces of legislation such as the CAA, the CWA, and the Safe Drinking Water Act. Although this arrangement made lots of sense decades ago, it arguably makes less sense today as we have come to understand that environmental issues transcend these traditional boundaries of water, waste, and so forth.

Another significant internal challenge has to do with administrative discretion. Our discussion in this chapter (and also in Chapters 5 and 6) conveys the complexities of taking vague statutory language and translating it into actionable regulations. The steps in the process often remove direct oversight from elected officials. Therefore, governmental administrators are relied upon to ensure successful implementation of the laws without direct oversight. Put differently, when Congress enacts policy, it neither supervises the day-to-day activities of rule-writers in the US EPA or state environmental agencies, nor is Congress out in the field with regulators, ensuring the ongoing compliance with the law.

As a result, these regulators exercise discretion, which has a variety of implications. On the positive side, this discretion allows the expert scientists, engineers, and other civil servants to go about protecting the environment free of the meddlesome nature of Congress. Indeed, Michael Milakovich and George Gordon (2013) remind us that these civil servants are, often, in a better position "to make decisions on the basis of the broader public interest" (94). For example, a regulator may be inspecting a printing facility as part of routine compliance monitoring and she finds one of the collection bins of solvent-soaked rags is uncovered, which is a permit violation. The regulator has discretion about how to respond to the facility's violation. She may elect to immediately write up the facility and suggest to her supervisor that a NOV be issued so the facility is formally reprimanded. Or she may decide that, as the facility is a model for its environmental stewardship, and of the ten bins, only one is uncovered, to simply draw attention to the problem; if the manager immediately sees the error and corrects it, the regulator then only makes a note of the issue in the inspection report. There are plenty of reasons to justify either course of action and the regulator's decision demonstrates administrative discretion. Of course, there is reason to be concerned about the abuse of power that coincides with the exercise of discretion; in the environmental arena, many of these concerns manifest themselves in debate over regulatory capture.

Concerns of Regulatory Capture

A pervasive fear that a regulator will succumb to the regulated community is the essence of capture. More formally, regulatory capture occurs when regulators become beholden to those they attempt to regulate. Furthermore, a regulatory agency or regulator could succumb to the control of outside influences ranging from the community they are responsible for regulating (Bernstein 1955). In the environmental arena, the now-defunct Minerals Management Service in the Department of Interior is thought to have demonstrated some aspects of regulatory capture, which came to light after the Deepwater Horizon spill (at the time of this writing, investigations are still ongoing). Fears of capture permeate all regulatory arenas, not just environmental policy; however, definitive conclusions about its presence remain elusive. Concerns stem from a host of issues, including worries that a regulator will behave a certain way in the hope of securing a job with industry, or concerns that a regulator is simply complacent and ambivalent about the regulatory apparatus he/she is tasked with enforcing, or even that a regulator is sympathetic to industry (cf. Makkai and Braithwaite 1992).

Concerns of regulatory capture are not entirely unfounded; however, "in crude terms, the idea of capture is a dramatic overstatement or even simply inaccurate and also an insult that impugns the integrity of many good people who have spent their careers working for public interest in regulatory agencies" (Cooper 2009, 11). James Q. Wilson (1980) and Paul Quirk (1981), among others, argue that regulatory capture is not common, and Toni Makkai and John Braithwaite (1992) find the presence of regulatory capture to be weak and situational. Stephen Croley (2008) not only refutes regulatory capture, but also points to how well the public interest has been served by regulatory bodies and their regulators. In the context of environmental regulation, we, too, raise doubts that capture should be an overriding concern about regulators. To get a better glimpse of the complexities of regulatory implementation and compliance, the following case study discusses a facility in Dayton, Ohio that has had its ups and downs in implementing environmental regulations.

Regulatory Realities and Clean Water, Limited

Located in Dayton, Ohio, Clean Water, Limited (CWL) is an industrial wastewater processor, which means that the company takes commercial wastewater and processes it before the waste can either sent to a landfill or released back into the sewer and water system. The facility in Dayton has existed for decades and was most recently bought by CWL, although its problems stem from its previous ownership, when the facility was called Perma-fix. Given the nature of its operations, this facility holds a variety of air and water permits, which means it has to deal with state water regulators and local government air regulators (in Ohio, the implementation of air regulations is delegated to local, regional authorities from the state environmental protection agency).

When CWL took over the facility, it inherited a lot of environmental compliance problems, and most of the environmental staff left the company within a year. Therefore, in many ways, the new facility management was starting from scratch, even though it had a litany of compliance problems. To make matters worse, the facility had a poor, long-standing relationship with its neighbors, a mostly residential, minority community. In addition, the new corporate structure of the facility had to contend with enforcement actions from the US EPA.

Many of the compliance issues surrounding this facility are complex and technical. When a facility such as CWL, or any other facility for that matter, wants to make modifications to its operations, it often has to report its intended changes and wait for approval from environmental regulators before moving forward. Although there are a variety of issues concerning the CWL facility, the crux of its problem concerns permit modifications that the facility moved forward with, without first receiving approval to make such changes. Facilities have to wait for approval in order to ensure that their modifications do not affect their environmental footprint or put them into a different category of regulatory requirements. However, CWL did not wait. As is the case in so many operations, the facility needs to do what it does, and delays from government agencies can stymie those operations. More recently, the facility's thermal oxidizer, which is used to filter air emissions, did not work for more than a week, which led to a citation by the US EPA. The thermal oxidizer and its venting system not working properly is releases pollutants into the air and causes noxious fumes for nearby residents.

Up until this point, the story may seem rather ordinary—a facility is getting in trouble for polluting the environment—but what makes this diverge from that plot a bit is the ability of the state environmental regulators assigned to CWL to work together to help get the facility on the path toward compliance. First, the community was outraged by the noxious fumes coming from the facility and lawsuits were filed by angry citizens. The regulators were equally upset with the ongoing compliance issues at the facility and were in search of a solution. In a unique effort, regulators from the Ohio EPA and the local air pollution control agency, the Regional Air Pollution Control Agency (RAPCA), worked together to help get the facility on track toward compliance and educate CWL about its regulatory requirements. These regulators even hosted community meetings in which they met with concerned citizens and officials from CWL to help open communication and rebuild the relationships between all the actors.

Instead of the regulators pursuing a path that simply entailed contentious enforcement activity, the regulators decided a different approach was needed. After all, the ultimate goal is compliance with environmental regulations and NOVs were not fixing the issue. Accordingly, regulators from multiple agencies (Ohio EPA, RAPCA, and Montgomery County public health officials) worked together with the facility and the community to educate all parties and address the ongoing issues at the facility. Although the facility still has challenges and the community is not entirely satisfied, the odors have diminished and appropriate permits are in place and all parties are better able to engage with one another. The cooperation exemplified in this case study helps demonstrate that regulatory interactions do not necessarily have to be confrontational and can be cooperative instead. As we look to the future of environmental regulations, an argument can be made that greater flexibility might allow for enhanced cooperation, which could lead to better regulatory outcomes for everyone involved. The final section of the chapter considers the future of regulation in light of critiques of the traditional command and control structure.

THE NEXT GENERATION OF ENVIRONMENTAL REGULATION

These discussions of the challenges associated with implementing environmental regulations bring up the broader critique of command and control regulations and a consideration of what the future may hold for environmental regulations. Before we can turn to alternative regulatory strategies that might prove advantageous for environmental protection, we must first consider the widespread critiques of command and control regulations in this arena.

Criticisms of Command and Control Regulation

An emerging theme in this chapter (and in conjunction with the history of environmental policy discussed in Chapter 2) is that environmental policy is a product of the time in which it was created. In the 1960s and 1970s, when most of the foundation of environmental policy was established, the rules and regulations that built upon those statutes reflected the times. For example, the environmental laws that responded to specific environmental problems were built around particular facets of the environment, notably air, water, and waste. Accordingly, the environmental laws focused independently on air, water, and waste concerns. Today, however, we have come to understand that environmental issues cannot be tackled independently of one another. Put differently, we cannot continue to deal with air quality issues in isolation without considering water or waste issues because progress in dealing with one particular issue might impact efforts in another area of environmental concern. With this media-specific approach, environmental protection agencies were set up based around environmental media; therefore, regulators become experts in particular areas of environmental concern and the regulated community has to interact with regulators from air, water, and waste (as their operations dictate). These organizational implications are significant and make collaboration across media and organizational boundaries challenging at times.

As we just discussed, the foundational environmental laws did much to address the pollution problems as we understood them decades ago. However, during the intervening years following the establishment of these laws, new scientific information has come to light, and we now better understand environmental issues; however, our existing regulatory structure has trouble keeping up with environmental issues today. For example, much of our regulatory structure is reactive to problems rather than proactive in preventing problems. Regulations have done much to curb pollution, but what about preventing pollution in the first place? Moreover, in the decades since most of these laws were passed, many environmental problems—including climate change and loss of biodiversity—have been identified, and these dated laws struggle to adequately address these contemporary issues.

Another theme that emerges with this regulatory approach is that it stifles innovation and fails to recognize the importance and even necessity of collaboration in environmental protection. As we discussed earlier in this chapter, most command and control regulations do exactly what the name indicates—they tell the regulated community what to do and how to control pollution. These commands may include specific emissions limits or the utilization of a particular pollution control technology. As a result, there is usually little opportunity for the regulated community to innovate and embrace new technologies or processes that might result in better environmental outcomes. Moreover, to devise these regulations, the burden is on the government to figure out the best methods of environmental protection, and there is little formal opportunity for those individuals who work in industry to devise cooperatively broader goals that allow industry to be creative. We have come to see that environmental protection is, frequently, a collaborative endeavor in which government and the regulated community have to work together to protect the environment; however, this regulatory structure can make that difficult, and even outright adversarial (cf. Eisner 2006; Fiorino 2006; Kettl 2002). There are growing calls for the regulatory approach to be more collaborative because environmental protection is achieved not by government alone, but through the partnership of government, the regulated community, and other public interests.

These criticisms of command and control regulations are poignant and significant, and further evidenced in growing discussions about the future of command and control regulation. However, moving away from this structure will be challenging, as the preceding conversation makes clear, and in light of the Trump administration's apparent efforts to dismantle the regulatory structure more broadly. As our study of environmental policy has progressed, we understand the complexities of changing policy in the United States.

The Future of Environmental Regulation

With these criticisms of the traditional command and control approach to environmental regulation, it becomes apparent that serious conversation about a "next-generation" of environmental regulation is needed. The good news is that this conversation is occurring and there are numerous ideas about how the regulatory structure can and should evolve in order to meet twenty-first-century environmental challenges. In the final chapter of this text, we delve into these discussions as we look toward the future of environmental regulation in the United States. Innovative regulatory strategies are already being employed in some contexts and include provisions that allow for market-trading instead of command and control provisions, and more collaborative, systems-based approaches such as environmental management systems are proving useful. But that future remains uncertain as we may be experiencing a fundamental shift in the nation's attitudes to environmental protection more broadly.

CHAPTER WRAP-UP

This chapter has explored how environmental policy is implemented, emphasizing the dominant regulatory tool—command and control regulations. Thousands of pages of regulations enable the implementation of the laws passed by Congress. Implementation also requires an array of regulatory actors—many of who garner little consideration in environmental policy. In particular, the efforts of those individuals on the frontlines of environmental protection, the regulators and the individuals at regulated facilities, are essential. And the interactions between these individuals constitute environmental protection on a daily basis. Scant attention is often paid to these interactions, but here we explore these interactions and discuss the necessity of cooperation among regulatory actors. As expected, there are challenges in implementing environmental regulation and while this regulatory approach has facilitated significant improvement in the nation's environmental health, its critiques are growing louder.

SUGGESTED RESOURCES

Reading and Websites

Durant, Robert F., Daniel J. Fiorino, and Rosemary O'Leary, eds. *Environmental Governance Reconsidered: Challenges, Choices and Opportunities*. 2nd edition. Cambridge: MIT Press, 2017.

Fiorino, Daniel J. *The New Environmental Regulation*. Cambridge: MIT Press, 2006.

Klyza, Christopher McGrory, and David Sousa. *American Environmental Policy: Beyond Gridlock*. Cambridge: MIT Press, 2013.

Mintz, Joel A. *Enforcement at the EPA: High Stakes and Hard Choices*. Revised edition. Austin: University of Texas Press, 2013.

Rechtschaffen, Clifford, and David L. Markell. *Reinventing Environmental Enforcement and the State/Federal Relationship*. Washington, DC: Environmental Law Institute, 2003.

Scheberle, Denise. *Federalism and Environmental Policy: Trust and the Politics of Implementation*. 2nd edition. Washington, DC: Georgetown University Press, 2004.

Films and Videos

A Civil Action. Directed by Steven Zaillian. 1998. Touchstone Pictures, Paramount Pictures, Wildwood Enterprises, Scott Rudin Productions. DVD.

Erin Brockovich. Directed by Steven Soderbergh. 2000. Universal Pictures, Columbia Pictures, Jersey Films. DVD.

War on the EPA. Directed by James Jacoby. 2017. PBS Frontline Documentary.

REFERENCES

Andrews, Richard L. *Managing the Environment, Managing Ourselves: A History of American Environmental Policy*. New Haven, CT: Yale University Press, 2006.

Arora, Seema, and Timothy N. Carson. "Why Do Firms Volunteer to Exceed Environmental Regulations? Understanding Participation in EPA's 33/50 Program." *Land Economics* 74 (1996): 413–432.

Ayers, Ian, and John Braithwaite. *Responsive Regulation: Transcending the Deregulation Debate*. New York: Oxford University Press, 1992.

Bardach, Eugene, and Robert A. Kagan. *Going by the Book: The Problem of Regulatory Unreasonableness*. New Brunswick, NJ: Transaction Publishers, 2002/1982.

Bernstein, Marver. *Regulating Business Through Independent Commission*. Princeton, NJ: Princeton University Press, 1955.

Birkland, Thomas A. *An Introduction to the Policy Process: Theories, Concepts, and Models of Public Policy Making*. Armonk, NY: M.E. Sharpe, 2011.

Blinder, Alan. "Donald Blankenship Sentence to a Year in Prison in Mine Safety Case." *The New York Times*, April 6, 2016. http://nyti.ms/2O7NUCI.

Braithwaite, John. *Corporate Crime in the Pharmaceutical Industry*. Boston: Routledge, 1984.

Braithwaite, John, John Walker, and Peter Grabosky. "An Enforcement Taxonomy of Regulatory Agencies." *Law & Policy* 9 (1987): 323–351.

Coglianese, Cary, and Jennifer Nash. *Regulating from the Inside: Can Environmental Management Systems Achieve Policy Goals?* Washington, DC: Resources for the Future, 2001.

Cooper, Philip J. *The War Against Regulation: From Jimmy Carter to George W. Bush*. Lawrence: University Press of Kansas, 2009.

Croley, Steven P. *Regulation and Public Interests: The Possibility of Good Regulatory Government*. Princeton, NJ: Princeton University Press, 2008.

Davies, J. Clarence, and Jan Mazurek. *Regulating Pollution: Does the U.S. System Work?* Washington, DC: Resources for the Future, 1997.

Dietz, Thomas, and Paul C. Stern. "Exploring New Tools for Environmental Protection." In *New Tools for Environmental Protection: Education, Information, and Voluntary Measures*, edited by Thomas Dietz and Paul C. Stern, 3–15. Washington, DC: National Academy Press, 2002.

Eisner, Marc Allen. *Governing the Environment: The Transformation of Environmental Regulation*. Boulder, CO: Rienner, 2006.

Environmental Council of the States. "Status of State Environmental Agency Budgets (EAB), 2013–2015." Environmental Council of the States, 2017. https://www.ecos.org/wp-content/uploads/2017/03/Budget-Report-FINAL-3_15_17-Final-4.pdf.

Fineman, Stephen. "Street-Level Bureaucrats and the Social Construction of Environmental Control." *Organization Studies* 19, no. 6 (1998): 953–971.

Fiorino, Daniel J. *The New Environmental Regulation*. Cambridge: MIT Press, 2006.

Gormley, William T. "Regulatory Enforcement: Accommodation and Conflict in Four States." *Public Administration Review* 57, no. 4 (July–August 1997): 285–293.

———. "Regulatory Enforcement Styles." *Political Research Quarterly* 51 (1998): 363–383.

Haines, Fiona. *Corporate Regulation, Beyond "Punish or Persuade"*. Oxford: Clarendon Press, 1997.

Harrison, Kathryn. "Is Cooperation the Answer? Canadian Environmental Enforcement in Comparative Context." *Journal of Policy Analysis and Management* 14, no. 2 (Spring 1995): 221–244.

Hawkins, Keith. *Environment and Enforcement: Regulation and the Social Definition of Pollution.* Oxford: Clarendon Press, 1984.

Hawthorne, Fran. *Inside the FDA: The Business and Politics Behind the Drugs We Take and the Food We Eat.* New York: Wiley, 2005.

Hoffman, Andrew J. *From Heresy to Dogma: An Institutional History of Corporate Environmentalism.* Expanded edition. Stanford: Stanford University Press, 2001.

Hutter, Bridget M. *Compliance: Regulation and Environment.* Oxford: Clarendon Press, 1997.

———. *The Reasonable Arm of the Law? The Law Enforcement Procedures of Environmental Health Officers.* Oxford: Clarendon Press, 1988.

———. "Variations in Regulatory Enforcement Styles." *Law & Policy* 11, no. 2 (April 1989): 153–174.

Joskow, Paul L., and Roger G. Noll. "Regulation in Theory and Practice: An Overview." In *Studies in Public Regulation,* edited by Gary Fromm, 1–65. Cambridge: MIT Press, 1981.

Kagan, Robert A., Neil Gunningham, and Dorothy Thornton. "Explaining Corporate Environmental Performance: How Does Regulation Matter?" *Law and Society Review* 37 (2003): 51–90.

Kamieniecki, Sheldon. *Corporate America and Environmental Policy: How Often Does Business Get Its Way?* Stanford: Stanford University Press, 2006.

Kettl, Donald. *Environmental Governance: A Report on the Next Generation of Environmental Policy.* Washington, DC: The Brookings Institution, 2002.

Klyza, Christopher McGrory, and David Sousa. *American Environmental Policy 1990–2006.* Cambridge: MIT Press, 2008.

———. *American Environmental Policy 1990–2006.* Revised and expanded edition. Cambridge: MIT Press, 2013.

Kraft, Michael E. *Environmental Policy and Politics.* 5th edition. New York: Longman, 2011.

Kraft, Michael E., Mark Stephan, and Troy D. Abel. *Coming Clean: Information Disclosure and Environmental Performance.* Cambridge: MIT Press, 2011.

Laffont, Jean-Jacques, and Jean Tirole. "The Politics of Government Decision-Making: A Theory of Regulatory Capture." *The Quarterly Journal of Economics* 106, no. 4 (November 1991): 1089–1127.

Levine, Michael E., and Jennifer L. Forrence. "Regulatory Capture, Public Interest, and the Public Agenda: Toward a Synthesis." *Journal of Law, Economics, & Organization* 6, no. Special Issue (April 1990): 167–1983.

Lipsky, Michael. *Street-Level Bureaucracy: Dilemmas of the Individual in Public Services.* New York: Russell Sage Foundation, 1980.

Lipton, Eric, and Danielle Ivory. "Under Trump, E.P.A. Has Slowed Actions Against Polluters, and Put Limits on Enforcement Officers." *The New York Times*, December 10, 2017. http://nyti.ms/2jDgT4c.

Makkai, Toni, and John Braithwaite. "In and Out of the Revolving Door: Making Sense of Regulatory Capture." *Journal of Public Policy* 12, no. 1 (January–March 1992): 61–78.

May, Peter J. "Compliance Motivations: Perspective of Farmers, Homebuilders, and Marine Facilities." *Law & Policy* 27, no. 2 (April 2005): 318–347.

May, Peter J., and Raymond J. Burby. "Making Sense Out of Regulatory Enforcement." *Law & Policy* 20, no. 2 (April 1998): 157–182.

May, Peter J., and Robert S. Wood. "At the Regulatory Front Lines: Inspectors' Enforcement Styles and Regulatory Compliance." *Journal of Public Administration Research and Theory* 13, no. 2 (2003): 117–139.

May, Peter J., and Søren Winter. "Reconsidering Styles of Regulatory Enforcement: Patterns in Danish Agro-Environmental Inspection." *Law & Policy* 22, no. 2 (April 2000): 143–173.

Maynard-Moody, Steven, and Michael Musheno. *Cops, Teachers, Counselors: Stories from the Front Lines of Public Service*. Ann Arbor: University of Michigan Press, 2003.

McCaffrey, David P., Amy E. Smith, and Ignacio J. Martinez-Moyano. "Then Let's Have a Dialogue: Interdependence and Negotiation in a Cohesive Regulatory System." *Journal of Public Administration Research and Theory* 17, no. 2 (April 2007): 307–334.

Milakovich, Michael E., and George J. Gordon. *Public Administration in America*. New York: Wadsworth, 2013.

Milazzo, Paul Charles. *Unlikely Environmentalists: Congress and Clean Water, 1945–1972*. Lawrence: University Press of Kansas, 2006.

Office of Management and Budget, Office of Information and Regulatory Affairs. "2016 Draft Report to Congress on the Benefits and Costs of Federal Regulations and Agency Compliance with the Unfunded Mandates Reform Act." 2016. Available at https://obamawhitehouse.archives.gov/sites/default/files/omb/assets/legislative_reports/draft_2016_cost_benefit_report_12_14_2016_2.pdf.

Pautz, Michelle C. "Perceptions of the Regulated Community in Environmental Policy: The View from Below." *Review of Policy Research* 26, no. 5 (September 2009): 533–550.

Pautz, Michelle C., and Sara R. Rinfret. *The Lilliputians of Environmental Regulation: The Perspective of State Regulators*. New York: Routledge, 2013.

Potoski, Matthew, and Aseem Prakash. "The Regulation Dilemma: Cooperation and Conflict in Environmental Governance." *Public Administration Review* 64, no. 2 (March/April 2004): 152–163.

Prakash, Asseem. *Greening the Firm*. New York: Cambridge University Press, 2000.

Press, Daniel, and Daniel A. Mazmanian. "Toward Sustainable Production: Finding Workable Strategies for Government and Industry." In *In Environmental Policy: New Directions for the 21st Century*, edited by Norman J. Vig and Michael E. Kraf, 230–254. Washington, DC: CQ Press, 2013.

Pressman, Jeffrey L., and Aaron Wildavsky. *Implementation: How Great Expectations in Washington Are Dashed in Oakland*. Los Angeles: University of California Press, 1984.

Quirk, Paul J. *Industry Influence in Federal Regulatory Agencies*. Princeton, NJ: Princeton University Press, 1981.

Rabe, Barry G. "Permitting, Prevention, and Integration: Lessons from the States." In *Environmental Governance: A Report on the Next Generation of Environmental Policy*, edited by Donald F. Kettl, 14–57. Washington, DC: The Brookings Institution, 2002.

———. "Power to the States: The Promise and Pitfalls of Decentralization." In *Environmental Policy: New Directions for the Twenty-First Century*, edited by Norman J. Vig and Michael E. Kraft, 34–56. Washington, DC: CQ Press, 2006.

Reiss, Jr., Albert J. "Selecting Strategies of Social Control Over Organizational Life." In *Enforcing Regulation*, edited by Keith Hawkins and John M. Thomas. Boston: Kluwer-Nijhoff Publishing, 1984.

Riccucci, Norma M. *How Management Matters: Street-Level Bureaucrats and Welfare Reform*. Washington, DC: Georgetown University Press, 2005.

Richardson, G.M., A.I. Ogus, and P. Burrows. *Policing Pollution: A Study of Regulation and Enforcement*. Oxford: Clarendon Press, 1983.

Rosenbaum, Walter A. *Environmental Politics and Policy*. Washington, DC: CQ Press, 2011.

Scholz, John T. "Cooperative Regulatory Enforcement and the Politics of Administrative Effectiveness." *The American Political Science Review* 85, no. 1 (March 1991): 115–136.

Scholz, John T., and Heng Wei Feng. "Regulatory Enforcement in a Federalist System." *American Political Science Review* 80, no. 4 (December 1986): 1249–1270.

Smith, Kevin B., and Christopher W. Larimer. *The Public Policy Theory Primer*. 2nd edition. Boulder, CO: Westview Press, 2013.

US Environmental Protection Agency, Office of the Inspector General. "Studies Addressing EPA's Organizational Structure." August 26, 2006.

———. "Our Nation's Air." U.S. Environmental Protection Agency, 2017. https://gispub.epa.gov/air/trendsreport/2017/#home.

———. "State NPDES Program Authority." 2018. https://www.epa.gov/sites/production/files/2015-10/documents/state_npdes_prog_auth.pdf.

————. "U.S. EPA Website." 2011. http://www.epa.gov.

————. "Watershed Assessment, Tracking, and Environmental Results." 2015. http://iaspub.epa.gov/waters10/attains_nation_cy.control.

US Government Accountability Office. "Major Management Challenges and Program Risks: Environmental Protection Agency." U.S. Government Accountability Office, 2003.

Viscusi, W. Kip, Joseph E. Harrington, and John M. Vernon. *Economics of Regulation and Antitrust.* 4th edition. Cambridge: MIT Press, 2005.

Wilson, James Q. *The Politics of Regulation.* New York: Basic Books, 1980.

Is It Working? Evaluating Environmental Policy (written by Jeffrey J. Cook)

Contents

From Texas to Washington: Cleaning the Air One City at a Time

In 2017, Houston, Texas had the 16th highest level of particle pollution (e.g., dust and soot) across United States metropolitan areas (American Lung Association 2017). High concentrations of particulates in the air can cause trouble breathing, heart attacks, and premature death. Houston's ranking represents an improvement since tracking began in 1996. However, this improvement has not been uniform across the metropolitan area. Galena Park, Texas is located east of Houston and is a predominately Hispanic and poor community sandwiched between heavily trafficked road, rail, and sea routes that serve the Port of Houston. This traffic generates significant particulate pollution, attributed to diesel exhaust that has exceeded the EPA's standards for annual exposure (Air Alliance Houston 2014).

Matthew Tejada recognized this environmental injustice while working for the Air Alliance Houston, a grassroots organization focused on improving environmental quality in the Houston metro (Goldfarb 2013). The EPA (2018a) defines environmental justice as, "the fair treatment and meaningful involvement of all people regardless of race, color, national origin, or income with respect to the development, implementation, and enforcement of environmental laws, regulations, and policies." To understand the scope of the problem in Galena Park, Tejada helped residents monitor pollution in their community (Goldfarb 2013). Once the community identified the disproportionally poor environmental conditions they experienced, they worked with Tejada to push policy makers to act. This included securing $9 million dollars to repave a deteriorated Clinton Drive, thereby reducing particulate emissions and improving quality of life (Goldfarb 2013).

Ultimately, Tejada played a pivotal role in empowering community members to achieve their environmental objectives, by serving as a bridge between the community and policy makers. As Director of Environmental Justice at the EPA, he serves that role for communities nationwide (EPA 2017a). Since accepting this position in 2013, Tejada has fought for environmental justice communities by incorporating justice considerations into all EPA decisions, securing funding for justice-related projects, and most importantly providing communities the data they need to become their own advocates. From Tejada's perspective "a lot of caring and a little bit of action can go a LONG way in this world to make people's lives and communities better" (EPA 2017a). One of the best ways to spark that interest is providing data to informed citizens.

Tejada's work to assess environmental inequities, identify policy solutions, and apply them is reflective of a broader and vital component of environmental policy, policy analysis, and evaluation. Although Tejada's work is focused on air quality, evaluation is a key aspect of all environmental policy from waste management to energy production. The goal is to determine how the policy works and most importantly how it can be improved to achieve objectives more effectively. No two people may come to an agreement on what constitutes "effective" and this is an ongoing challenge. This chapter's focus is on how scholars and practitioners assess the performance of environmental policy in the twenty-first century.

POLICY ANALYSIS AND EVALUATION

Policymakers and practitioners have regularly assessed the effectiveness of all major environmental laws to ensure that they are achieving their goals, whether it is clean air, water, or environmental justice. As a result, an entire field—policy analysis—has been dedicated to the evaluation of policy (Dunn 2008; Lasswell 1971; Quade 1989). Although definitions of policy analysis vary, for the purpose of this chapter, we suggest policy evaluation is simply the act of critically examining a policy, or as Michael Kraft and Scott Furlong (2013) succinctly suggest, "[a]nalysis means deconstructing an object of study–that is, breaking it down into basic elements to understand it better" (8).

Policy evaluation is a profession conducted by policy analysts or program evaluators. These individuals have varying skills, expertise, and educational backgrounds depending upon the policy they study (Bardach 2004). More specifically, in the environmental arena, policy analysts may have backgrounds in biology, ecology, political science, economics, or sociology, among other fields. In addition, policy analysts are employed by consulting firms, private corporations, public agencies, trade associations, and a host of other entities.

Just as these analysts' backgrounds may differ, the types of policy evaluation they conduct can also vary. For example, an analyst could take a macro approach to evaluate the cost and benefit of all environmental regulation published by the EPA, which means that this analyst would examine each air, water, and land regulation's impact on overall environmental quality in the United States. In turn, an analyst might approach the evaluation of environmental regulation through a micro lens. Here, an analyst might evaluate the impact of one regulation to measure its impact in relation to costs. For instance, under this guise, a policy evaluator could examine the EPA's regulation of greenhouse gas (GHG) emissions from passenger vehicles and light trucks to assess its impact on climate change. The purpose of this brief comparison is to illustrate that policy analysts have a variety of approaches at their disposal to assess environmental policy, which is the focus of this chapter.

Accordingly, this chapter begins with a discussion of why policy evaluation is necessary, the theoretical underpinnings that structure its processes, and a discussion of how it occurs in practice. Second, we address some of the issues associated with how policy evaluation is employed and the difficulties of examining one evaluative criterion: environmental justice. Third, we provide an assessment of the overall record of environmental policy in achieving environmental outcomes to date, and what is needed to improve these assessments for the future. Lastly, the chapter concludes with a discussion of the evolution of coal ash policy and the role environmental justice played in shaping this arena.

The goal of this chapter is to provide a basic understanding of the promise and pitfalls of policy evaluation within an environmental context. Therefore, after reading this chapter, the reader should be able to take away a few important lessons. The first lesson is that policy evaluation or analysis is essential to understanding if environmental laws or policies are indeed, working. Making this determination is not without its challenges, given that stakeholders may view the goals and related performance of programs differently. This challenge is like those associated with problem definition as outlined in Chapter 2. If a given policy is "working," the second lesson is for policymakers and the public to pay attention to how benefits are distributed. Cases of environmental justice demonstrate that it may not be enough to show improved national outcomes when local conditions may stagnate or decline. Third, policy analysis often names winners or losers—and those pronouncements have consequences. Therefore, we need to pay attention to who is conducting the evaluation or who is funding it.

THE PURPOSE OF POLICY EVALUATION

Environmental policy can be costly, and how programs are implemented and achieve their goals is important to understand. Although there is significant agreement that environmental policy should be evaluated frequently, there is far less agreement on the best approach to evaluate these policies. For instance, there is some acceptance of the US Government Accountability Office (GAO) and the National Academy of Sciences (NAS) assessments of policy as sources of unbiased and accurate analyses: however, these are not the only entities that provide policy evaluation

(Kraft 2018, 272–277). There is a whole host of other federal agencies, think tanks, trade associations, environmental interests, and other entities that provide policy evaluations, and the results of these analyses can vary.

For example, when the EPA developed its GHG emission regulations for passenger vehicles and light trucks from 2017–2025, the agency found the regulation's benefits outweighed the costs by more than $450 billion dollars (EPA 2012). As a result, the EPA argued that the rule-making was justified to improve environmental quality. Other organizations have conducted their own analyses of EPA regulations, and come to varying conclusions. Analysts at the Council on Foreign Relations (2015) have argued that current vehicle regulations actually provide more benefits than the EPA suggested, despite lower oil prices. In comparison, the U.S. Chamber of Commerce (2014), a business trade association, concluded that the cost of passenger vehicle regulation exceeds total benefits by nearly $10 billion.

Some of the difference in the assessments of passenger vehicle regulations could be the result of a biased policy evaluator—the analyst responsible for conducting the evaluation. However, any policy analyst will tell you, the goal is for an analyst to remain value-neutral and not to insert biases into the evaluation of the policy or program. More specifically, a policy analyst is not supposed to inject their values or beliefs into the analysis. This allows the evaluator to provide an evidence-based policy analysis that includes all relevant factors so that policymakers can make changes or modifications based upon that objective information (Dunn 2008).

It is more likely that the aforementioned differences in policy evaluation actually stem from variation in policy evaluation design. The act of policy evaluation is not simple (Dunn 2008; Lindblom 1959, 1979; Ostrom 1990; Rhoads 1985; Weimer and Vining 2011). Policy analysts do not have unlimited resources to acquire data regarding a policy problem; thus, they cannot identify all the factors that impact a program or policy (Weimer and Vining 2011). Accordingly, how an evaluator structures analyses may elevate some priorities over others based upon necessity, or blatant or latent political, ideological, or ethical grounds (Dunn 2008). Finally, the supporter of the evaluation (the person funding the project) may also sway the overall outcome of the analysis based upon his own values (Bardach 2004; Weimer and Vining 2011). For instance, if a member of city council, who believes renewable energy is costly and unreliable, pays a private firm with an interest in fossil-fuels to conduct an evaluation of a community's 100% renewable energy program it is possible the results from this evaluation will support his original perspective. Despite these challenges, the overall goal of these and other policy evaluations is to suggest that a policy or program is either working, should be improved, or is no longer needed (Dunn 2008).

THE STAGES OF POLICY EVALUATION

Although judgments may be superimposed on evaluations, analysts follow a set process that is designed to help standardize analyses. This process includes (see Fig. 8.1): (1) identifying policy or program goals, (2) selecting evaluative criteria, (3) producing recommendations, and (4) disseminating the final product (Bardach 2004; Weimer and Vining 2011). Evaluators' decisions at each step in the process can influence the

Fig. 8.1   Stages of policy evaluation

results and this section provides an overview of what occurs within each stage.

First, policy evaluation begins by identifying the original intent of the policy or program (Bardach 2004). At this stage in the process, policy analysts examine the specific goals of the policy or program. Let us assume the city of Burlington, Vermont has implemented a program to achieve 100% renewable energy consumption citywide and the city's stated goal of the program was to provide residents and businesses with clean, reliable, and low-cost renewable electricity. After an analyst has confirmed the goals of a given policy, the analyst then must determine what happened after the policy was adopted. Simply stated, what are the outcomes of the program? For our Burlington example, the evaluator might compare how much electricity is served by renewable energy sources after the program was implemented versus before the program. The evaluator might also review how the cost of electricity compares to previous rates with lower renewable energy content or improvements in public health resulting from lower electricity-related emissions.

In order to determine whether the outcomes of the program actually achieved the goals of the program, an analyst may use a number of evaluative criteria—effectiveness, efficiency, equity, responsiveness, and appropriateness—which drive the second stage of the process (Bardach 2004; Dunn 2008). Each one of these criteria answers a different question regarding how well a policy is achieving its goals. First, effectiveness assesses whether a program has resulted in a valued outcome; basically, has the policy worked, and in our example, does the city consume 100% renewable electricity? The efficiency criterion evaluates how much effort, or, commonly, how much money was required to achieve a valued outcome. For Burlington, the city might be interested in how electricity costs differ as compared to before they implemented the 100% renewable program. Are costs comparable or lower than what the city used to pay for fossil fuel-generated electricity? Equity assesses how the desired outcomes are distributed between groups (e.g., do impacts vary by race, gender, income group). Here, Burlington policymakers may be interested in how differences in electricity rates benefit or harm certain constituents based on income. Responsiveness, then, determines whether the valued outcomes are actually valued by the public.

More succinctly, does the public want their electricity to come from renewable energy? Finally, appropriateness is related to responsiveness in some ways, as it assesses whether the objectives or valued outcomes are, in fact, useful or important (Dunn 2008). In short, is low-cost, clean electricity good for the city? Each of the evaluative criteria is often referred to as the lifeblood of policy evaluation, which will be discussed in more detail in the next section of this chapter (Kraft and Furlong 2013).

The result of applying these evaluative criteria to a policy is analyzed to understand the overall impact of that action and next steps. This is where the third stage, policy recommendations, comes in. Policy analysts provide pros and cons associated with a policy. Our policy analysts in Burlington, Vermont might suggest the program achieved its objective of achieving 100% renewable energy consumption, with some additional cost than would have occurred absent the policy. They may find that this negatively affects low-income residents who pay disproportionally more on energy bills than more affluent residents. They might also suggest developing a new fund, paid by all electricity customers to help offset low-income resident's energy bills. However, it is up to local policymakers to determine the best course of action based upon the evidence provided by policy analysts. Therefore, at this stage, policymakers may take this information and adjust, terminate, or continue to support the policy or program (Bardach 2004; Dunn 2008).

The overall goal of policy evaluation is an assessment of how well various laws, regulations, and programs are achieving the objectives set out by their architects (such as legislators and rule-writers). Thus, if policy analysts determine that a policy or program is not achieving the valued outcomes, or simply that the problem does not exist anymore, it is up to analysts to disseminate that information to policymakers and the public. Policymakers can take this information and use it to redirect resources towards other problems. As a result, evaluation is critically important in the policymaking process in assessing how well programs achieve their objectives, but it is critical that the evaluation is credible. Overall, policy analysis is not a strictly scientific field, and value judgments can permeate the process. These value judgments are often most pronounced in the selection and application of evaluative criteria. The next section outlines the methods used by evaluators to apply these criteria and the controversies that can occur.

EVALUATIVE CRITERIA: THE LIFE BLOOD OF POLICY EVALUATION

In theory, policy analysts would apply all the available evaluative criteria (effectiveness, efficiency, equity, responsiveness, and appropriateness) to a policy (Weimer and Vining 2011). However, evaluators are constrained with the type of analysis they can conduct due to limits on time and resources. We spend the following pages examining the pros and cons associated with the most frequently applied evaluative criteria—effectiveness, efficiency and equity (Bardach 2004; Weimer and Vining 2011).

Assessing Effectiveness and Efficiency

Of all the available criteria, effectiveness is, often, the most straightforward. Recall that the effectiveness criterion is used to determine whether a policy has achieved the intended outcome. As a new example, a policy analyst might evaluate the performance of the Clean Water Act (CWA) by assessing its effectiveness in improving water quality. The analyst could evaluate pollutant levels, such as heavy metal content, and track improvement over time. However, the effectiveness criteria may not always be so straightforward. One could attempt to assess the effectiveness of the CWA in improving ecosystem health, where the outcomes of the program are much more difficult to determine. This is because scientists and practitioners have not agreed upon metrics to determine the health of ecosystems (Kraft 2018, 273).

By way of comparison, no criterion has been subject to more controversy than the efficiency criterion. This controversy generally revolves around how benefits of environmental programs are quantified. The cost of environmental programs can be high, and these expenses are generally easy to add up. For example, the cost to purchase and install pollution control equipment and the cost of managing and operating that equipment are usually easy to locate, record, and forecast into the future. In some cases, virtually anyone with an Internet connection, and a significant amount of free time could come up with these costs. However, assessing, compiling, and quantifying benefits of environmental programs are far more complex. As a result, practitioners use several methods to determine these benefits and compare them to costs, with the two most common methods—Cost-Effectiveness Analysis (CEA) and Cost-Benefit Analysis (CBA) (Weimer and Vining 2011). Table 8.1 offers a comparison of the two different approaches.

Table 8.1   Comparing cost-effectiveness and cost-benefit analyses

Cost-effectiveness analysis characteristics	Cost-benefit analysis characteristics
• Used infrequently in environmental policy • Comparison between cost and effectiveness • Useful when used to compare competing policies or programs • Typically used for transportation or criminal justice policy analysis	• Used frequently in environmental policy • Comparison between costs and benefits across all policies or programs • Can be controversial due to scientific uncertainties • Difficult to use as a single measurement to determine the effectiveness of a program

Typically, a CEA compares monetary cost against effectiveness in achieving a given outcome (Boardman et al. 2018). For example, what is the cost of adding a new pollution control technology to a facility, and how does this compare to the benefit accrued in terms of reduced pollution from that technology? If evaluators have this information, they can provide a per unit ratio of costs to benefits. This is useful when, for instance, comparing one specific pollution abatement technology with another. Typically, this type of analysis has been employed for criminal justice, transportation, health, and defense policy (Dunn 2008). However, the common criticism of CEAs is the inability of analysts to compare across policy areas because the metrics and ratios are inherently different because they are using different units of measure (Boardman et al. 2018).

In comparison, CBA is the most common method to evaluate policy within the environmental policy arena. For instance, administrative agencies must employ CBA as a component of their Regulatory Impact Assessments (RIAs) for all significant rules. This is because CBA has been mandated by policymakers (mostly, presidents) because it provides analysts with the ability to evaluate *all* costs and benefits within one common unit of value—the dollar (Boardman et al. 2018). The goal of CBA is to determine if a program is providing a net benefit to society.

Because CBA is such an integral component of governmental policy evaluations, it is relevant to discuss how it is conducted. CBA unfolds throughout five stages: (1) identifying the costs and benefits of a program, (2) applying values to those benefits and costs, (3) discounting those values to present dollars, (4) conducting sensitivity analyses on the data, and (5) subtracting costs from benefits to determine the benefits to society. Although it seems straightforward, each step is complex and fraught with uncertainty.

The uncertainty starts at the outset of the process when analysts must determine all the costs and benefits of a program. As one might think, this is difficult to do in practice, but scholars have outlined a structure to determine these values. First, evaluators must set boundaries around a problem area, or what a program does, and who it affects (Boardman et al. 2018). Then, analysts determine what the internal and external costs are of a given program, along with the external costs and benefits. Internal costs and benefits refer to those that are included within the market setting (e.g., cost of a program's implementation). External costs and benefits then refer to those values that are not included in the internal costs; these can be either negative harms or positive benefits to society that are not accounted for in the market price (Dunn 2008). These negative external costs are often present in the environmental arena, as air, water, and land pollution impacts.

After determining what costs and benefits exist both internally and externally, analysts must determine which are directly and indirectly measurable. More specifically, directly measurable values refer to the tangible costs and benefits that have a market price (e.g., pollution control equipment), whereas indirectly measurable values are those that are intangible and do not have a definitive market price (e.g., clean air; see Dunn 2008).

One presumption in the preceding discussion is that an analyst can make several assumptions during a CBA that could lead to significant differences in determining the efficiency of a program. This may help explain why the Council on Foreign Relations, EPA, and the U.S. Chamber of Commerce-supported analyses provided such varied results on the cost and benefits of vehicle emission regulations. In the context of environmental regulation, analyst decisions relating to the benefit from lives saved, GHG emissions avoided, and the inclusion of co-benefits often contribute to the dramatic differences in CBAs. The following pages provide a snapshot of the controversies that are associated with these components of a CBA.

Environmental regulation can save lives, by reducing citizen exposure to hazardous pollution. Though this much is clear, policy analysts have struggled to quantify this value for inclusion in CBA. A variety of methods have been proposed to monetize lives. The two most common methods are the Value of Statistical Life Years Saved (VSLYS) and Quality-Adjusted Life Years (QALY). These methods are similar. The VSLYS method places a value on 1 year of life and multiples that by the number of life years saved. The QALY method is similar to the VSLYS, but makes one adjustment—value is placed upon how old the individual is, as a younger individual would likely have more quality life years left than an elderly person (Cooney 2003). After the Bush Administration was criticized for briefly applying the QALY method, nicknamed the "senior death discount" (Cooney 2003; Seelye and Tierney 2003), the administration returned to using the VSLYS, but controversy around the value of a life saved has persisted. While the Bush administration was ridiculed for reducing the value of a human life and thereby the benefits of regulation, the Obama administration was criticized for increasing it (Appelbaum 2011; Bastasch 2016). Regardless, the decisions made applying VSLYS have significant impacts on overall costs and benefits and can go unnoticed absent careful review of a CBA's methodology.

Regardless, if all environmental CBA's quantify lives saved, incorporating the benefit of avoided GHG emissions may not be universal. The analyst, and more likely the funder, must believe that climate change is a real environmental problem that negatively effects the public before including it in a CBA. If, as in most cases, the benefit of avoided GHG emissions is included, policy analysts must still determine how to value these avoided emissions. In 2010, the Obama Administration introduced the social cost of carbon (SCC) as the means for agencies to quantify the climate change benefit of regulatory actions (Interagency Working Group on Social Cost of Carbon 2010). The SCC offered a range of costs that could be incorporated into CBAs and the Obama administration periodically updated, and increased, the SCC. The administration defended these increases, arguing that the costs of climate change were increasing (Cook and Rinfret 2013; Interagency Working Group on Social Cost of Greenhouse Gases 2016).

When the Trump administration entered office they reduced the SCC from an inflation-adjusted $45 per ton in 2020 to between $1 and $6 per ton in 2020 (Mooney 2017). The Trump administration supported the move, arguing that the Obama era SCC estimated global climate benefits associated with regulatory actions, rather than domestic impacts. This may seem reasonable for assessing the costs and benefits of domestic programs, but others contend that climate change is a global problem. Depending on which metric is used, the benefit of regulations that reduce GHG emissions vary substantially.

In addition to considering the benefit of avoided GHG emissions, policy analysts might also include co-benefits in their CBA. Co-benefits, in the environmental context, refer to benefits from the reduction of pollutants not directly subject to regulation that will also decline from the application of certain control technologies. The controversy surrounding this variable in a CBA is best illustrated by the EPA's adoption of the Mercury and Air Toxic Standards (MATS) for power plants in 2011. The EPA argued that the MATS would result in $90 billion in annual benefits, as compared to $10 billion in costs (*The Economist* 2012). The clear majority of these benefits are not associated with reducing mercury, which was the subject of the regulation, but rather associated with reduced particulate matter. Critics of the MATS have argued that the efficiency of the regulation designed to reduce mercury, should not be based on the value generated from the co-benefits of the action. Assessing the rule in this context, may suggest it provides more costs than benefits. Others might argue that the goal of the rule is to improve environmental quality, and as such co-benefits including reductions in particulate matter should be included. The Obama administration believed this, but the Trump administration did not. In fact, the agency, in 2018, is reconsidering MATS. However, most facilities have already installed technology necessary for compliance with the Obama standards (Walton 2017).

These three examples demonstrate that quantifying benefits is not a simple task, nor is it apolitical. Fundamentally, policy analysts need to decide what benefits to include and a metric to quantify them. These questions can be philosophical, as they deal with individual values and ethics, making it difficult for bureaucrats—or anyone, for that matter—to agree on a standardized value. Given this challenge, most policy analysts attempt to incorporate a range of values to subsequently provide a range of benefits. Even so, two well-meaning policy analysts may produce widely different CBA results. Scholars are aware of this challenge and thus argue that CBA alone should not be used to determine whether an individual policy is useful or valuable (Boardman et al. 2018; Kraft 2018; Weimer and Vining 2011; Olmstead 2018).

Assessing Equity

Effectiveness and efficiency are the two most common criteria to assess environmental policy; however, the incorporation of equity has become more prevalent, and we turn to examples of environmental justice to understand why. Much like efficiency, this criterion is subject to significant controversy. Overall, the argument is that the benefits of environmental policy decisions as well as the harms should be evenly distributed across society.

Consideration of environmental fairness and justice concerns came about in the 1980s amidst protest by a predominantly African-American community in Warren County, North Carolina, which was designated for a hazardous waste landfill. The National Association for the Advancement of Colored People (NAACP) held a protest against the designation, and it garnered significant media attention when 500 individuals were arrested (Department of Energy 2013). This protest, along with others, led politicians to request a report from the GAO to determine if low-income and minority communities were disproportionately targeted for these facilities. The GAO found that three of the four hazardous waste landfills it analyzed were sited in minority communities, and all four were sited in locations where at least 26% of the population was below the poverty line (GAO 1983). Several other studies in the 1980s and early 1990s confirmed these results: the poor and minorities are more likely to have increased rates of exposure to toxic chemicals and other environmental harms (Bryant and Mohai 1992; Hill 2009; UCC 1987; US EPA 1992).

As a result, in 1994, President Clinton issued Executive Order 12898 titled *Federal Actions to Address Environmental Justice in Minority Populations and Low-Income Populations.* Executive Order 12898 required that each:

> federal agency shall make achieving environmental justice part of its mission by identifying and addressing, as appropriate, disproportionately high and adverse human health or environmental effects of its programs, policies, and activities on minority populations and low-income populations in the United States.

This Executive Order put the EPA in charge of overseeing the implementation of this directive. As noted, the EPA has subsequently defined environmental justice as "the fair treatment and meaningful involvement of all people regardless of race, color, national origin, or income with respect to the development, implementation, and enforcement of environmental laws, regulations, and policies" (EPA 2018a). Ultimately, the Office of Environmental Justice within the EPA is in charge of integrating these principles into the operations of the agency.

Though environmental justice has had a home at the EPA since the 1990s, the GAO published a report in 2011 suggesting that the EPA should do more to address environmental justice concerns when creating rules. More specifically, the GAO (2011) recommended that the agency develop a strategy to define key terms in order to establish a "consistent and transparent approach for identifying potential communities with environmental justice concerns" (32). Furthermore, the GAO (2011) suggested that the EPA needed to assess the resources needed to carry out its goals, and it needed to develop a plan for how the agency will measure its performance in achieving those goals.

After the publication of the report, the EPA issued Plan EJ 2014, which the agency considered a roadmap to integrating environmental justice into the activities of the agency. The goals of the plan were to protect health in communities overburdened by pollution, empower community residents to take action to improve their health and environment, and to establish partnerships with local, state, tribal, and federal agencies to achieve healthy and sustainable communities (EPA 2013). In line with the goals of this plan, the EPA launched EJSCREEN in 2015 a web-based tool that identifies areas with minority and low-income populations, along with environmental quality issues that are greater than usual. The tool is a common starting point to identify potential environmental justice communities, build community awareness, and prioritize communities for targeted policy and programs to resolve injustices. The tool is a key component of the EPA's (2016a) newest EJ 2020 vision to improve on-the-ground results for environmental justice communities.

Despite the development of this strategy, how environmental justice is assessed is problematic because it has not been adequately explained. For example, there is likely to be some variation in the distribution of benefits and harms. The EPA and other federal agencies have not answered this question making it difficult for policy analysts to incorporate a standardized metric into their analyses. Even so, the development of EJSCREEN is likely to increase citizen awareness of environmental justice communities and subsequent calls for including an analysis of equity in policy evaluation going forward.

EVALUATING PROGRAMS AND ACHIEVING GOALS

As indicated throughout this chapter, most evaluations assess specific aspects rather than a holistic discussion of the environment. More specifically, analysts have evaluated the effectiveness of implementing laws like the Clean Air Act (CAA), the CWA, and the Endangered Species Act (ESA) to provide some insight into how the United States is doing in achieving its most important environmental goals. Thus, in this section, we provide a brief overview of how the nation is doing in achieving these goals.

We begin with a discussion of the implementation of the CAA. Since the law was enacted in 1970, the six most common air pollutants including particulate matter, sulfur dioxide, nitrogen oxides, volatile organic compounds, carbon monoxide, and lead have dropped 71% (EPA 2016b). Meanwhile, gross domestic product, a metric of economic growth, has increased 246% and population has increased 57%. Despite these impressive improvements, GHG emissions have increased 28% (EPA 2016b). During the Obama administration, the EPA took steps to address these emissions. Subsequently, the Trump administration has dialed back regulation including the aforementioned GHG regulations from passenger vehicles (Eilperin and Dennis 2018), which may result in higher GHG emissions and more damaging climate change impacts.

The EPA has been less successful in implementing the water quality goals of the CWA. This is in part because water pollution is generated by a wide variety of sources. For example, the nutrients from misapplied lawn fertilizers can run-off and pollute waterways after rain events. Though this pollution may be negligible on a per home basis, collectively it can result in dead zones in rivers and streams. For example, nutrient pollution from the Mississippi River has resulted in an estimated 9000 square mile dead zone in the Gulf of Mexico (Smith 2017). Even so, regulating homeowner's lawn care practices may not be practical, which will impact agency performance on improving water quality. Overall, the EPA (2017b) concludes that 46% of rivers and streams are in poor biological condition. In comparison, 32% of wetlands, 21% of lakes, and 18% of coastal waters are in poor condition. Although there has been improvement in these numbers over time, emerging challenges in urban water pollution and drinking water quality are rising as exemplified by lead-poisoning in Flint, Michigan (Vig and Kraft 2018).

In addition to air and water quality, land protection is also an important area for investigation. The assessment of improved land quality has historically been based on the amount of land that has been set aside for protection (WSTB 2004). Under this measure, the United States has been quite successful. Land set aside for national parks, wilderness areas, and the national wildlife refuge system has increased since the 1970s (Kraft and Vig 2013). However, this is an insufficient metric to determine the value of natural resource conservation (Jenkins et al. 2015). Jenkins et al. (2015) map conserved land to areas of threatened biodiversity and conclude that the United States is not protecting the land, predominantly in the southeast, where biodiversity is most threatened. Therefore, more may need to be done to protect unique land.

Accordingly, what may be more indicative of US protection of natural resources is an assessment of US efforts to protect endangered species and biodiversity under the ESA. The U.S. Fish and Wildlife Service (USFWS 2016), which implements the ESA, listed 1478 species as endangered (1171) or threatened (307). First, many species that were listed at the inception of the program are still on the list and since its last biennial report the agency has added 141 additional species. In addition, the USFWS has conducted five-year reviews on 1099 listed species and concluded that 92% had no change in status, 4% could be delisted from endangered to threatened, and 2% could be delisted (USFWS 2016). Delisting may be considered a success. However, half of these species were recommended for delisting because of extinction. In short, policy evaluators should assess these numbers differently. One could argue that the program has been a success in avoiding species extinction, given 4% of species have been delisted from endangered to threatened, and a few species have been delisted from threatened. Another could argue that the results are more mixed given that the law has done nothing to improve the status of 92% of species, and some have gone extinct.

Ultimately, policy analysts can come to different conclusions regarding environmental policy effectiveness in reducing air, land, and water pollution. Perhaps, an even stronger argument can be made regarding whether they have been efficient. Although the United States has reduced air pollution, scholars argue that these environmental benefits, associated predominately with command and control regulation, may have come at a much higher cost than necessary (Portney 1994; Freeman 2006; Fiorino 2009; Olmstead 2018).

POLICY EVALUATION IN THE TWENTY-FIRST CENTURY

This chapter has defined and documented the various pros and cons associated with policy evaluation, the tools or methods associated with it, and overall environmental performance. However, for the future of environmental policy, policy evaluation must improve. First, a fundamental component of environmental policy evaluation is efficiency. CBA is often used to examine this element, and this chapter has demonstrated that policy analysts can come to widely different conclusions about the efficiency of programs using this tool. One factor of this variation is the lack of agreed-upon environmental indicators or cost and benefit values for ecological services. This disagreement sheds doubt on the objectivity of the field. To solve this problem, researchers have diligently attempted to identify and quantify environmental benefits. If these values can be developed, and agreed upon, policy evaluation's most controversial component, the CBA, may actually be the objective tool its supporters suggest it is. Though these efforts could be valuable, it is important to bound optimism. Having accurate and consistent costs and benefits may not be enough to push policymakers to act. For example, a Cornell study suggested that pollinators, including bumblebees, contributed $29 billion to the US economy in 2010 (Ramanujan 2012). Yet, in 2016 one third of the nation's honeybee colonies died (Rossman 2017) and wild pollinator populations declined worldwide (Schwartz 2016). Having a better understanding of the value of pollinators did not result in a subsequent policy designed to protect these species. Ultimately, policy evaluation may show significant *societal* benefits of action, but policymakers will still need to be convinced that these benefits outweigh near-term likely negative impacts on constituents.

Second, most policy evaluation is conducted in a media-specific, piecemeal fashion. For example, policy evaluators might argue that emission control equipment at power plants is quite successful in reducing heavy metal concentrations released to the air because they are precipitated out as physical waste. The evaluation typically ends there and does not consider the impacts associated with that physical waste. If poorly handled, this waste may have more significant, negative impacts on land and water quality. This problem is in part a function of the media-specific legislative design of the environmental policy framework in the United States. The focus of each law is on reducing pollution from the air, land, OR water and not necessarily all three (Bryner and Duffy 2012). The problem then is that individual policy evaluations might show an improvement, but a holistic analysis may not. Solving this problem may require legislative action and there are some efforts to integrate policies in the United States (Duffy and Cook 2018). Additional research evaluating the performance of these integrated policies and comparing that performance to typical media-specific approaches is essential to provide more holistic assessments of environmental policy performance.

Finally, if environmental justice is going to become an integral evaluative tool in terms of assessing environmental policy, it is critical that experts come to a consensus on what environmental justice means and when a community is subjected to an injustice. If a community has been disproportionally impacted, decision-makers then need to clarify how to act upon this finding. Should certain facilities be prohibited from locating in environmental justice communities and rather be in more affluent communities? What economic impacts might this have on environmental justice communities that already may lack economic growth opportunities? Alternatively, should more affluent communities compensate environmental justice communities for the additional harm they are subjected too? Answering these questions requires quantifying the cost of environmental injustices, which will face similar challenges to those debated in the efficiency arena. Inevitably, there are real environmental justice concerns and our chapter's case study makes this point.

Understanding Environmental Justice: Lessons for the Future
As noted, poor and minority communities are more likely to be exposed to environmental harms than affluent, white communities. Environmental justice advocates have long argued this is because these communities have been targeted for the siting of significant polluters. For these individuals, policy should be adopted to correct these imbalances. Meanwhile, others have contended that these injustices have not resulted from vindictive actions. Rather, the poor and minorities have chosen to locate in areas near these pollution sources because they offer lower costs of living. From this perspective, no policy change is necessary, because the poor and minorities willingly moved to these locations. This disagreement has persisted for decades because there was limited research into environmental justice claims and variation in methodological assumptions resulted in conflicting conclusions (Niles and Lubell 2012; Mohai and Saha 2015).

In 2015, Mohai and Saha conducted a seminal, nationwide study of commercial hazardous waste facilities sited from 1966–1995 to address this debate. They show that new hazardous waste facilities were located in areas that already had higher concentrations of poor and minority communities. These concentrations then increased after these facilities located in the community. The authors argue that this shows a pattern of commercial facilities searching for the path of least resistance, when siting new facilities. The goal of these companies is to find communities that are less likely to generate a protracted battle to receive approval and construct the facility. For these scholars, this explains why minority communities compose more than 50% of all people living within 3 kilometers of a hazardous waste facility. These conclusions support the perspective of environmental justice advocates that the poor and minorities have been targeted for these facilities and have thus been disproportionally impacted by environmental harms. However, Mohai and Saha's research will need to be validated and confirmed by other scholars before this debate is settled.

Ultimately, Mohai and Saha (2015) evaluated one potential industry that has generated environmental justice concerns surrounding coal ash. Coal ash is generated from burning coal for electricity production. According to the EPA (2018b), coal ash is one of the largest sources of industrial waste with over 110 million tons of ash produced in 2012. About half of this ash is beneficially reused as a strengthening agent in cement for roads and bridges, while the other half is often laced with heavy metals (e.g., arsenic, mercury, and selenium) and is stored in large shallow ponds near coal plants (Dilts 2014). These ponds went largely unnoticed until December 22, 2008 when a dike failed at the Tennessee Valley Authority's Kingston coal-fired power plant. This failure released 5.4 million cubic yards of toxic coal ash into the nearby Emory and Clinch River's in Tennessee (Gang 2013). TVA spent $1 billion to clean up the ash, buy impacted property, develop new parks, and monitor wildlife (Gang 2013). In addition, TVA stopped holding coal ash in ponds on-site and began transporting it to a landfill in Alabama.

Though the Kingston spill spurred concern, policy change was slow to follow. After this spill, 200 coal ash sites were associated with subsequent air and water pollution including the Dan River spill in 2014 where 27 million gallons of coal ash contaminated wastewater was released in North Carolina (Bienkowski 2016). Significant discharges like that at Dan River are noticeable and negatively affect the entire watershed. However, smaller discharges near coal ash ponds may go unnoticed. This is most problematic for those individuals that live closest to these facilities, including an estimated 1.5 million people of color. In response to the growing concerns about coal ash pits, the EPA promulgated new rules in 2014 that required groundwater monitoring near pits, stronger pit liners, and limits on coal ash discharge into rivers (Bienkowski 2016). In response to regulation and spills, some utilities have taken the approach of TVA and have started to transport their coal ash to landfills. This represents a victory for the individuals living closest to coal plants, as they may face fewer risks of air and water pollution.

If the case study ended here, this story might be considered an environmental justice success. Yet, the conclusion to this story is more complicated. Returning to TVA's Kingston spill. TVA began to ship the coal ash to the Arrowhead Landfill, near Uniontown Alabama (Dewan 2009). The town is about 90% black with a median income 74% below the national average as compared to Kingston a predominantly white, middle-class town (Bienkowski 2016). Local politicians supported the agreement citing the $3 million that would be added to the county's $4.5 million budget, and the addition of 30 local jobs (Dewan 2009). From the beginning, residents voiced concerns about the safety of the project, the honesty of their elected officials, and the intimidation tactics of the landfill owners that has included defamation lawsuits (Cerullo 2018; Milman 2018). Since the landfill began accepting coal ash, residents have complained of a host of illnesses including nosebleeds and cancers that have not yet been studied for potential links to coal ash (Milman 2018). In addition, residents are concerned with the impacts of the landfill on an adjacent unmanaged cemetery, where land, owned by the landfill, had been cleared making it difficult for some to locate their ancestral remains (Pillion 2015). The residents of Uniontown filed a complaint against the project to the EPA under Title VI of the Civil Rights Act in 2013.

The EPA held hearings on the issue in 2016 and has since closed the case arguing there was "insufficient evidence" that authorities in Alabama breached the Civil Rights Act in allowing the facility to locate in the town (Milman 2018). The EPA decision in this, and other recent environmental justice cases has been criticized as partisan, given the Trump administration's interest in deregulating industry and coal ash ponds in particular (Milman 2017). Given these concerns, and ongoing tensions in the community, it is unlikely that either supporters of the project or opponents will come to an agreement on the impact of the facility to the community.

The complicated outcome associated with cleaning up the coal ash pit in Kingston illustrates two key questions worth discussing in more detail (1) what constitutes an environmental justice issue and (2) what should be done about identified or potential cases? Clearly, this case demonstrates that waste was moved from one, more affluent community to a poorer one. In addition, the waste can cause public health impacts if handled improperly. As a result, there is a risk that the Alabama residents will be negatively impacted by the transfer of waste. The question is has this occurred and resulted in an environmental justice concern? For Uniontown, there have not been studies on the impact that this waste has had on the community making it difficult to assess injustice. It is possible that the landfill has not caused increased public health problems, suggesting there is no impact as landfill supporters might suggest. Alternatively, it could be causing yet-to-be-seen health complications, suggesting that the community is a toxic experiment. Understandably, residents may not be comfortable waiting to see which result is accurate. Nevertheless, future analysis addressing these claims is necessary to determine if an injustice has occurred in Alabama.

If these residents do face disproportionate risks, what should be done? In Uniontown, the community is benefiting from compensation from accepting the waste. In addition, many more people may be benefitting from the fact that fewer coal ash ponds are being breached nationwide. However, it is unclear whether the compensation for this individual community is enough to offset potential environmental harms. Moreover, once the landfill is full the facility will no longer receive compensation which could make it difficult to mitigate future environmental and public health problems should they arise. As a result, it is unclear whether the town's current compensation adequately matches the risk they are assuming. Ultimately, the residents of Uniontown might have argued that more research needed to be done before the facility was built to assess these risks and determine compensation. Though this would have been valuable, in reality, most communities will have to make decisions with limited information as new technology and associated environmental challenges are just emerging. This is not lost on environmental justice advocates, who counter that even in situations with limited information community members need to be informed of the potential risks they face and be included in decision-making processes. In the case of Uniontown, many residents felt that they had been excluded from this process, generating mistrust from the start. Determining just how to include community members in decision-making processes and provide the relevant information to make decisions that mitigate environmental justice impacts will be an ongoing challenge.

Overall, this coal ash case study demonstrates that minorities and the poor are more likely to be exposed to environmental harms. Determining whether an individual claim is justified and warrants remediation is challenging, which helps explain why incorporating environmental justice into policy evaluation and broader policy processes has been challenging. This case also illustrates the fundamental role policymakers must play in answering the question: how much environmental harm is too much, and what should be done to address it.

CHAPTER WRAP-UP

This chapter provides four key insights. First, policy evaluation is a valuable component of the environmental policymaking process because it provides policymakers and practitioners with data regarding how effective policies are in achieving outcomes. Moreover, these analyses are useful when Congress and agencies must make difficult decisions about how to prioritize resources. Because of these inherent values, in theory, evaluation is supported by virtually all players in the environmental policy arena.

Second, we cannot forget that policy evaluation often suffers because experts do not agree about policy performance. These challenges are compounded by the fact that asking questions such as how much is a life worth or how much environmental harm is too much, are value-laden questions that are difficult to answer, no matter the circumstances. Therefore, attempts to apply CBA, in particular, have been criticized as thin veils over political activities.

Third, despite these concerns, policy evaluations have shown that the environment has improved in the United States. The air, water, and land are cleaner than they were in the 1970s. However, for policy evaluation in the environmental arena to shed the controversy surrounding it, more scientific consensus is necessary on measuring policy outcomes, as well as more definitive determinations on the values of those outcomes to society.

Lastly, this chapter demonstrates that the policy evaluation field is robust and evolving. There are many opportunities to join this field conducting evaluations, quantifying environmental services, or critiquing results. If this sounds appealing, becoming a policy evaluator may be the most rewarding career for you. After all, understanding whether a policy is effective is essential to the future of environmental policymaking in the United States.

Suggested Resources

Readings and Websites

Ackerman, Frank, and Lisa Heinzerling. "Pricing the Priceless: Cost-Benefit Analysis of Environmental Protection." *University of Pennsylvania Law Review* 150 (2002). Accessed May 4, 2018. https://scholarship.law.upenn.edu/cgi/viewcontent.cgi?article=3277&context=penn_law_review.

Bullard, Robert D., Paul Mohai, Robin Saha, and Beverly Wright. *Toxic Wastes and Race at Twenty 1987–2007* (March 2007). Accessed May 4, 2018. https://www.nrdc.org/sites/default/files/toxic-wastes-and-race-at-twenty-1987-2007.pdf.

Cole, Luke W., and Sheila R. Foster. *From the Ground Up: Environmental Racism and the Rise of the Environmental Justice Movement*. New York: New York University Press, 2000.

GAO. *Natural Resources and Environment* (2018). Accessed May 4, 2018. https://www.gao.gov/browse/topic/Natural_Resources_and_Environment.

Hill, Barry E. *Environmental Justice: Legal Theory and Practice*. Washington, DC: Environmental Law Institute, 2009.

Ihab, Mikati, Adam, F. Benson, Thomas J. Luben, Jason D. Sacks, and Jennifer Richmond-Bryant. "Disparities in Distribution of Particulate Matter Emission Sources by Race and Poverty Status." *American Journal of Public Health* (2018). https://ajph.aphapublications.org/doi/pdf/10.2105/AJPH.2017.304297.

Sierra Club. *Environmental Justice*. Accessed May 4, 2018. https://www.sierraclub.org/environmental-justice.

US EPA Toxics Release Inventory (TRI) Program. Accessed May 4, 2018. https://www.epa.gov/toxics-release-inventory-tri-program.

US EPA EJSCREEN. Accessed May 4, 2018. https://www.epa.gov/ejscreen/purposes-and-uses-ejscreen.

Films and Videos

Coal Country a New Civil War. Directed by MariLynn Evans and Phylis Geller. 2009. Evening Star Productions. DVD.

Erin Brockovich. Directed by Steven Soderbergh. 2000.Universal Pictures. DVD.

Toxic Bust: Chemical and Breast Cancer. Directed by Megan Siler. 2006. Plumb Pictures. DVD.

References

Air Alliance of Houston. "Air Pollution and Public Health in Galena Park, Texas." 2014. Accessed May 4, 2018. http://airalliancehouston.org/wp-content/uploads/Galena-Park-Monitoring-Report-FINAL.pdf.

American Lung Association. *State of the Air 2017*. 2017. Accessed May 4, 2018. http://www.lung.org/assets/documents/healthy-air/state-of-the-air/state-of-the-air-2017.pdf.

Appelbaum, Binyamin. "As U.S. Agencies Put More Value on a Life, Businesses Fret." *New York Times*, 2011. Accessed May 4, 2018. https://www.nytimes.com/2011/02/17/business/economy/17regulation.html.

Bardach, Eugene. *Practical Guide for Policy Analysis: The Eightfold Path to More Effective Problem Solving*. 2nd edition. Washington, DC: CQ Press, 2004.

Bastasch. Michael. "Rep. Chaffetz Worries EPA Is Fudging the Numbers to Justify Costlier Regs. *The Daily Caller*, 2016. http://dailycaller.com/2016/07/15/rep-chaffetz-worries-epa-is-fudging-the-numbers-to-justify-costlier-regs/.

Bienkowski, Brian. "Toxic Coal Ash Hits Poor and Minority Communities Hardest." *Scientific American*, 2016. Accessed May 4, 2018. https://www.scientificamerican.com/article/toxic-coal-ash-hits-poor-and-minority-communities-hardest/.

Boardman, Anthony, David Greenberg, Aidan Vining, and David Weimer. *Cost-Benefit Analysis*. 4th edition reissued. Upper Saddle River, NJ: Prentice Hall, 2018.

Bryant, Bunyan, and Paul Mohai. *Race and the Incidence of Environmental Hazards: A Time for Discourse.* Boulder, CO: Westview Press, 1992.

Bryner, Gary C., and Robert J. Duffy. *Integrating Climate, Energy, and Air Pollution Policies.* Cambridge, MA: MIT Press, 2012.

Cerullo, Megan. "Alabama Residents Blast EPA for Allowing Massive Coal Ash Landfill to Operate Nearby Largely Black Town." *NY Daily News*, 2018. Accessed May 4, 2018. http://www.nydailynews.com/news/national/alabamians-blast-epa-coal-ash-landfill-poor-black-town-article-1.3858923.

Cook, Jeffrey J., and Sara Rinfret. "Adjusting the Social Cost of Carbon: A Commonsense Revision." *The Regulatory Review*, 2013. Accessed May 4, 2018. https://www.theregreview.org/2013/08/20/20-cook-rinfret-scc/.

Cooney, Catherine M. "Gauging the Price of Good Health." *Environmental Science and Technology: American Chemical Society* (2003): 365A–368A.

Council on Foreign Relations. *Discussion Paper Automobile Fuel Economy Standards in a Lower-Oil-Price World.* 2015. Accessed May 4, 2018. https://cfrd8-files.cfr.org/sites/default/files/pdf/2015/10/CAFE_Standards_Paper.pdf.

Department of Energy (DOE). "Environmental Justice History." 2013. Accessed May 4, 2018. http://energy.gov/lm/services/environmental-justice/environmental-justice-history.

Dewan, Shaila. "Clash in Alabama Over Tennessee Coal Ash." *The New York Times*, 2009. Accessed May 4, 2018. https://www.nytimes.com/2009/08/30/us/30ash.html.

Dilts, Elizabeth. "After North Carolina Spill, Coal Ash Ponds Face Extinction." *Reuters*, 2014. Accessed May 4, 2018. https://www.reuters.com/article/us-usa-coal-spill-regs-analysis/after-north-carolina-coal-ash-ponds-face-extinction-idUSBREA2D1G720140314.

Duffy, Robert, and Jeffrey J. Cook. "Overcoming Bureaucratic Silos? Environmental Policy Integration in the Obama Administration." *Environmental Politics* (2018, Forthcoming).

Dunn, William N. *Public Policy Analysis: An Introduction.* 4th edition. Upper Saddle River, NJ: Pearson Prentice Hall, 2008.

Eilperin, Juliet, and Brady Dennis. "EPA to Roll Back Car Emissions Standards, Handing Automakers a Big Win." *The Washington Post*, 2018. Accessed May 18, 2018. https://www.washingtonpost.com/national/health-science/epa-to-roll-back-car-emissions-standards/2018/04/02/b720f0b6-36a6-11e8-acd5-35eac230e514_story.html?utm_term=.2d4872114329.

EPA. *Regulatory Impact Analysis: Final Rulemaking for 2017–2025 Light Duty Vehicle Greenhouse Gas Emission Standards and Corporate Average Fuel Economy Standards.* 2012. Accessed May 4, 2018. https://nepis.epa.gov/Exe/ZyPURL.cgi?Dockey=P100EZI1.TXT.

———. "Plan EJ 2014." 2013. Accessed May 4, 2018. https://www.epa.gov/environmentaljustice/plan-ej-2014.

———. "Plan EJ 2020." 2016a. Accessed May 4, 2018. https://www.epa.gov/environmentaljustice/about-ej-2020#goals.

———. "Our Nation's Air Status and Trends Through 2015." 2016b. Accessed May 4, 2018. https://gispub.epa.gov/air/trendsreport/2016/.

———. "Profiles of Hispanics at EPA: Matthew Tejada." 2017a. Accessed May 4, 2018. https://www.epa.gov/careers/profiles-hispanics-epa-matthew-tejada.

———. *National Water Quality Inventory: Report to Congress.* 2017b. Accessed May 4, 2018. https://www.epa.gov/sites/production/files/2017-12/documents/305brtc_finalowow_08302017.pdf.

———. "Environmental Justice." 2018a. Accessed May 4, 2018. https://www.epa.gov/environmentaljustice.

———. "Coal Ash (Cola Combustion Residuals, or CCR)." 2018b. Accessed May 4, 2018. https://www.epa.gov/coalash.

EPA, Office of Policy, Planning, and Evaluation. "Environmental Equity: Reducing Risk for All Communities." *EPA 1992* 2. Washington, DC: GPO, 1992.

Fiorino, Daniel. "Regulating for the Future: A New Approach for Environmental Governance." In *Toward Sustainable Communities: Transformations and Transition in Environmental Policy*, edited by Michael E. Kraft and Daniel A. Mazmanian. Cambridge: MIT Press, 2009.

Freeman, Myrick A. "Economics, Incentives, and Environmental Regulation." In *Environmental Policy*, edited by Norman E. Vig and Michael E. Kraft. Washington, DC: CQ Press, 2006.

Gang, Duane W. "5 Years After Coal-Ash Spill, Little Has Changed." *USA Today*, 2013. Accessed May 4, 2018. https://www.usatoday.com/story/news/nation/2013/12/22/coal-ash-spill/4143995/.

Golfarb, Ben. "An Advocate in Pursuit of Environmental Justice at the EPA." *Yale Environment 360*. 2013. https://e360.yale.edu/features/interview_with_epa_environmental_justice_director_matthew_tejada.

Government Accountability Office (GAO). "Environmental Justice: EPA Needs to Take Additional Actions to Help Ensure Effective Implementation." 2011. Accessed August 11, 2013. http://www.gao.gov/new.items/d1277.pdf.

Government Accountability Office (GAO). *Siting of Hazardous Waste Landfills and Their Correlation With Racial and Economic Status of Surrounding Communities.* 1983. Accessed August 11, 2013. http://archive.gao.gov/d48t13/121648.pdf.

Interagency Working Group on Social Cost of Carbon. *Technical Support Document: Social Cost of Carbon for Regulatory Impact Analysis—Under Executive Order 12866.* 2010. Accessed May 4, 2018. https://obamawhitehouse.archives.gov/sites/default/files/omb/inforeg/for-agencies/Social-Cost-of-Carbon-for-RIA.pdf.

Interagency Working Group on Social Cost of Greenhouse Gases. *Technical Support Document: Technical Update of the Social Cost of Carbon for Regulatory Impact Analysis Under Executive Order 12866.* 2016. Accessed May 4, 2018. https://www.epa.gov/sites/production/files/2016-12/documents/sc_co2_tsd_august_2016.pdf.

Jenkins, Clinton N., Kyle S. Van Houtan, Stuart L. Pimm, and Joseph O. Sexton. "US Protected Lands Mismatch Biodiversity Priorities." *Proceedings of the National Academy of Sciences of the United States of America.* 2015. Accessed May 4, 2018. https://www.ncbi.nlm.nih.gov/pmc/articles/PMC4413281/.

Kraft, Michael E. *Environmental Policy and Politics.* 7th edition. New York: Routledge, 2018.

Kraft, Michael E., and Norman Vig. "Environmental Policy Over Four Decades Achievements and New Directions." In *Environmental Policy*, edited by Norman J. Vig and Michael E. Kraft, 206–229. Washington, DC: CQ Press, 2013.

Kraft, Michael E., and Scott R. Furlong. *Public Policy: Politics, Analysis, and Alternatives*, 4th edition. Washington, DC: CQ Press, 2013.

Lasswell, Harold D. *A Pre-view of Policy Sciences.* New York: American Elsevier, 1971.

Lindblom, C. E. "The Science of 'Muddling Through'." *Public Administration Review* 19, no. 2 (Spring 1959): 79–88.

———. "Still Muddling, Not Yet Through." *Public Administration Review* 39, no. 6 (1979): 517–526.

Milman, Oliver. "A Civil Rights 'Emergency': Justice, Clean Air and Water in the Age of Trump." *The Guardian*, 2017. Accessed May 4, 2018. https://www.theguardian.com/us-news/2017/nov/20/environmental-justice-in-the-age-of-trump.

———. "Environmental Racism Case: EPA Rejects Alabama Town's Claim Over Toxic Landfill." *The Guardian*, 2018. Accessed May 4, 2018. https://www.theguardian.com/us-news/2018/mar/06/environmental-racism-alabama-landfill-civil-rights.

Mohai, Paul, and Robin Saha. "Which Came First, People or Pollution? A Review of Theory and Evidence from Longitudinal Environmental Justice studies." *Environmental Research Letters* 10, no. 12 (2015): 1–9.

Mooney, Chris. "New EPA Document Reveals Sharply Lower Estimate of Cost of Climate Change." *The Washington Post*, 2017. Accessed May 4, 2018. https://www.washingtonpost.com/news/energy-environment/wp/2017/10/11/new-epa-document-reveals-sharply-lower-estimate-of-the-cost-of-climate-change/?utm_term=.03cbade750e8.

Niles, Meredith T., and Mark Lubell. "Integrative Frontiers in Environmental Policy Theory and Research." *The Policy Studies Journal* 40, no. S1 (2012): 41–64.

Olmstead, Sheila M. "Applying Market Principles to Environmental Policy." In *Environmental Policy*, edited by Norman J. Vig and Michael E. Kraft, 245–268. Washington, DC: CQ Press, 2018.

Ostrom, Elinor. *Governing the Commons: The Evolution of Institutions for Collective Action*. Cambridge, MA: Cambridge University Press, 1990.

Pillion, Dennis. "Cemetery Dispute the Latest Conflict Between Arrowhead Landfill, Uniontown Residents." *Al.com*, 2015. Accessed May 4, 2018. https://www.al.com/news/index.ssf/2015/12/arrowhead_landfill_uniontown_r.html.

Portney, Paul R. "Does Environmental Policy Conflict with Economic Growth?" *Resources* 115 (1994): 21–23.

Quade, Edward S. *Analysis for Public Discourse*. 3rd edition. New York: North Holland Publishing, 1989.

Ramanujan, Krishna. "Insect Pollinators Contribute $29 Billion to U.S. Farm Income." *Cornell Chronicle*, 2012. http://news.cornell.edu/stories/2012/05/insect-pollinators-contribute-29b-us-farm-income.

Rhoads, Steven E. *The Economist's View of the World*. Cambridge, MA: Cambridge University Press, 1985.

Rossman, Sean. 2017. "A Third of the Nation's Honeybee Colonies Died Last Year: Why You Should Care." *USA Today*, 2017. Accessed May 4, 2018. https://www.usatoday.com/story/news/nation-now/2017/05/26/third-nations-honeybee-colonies-died-last-year-why-you-should-care/348418001/.

Schwartz, John. "Decline of Pollinators Poses Threat to World Food Supply, Report Says." *The New York Times*, 2016. Accessed May 4, 2018. https://www.nytimes.com/2016/02/27/science/decline-of-species-that-pollinate-poses-a-threat-to-global-food-supply-report-warns.html?hp&action=click&pgtype=Homepage&clickSource=story-heading&module=second-column-region&region=top-news&WT.nav=top-news&_r=0.

Seelye, Katharine Q., and John Tierney. "E.P.A. Drops Age-Based Cost Studies." *New York Times*, 2003. Accessed May 4, 2018. http://globalag.igc.org/elderrights/us/seniordiscount.htm.

Smith, C. "New Jersey-Size 'Dead Zone' Is Largest Ever in Gulf of Mexico." 2017. Accessed May 4, 2018. https://news.nationalgeographic.com/2017/08/gulf-mexico-hypoxia-water-quality-dead-zone/.

The Economist. "The Rule of More." *The Economist*, 2012. Accessed May 4, 2018. https://www.economist.com/node/21547772.

UCC. *Toxic Wastes and Race in the United States*. New York: United Church of Christ Commission for Racial Justice, 1987.

US Chamber of Commerce. "Charting Federal Costs and Benefits." 2014. Accessed May 4, 2018. https://www.uschamber.com/sites/default/files/021615_fed_regs_costs_benefits_2014reportrevise_jrp_fin_1.pdf.

USFWS. "Report to Congress on the Recovery of Threatened and Endangered Species: Fiscal Years 2013–2014." 2016. Accessed May 4, 2018. https://www.fws.gov/endangered/esa-library/pdf/Recovery_Report_FY2013-2014.pdf.

Vig, Norman J., and Michael E. Kraft. *Environmental Policy: New Direction for the 21st Century*. Washington, DC: CQ Press, 2018.

Walton, Robert. "EPA to Review MATS Rule Limiting Mercury Emissions from Coal Plants." *Utility Dive*, 2017. Accessed May 4, 2018. https://www.utilitydive.com/news/epa-to-review-mats-rule-limiting-mercury-emissions-from-coal-plants/440850/.

Weimer, David L., and Aidan R. Vining. *Policy Analysis*. 5th edition. Boston, MA: Longman Pearson, 2011.

WSTB. *Valuing Ecosystem Services: Toward Better Environmental Decision-Making*. Washington, DC: National Academies Press, 2004.

The Intersection of Natural Resource and Energy Policy

Contents

A Relic of the Past

The American West's picturesque landscapes and vast blue skies are unforgettable. The grandeur of Wyoming's Grand Teton National Park or the "Big Sky Country" of Montana is memorable. To promote westward expansion and to protect the splendor of the West, President Theodore (Teddy) Roosevelt set aside much of these lands as federal public lands—meaning the government owns and manages them.

© The Author(s) 2019   287
S. R. Rinfret and M. C. Pautz, *US Environmental Policy in Action*,
https://doi.org/10.1007/978-3-030-11316-2_9

The managers of public lands in the United States are a number of federal agencies, including the U.S. Fish and Wildlife Service, the U.S. Forest Service, the National Park Service, and the Bureau of Land Management. Overseeing public lands is not an easy endeavor because it requires the supervision of multiple uses of those lands, and those multiple uses often conflict with one another. The National Park Service, for example, simultaneously manages land for multiple objectives: preservation, extraction, and recreation. Within a park, a manager could be tasked with preserving an endangered species while determining how snowmobiles affect its habitat, for instance.

Overseeing resource extraction from public lands is another example. Uranium mining in the Grand Canyon is an illustration of the multiuse quagmire. Created in 1919, Grand Canyon National Park (in Arizona) is one of the most magnificent parks in the United States. The Park is home to eleven Tribal communities, contains human artifacts more than 12,000 years old, and receives millions of annual visitors (Grand Canyon National Park 2018). Within the park's borders are some of the richest deposits of uranium in the world, which is governed by the General Mining Act of 1872.

For some, the General Mining Act of 1872 is a relic of the past. The aim of this Act was to promote expansion into the American West, without consideration for the effects on the natural environment (Vaughn 2007). The Act allows for any US citizen or corporation to stake a claim to explore for hard rock minerals (e.g., copper, gold). Until 1969, the Orphan Mine maintained mining operations in the South Rim of the Grand Canyon, but eventually halted work due to decreased market demand. Its remnants leach into the nearby Horn Creek, with unacceptable levels of uranium mining decay, placing restrictions on swimming and drinking water for visitors.

With the potential for future development of uranium, Representative Raul Grijalva (D-Arizona) took the lead combating such instances. Grijalva, born and raised in Tucson, Arizona, is a 5-hour drive to Grand Canyon National Park.His father, who lived most of his entire adult life in Arizona, did not visit the Grand Canyon until the age of 74. Grijalva drove his father to the Park and described the experience as both "strange and exhilarating" (Grijalva 2016). Upon arrival, his father took some time to look inside the rim of the Grand Canyon and returned to the car—he was ready to go home. As Grijalva recalls, "It wasn't that he didn't enjoy the experience, nor that he failed to appreciate the scene. He just didn't need to linger. He got it immediately, and that was enough for him. There are places that are beyond words. Places that are beyond description. Places worthy of reverence and permanent protection. Without a doubt, the Grand Canyon is one of them. Through my father's eyes, I saw the natural world for what it is: a constant source of inspiration regardless of how much time we spend there. Even if we only rarely hike through wilderness or canoe down wild rivers, it is our responsibility to protect those experiences and ensure the lasting conservation of the natural world" (Grijalva 2016).

Girjalva's experiences as a native Arizonan defined his impetus to protect the Grand Canyon, and in 2008, he proposed the Grand Canyon Watershed Protection Act. The mining for uranium, in his eyes, is objectionable and a detriment to the future enjoyment of the Park. The purpose of his proposed Act was to set aside one million acres surrounding Grand Canyon National Park to prohibit mining (Grijalva 2018). In 2009, David Kreamer, a professor of geology at the University of Nevada, Las Vegas, provided testimony to Congress, arguing: "Scientific evidence suggests that the exploitation of uranium resources near the Grand Canyon will be intimately connected with the groundwater aquifers and springs in the region. The hydrologic impacts have a great potential to be negative to people and biotic systems. I believe that an assumption that uranium mining will have minimal impact on springs, people and ecosystems in the Grand Canyon is unreasonable, and is not supported by past investigations, research and data" (McKinnon 2007). Although Representative Grijalva's Act did not pass in Congress, his efforts were noted by former Department of Interior Secretary Ken Salazar who placed a 20-year ban on mining in the Grand Canyon. This ban could change under the directive of President Trump, who believes exploration on public lands in the West is necessary for our energy security and independence. Nevertheless, the 1872 Mining Law, a relic of the past, continues to shape our natural resource and energy policy future.

The 1872 General Mining Law serves as an important lesson—it illuminates the interconnectedness of public lands, natural resource and energy policy. Most importantly, natural resource policy is guided by multiuse laws by which federal managers must reconcile how to best use the land, preserve the land for future generations, and the land for economic benefits. At the crux of this debate is the protection of public lands versus the advancement of extractive resource industries. This is a simplistic explanation and this chapter will investigate the complexities of these issues and the multiple layers of government and actors that are involved. More specifically, in this chapter, we begin with an overview of the topic, defining public lands and exploring the four central agencies for managing these lands—U.S. Fish and Wildlife Service (USFWS), the National Park Service (NPS), the United States Bureau of Land Management (BLM), and the U.S. Forest Service (USFS). Within this context, we delve into some of the multiuse natural resource policies that provide broader linkages to US energy policy. The chapter concludes by considering issues and concerns, such as water scarcity in the American West. Readers of this chapter will be able to convey the myriad of actors involved (institutional and noninstitutional) that define how we manage the use of natural resources on public land. Simply put, the way in which we manage our public land affects the future of our environment. By no means can we cover every single topic related to natural resource and energy policy. Instead, our goal here is simple—to introduce you to the primary actors involved and some of the dilemmas they confront.

Defining the Intersection

As we have noted throughout this text, environmental policy is complex, involving multiple layers. How we use natural resources on public lands helps us understand the driving components of energy policy—the building blocks to the messy nature of environmental policymaking. As *The Lorax* depicts in Chapter 1, the decisions we make about the use of our public lands affect all of us. If we decide to open the Grand Canyon National Park to uranium mining, its impacts are far-reaching. Here is a plausible list of environmental consequences of such action in this particular national park:

1. Contamination of the Havasupai Tribe's travertine waterfalls and drinking water supply;

2. Tusayan, Arizona (community outside of the South Rim, Grand Canyon) local economy plummets because Grand Canyon National Park visitation decreases due to mining activity; and/or
3. Uranium mining tailings contaminate the Colorado River, a drinking water source for seven states—Colorado, Arizona, New Mexico, California, Utah, Wyoming, and Nevada.

Uranium mining is just one example of the connections between natural resource and energy policy in the United States. We begin our discussion of defining this natural resource and energy policy intersection through the lens of public lands in the United States.

Public lands are designated lands for the use and enjoyment of the American people and are managed by the federal government. However, over time, the concept of public lands has shifted from selling the land to preservation of the land. As Jacqueline Vaughn (2007) defines, "When the United States was at its infancy 'public lands' referred to the area between the Appalachian Mountains and the Mississippi River that were held by seven of the original 13 colonies – the land claim states" (111). As payment for fighting in the Revolutionary War, soldiers were compensated with land to raise revenue for the United States. By 1842, up to 160 acres of land would be provided if a person would be willing to fight Indians in Florida or couples could settle the Oregon Territory, receiving 640-acre parcels (Vaughn 2007).

The American Antiquities Act of 1906 changed the direction of the federal government's approach from selling land for a profit to conservation of the land. Under the Act, the president of the United States can designate land as a national monument to protect the land for scientific, cultural, or archeological purposes, to name a few reasons. Catalysts for this legislation were related to the writings from Henry David Thoreau and Ralph Waldo Emerson. Both poets, Thoreau and Emerson wrote about the beauty of the natural landscape of the Western United States and did not want a future where the commodification of the land would deplete all of its resources, stifling future enjoyment of the land's magnificence (Andrews 2006).

Roughly, 640 million acres, or 28%, of all the land in the United States are federal public lands. The vast majority of this land resides in the Western United States because much of this land was undeveloped during the origins of the United States and because, "[m]any mountainous, arid and difficult-to-reach tracts of land in the West simply weren't

Table 9.1 Public lands in the United States

State	Total federal acreage	% of state
Alabama	867,360	2.7
New York	188,537	0.6
Ohio	307,180	1.2
Montana	27,049,302	29
Wyoming	30,183,609	48.4
Idaho	32,623,376	61.6

Source https://fas.org/sgp/crs/misc/R42346.pdf

attractive to farmers. Settlers claimed the few valleys where farming was feasible and built towns. The only thing most of the remaining land was good for was grazing, but cattle ranchers and sheepherders needed large tracts of land to feed their livestock, not the smaller parcels they could claim through homestead policies" (Quoctoring and Sanger-Katz 2016, npn).

Table 9.1 uses a few state examples to differentiate the amount of federal public land per state. Alabama's landmass includes 22 million acres and 2.7% is federal public lands (867,360 acres). Idaho, in contrast, has approximately 4.9 million acres, and 61.6% of this is federal public lands.

America's public lands encompass many different categories, including national parks, national forests, national conversation areas, national wildlife refuges, national monuments, national historical areas, wilderness areas, national recreation areas, national battlefields, national seashores and lakeshores, scenic areas, and national trails (U.S. Department of Interior 2016). We compare a few of these land types to convey some of the differences. A national park (e.g., Grand Canyon, Yellowstone) is land designated by the federal government to preserve this land and the future enjoyment of its environment. A national forest, by way of comparison, is also land designated by the federal government but contains many uses—timber harvesting, recreation, wildlife, or fishing. A national battlefield is designated to commemorate historical point in US history.

Public lands contain natural resources—renewable and nonrenewable. A renewable natural resource is replaceable by nature or human intervention (e.g., trees, water, soil, wildlife). In comparison, a nonrenewable resource has a set amount available, which cannot be replenished (e.g., coal, petroleum, natural gas). Public lands in the United States are inevitably a unique treasure and an envy of the world (Davis

2018). These lands are managed in a variety of ways and serve multiple purposes. As Davis (2018) notes,

> They provide critical and otherwise unavailable habitats for precious biodiversity. They churn out trillions of dollars of ecological services, generally unpriced yet vital to life. They provide recreation and aesthetic wonders that undergird entire global economies. They provide stable access to such resources as timber, minerals, energy, and pasture that also support local economies. They also provide untold intangible benefits: wonder, reverence, solitude, psychological and physical health, history, national and community pride, connections to land and place, and intergenerational continuity in an increasingly turbulent and confusing world. (209)

Creating public lands does not come without conflict and controversy. For example, do you allow for the creation of a new natural gas power plant or protect the habitat of an endangered species? Nevertheless, the management of federal lands is not an easy undertaking. The estimated cost to oversee these lands is approximately the same price for one hundred F-35 fighter jets (Davis 2018). We examine the four largest managers of public lands to understand some of the difficulties involved.

THE FEDERAL LANDLORDS

As we learned in Chapter 6, Congress delegates its authority to the bureaucracy for the interpretation and implementation of environmental laws. Ninety-six percent of federal public lands are managed by four federal agencies, which fall under the U.S. Department of Interior, (except the U.S. Forest Service, which is within the United States Department of Agriculture): BLM, USFWS, USFS, and NPS. Each of these agencies must reconcile multiple use on federal public lands—recreation, preservation, and development of natural resources. As stated previously, multiple use simply means that the land has been designated by the federal government for a variety of purposes (see explanation of national forests above).

Bureau of Land Management: The BLM, the youngest of the federal land agencies, oversees the largest amount of federal public lands—248 million acres. This acreage is primarily within eleven Western states in arid rangeland or desert. In 1946, the BLM was created through the merger of two existing agencies—the Grazing Service and the General

Land Office. The permanent protection of these lands occurred in 1976 with the passage of the Federal Land Management Policy Act (FLPMA). The Taylor Grazing Act of 1934 and Public Lands Rangeland Improvement Act of 1978 are two essential pieces of legislation that BLM agency officials grapple with. Under these Acts, BLM officials oversee grazing districts whereby western ranchers rent the land for their cattle to graze. Concerns about rangeland management and overuse is a constant concern for the BLM to reconcile with ranching and environmental interests (Andrews 2008). The approach taken is animal unit month (AUM) which is the carrying capacity for forage on a pasture. More specifically, an AUM means an animal unit (AU) is a mature cow weighing approximately 1000 pounds that requires 26 pounds of dry matter or food per day (DM). This is a system to standardize the forage (hay, grass) needs of cattle (or other grazing animals—sheep, horses) and the forage available. The BLM manages approximately 18,000 leases for cattle ranchers to graze on public lands. The grazing fee for 2018 is $1.41 per AUM (U.S. Department of Interior 2018).

In 2014, Cliven Bundy, a longtime Nevada rancher declared war against the federal government, noting he should not have to pay for his cattle to graze on public lands. After three ignored court orders, the BLM impounded his cattle due to failure to pay. This led to an armed standoff between Bundy, his militia supporters, and federal officials (Childress 2018). Movements like this are not uncommon and were also attempted by individuals during the Reagan administration Sagebrush Rebellion—during the 1980s a group of individuals in the American West organized and argued to have more state and local control over federal lands.

U.S. Fish and Wildlife Service: The origins of the USFWS date back to two federal agencies established in the early nineteenth century. The intent of each agency was to oversee the nation's fish and wildlife supplies, respectively. The Commissioner of Fish and Fisheries studied the supply of coastal and lake fisheries, which later become the Bureau of Fisheries in the Department of Commerce. In 1905, the Bureau of Biological Survey in the Department of Agriculture was established, with the stated mission of studying birds and mammals in the United States. By 1939, the Bureau of Fisheries and the Bureau of Biological Survey were consolidated, which created the USFWS.

The primary responsibilities of USFWS are to manage migratory birds, develop hunting regulations, acquire/protect habitat, and enforce international treaties that protect migratory birds. The broadest sources of statutory authority for the USFWS are the National Environmental Policy Act (NEPA) of 1969, and the Endangered Species Act of 1973. NEPA serves as a formal vehicle for USFWS to analyze the impact of projects on all types of fish and wildlife through environmental assessments. The other key directive for USFWS came in 1973, with the passage of the Endangered Species Act (ESA) to protect endangered or threatened plants and animals. Under the ESA, USFWS, along with the Department of Commerce, is responsible for carrying out this law through rulemaking processes (see Chapters 6 and 7 for more detail). The language of the ESA directs USFWS to use only the best scientific data to list a species, develop a recovery plan, and designate critical habitats once a species goes through the rulemaking process and is listed as endangered or threatened. In 2017, the USFWS decided to delist the grizzly bear as an endangered species, changing its classification to threatened in the Greater Yellowstone Ecosystem. Lawsuits from numerous environmental groups claimed that the USFWS did not use the best available science to make this delisting and the battle continues as we write this book (Miller 2017).

The U.S. Forest Service: Created in 1905, the USFS oversees our national forests and grasslands. The origins of the USFWS are rooted in the ideals of Gifford Pinchot (former governor of Pennsylvania, forester, and first administrator of the USFS) who viewed the forest through a utilitarian lens. Simply put, the forest would be used for multiple uses—resource extraction, recreation, or wildlife (Davis 2018).

The Multiple Use Sustained Yield Act (MUYSA) of 1960 serves as a prominent legislative directive for the USFS. MUYSA mandates that the agency not only mange the forest but also produce sustained yield—total amount of timber which can be removed from any forest at any time (Davis 2018). Recall from Chapter 5, Daniel McGowan ardently opposed USFS practices, used violent protest mechanisms, and as a result, classified as ecoterrorism.

Although USFS is often criticized for its approach to multiple use, there are additional concerns. The USFS continues to struggle with wildland fire management. Some critics contend that the development of national forests (e.g., timber) coupled with climate change has led to record seasons of wildland fires. As of September 2018, approximately ninety large fires across twelve states burned across the American West (National Interagency Fire Center 2018). With decreasing agency budgets, fighting forest fires is at the forefront. The USFS often spends 50% of its budget fighting fires and does not have enough resources for prevention, as a result. President Trump is considering new management approaches, and vehemently maintains because "It is not a global warming issue, it is a management issue" (Ebbs 2018, npn). However, others question whether the USFS should be in the firefighting business or if forests should naturally burn. Christopher Stone's (USC law professor) famous 1972 law review article—*Should Trees Have Standing*—goes one step further—asking the question who really speaks for the trees. Stone stresses that trees are indeed objects and should have standing to sue. Supreme Court Justice Douglas even cited his argument in one of his dissenting opinions (*Sierra Club v. Morton*).

The National Park Service: In 1916, the NPS was created as part of the Organic Act—often referred to as a dual mandate. This dual mandate provides that the NPS is designated by Congress to provide recreational enjoyment for the people as well as preservation of the land. The NPS maintains 79.7 million acres of national parks, preserves, monuments, battlefields, lakeshores, and historic sites (Davis 2018). Much like the USFWS, the NPS uses NEPA and the ESA for guidance for species protections within park boundaries.

However, the Antiquities Act provides US presidents authority over the designation and creation of national monuments, often increasing the amount of management for NPS officials. Presidents can designate national monuments through executive orders under the Antiquities Act of 1906. President Obama was classified as the "monument man" for creating the most national monuments since President Teddy Roosevelt under one administration—1.65 additional acres. However, the Trump administration has considered rolling these endeavors back and, as we write this chapter, these policies are pending.

The aforementioned history provides basic background information about the origins of the four federal landlords and some issues each confronts. Inextricably, these federal landlords confront a deluge of issues. Certainly, answers to how best to use natural resources on public lands is multifaceted and involves numerous institutional and noninstitutional actors. We could fill pages of several chapters about the management approaches for each respective public lands agency. Nevertheless, our purpose here is simple—to introduce the reader and to investigate one of the larger nuances that federal public land manager's face—reconciling energy development and preservation. Much like the opening pages of this chapter, and Chapter 1, how do we reconcile preservation of public lands while providing energy for Americans?

ENERGY POLICY AND PUBLIC LANDS

Energy development is at the epicenter of the public lands debate. Much like with management of public lands, an essential piece of energy policy is how do we effectively manage the land under multiple use mandates? Energy policy concerns the management and use of the nation's energy resources, both renewable sources (e.g., solar or wind power) and nonrenewable (e.g., coal, natural gas, petroleum) sources of energy. And, public lands are one of *the* sources of nonrenewable resources of energy.

The federal government manages public lands. Energy policy, by way of comparison, refers to government action or inaction that deals with issues related to the production, distribution, transportation, and consumption of energy (Rinfret et al. 2018). However, energy resources are located on public lands, as is the case with uranium deposits in the Grand Canyon. Additionally, energy is at the forefront of Americans' minds because it affects our daily lives—from filling up our car with gasoline, to paying our monthly energy bill, to receiving a tax credit for the solar panels on your rooftop.

Energy production, as Fig. 9.1 illustrates, is an economic driver for several state economies. Wyoming, Colorado, and North Dakota are all within the top 10 energy producers for the United States. These same states contain a significant portion of federal public land.

In addition to energy production, we also need to consider our consumption. We can use information from the US Energy Information Administration (EIA), which tracks our energy consumption over time. In 2017, according to the US EIA, we consumed 97.7 quadrillion Btus. The US consumption in 2017 is driven by electric power (38%); transportation (29%); industry (22%), residential (6%), and commercial (4%) (US Energy Information Administration 2017). By way of comparison, consumption of renewable energy (e.g., wind, solar) has more than doubled since 2008. It remains to be seen if this will be affected by President Trump's disinvestment from renewable energy sources.

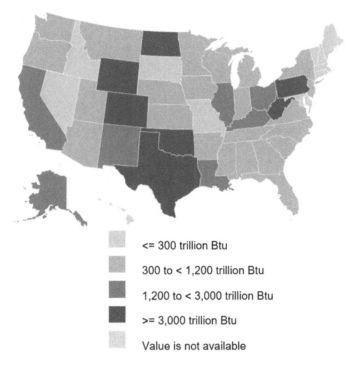

<= 300 trillion Btu

300 to < 1,200 trillion Btu

1,200 to < 3,000 trillion Btu

>= 3,000 trillion Btu

Value is not available

Fig. 9.1 Total energy production per state (*Source* https://www.eia.gov/state/rankings/?sid=US#/series/101)

FEDERAL ENERGY MANAGERS

Although we have already extensively discussed the federal public land managers, these same individuals often work with individuals within energy agencies or commissions to determine the relevancy of energy production on public lands or its impact on species. Two of the key guiding policies for federal energy managers include the Energy Policy Act of **2005** and the Energy Independence and Security Act of **2007**. The Energy Policy Act of **2005** was the result of an energy task force, headed by Vice President Dick Cheney. The focus is to find ways to increase domestic sources of energy, such as coal, providing grants for development of various energy technologies. The act includes provisions for tax credits for homeowners who make energy improvements. The Energy Independence and Security Act of 2007 promotes energy independence from foreign sources by focusing on fuel economy, biofuel development, fuel efficiency of vehicles, and improving the energy efficiency of public buildings. These policies serve as laws for federal energy managers to implement. We consider a few energy agencies and commissions to better understand their intersection with public land managers.

Department of Energy: Most notably is the US Department of Energy (DOE). Its agency mission is "to ensure America's security and prosperity by addressing its energy, environmental, and nuclear challenges through transformative science and technology solutions." The agency implements policies involving nuclear power, fossil fuels, and alternative energy sources. It is organized around three major offices: nuclear security, science and energy, and management and performance and it is overseen by a cabinet secretary, currently Rick Perry (Rinfret et al. 2018). The DOE often works with the BLM regarding placement of solar and wind energy products on western public lands, for example.

Federal Energy Regulatory Commission: FERC manages the interstate sale and transmission of energy which includes the sales, licensing, pricing, and pipeline rates. It is a self-funding entity, meaning that it pays for its operations from the fees it charges the energy industry, which it regulates (Rinfret et al. 2018). In 2018, FERC is working with the BLM to conduct an environmental impact statement to determine the effect of building the Mountain Valley Pipeline. This proposed pipeline would cross public lands in Virginia and West Virginia. The agencies are working together to determine, as we write this book whether or not to move forward with the natural gas pipeline.

Nuclear Regulatory Commission: This NRC is responsible for the safe use and environmental security of nuclear energy for nonmilitary purposes. This includes the operation of nuclear reactors, materials, transportation, storage and disposal of nuclear waste. The NRC is overseen by five commissioners, appointed by the president for fixed terms. This commission was created in 1974 and its headquarters are in Rockville, Maryland with four regional offices throughout the country. Most importantly, the NRC is tasked with the safe storage of radioactive waste which has been a topic surrounding the use of Yucca Mountain, Nevada as a geological repository for nuclear waste. It is yet to be determined if this site will be used to store waste.

Nevertheless, presidential policy directives also define US energy production. These policies can make it difficult for public land management. To provide context, we briefly examine presidential energy policy approaches from 2001 to 2018 as a foundation for our chapter's case study—Keystone Pipeline XL.

NATIONAL SECURITY, ENERGY, AND PRESIDENTIAL DIRECTIVES

Post-9/11, energy policy in the United States has been defined through the lens of a national security. President George W. Bush framed energy policy as a national security when he charged his Vice President, Dick Cheney, with the responsibility of overseeing an energy taskforce. He wanted the Vice President to investigate environmental regulations that would stifle energy production on public lands. For example, one of the recommendations of the Taskforce was to open the Alaska National Wildlife Refuge to the drilling of oil and gas. The Taskforce underwent scrutiny because its makeup consisted of energy industry representatives without the input from environmental interests (Rinfret et al. 2018). Although the Republican Party maintained control of the U.S. House of Representatives, the U.S. Senate was divided during Bush's tenure. Therefore, many policy directives fell flat (e.g., drilling for oil in ANWR).

President Obama took a different approach toward energy policy on public lands. The American Recovery and Reinvestment Act of 2009 provided tax incentives and favored the use of renewable energy. President Obama's approach was for a clean energy future on public lands. For example, the BLM approved plans for 15,000 megawatts of renewable power (e.g., solar and wind). Additionally, President Obama urged public land agencies to undergo climate change assessments and its effects on management practices. The NPS, for example, did not have a climate program prior to President Obama, but conducted 235 climate assessments out of its 413 parks during his tenure (Shogren 2017).

President Trump's approach to energy policy is to prioritize energy production on all public lands. *Outside Magazine*, in 2018, defined President Trump as the rollback president with energy first and public lands second. To illustrate this label, President Trump has repealed regulations that prevent mining companies for dumping their waste into rivers. Most notably, President Trump was successful in opening ANWR to oil and gas development (Outside Editors 2018).

PUBLIC PERCEPTIONS IN THE WEST

Presidential approaches inherently affect the use of natural resources on public lands, but public opinion matters because voters effect policy change (see Chapter 2). In 2017, Colorado College conducted a telephone survey of voters in seven Western states (Montana, Wyoming, Utah, Colorado, Nevada, Arizona, New Mexico) to assess perspectives about how public lands should be managed. Their findings suggest five overarching findings:

1. More than 68% of respondents want to protect clean water, air, and wildlife habitat on national public lands;
2. Only 22% want more energy production on public lands;
3. Respondents placed a greater emphasis on conservation over energy production;
4. Approximately 62% oppose oil and gas companies to drill in new areas on public lands; and
5. Respondents are happy with the management of public lands by the four major agencies (Colorado College 2017).

These Western state perspectives are consistent with national trends. In 2017, Pew Research Center found that 65% of Americans support the development of alternative energy sources. Comparatively, only 27% want to expand US production of fossil fuel sources of energy development (Kennedy 2017).

Now that we have a basic understanding of why energy policy is connected to the use of natural resources and public lands management, it is helpful to contextualize this through the case of Keystone XL Pipeline. This case helps to illuminate the broader connections within this text—institutional and noninstitutional actors and how policy is implemented.

Keystone XL
Throughout this chapter, natural resources on public lands sit center stage. The Keystone XL Pipeline sheds light on the convergence of institutional and noninstitutional actors on the use of natural resources on public lands and its long-term development effects on the environment. The figure depicts the key actors in describing this case (Fig. 9.2).

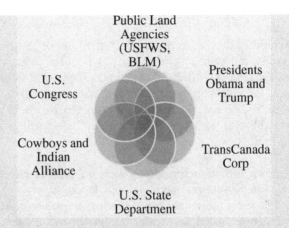

Fig. 9.2   Understanding the players

In 2008, TransCanada Corporation proposed a presidential permit application to the U.S. Department of State for the construction of a pipeline from Alberta, Canada to Texas to carry hundreds
of thousands of oil sands crude oil. This pipeline would trav-
erse Montana, North Dakota, South Dakota, Nebraska, Kansas,
Oklahoma, and Texas. As part of the application process, the U.S.
Department of State in 2010, conducted an environmental impact
assessment under the National Environmental Policy Act to determine environmental effects. Agencies such as the USFWS and
BLM conduct assessments to determine impacts on land and species habitats (Canadian Press 2017).

The U.S. Department of State released its environmental assessment in 2011, stating there would be limited impact on the environment. As a result, hundreds of protesters such as Canadian
activist Naomi Klein protest for two weeks in front of the White
House to prevent the development of the Keystone XL Pipeline.
Soon after, additional research from the U.S. Department of State
suggests there would be sensitive areas in Nebraska's protected
Sandhills and the developers of the pipeline would need to come
up with a new route. The TransCanada Corporation agrees to
reroute the pipeline. The U.S. Congress passed legislation stating
President Obama must make a determination about the pipeline

within 60 days. January 2012, President Obama rejected the Keystone Pipeline proposal arguing there was not enough time to evaluate the reroute proposal and its effects (Canadian Press 2017).

In response, TransCanada stated it would only build the southern leg of the pipeline from Oklahoma to Texas' Gulf Coast. Their argument was that since it does not cross international borders, it no longer needed presidential approval, but submitted a new request to the U.S. Department of State for review. During their review, the U.S. Department of State suggested less greenhouse gases would be emitted through the pipeline as opposed to transporting by truck. April 2014, the Cowboys and Indian Alliance (e.g., ranchers, conservationists, and Tribes), protested outside of the White House to reject the pipeline to protect public land. However, in August 2014, the State Department suspended its review process indefinitely because of a pending lawsuit in Nebraska—the Governor decided to approve the pipeline construction, but opponents sue stating it violated their state constitution (Canadian Press 2017).

December 2014, the Republican Party gained control of the U.S. Congress and passed legislation for the construction of the Keystone Pipeline. On February 24, 2015, President Obama vetoed the legislation. January 2016, TransCanada filed a lawsuit against the Obama administration for exceeding his powers by denying construction of the project. November 2016, Trump elected president. January 2017, President Trump signed a memorandum for the reconsideration of the construction of the pipeline if the company used US steel (Canadian Press 2017). March 2017, the U.S. Department of State, under President Trump issued a permit to TransCanada for the construction of the Keystone XL Pipeline. In November 2018, Judge Brian Morris of the US District Court in Montana blocked the construction of the pipeline, stating the Trump administration failed to provide fact-based evidence for its decision to move forward with construction.

This case occurred over several years and involved numerous actors, but access for energy development on public lands took precedence and as of November 2018, the outcome of this case is to be determined. As this chapter depicts, public land managers

routinely confront how to manage the land, reconciling preservation, recreation, and development. Vague presidential and congressional instruction leaves agency officials interpreting vague statutes
from implementation. This case demonstrates that energy production was a top priority for President Trump. Therefore, if a spill
occurs, it will be up to public land managers to develop approaches
to protect species and the environment. This embodies a reactionary approach to the implementation of US environmental policy.

ISSUES AND CONCERNS

Natural resource and energy policy is characterized by how we use and
manage our public lands. Although our federal managers confront a
host of issues, new concerns are on the horizon and they are tasked with
coordinating plausible solutions. We explore four issue areas: the evolution of natural resource economies; devolution of federal public land
oversight to state officials; the effects of the #MeToo movement; and
water scarcity in the West.

THE EVOLVING WEST AND NATURAL RESOURCE ECONOMIES

As evidenced throughout this chapter, tradition and natural resource
extraction economies (e.g., coal, uranium), often explain American
Western communities. After the Revolutionary War, many soldiers,
instead of receiving salaries, were provided payment in the form of a
Western land parcel. Moreover, homesteaders traveled West in hopes of
making it rich through the exploration of gold or uranium.

Families have lived on these lands for generations and are suspect of
outsiders. In Montana, for example, you define your family by generation—"I am fifth generation Montanan," which is essential for running
for local or statewide office. Such sentiments were dramatized in Kevin
Costner's 2018 *Yellowstone* series where a ranching family confronts
nearby development. These long-standing family traditions collide as "outsiders" move to rural Western states (e.g., Montana, Wyoming) with different viewpoints. The "old" West is defined by tradition and the "new"
West through the lens new perspectives on how best to manage the land.

Regardless, as more individuals move to the American West, perspectives about public lands have changed—specifically, how we define

natural resource extraction economies. Colorado, for example, contained 1.75 million people in 1960. In 2017, the population has grown to over 5 million. As Kerklivet (2017) suggests, "Old economies are simple and easy to see. A ton of coal is mined, shipped to a power plant, and the miner is paid. New economies are more complex and links between production and payment are less easily seen" (npn). Nonetheless, rural, Western communities are accustomed to extraction producing jobs and monetary support for local communities. However, land is symbolic for conservation efforts and if contaminated it could be destructive for local economies. President Obama's Clean Power Plan Rule challenged the rural West to consider new ways to use the land (e.g., wind and solar) to produce energy. States and federal agencies were tasked with cocreating plans for a new energy future.

The Western United States is facing the choice of "old" (economy based upon resource extraction) or "new" (economy based upon clean environment, renewable energy). At the heart of the debate are public land agencies attempting to reconcile these old and new ideals searching for new ways to shepherd bargain and compromise. Arguably, research suggests respecting the long-standing cultural norms without predetermined solutions (Nie 2009). The most important reminder for public land agencies is, as Wyoming rancher stated, "It's the leanin' against the pickup conversation where you let your guard down because you build up trust, that's where the magic starts. This takes decades of trust building, rather than walking in and telling you what to do" (Partners for Collaboration 2018). Nonetheless, if the American West continues to consider transitioning from coal extraction to wind power, bringing individuals to the table for a discussion could prove fruitful.

STATE OR FEDERAL CONTROL

The Trump administration has set forth a movement to federal control and oversight of public lands to states. It is uncertain if President Trump would remove all federal control or only a portion. The idea is that the U.S. Congress would create a land transfer bill. As previously mentioned, this would appease individuals, such as Cliven Bundy, who vehemently oppose federal control of public lands. This is not a new approach and was attempted during the Reagan administration during the Sagebrush Rebellion to devolve more power to state governments to oversee federal public lands.

Proponents of the management transfer of public lands use the Constitution as their guide—that federal ownership of land is a prohibited activity. However, opponents of transfer from federal to state authority use the Constitution's Property Clause to articulate that the federal government can own and control land (Davis 2018). Regardless of perspective, if states were transferred control of all federal public lands, who has access and who pays for the management?

Another component in this conversation are Native American groups. As Davis (2018) succinctly states, "Despite losing their ancestral homes to the establishment of public domain, many Native Americans are steadfast opponents of privatization, as public lands, at their best, can act to protect sacred sites, resources, landscapes, with at least some accountability and accessibility for tribes" (197). Regardless, if you are a proponent or opponent, if management shifts from federal to state control, what role do the BLM, USFWS, USFS, and NPS play in its future? As noted previously, Colorado College's survey of the American West stresses the desire for respondents is to maintain federal oversight of their public lands (Weigel 2017).

WATER SCARCITY

Many of us might not realize this, but there is a looming water crisis in the American West. Take the example of Lori Paup, resident of Sulphur Springs Valley, Arizona. Lori and her family moved to Arizona in 2014 from Pennsylvania. The home they purchased contained a well—something that most individuals have in rural parts of the Midwestern United States. However, on numerous occasions (laundry, bath time), Lori's water was cloudy or did not contain a steady flow of water. Her family had their well inspected to investigate. The well inspector concluded, "you are running out of water" (Shannon 2018, npn).

Homeowners and farmers began to confront one another—who was using all of the water resources. The alternative—drill deeper water wells for the hefty price of $15,000–30,000. However, since 1915, cattle ranchers and homesteaders adopted the oil industry's approach to extract oil from the ground using turbine pumps to extract water to irrigate farmland using Aquifer water across the American West (Shannon 2018).

Due to less rain and snowmelt reaching the floor of dry, arid Western lands, public land managers are now confronting a new term—groundwater mining—water withdrawal exceeds the rate of replenishment (Shannon 2018). Presumably, water in the American West is becoming a semi-renewable infinite resource. Because of this, public land managers, states, and vested interests need to design collective solutions. Finding new water sources is not easy or cheap. Moreover, conservation mechanisms are troubling for individuals accustomed to providing water supplies for cattle and agricultural practices. Experts are considering measures such as toilet to tap (recycle wastewater for consumption) or the construction of desalination plants (remove salt from seawater for and make it drinkable).

The underlining question is who owns water on federal public lands. In 2016, Colorado passed the Colorado Water Rights Protection Act, which reaffirms their right to water on federal land. Legislation defining water on federal public lands has yet to pass the U.S. Congress (Kaufman 2018). This leaves federal public landowners at the eye of yet another battle.

#METOO AND PUBLIC LAND AGENCIES

In our final example for issues and concerns for consideration surrounds the makeup of those within public land agencies. Even before the #MeToo Movement, the USFS and NPS have been under investigation for discriminatory behavior against women. Kathryn Joyce (2018) from *Outside Magazine* spotlighted the stories of Bush and Szydlo.

Bush was an established forester with nineteen years of service for the USFS. In 2011, Bush accepted a position as an engine captain for Sequoia National Forest. Within this position, she was responsible for engine maintenance and physical training (e.g., hiking or running). When Bush became pregnant with twins, she declined to take the fitness test required for training. This test included a three-mile hike with a 45-pound load to be completed within 45 minutes. She asked her boss for a transfer of assignment until post-pregnancy. Reportedly, Bush's boss stated she was useless for the position.

In 2017, Bush et al. *v Purdue 2017*, is a class action lawsuit against the USDA. Under the Equal Employment Opportunity Commission (EEOC) Bush is the lead for a class action complaint against the USFS. The outcome of this case is pending as we write this text.

NPS practices are also of concern. Szydlo, a biologist, was selected to conduct field research for the Grand Canyon National Park. However, she shares a story of sexual harassment from 2006 while on the Colorado River. Her story describes a series of sexual advances from a colleague, the boatman on the river—guiding her from one spot to the next. She recounts countless sexual advances from this individual and concerned sexual assault would ensue. Joyce (2007), in an interview with Szydlo, describes a specific example, "Loeffler slowed the motorboat to a crawl, stopping at nearly every beach. Finally, in the middle of a channel, she heard the motor go quiet. Loeffler came up behind her, grabbed her shoulders and asked her to describe her sexual fantasies so he could act them out" (Joyce 2007, npn). Syzdlo documented her experiences, with countless other women, which led to a full investigation of the Grand Canyon's practices.

There is a much deeper story here that far surpasses discriminatory behavior in the USFS and sexual harassment in the NPS. It is about the treatment of individuals within public land agencies. These are the agencies responsible for reconciling preservation, recreation, and development on our federal lands. These individuals are on the front-lines of implementing policy that affect the future of our environment. If agencies are ill-equipped to ensure fairness within an agency, how can we tackle any of the aforementioned issues and concerns that confront the future of US environmental policy? Joyce reminds us, "Ever since the U.S. created institutions to protect its wilderness, those agencies have been bound up with a particular image of masculinity. The first park rangers in the U.S. were former cavalrymen, assigned to protect preserves like Yellowstone and Yosemite from poachers and fire. The public quickly became enamored by these rugged, solitary figures" (npn).

These four issues have broader consequences for US environmental policy. Consider the consequences the devolution of federal oversight of public lands to states—would this mean that we would eliminate agencies such as the BLM, USFWS, NPS, and USFS. If we did this, would states have the monetary resources to manage the vast amount of federal land in their state? Moreover, if the American Southwest runs out of water—would we then have an extreme case of environmental justice, as discussed in Chapter 8? Regardless, each captures stories across the American West. The "doers" within our public land management agencies are charged with tackling such issues for our future.

Chapter Wrap-Up

Our natural resource policies lead to the management practices of public lands. The way in which we use public lands at the heart of the debate. This chapter provides three broader themes. First, the use of public lands in the American West is riddled with conflict. At the cross-roads, are public land managers within the BLM, USFS, USFWS, and NPS tasked with the interpretation of dated congressional statutes and ever-changing presidential directives. Second, and by design, our public land agencies have dual or multiple mandates by Congress—manage for the future enjoyment of the public while preserving species and be open to energy extraction. Finding a balance across these elements have evolved over time. President Obama sounded the environmental alarm, asking public land agencies to extensively study their practices in the era a changing environment. President Trump in a dramatic roll-back has set energy development as the premiere purpose of our public lands.

Often missing from these conversations is the "public" in public lands. As evidenced throughout this chapter, the public, as defined by public opinion polls are findings that support conservation of our public lands so future generations can indeed enjoy. If we reopened the Grand Canyon, one of our nation's crown jewels to uranium mining, would our parents, like Grijalva's father be able to experience deep the vastness of the canyon and the indescribable beauty of the American West?

Suggested Resources

Readings and Websites

Andrews, Richard L. *Managing the Environment, Managing Ourselves: A History of American Environmental Policy.* New Haven, CT: Yale University Press, 2006.

Andrews, Richard L. 2008. https://www.amazon.com/Managing-Environment-Ourselves-American-Environmental/dp/030011124X.

Childress, Sarah. "The Battle of Bunkerville." 2018. https://www.pbs.org/wgbh/frontline/article/the-battle-over-bunkerville/.

Davis, Chuck. *Western Public Lands and Environmental Politics.* Boulder: Westview Press, 2001.

McKinnon, Taylor. 2007. https://www.npca.org/articles/1061-the-end-of-a-radioactive-proposal.

NASA. 2018. "Fire and Smoke." https://www.nasa.gov/mission_pages/fires/main/index.html.

Nie, Martin. *The Governance of Western Public Lands: Mapping the Present and Future.* Lawrence: University of Kansas Press, 2009.

Rasband, James, James Salzman, and Mark Squillance. *Natural Resources Law and Policy.* New York: Foundation Press, 2009.
Vaughn, Jacqueline. *The Public Land Debate.* Belmont, CA: Thomson Wadsworth, 2007.

Films or Videos

Promise Land. Directed by Gus Van Sant. 2013. DVD.
The National Parks: America's Best Idea. Directed by Ken Burns. 2009. Public Broadcasting Service. DVD.
Yellowstone. Directed by Taylor Sheridan. 2018. Paramount. American Drama Series.

REFERENCES

Andrews, Richard L. *Managing the Environment, Managing Ourselves: A History of American Environmental Policy.* New Haven, CT: Yale University Press, 2006.
Canadian Press. 2017. https://www.cbc.ca/news/politics/keystone-xl-pipeline-timeline-1.3950156.
Colorado College. 2017. https://www.coloradocollege.edu/stateoftherockies/conservationinthewest/.
Davis, Steven. *In Defense of Public Lands: The Case Against Privatization and Transfer.* Philadelphia, PA: Temple University Press, 2018.
Ebbs, Stephanie. "Trump Administration to Take a Smarter, More Aggressive Approach to Prevent Wildfires." 2018. https://abcnews.go.com/Politics/trump-administration-smarter-aggressive-approach-prevent-wildfires/story?id=57218357.
Grand Canyon National Park. *Culture and History.* September 1, 2018. https://www.nps.gov/grca/learn/historyculture/index.htm.
Grijalva, Raul. 2016. https://www.sierraclub.org/sierra/2016-4-july-august/last-words/us-representative-ra-l-grijalva-where-he-found-his-passion-for.
———. 2018. https://grijalva.house.gov/protecting-the-grand-canyon/.
Joyce, Kathryn. 2007. https://highline.huffingtonpost.com/articles/en/park-rangers/.
———. 2018. https://www.outsideonline.com/2334781/forest-service-silencing-women-harassment-discrimination?utm_source=facebook&utm_medium=social&utm_campaign=facebookpos.
Kaufman, Rachel. "Water Crisis in the West." 2018. library.cqpress.com/cqresearcher/document.php?id=cqresrre2018051100.

Kennedy, Brian. "Two-Thirds of Americans Give Priority to Developing Alternative Energy Over Fossil Fuels." 2017. http://www.pewresearch.org/fact-tank/2017/01/23/two-thirds-of-americans-give-priority-to-developing-alternative-energy-over-fossil-fuels/.

Kerklivet. 2017. https://newwest.net/city/article/what_is_a_new_west_vs_old_west_economy/C396/L396/.

Miller, Kathryn. "Legal Developments in the ESA Status of the Grizzly Bear." 2017. http://wildlife.org/legal-developments-in-the-esa-status-of-the-grizzly-bear/.

National Interagency Fire Center. 2018. https://www.nifc.gov/fireInfo/nfn.htm.

Outside Editors. "A Timeline of President Trump's War on Public Lands." 2018. https://www.outsideonline.com/2277446/public-lands-war-timeline.

Partners for Collaboration. 2018. https://www.partnersforconservation.org/lessons-learned-from-the-greater-sage-grouse-collaboration/.

Quoctrung, Bui, and Margot Sanger-Katz. "Why the Government Owns So Much Land in the West." *The New York Times*, January 6, 2016, Wednesday. Retrieved from Nexis Uni.

Rinfret, Sara, Denise Scheberle, and Michelle Pautz. 2018. *Public Policy: A Concise Introduction*. Washington, DC: CQ Press. https://us.sagepub.com/en-us/nam/public-policy/book249415

Shannon, Noah Gallagher. 2018. https://www.nytimes.com/2018/07/19/magazine/the-water-wars-of-arizona.html?smid=fb-nytimes&smtyp=cur.

Shogren, Elizabeth. 2017. https://www.wired.com/2017/01/obamas-energy-legacy-west-outlast-trump-administration/.

Stone, Christopher. "Should Trees Have Standing? Towards Legal Rights for National Objects." *Southern California Law Review* 45 (1972): 450–501.

U.S. Department of Interior. "Public Lands Explained." 2016. https://www.doi.gov/blog/americas-public-lands-explained.

U.S. Department of Interior. "Livestock Grazing." 2018. https://www.blm.gov/programs/natural-resources/rangelands-and-grazing/livestock-grazing.

Weigel, Lori. 2017. https://www.coloradocollege.edu/other/stateoftherockies/conservationinthewest/2018/release/18002%202018%20SOR%20Poll%20Presentation%20FINAL.pdf.

CHAPTER 10

The Politics and Policies of Food

Contents

© The Author(s) 2019   313
S. R. Rinfret and M. C. Pautz, *US Environmental Policy in Action*,
https://Doi.org/10.1007/978-3-030-11316-2_10

Outrage Over the Vegetable Garden at the White House

It may be hard to imagine, but the announcement that the then First Lady of the United States, Michelle Obama, was going to plant and oversee a vegetable garden on White House grounds set off a good deal of controversy at the start of Barack Obama's first term as president. Before we can unpack the details of the outrage, let us first situate the events in context. Michelle Obama was not the only First Lady to speak out about a vegetable garden at the White House; during World War II, Eleanor Roosevelt planted a garden—called a victory garden—as she was the one to start the movement nationwide for other gardens of the same name (NPR 2012). And since the Roosevelt administration, there have been other administrations that have engaged in vegetable growing activities at the White House.

While she was First Lady, Michelle Obama wanted an organic garden, comprised of raised beds that would provide food for the first family's meals and even formal White House dinners. The garden would grow more than 50 varieties of vegetables, including lettuce, spinach, tomatillos, hot peppers, snap peas, as well as herbs like cilantro. The gardens would be fertilized by compost generated by the White House as well as crab meal from the Chesapeake Bay and ladybugs and praying mantises would help control bugs (Burros 2009). In addition to the functionality Mrs. Obama wanted from the garden, she also wanted the garden to educate children about healthy, locally grown fruits and vegetables, stating "[m]y hope is that through children, they will begin to educate their families and that will, in turn begin to educate our communities" (Obama as quoted in Burros 2009). Local elementary school children would help plant and maintain the garden. These actions were part of Ms. Obama's broader efforts to combat childhood obesity.

To many, a White House garden would not seem controversial; but, Ms. Obama's vegetable garden drew criticism because it focused on local, organic food and healthy eating. Critics saw Ms. Obama's garden as an attack on industrial farming, the pesticide industry, and professional farmers (Evich 2016; Beam 2009). The American Farm Bureau Federation said that while backyard gardens are fine, people should not think they could economically feed their families that way (Beam 2009). Along similar lines, the Chilean Exporters Association noted that the garden is "...charming...but it's not practical" (Beam 2009). The United States imports a good deal of fruits and vegetables from Chile, so it is not surprising this trade group had a perspective on Ms. Obama's actions. Additional critiques centered on whether or not the emphasis on organic and local farming would undermine the contribution that industrial agriculture has made to the well-being of society with its ability to provide food for Americans cheaply and efficiently.

Eventually the uproar subsided, and the garden grew to more than 2800 square feet, producing about 2000 pounds of produce a year (Evich 2016). Prior to leaving the White House, Michelle Obama helped secure private funding of $2.5 million to support the ongoing maintenance of the garden so it would not burden taxpayers with its upkeep. Upon entering the White House, Ms. Obama's successor, Melania Trump announced that she intends to keep and maintain the garden (Reilly 2017). Time will reveal whether or not this once controversial garden remains a fixture at the White House.

Perhaps after reading about this controversy you are wondering why something as benign as a vegetable garden would engender such conflict. The point here is that even food can quickly become controversial, just as other major topics in environmental policy, like climate change. What we eat and how that food is grown and produced brings together a multitude of actors with varying interests and concerns that can make even vegetables politically contentious.

On first glance, a chapter on food may seem out of place in a book devoted to environmental policy; but a closer examination quickly reveals how intertwined food is with the environment. The health and the well-being of the natural environment is critical for the production of food that humans need to grow and flourish—indeed, the two are inextricably linked. Growing and producing food humans need impacts the environment, often in a negative way due modern agricultural practices (e.g., nonpoint source pollution). Accordingly, this chapter will investigate the intersection of environmental concerns with the food system in the United States. To do so, we start at the foundation and examine what we mean by food policy and politics, then we discuss the agricultural sector in the United States to not only understand the direct effects on the environment but also to get a sense of the scope and scale of agriculture. From there, we explore patterns of food consumption, nutrition, and public health so that we can grapple with food safety and nutrition assistance. The final section of the chapter turns our attention to culture and food as the role of the public is instrumental in investigating food policy.

Food Policy and Politics

Food policy refers to the decisions and actions surrounding food taken by, or instigated by the government. These steps may include laws, regulations, and actions by government agencies that affect the growth, production, distribution, and consumption of food. Often, these decisions incorporate political, economic, and cultural dimensions. Food politics is a term that incorporates the dilemmas and tensions associated with these decisions about food; and to paraphrase Theodore Lowi, food politics is about who gets what, when, and how regarding food. Both food policies and food politics encompasses the food industry, which includes all the organizations and "...companies that produce, process, manufacture, sell, and serve food, beverages, and dietary supplements" (Nestle 2002, 11).

The size and scale of the food industry in the United States is massive. About 1% of the nation's Gross Domestic Product (GDP) comes from the output of American farms, or about $136.7 billion annually (USDA 2018b). According to the US Department of Agriculture (USDA), the food service industry, which encapsulates restaurants and operations that sell or provide food, is worth approximately $1.46 trillion dollars (USDA 2018a). More than 20 million jobs, both full-time and part-time, come from the agriculture and food sectors (USDA 2018b). Americans spend about 13% of their household budgets on food, which is lower than the majority of nations in the world (USDA 2018b, Bosso and Tichenor, 195). In other words, most Americans spend a much smaller portion of their money on food than people in other nations, indicating that food is comparatively cheap for Americans. At the beginning of the 1900s, Americans spent around 40% of their budgets on food, indicating that food was nearly four times as expensive than as it is today (Paarlberg, 36). Furthermore, crops and food products play a major role in the nation's trade, both imports and exports. The economic dimensions of the food system in the United States should be sufficient to compel attention to this complex policy area, but with our primary focus on the natural environment, the connections to the environment are significant.

Connections Between Food and Environmental Issues

The environment plays a central role in the nation's food system because without the physical environment—meaning the air, water, and land—we would not be able to grow crops. Without the health of grasslands, corn would not grow, which is a common part of animal diets and the key ingredient in many processed foods. And the impacts of agricultural practices on the environment are significant; approximately 7% of the greenhouse gas emissions in the United States come from agriculture, and this does not include the emissions that result from the processing, transportation, and distribution of the food products (Wilde, 48). This means that growing and producing food has a substantial impact on climate change. Additionally, runoff from agricultural fields is a major contributor to non-point source pollution. As we will see in the coming pages, the centrality of the environment in food policy and politics is very clear, and examination of environmental issues has to involve food politics and policy.

THE AGRICULTURAL SECTOR IN THE UNITED STATES: ITS SIZE, SCOPE, AND ENVIRONMENTAL IMPACT

Discussions of farming and its role in society often gravitate to idyllic notions of a farmer and his family working hard on their small plot of land to grow crops and raise animals. Although there are still small farms throughout the nation, most farming is tied to the enormous agriculture industry and small farms are often connected to large corporations. Therefore, to explore the agricultural sector in the United States and grapple with its connections with the environment, we start by considering the scope of the sector.

The majority of farms today are large operations that employ the latest technologies to cultivate the crops we eat. The USDA reports that in 2016 there were around two million farms nationwide (USDA 2017, 4). By way of comparison, in 1935, there were about six and a half million farms in the United States (Bosso and Tichenor, 195). Approximately 911 million acres are farmed in the United States with the average farm more than 440 acres (USDA 2017, 4). As the number of farms has been declining steadily for years, the average size of farms has grown (USDA 2017, 7). Around 4% of farms account for two-thirds of farm products in the market; in other words, a small handful of farms produce about two-thirds of the agricultural products (Bosso and Tichenor, 195). These figures offer the evidence that small, family run farms are not the principle type of farm used to produce the nation's food. Moreover, these large farms do not necessarily employ legions of workers to run as technology is increasingly relied on in agriculture. Around 1% of the American workforce today is involved in farming whereas in 30 years ago that figure was about 3%, down dramatically from 50% in 1870 (Paarlberg, 3).

There are many different ways to categorize farms, including by area of the country, type of farm, or industry group. The Heartland, as labeled by the USDA, comprises Iowa, Illinois, Indiana, and Missouri and it is the most productive region of the nation for farming. Broadly there are two major types of farms: farms that produce crops (e.g., grains, feed for animals, vegetables) and farms that produce livestock (e.g., dairy, poultry, cattle). In terms of value, the biggest sectors are in cash grains and soybeans and other high value crops, like fruits and vegetables (Park et al. 2011, 10) (Fig. 10.1).

Another way to consider the different types of farms is by industry groups: grain and oilseeds, fruits and vegetables, cattle, dairy, and hogs, poultry, and eggs. Grain and oilseeds include corn, which is most often used for animal feed, and soybeans which is also used in animal feed, vegetable oil, and manufactured foods. This is the industry sector that receives the largest share of farm subsidies and most of the production in this sector comes from America's Heartland (Wilde, 18–19). Fruits and vegetables represent the smallest percentage of farmland in the U.S., but the harvest is very valuable. This sector includes crops such as grapes, oranges, apples, almonds, strawberries, lettuce, and potatoes. Most of these crops come from California and Arizona, along with Idaho for potatoes. The cattle sector is found in areas in the western United States where the land is not as ideal for growing crops but land is plentiful since raising cows requires a lot of land—indeed, 40% of the agricultural land in the country is used for cattle (Wilde, 20). There are two primary types of cattle farm: farms were cows are born and farms called feedlots, where cows are fattened up for slaughter. Dairy farms are found mostly in Wisconsin, Minnesota, and New York (Wilde, 20). The primary

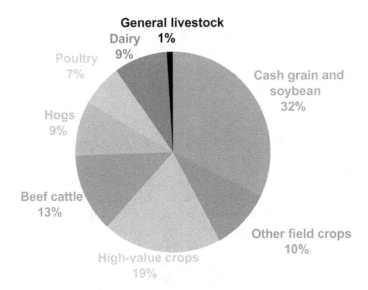

General livestock
Dairy   1%

Poultry   9%
7%

Cash grain and
soybean
32%

Hogs
9%

Beef cattle
13%

Other field crops
10%

High-value crops
19%

Fig. 10.1   US net farm income by farm production specialty (*Source* Adapted from Park et al. 2011, 10)

function of this sector is to turn animal products into cheese, milk, and butter. Finally, the hogs, poultry, and eggs sector is largely found in the Heartland, but North Carolina has seen a dramatic increase in this sector. This agricultural sector in particular has come to be dominated by large corporations and food manufacturers, such as Tyson, Smithfield, and Perdue. And this sector has experienced rapid technological innovations in recent decades.

Much more could be said about the modern agricultural sector in the United States today, but in keeping with our focus on the intersection of food and environmental policy, this brief overview enables us to grasp the scale of the sector and recognize that farming in reality may not comport with the images we have in our minds about farming. To that end, consider some of the summary points Bosso and Tichenor (2015) offer about today's agricultural sector: efficiency, specialization, technologized, energy dependent, globalized. Agriculture is well developed, harnessing technological innovations to enable it to efficiently and economically produce for its customers. These improvements in farming have enabled Americans to see the portion of their budgets they have to spend on food drop dramatically. However, the effects of agriculture and food production on the natural environment are significant. In fact, in some areas, agriculture is the biggest contributor to environmental degradation, from non-point source pollution to methane emissions. And this sector of the economy uses a lot of energy.

Environmental Impacts of Agriculture

The sheer size of the agricultural sector alone helps us start to grasp the potential environmental impact of this sector. With more than 900 million acres utilized for farming in the United States, the connection with the natural environment is apparent. More specifically, food production impacts the following environmental resources: water, air, land and soil quality, and native species. The use of chemicals and the generation of waste has additional environmental implications. Agriculture uses more than 70% of the planet's freshwater—and more than 90% in some areas of the western United States (Anderson 2015, 59). More specifically, the agricultural activities that impact water quality include: tillage and plowing, fertilization, spreading manure, raising animals in feedlots, applying pesticides, irrigating, and aquaculture. Much of the contamination of groundwater and surface water is a result of agriculture (Anderson, 61).

As we have seen in previous chapters, the United States has an array of laws that deal with water quality. The Clean Water Act addresses point-source pollution, which means water contamination that is attributable to particular source (e.g., a pipe draining into a waterway). When it comes to agriculture, though, the water contamination issues stem from runoff, which is a nonpoint source of pollution. This means it is difficult to pinpoint a specific pollutant and level of contamination from an individual source, therefore it can be difficult to use the Clean Water Act to address water quality concerns from agriculture (Angelo and Choate 2013). The primary manner in which the CWA addresses water quality is through the issuance of National Pollutant Discharge Elimination Systems (NPDES) permits and agriculture is not subject to these permits. In fact, most agricultural practices are exempt from water quality protections. Runoff from agriculture can be addressed through Total Maximum Daily Loads (TMDLs) that are established for a given waterway, but TMDLs only specify how much of a particular pollutant a waterway can handle and then requires states to take action to meet water quality standards. This is not to imply that there are no government efforts addressing water quality concerns and runoff from agriculture. Various provisions of the farm bill provide subsidies for farmers to restore habitats, prevent erosion, and utilize best management practices for addressing runoff.

Air quality is another concern when it comes to agriculture. In the United States, 7% of all greenhouse gas emissions are attributable to agriculture (Wilde, 48). Worldwide, farming accounts for about 30% of GHGs (Anderson, 64). Livestock production, along with farming equipment, generates significant amounts of air pollution. Additionally, application of fertilizers can contribute to air pollution along with the release of particular matter into the atmosphere from soil tiling and erosion. Confined Animal Feeding Operations (CAFOs) are a concentrated source of air pollutants, often from animal waste, that range from ammonia, hydrogen sulfide, particulate matter, volatile organic compounds (VOCs), hazardous air pollutants (HAPs), and odor. The Clean Air Act regulates these pollutants, but most of the regulations focus on "major" sources of air pollution and often, farms, even large industrial ones, do not meet the threshold standards for major sources, according to the US EPA (Clemmer 2013, 163).

Although the EPA has been somewhat reluctant to regulate farms as stringently as other industries under the Clean Air Act, some states have taken steps to address air pollution from agriculture (Clemmer, 176). A handful of states, including Colorado, Missouri, and Illinois, have implemented odor standards for factory farms and some have also specified construction standards as well as operational requirements (Clemmer, 181). To date, though, air pollution from agriculture remains largely uncontrolled (Clemmer, 184).

Growing crops and raising livestock can degrade the land's quality. Soil degradation can come from a range of agricultural activities from deforestation and tilling to excessive vehicle and equipment traffic, too much irrigation, and application of fertilizers. The use of chemicals in farming can fall under the Federal Insecticide, Fungicide, and Rodenticide Act, but FIFRA only applies to the manufacturing of chemicals and not their use or application on land. Further, animal waste can pose a significant environmental impact, particularly massive amounts of waste in Confined Animal Feeding Operations (CAFOs). However, unlike waste we generate in our households and hazardous wastes, there are not environmental statutes that tackle mountains of animal manure, for example, and address the environmental impacts of its generation.

Agriculture and food production have effects on every facet of the natural environment and contribute to the majority of environmental issues we contend with today, from climate change to biodiversity loss.

There are a number of ways that the government is involved with agriculture that do not directly pertain to environmental concerns. The nation has long provided price supports for farmers and their crops (e.g., subsidies) and helped to control the supply in order to make farming profitable for those in the industry and make food affordable. The federal government has also been very involved in providing insurance to farmers as their livelihoods are often at the mercy of weather patterns and pests.

There are two additional pieces of legislation that merit mention here that pertain to agriculture. The farm bill,[1] which is the term for a collection of laws passed by Congress every five or so years, deals with many facets of agriculture. The first farm bill was first passed in 1933 and called the Agriculture Adjustment Act as part of Franklin D. Roosevelt's New Deal. The farm bill covers a range of agricultural issues from subsidies for the industry to research to international trade and environmental conservation. Up until recent years, the passage of the farm bill has been largely noncontroversial and enjoyed bipartisan support—after all, the nation thinks well of its idyllic farms. The farm bill has engendered controversy in recent iterations as provisions were included to make changes to the food stamp program (more on that program is in the next section) as well as the sheer size of the bill and its cost. The last farm bill, the Agricultural Act, was passed in 2014 and runs through 2018.

The 2007 Energy Independence and Security Act may not seem relevant to agriculture but a provision in this law has major implications for the industry. The law, which was passed during the George W. Bush administration, is an effort to make the U.S. more reliant on domestic sources of energy rather than relying on energy imported from around the world, including volatile places such as the Middle East. Part of the law promotes alternative energy sources other than fossil fuels and requires the increased use of ethanol, which is made from corn, which

---

[1] Various names have been used for specific farm bills, including the Food, Conservation, and Energy Act of 2008 or the Agricultural Adjustment Act of 1938. The term "farm bill" refers to a category of legislation that is the primary means of federal government policy surrounding agriculture and food.

has agricultural and environmental implications. While ethanol is a fuel source that is not a traditional fossil fuel, it requires a lot of fossil fuels to produce. Corn farmers are understandably thrilled with mandates for a larger share of the nation's energy to come from their product, but many other interests are less enthusiastic, from environmentalists to the renewable energy sector.

Agricultural practices can have significant impacts on the environment, notably pertaining to air quality, water quality, land quality, and the generation of waste. Most environmental laws in the United States do not address agricultural practices and their impact on the environment directly, and as mentioned previously, much of the sector is exempt from environmental regulatory provisions. Regardless of one's perspective on farming, we should recognize there is a direct and substantial impact on the environment, but addressing those concerns are not easy given the centrality of food to human well-being. These considerations do not account for the environmental impacts that result from transportation crops and animals nor do they address the environmental inputs needed to process and manufacture the food products that we buy, cook, and consumed daily.

FOOD CONSUMPTION, NUTRITION, AND PUBLIC HEALTH

The evolution of agriculture in the United States and the increased mechanization of it supported urbanization, thereby contributing to the host of environmental issues brought about as the population shifted. No longer did people have to spend most of their time growing and preparing food to survive as those activities could be done by a smaller and smaller percentage of the population more efficiently and economically. With American involvement in both World Wars, more and more people entered the workforce and moved away from the fields, so foods that were convenient were increasingly necessary. Women joined the workforce in large numbers during World War II in particular and this led to the rise of Betty Crocker's cake mixes and Swanson's TV dinners (Wilde, 87). Food had to be more convenient and have a longer shelf life. And these changes had major implications for agricultural practices, nutrition and health, and the environment. Accordingly, the food system in the United States grew in size and complexity and while it became more convenient for people as less time was required to prepare food, there are important health and environmental implications as a result of these changes in consumption patterns. And these implications help explain the role the of government in these topics. As we will see in this section, the role of government—from legislation to rulemaking and implementation—is significant and complex.

Dietary Guidance from the Government

In the U.S., and elsewhere, there is widespread public confusion about nutrition and the government plays a role in all of this. And we do know that in the United States, Americans are eating more calories than they did generations ago. Forty years ago, Americans averaged around 1875 calories per day and that figure has climbed to nearly 2100 calories (Moshfegh 2015, 379). More of those calories are coming from carbohydrates while we consume less calories from fats.

The US government has long been concerned with nutrition and dietary guidance. In 1862, the USDA was created to ensure a sufficient and reliable food supply and to provide information to the nation on agricultural matters (Nestle 2002, 33). By the early 1900s, the government became particularly worried about nutritional deficiencies and the disorders that resulted. The USDA issued its first dietary recommendations in 1917 in a 14-page booklet entitled *How to Select Foods* and offered five food groups during the 1920s (Nestle, 34). In the following decade, the USDA identified some "protective" foods that offered important vitamins and nutrients. Then in 1941, the Food and Nutrition Board offered Recommended Dietary Allowances. The four basic food groups—milk, meat, fruits and vegetables, and breads and cereals—were introduced in the 1950s along with recommended dietary allowances for each group. The 1960s saw the government make its first statements that some foods might be "bad" or "unwise;" these included foods that were high in fat, cholesterol, salt, sugar, and calories.

Since the 1970s, the federal government has regularly updated its dietary guidance for Americans. In 1977, the *Dietary Goals for the United States* encouraged increased consumption of carbohydrates but decreased consumption of fats. This guidance was greeted with outrage from various sectors, including cattle ranchers, dairy farmers, and egg producers among others, because they viewed the government's guidance as telling Americans that their products were bad. Similar politics were involved in the guidance released in 1980. The *Dietary Guidelines for Americans*

Fig. 10.2 Food guide pyramid (*Source* https://www.cnpp.usda.gov/food-guide-pyramid-graphic-resources)

recommended that people eat a variety of foods, maintain their ideal, weight, and avoid too much fat, cholesterol, sugar, and sodium. Initially these guidelines included phrases such as "eat less" but that wording was not politically palatable, so language was amended to encourage Americans to avoid too much (Nestle 2002, 46). Revisions to these guidelines and wordsmithing continued throughout the 1980s.

It was during the aforementioned decade that work began on a symbol of healthy eating that you are probably familiar with: the food pyramid (see Fig. 10.2).

First released in 1991, and updated several times since then, the food pyramid reflected the government's efforts to encourage healthy eating by helping Americans make sense of all the messages around nutrition and health guidance. Controversy surrounded the release of the pyramid

Fig. 10.3   MyPlate (https://www.choosemyplate.gov/)

because various food producers were upset that the government would seemingly convey an endorsement of certain food sectors over others. So, in 1992 a revised *Food Guide Pyramid* was released by the USDA. Language was changed to appease the food industry, especially Kraft Foods, and "eating right" became "food guide" (Nestle 2002, 64). Instead of telling Americans to eat two to three servings of a particular food category, the language was updated to say "at least" two to three servings. More updates followed about every five years.

Alas, in 2011, the Pyramid was replaced by MyPlate (see Fig. 10.3). The MyPlate initiative from the USDA was an effort to convey better nutrition information in a more visually appealing manner—via a place setting. According to the USDA, "MyPlate is designed to remind Americans to eat healthfully, and is not intended to change consumer behavior alone" (USDA 2018c). Note the careful language from the agency about its aim; undoubtedly the language was deliberate in an effort to be mindful of past controversies around federal government nutrition and dietary guidance.

This is unlikely to be the federal government's last effort in providing dietary and nutrition guidance, especially given the government's interest in the overall health of the general public.

Public Health

At this point, you might be wondering why the government would even go through such efforts surrounding dietary guidance if it raises so much ire from the food industry. These efforts stem from concern over the health of Americans. During the first part of the twentieth century, the government was very concerned about malnutrition and conditions that resulted from nutrient deficiencies. These worries grew as the government had challenges recruiting people for the military. Today, the concern is less about lack of nutrients and more about the excessive intake of food as diet is linked to four of the top ten leading causes of death in the United States (heart disease, cancer, stroke, and diabetes) (Paarlberg, 81–82). Thirty-six percent of American adults were obese in 2010, which is double the percentage from 1971 (Paarlberg, 82). By 2014, that figure grew to 38% (CDC 2018a). More than two-thirds of Americans are either overweight or obese (NIDDK 2018).

Another mechanism that the government employs to encourage healthy food choices is food labeling. Various pieces of legislation—and subsequent rulemaking—require country of origin labeling and the listing of potential allergens. The Nutrition Facts Panel, or the nutrition information label, adorns most packaged food in the United States to help Americans understand what is in the food they are eating. The first labels of this kind appeared in 1990 under direction of the US Food and Drug Administration and have undergone a variety of updates. The most recent rules came about in 2016 and include revisions to the serving size to make it a better reflection of how much a person might consume and additional information about any sugars that were added to the food during the production process. Unsurprisingly, there was strong objection to these revisions, particularly the updates about sugar additions (see Fig. 10.4 for the original and revised nutrition label).

Beyond the government's role in providing Americans information about the food they eat and helping clarify the best science of nutrition guidance, the government is very involved in ensuring the safety of the food we eat and helping ensure access to food for those individuals who may otherwise go hungry. The next section investigates government programs and regulations surrounding food safety and hunger.

Nutrition Facts

Serving Size 2/3 cup (55g)
Servings Per Container About 8

Amount Per Serving

Calories 230   Calories from Fat 40

                                    % Daily Value*

Total Fat 8g	**12%**
Saturated Fat 1g	**5%**
Trans Fat 0g	
Cholesterol 0mg	**0%**
Sodium 160mg	**7%**
Total Carbohydrate 37g	**12%**
Dietary Fiber 4g	**16%**
Sugars 1g	
Protein 3g	

Vitamin A	10%
Vitamin C	8%
Calcium	20%
Iron	45%

* Percent Daily Values are based on a 2,000 calorie diet.
Your daily value may be higher or lower depending on
your calorie needs.

	Calories:	2,000	2,500
Total Fat	Less than	65g	80g
Sat Fat	Less than	20g	25g
Cholesterol	Less than	300mg	300mg
Sodium	Less than	2,400mg	2,400mg
Total Carbohydrate		300g	375g
Dietary Fiber		25g	30g

Nutrition Facts

8 servings per container
Serving size   2/3 cup (55g)

Amount per serving

Calories   230

                                    % Daily Value*

Total Fat 8g	**10%**
Saturated Fat 1g	**5%**
Trans Fat 0g	
Cholesterol 0mg	**0%**
Sodium 160mg	**7%**
Total Carbohydrate 37g	**13%**
Dietary Fiber 4g	**14%**
Total Sugars 12g	
Includes 10g Added Sugars	**20%**
Protein 3g	

Vitamin D 2mcg	10%
Calcium 260mg	20%
Iron 8mg	45%
Potassium 235mg	6%

* The % Daily Value (DV) tells you how much a nutrient in
a serving of food contributes to a daily diet. 2,000 calories
a day is used for general nutrition advice.

Fig. 10.4 Original and revised nutrition labels (*Source* https://en.wikipedia.org/wiki/Nutrition_facts_label)

THE ROLE OF GOVERNMENT IN FOOD SAFETY AND NUTRITION ASSISTANCE

Since the government is concerned about the health and well-being of its citizens, there are two specific policy areas to explore: food safety and nutrition assistance programs.

Food Safety

The Centers for Disease Control (CDC) estimates that every year, one in every six Americans will become sick from eating contaminated food,

128,000 people will be hospitalized because of it, and that approximately 3000 Americans die every year as a result of contaminated food, resulting in costs of more than $15 billion dollars annually (CDC 2018b, c). There are more than 250 foodborne diseases that result from a variety of bacteria, viruses, and pathogens including *salmonella, listeria, clostridium perfringens,* and *e. coli.* It is difficult to monitor and measure the exact figures since most Americans have likely experienced some form of food poisoning and they may or may not have sought professional medical care and had their illness tracked. It is also complicated by a web of actors who are involved in food safety from growers and producers to local health departments and medical professionals to the CDC and USDA.

In today's world, food is far safer with than it used to be even a century ago as sanitary practices, safer packaging, and refrigeration are mainstays of food production and consumption. But as the statistics above indicate, food contamination is still common as food can be contaminated at numerous points from production to transportation to cooking and consumption. In the production process, contaminants can be introduced in slaughterhouses, through insufficient manufacturing processes and monitoring and the adulteration processes of many manufactured foods, and even in agricultural fields. Common sources of contamination in food preparation include unwashed hands and cutting boards as well as poor refrigeration and insufficiently cooked meats. The US Department of Health and Human Services (DHHS) maintains a website (http://www.foodsafety.gov) in which current recalls and food safety alerts are updated continuously. At the time of writing, a review of this site indicates recalls on everything from frozen, ready to eat green beans to beef stew to pre-made penne pasta. Most of these recalls garner little converge in the news media, but there are notable examples of major, nationwide recalls. In 2009, the Peanut Corporation of America recalled more than 2100 products made by 200 companies in 43 states because of tainted peanuts. Nestle recalled 300,000 cases of premade cookie dough in the same year because of *e. coli.* In 2008, Hallmark Beef recalled 143 million pounds of beef and Cargill pulled 36 million pounds of ground turkey in 2011. And if you think it is just processed food or meat products, remember that in 2006 five people died eating spinach contaminated by *e. coli.*

The government has a long history of trying to mitigate these episodes and there are some notable pieces of federal legislation that address food safety. In 1906, the Pure Food and Drug Act was the first of its kind and required accurate labeling of food and drug products and created the Food and Drug Administration. During the same year, the Meat Inspection Act was passed focusing on the processing of meat. Mandatory factory inspections by the government came in 1938 with the Federal, Food, Drug, and Cosmetic Act after more than 100 people were killed from a toxic product. More recently, the 2004 Food Allergy Labeling and Consumer Protection Act requires foods to be labeled if they contain or may contain common allergens. And the Food Safety Modernization Act passed in 2010 gives the FDA additional authority to regulate how foods are grown and processed, and came about after many of the food safety recalls mentioned earlier. This was the first major legislation since 1938 to address food safety.

To implement these laws and ensure the safety of the nation's food supply, numerous government agencies are involved at multiple levels of government. At the federal level, the Department of Health and Human Services houses the Food and Drug Administration and the Centers for Disease Control. The FDA is primarily responsible for the safety of most food products, with the exception of meat, poultry, and processed eggs. And the CDC monitors and investigates foodborne illnesses. The USDA includes the Food Safety Inspection Service (FSIS), the Animal Plant Health Inspection Service, and the Agricultural Marketing Service. The FSIS is responsible for the safety of meat, poultry, and processed eggs. Here it is important to underscore that two major and distinct federal agencies are responsible for food safety and each agency—the USDA and DHHS—have a very different mission from the other. The Agricultural Marketing Service establishes the quality and marketing grades and standards for dairy products, fruits, vegetables, and meats. In addition to these agencies, the EPA is involved in food safety as it regulates the pesticides that are used in agriculture and the National Oceanographic and Atmospheric Administration within the U.S. Department of Commerce oversees the voluntary seafood safety and quality inspection services. And US Customs and Border Protection within the Department of Homeland Security inspects food products that are imported from other countries. In addition to the work of these federal level agencies, state and local government agencies are involved, especially public health entities. Needless to say, there are a lot of organizations involved just from the government side of food safety without even enumerating the food manufacturers, retailers, associations, and interest groups that are also concerned with food safety.

Hunger and Food Insecurity

With all of this investigation of food and worry about keeping it safe, it is imperative to note that significant numbers of Americans suffer from hunger and food insecurity. Hunger can be defined as "the uneasy or painful sensation caused by a lack of food," according to the Life Sciences Research Office of the Federation of American Societies for Experimental Biology (as quoted in Christaldi and Castellanos 2018, 16). And hunger is often used to reference chronic undernutrition, which is the long-term condition that includes deficiencies in diet (Paarlberg, 31).

Food insecurity, according to the USDA, encompasses "households [that] were uncertain of having, or unable to acquire, enough food to meet the needs of all their members because they had insufficient money or other resources for food" (USDA 2018d). Among those households that are food insecure, there are additional delineations of low food security and very low food insecurity. In 2016, 12.3% of American households, or 15.6 million households, were food insecure, which is roughly the same figure from the previous year (USDA 2018d). Put differently, 41.2 million people in the U.S. were food insecure and 6.5 million children live in food insecure households (USDA 2018b). The consequences of food insecurity can be profound, including adverse psychosocial and health effects (Christaldi and Castellanos, 19). Stress, anxiety, and depression are common with food insecurity and for children, this can mean poor performance in school, higher rates of absenteeism, and altered social skills (Christaldi and Castellanos).

Historically, hunger and food insecurity garnered attention as the nation transitioned from an agrarian society to an industrial one. And then during the Great Depression, hunger again became a prominent societal concern and the New Deal included federal government efforts to curb hunger. As the nation became embroiled in World War II, the nation was again focused on hunger as 40% of potential draftees were rejected by the military because of malnutrition (Christaldi and Castellanos, 17). Later in the twentieth century, a CBS documentary on *Hunger in America* concentrated the nation's attention on malnutrition when it first aired in May of 1968. Viewers were astonished to see the problem of hunger rampant in their own nation, as many assumed hunger to be a problem that beset other nations, and demanded the government take action to alleviate the issue. Each of these historical circumstances resulted in policy action about hunger, ranging from school food programs that started in the 1940s to nutrition assistance programs in the 1960s. In reviewing this history, it is important to note that American society continues to face challenges ensuring that people have enough to eat and that the food available is nutritious. During this time in American history, the wealth and prominence of the country has continued to grow, but a sizeable portion of Americans still do have reliable access to food. And this concerns Americans.

A Spring 2017 Gallup Poll found that concerns about hunger in America are rising. When asked if they worry about hunger and homelessness in the United States, 47% of respondents to the poll said they worried a great deal, which holds steady from 2016 but is up dramatically from 35% of respondents expressing the same concern in 2004 (Jones 2017).

Americans' concern about hunger has historically led to a variety of federal government programs to combat hunger. During the Great Depression, the first federal government food assistance program was created, known as food stamps. The program started in the Department of Agriculture where recipients got orange or blue stamps that could be used to buy food and lasted for just a few years. In 1964 the Food Stamp Act was passed by Congress as part of President Lyndon B. Johnson's "War on Poverty." Essentially, the modern food stamp program was a federal aid program run by the Department of Agriculture that helped those individuals and families with no or low incomes buy food with "stamps" or "coupons" at local grocery stores and markets. Since the 1960s, the program has gone through a variety of revisions, including eligibility requirements and the process to determine eligibility. The program has seen varying levels of support over the decades. Significant changes came in the 1990s when welfare programs, including food stamps, saw alterations including changes in requirements to receive aid and the conversion of the books of stamps to an electronic benefits transfer (EBT) card that looks and acts much like an ATM card. The 2008 farm bill renamed the food stamps program the Supplemental Nutrition Assistance Program (SNAP).

The program is still administered by the Food and Nutrition Service in the USDA today; however, the benefits are distributed to state governments who in turn administer the program within the state. To qualify for SNAP benefits, individuals and households must earn 130% or less of the federal poverty limit; put another way, if an individual's gross income is less than $1245 a month or a household of four's income is less than $2552, they qualify for SNAP. There are restrictions about what SNAP recipients can and cannot buy with their EBT cards. For example, paper towels and napkins cannot be purchased under SNAP nor can alcoholic beverages. In 2018, approximately 43.7 million people received SNAP benefits, up slightly from the previous year (Food and Nutrition Service 2018a). The average household received $278.51 a month in SNAP benefits (Food and Nutrition Service 2018a). Another program that is similar in some ways is the Special Supplemental Nutrition Program for Women, Infants, and Children, better known as WIC. This program provides similar benefits to women who are pregnant and women who have children under the age of five. In 2017, approximately 7.3 million people participated in this program, receiving about $41 a month (Food and Nutrition Service 2018b). Like SNAP, WIC is overseen by the USDA but administered through state governments.

The school lunch and breakfast programs represent other government efforts to ensure children have access to food. The National School Lunch Program (NSLP) was created during Harry Truman's administration to provide food for kids and, perhaps more importantly, to help the nation's farmers with their surplus crops. Passed in 1946, the National School Lunch Act was a fascinating compromise between those politicians who were concerned about nutrition and children and those politicians concerned about the state of agriculture in the United States (Levine 2008, 72). Farmers were experiencing dropping prices and an excess supply of crops and, at the same time, there were growing concerns about childhood nutrition. So the school lunch program was born in an effort to help the agricultural sector by having a customer for their excess crops and to provide some price stability while also providing food to school kids. This explains why the program was then, and is still now, run out of the USDA, rather than health or education focused agencies. In the 1960s, the school breakfast program was added.

These programs provide free or reduced priced meals to school children. In 2016, school cafeterias served more than 30 million kids under this program (Food and Nutrition Service 2018c). As with the SNAP and WIC programs, the USDA oversees the program, but it is administered at the state level. Schools, both public and private, participate in the program and receive cash subsidies to provide meals to children as well as the ability to obtain food from the USDA Foods program (which distributes agricultural surplus foods). Schools are reimbursed at various rates for the meals they serve; they receive between $2.83 and $3.06 for a reduced priced lunch and between $3.23 and $3.46 for a free lunch. The point here is that a school has to figure out how to serve a meal that meets nutritional guidance set by the government that is also appealing a child that costs just a few dollars! Children whose families have incomes at or below 130% of the federal poverty level are eligible for free meals and children whose families have incomes between 185 and 130% of the federal poverty level are eligible for meals at reduced prices of no more than forty cents.

In 2010, the Healthy Hunger-Free Kids Act was passed by Congress that reauthorized these programs. For the first time since 1995, the USDA updated the nutritional standards of the meals served in these programs, doubling the amount of fruits and vegetables required—now there is a weekly requirement for a dark green, a red or orange vegetable, and beans and peas. Also required are whole grains and a reduction of sodium and elimination of trans fats from meals. Additional nutritional guidelines came in 2012. These programs are under scrutiny with the Trump administration. In December 2017, the administration announced that it is not going to pursue additional reductions in salt in school lunches that the Obama administration put in place. USDA Secretary Sonny Perdue indicated that relaxing the salt restrictions is necessary since kids do not eat healthier food (Danilova 2017). These programs are some of the major avenues that the federal government is involved in reducing hunger and food insecurity in the United States.

Concern about the food Americans eat and the access they have to that food has been and will continue to be a concern of the government. And we have seen from the discussion in this section that determining and disseminating nutritional information about food is complex, just as making sure that the food is safe to eat and available to those individuals and families who suffer from food insecurity is as well. The role of government in these pursuits is longstanding and that history brings may actors into the process, making it complex. Not only are there environmental implications to the growing and production of the food we eat, but there are implications for the work of federal, state, and local governments and the other public sector organizations that work alongside the government.

Voices from School Cafeterias: Smart Snacks Regulations

The federal government has been involved in providing meals for school children and ensuring nutritious food for more than eighty years, but that does not mean it is all figured out. In the 2010 Healthy Hunger-Free Kids Act, Congress sought improvements in providing kids with healthy food. Under this law, the USDA got to work crafting new standards for the snacks available to kids in schools. Through the rulemaking process described in Chapter 4, the USDA put together new regulations about what can and cannot be sold in school vending machines, snack shops, and through fundraisers. These regulations also set limits for fats, salt, and sugar. These changes went into effect for the 2014–2015 school year. As often happens in rulemaking, the results may not always meet expectations. Here we highlight a couple of the fascinating dimensions of this rulemaking and the ramifications for those individuals on the front-lines: school cafeteria workers. As *New York Times* reporter Nicholas Confessore reports, the work of "lunch ladies" has taken on new political significance (Confessore 2014).

For decades, many schools have struggled to provide meals to their students—many of whom would go without meals if it were not for the school meals, to make food that is appealing to kids, and to ensure fiscal responsibility—often per the demand of the local school board. Providing meals that kids will eat and that cover all the costs of running a school cafeteria and buying food is a delicate balancing act and food service workers in school cafeterias have a lot to juggle. Many schools have looked to ways to supplement the funds they receive through the federal lunch and breakfasts programs and local tax dollars with revenues from vending machines and other food sales. In the Smart Snacks rule, food sold in other places besides the cafeteria line, such as vending machines, has to meet nutritional standards. Huge food manufacturers can adjust portion sizes or modify other aspects of the production process to help meet these guidelines and economies of scale make it worthwhile. For cafeteria workers, though, it can be harder. Interviews with lunch ladies (and gentlemen) reveal countless, intriguing stories of how these individuals strive to meet the demands of their students (and parents) and school boards

(Pautz et al. 2018). Perhaps the implementation of the Smart Snacks regulation is best summed up by one school food service director who reports that the manufacturer of Red Bull (an energy drink) is able to meet the guidelines for sale in a school cafeteria by providing a diet version with less sugar and sodium, but she is no longer able to serve a cafeteria-made vegetable barley soup because its sodium content exceeds the regulations (Pautz et al., 126–130). These new realities leave the director scratching her head. Here we see that there are some interesting side effects, if you will, to a regulation, mandated by the Healthy Hunger-Free Kids Act. It may defy logic that government efforts to promote health and provide access to good food to school kids enables a highly processed energy drink to find a place in a school but vegetable barley soup does not. The point is that figuring out what to serve in a school cafeteria is wrought with challenges when political forces and fiscal demands have to coincide with nutritional and health standards. After all, anyone who has experience trying to get school-aged kids to eat healthy meals knows, just figuring out what kids will eat can be hard enough, not to mention dealing with what government and school boards say they should eat and at what cost! These decisions and actions have ramifications for the environment since the land, water, and air are required to produce the food; and this production effects the well-being of the environment.

FOOD AND CULTURE

A discussion of food policy and politics would be incomplete if we did not consider the role of culture on our food consumption. As we have seen already in this chapter, Americans' concerns about food and nutrition have changed quite a bit since the 1800s along with the availability of food items. Our nation is more concerned now with overconsumption of foods, particularly foods that have limited nutritional value, than we were in the early twentieth century. Part of the overconsumption of food stems from the fact that there is also far more variety and choice of foods at the ready, at least for Americans who do not live in food deserts (more on food deserts in a bit). In the second decade of the twenty-first century, supermarkets carry an average of 42,000 different items, which represents a significant increase from the roughly 14,000 items they carried in 1980 (Moshfegh 2015, 376). And with this increase in choice, food comprises a smaller percentage of our household spending than it did just a few decades ago for many Americans. But with all of these changes, we must wonder about our food literacy. The Food Literacy Center defines food literacy "as an understanding of the impact of food choices on health, the environment, and [one's] community" (as quoted in Jones, 232). Keep in mind this concept as we explore various facets of food in our society.

As the lifestyle of so many Americans seems to get busier, the convenience of food is increasingly important. Just think about the availability of foods that are single-serve, easy to consume and equally easy when it comes to disposal. Keurig's single-cup coffee makers, or K-cups, has transformed access to coffee (and other hot beverages). Approximately one in three American homes has a single-serve coffee machine and in 2014, 9 billion K-cups were sold (Hamblin 2015). While exceedingly convenient in offices and homes alike, the waste generated from those seemingly small, single serve cups is significant as they are not recyclable or biodegradable.

Along these lines, consider the growing sector of "fast causal" restaurants that offer convenience and purportedly better food than fast-food franchises, such as McDonald's, without the table-service one would find in a restaurant. Examples of this type of dining option include Panera Bread, Chipotle Mexican Grill, Five Guys Burgers & Fries, and Boston Market. If you have eaten at any one of these, or similar, establishments, consider the disposable, single-use nature of the plates, wrappers, and other dining items you find there. And then think about the nutritional value of what you ordered (or perhaps not!).

It was not too long ago when most families, most of the time ate all their meals at home. Families cooked food together from scratch. There was little in the way of pre-made meals that enabled a few, quick steps to produce a healthy, tasty meal for all. Growing numbers of Americans do not even know how to cook or prepare the simplest of meals. According to a Harris Poll, 14% of Americans do not like to cook, 7% do not cook at all and only 41% of Americans prepare home cooked meals five or more times a week (Jones, 231). In the mid 1960s, approximately 112 minutes a day was spent cooking; and in the early twenty-first century, that figure is down to 66 minutes (Jones, 231). When we think about food in today's society, we increasingly think about convenience.

The emphasis on convenience may stem from the mixed messages we receive about food and nutrition. The research and information about food, what we should and should not eat and in what amounts evolves and it can be difficult to stay abreast of that information. This is a major motivation in the government's efforts to provide Americans guidance through food pyramids and other information. However, as we have seen, that information is not always the summation of the most up-to-date information as politics can and does play a role in providing that guidance. And, as Marion Nestle (2002) argues, the food industry would prefer the public to stay confused about what they should and should not eat. The marketing and advertising of food and related products is big business and the industry would rather provide their own messages to consumers. Have you ever stopped and thought about the placement of products on supermarket shelves? Most of us have not, but it is big business and manufacturers pay not inconsequential sums of money for their product to be eye level of kids shopping with the adults in their lives for their products that are marketed to kids.

Beginning in the 1990s, food manufacturers have also taken to fortifying foods with additional supplements in an effort to add to the nutritional benefits you may receive by eating their products. But these additions may or may not be substantiated by science. Often called "functional foods," these food products are foods that "…tempt consumers with a variety of health and welfare claims from the prevention of heart disease to better gastrointestinal health to cancer prevention. The producers who design and market them seek to capture consumer dollars, and if the claims made by functional food proponents are to be believed, these products create a new bridge, lucrative both to the corporations that produce them and beneficial to the people who consume them, between food and health" (Thomas 2018, 94). The first two decades of "functional foods" saw many food products enhanced with specific nutrients, such as high fiber chicken or omega-3 yogurts; most of these products failed (Thomas, 95). More recently, a second generation of functional foods tries to emphasize what consumers want with "naturally functional" foods, such as probiotic yogurts, which make sense while probiotic pizza does not (Thomas, 95). Ultimately, the efforts by food producers and manufacturers are focused on giving consumers what they want and making a profit at the same time. The challenge lies in whether or not the advertising claims are based on sound science and data and what, if anything, the government should do regarding the claims made. Current guidelines from the Food and Drug Administration permit the labeling of a product as a whole grain food if it has 51% or more whole grain ingredients by weight and a whole grain food may let consumers know that "diets rich in whole-grain foods and other plant foods and low in total fat, saturated fat, and cholesterol, may help reduce the risk of heart disease and certain cancers" (Thomas, 93). Of course, it is up to the manufacturer the font sizes and graphics used to convey this health information.

Interest in health and nutrition has fueled various diet trends and movements in the United States. Different fads in diets, whether it is the no carbohydrate diets or the diets predicated on only raw foods, impact food consumption patterns and the products provided by food manu-facturers. And, in turn, there are policy implications as well as environ-mental impacts. It is difficult to track the number of individuals who are vegetarians or vegans and whether or not more Americans embrace diets without animal products is about the same or growing over time, but restaurants and grocery stores are increasingly hospitable to those dietary patterns. And food manufacturers are offering more and more products that align with these consumption patterns.

One aspect of food preferences and trends that has seen government take action on is the organic food movement. Organic foods are foods that are produced without any human made fertilizers, pesticides or pre-servatives. This movement began in Europe in the early twentieth cen-tury and has become firmly established in the United States (Paarlberg, 167). If an individual wants to make choices about food that does not have any of these additives or chemicals in the production process, that individual needs to know information that the typical consumer is unlikely to have. As a result, the federal government has taken steps to ensure that claims made around organic foods are not erroneous. In 1990, the Organic Foods Production Act was passed and stipulated that the USDA create the National Organic Program to set standards regard-ing organic labeling. According to studies from the Mayo Clinic, there is no conclusive evidence that organic food is safer or more nutritious, and there are some positive benefits for the environment as well as some additional burdens in organic farming (Paarlberg, 173). More research is needed to determine the benefits and costs associated with organic foods, but the government is increasingly getting involved in this dimen-sion of food policy.

Without a doubt, the cultural dimension of food is significant. What we value in our food choices and what we demand of food manufacturers will drive much of the actions of the industry and the government around food. And these demands have implications for the natural environment. This section offers a mere introduction to the complexity of food and culture topics. And the discussion thus far has focused largely on these topics generally without exploring the socioeconomic dimensions of them. For example, the ability of an individual to pursue organic foods and make dietary choices based on the social responsibility (or perceived responsibility) of a manufacturer has much to do with that individual's income and wealth. And, if someone wants to ensure that the food she eats is grown organically and fair trade practices are followed, having a Whole Foods Market nearby might be advantageous. She may not realize that there is a large and growing percentage of Americans that do not have easy access to any grocery store, let alone a Whole Foods. A food desert is an area that has limited access to affordable and healthy foods, particularly fresh fruits and vegetables. Food desserts are particularly common in low-income areas. In 2010, more than 18 million Americans live in food deserts according to the USDA (Lee 2017).

Ultimately the choices we make about food are a function of many dimensions, from health and nutrition to income and access to convenience and culture. For some of us, the choices are manifold and growing while for some of us those choices are limited and perhaps even diminishing. And policy decisions about food have environmental ramifications. When you started reading this section, you might not have thought much about the cultural dimensions of food, but they are varied and many.

Challenges in the Future

As we consider the many dimensions of food policy and politics, there are a number of challenges facing citizens and politicians alike, including: the multitude of stakeholders and interest areas; the consumption of scientific information, and continually evolving cultural and societal norms about food.

Multitude of Interests

Food policy and politics encompasses a huge range of stakeholders and interest areas that make a single chapter a meager introduction. Starting with the growing of crops and the raising of livestock, there are many individuals and organizations that are involved in food production, including farmers, ranchers, and associations including the American Farm Bureau and the National Cattlemen's Beef Association, as examples. Then there are the individuals and companies that produce the supplies farmers and ranchers need from animal feed to pesticides and fertilizers. Once crops are grown and animals raised, transportation companies help facilitate the production of food along with the food manufacturers. Once food products are ready for consumers, they have to be transported to grocery stores and restaurants, for individuals to purchase and consume the food. Throughout this entire journey, waste is produced that requires disposal. All of these actors represent a wide range of interests when it comes to food policy and politics. This list does not include nutritionists and public health officials, school kids and cafeteria food service directors, or chefs and food celebrities. These stakeholders have varying interests that elected leaders in Congress and state legislatures and civil servants in government agencies from local health departments to the FDA have to contend with as they strive to create and maintain a coherent approach to food policy in the United States. The point is that something as seemingly uncontroversial as food because exceedingly complicated with this number of stakeholders and their various interests.

Understanding and Conveying Scientific Information

Complicating matters further is how Americans consume scientific and technical information. Picking up on some of the discussion in Chapter 2, the methodical and incremental nature of scientific research often has difficulty aligning with the media environment of twenty-first century America. More specifically, it takes lots of time and scientists take incremental steps in their efforts to understand the world around us. Figuring out what is and is not nutritious, for example, is not a one study endeavor; rather, it takes lots of studies that explore all facets of a particular nutrient and how it may affect the human body. Researchers are unlikely to definitively conclude something is good for everyone or something is bad for everyone, yet the media often engage their viewers and readers with headlines touting the latest research conclusions that chocolate is good for us or chocolate is bad for us. How many of us actually track down the scientific journal article that the news is reporting on? Few, if any of us. But many of us rely on the news media, and perhaps a medical professional for dietary advice. Ultimately, researchers, the media, and citizens have a responsibility to understand what we understand about health and food and to use that information to make decisions.

Evolving Cultural Values Around Food

Our decision-making around food has a lot to do with our values and the culture in which we live in, and these values and notions are constantly evolving. As we discussed previously, consider the rise in popularity of single-serve coffee pods that make coffee—as well as caffeine, and other sugary beverages—all the more convenient and accessible. This creates more waste than brewing coffee or hot chocolate in more conventional ways. Additionally, the dramatic growth of food services such as Blue Apron and other mail order meal kits are increasingly popular—at least among those demographics that can afford to have food delivered to their home daily or weekly in pre-portioned ingredients to make cooking quick and easy. This is important as fewer and fewer Americans have the time or inclination to cook or even prepare ingredients to make a meal. These manifestations of cultural values will shape the kinds of foods that are grown, prepared, and manufactured for us to consume and it remains to be seen what the health or environmental impacts might be; however, suffice it to say, these trends towards convenience do tell a lot about values and priorities around food. Additionally, the portions of food the average American eats at any given meal has grown and grown. Portion size has implications for the health and the environment. Time will help us better understand the true implications. Seemingly our culture values convenience.

Political Environment

All of these considerations must be taken in context of the ever-changing political environment of the nation. As we have seen in this chapter, the politics of food are more than the implementation of food programs for school-aged children or the research surrounding the latest health and dietary information. These initiatives and policy steps have to take place in the broader political environment. This includes political control of state legislatures and Congress, as well as the occupants of these offices. At the outset of the chapter, one may have thought that food could hardly be controversial—after all, everyone needs to eat and food is not about saving the whales, for instance. But as we have seen, these issues are fraught with political tensions and controversies and will likely be for the foreseeable future.

CHAPTER WRAP-UP

In this chapter, we have explored an area of policy that might seem out of place in a book devoted to environmental policy and an area of policy that might not appear as an area of policy and politics at all—food. The growing, production, and transportation of food have significant implications for the health and well-being of the natural environment. These areas of public policy are not as coordinated as one might expect to find them, thereby compounding challenges to address real problems, such as hunger and food insecurity in the United States, and to move forward in a coherent manner to think more holistically about the food system in the country and its effects on the natural environment.

SUGGESTED RESOURCES

Angelo, Mary Jane, Jason J. Czarnezki, and William S. Eubanks. *Food, Agriculture, and Environmental Law*. Washington, DC: ELI Press, 2013.
Bosso, Christopher. *Framing the Farm Bill: Interests, Ideology, and the Agricultural Act of 2014*. Lawrence: University Press of Kansas, 2014.
Food, Inc. Directed by Robert Kenner. 2008. Magnolia Pictures, Participant Media, River Road Entertainment.
Levine, Susan. *School Lunch Politics: The Surprising History of America's Favorite Welfare Program*. Princeton, NJ: Princeton University Press, 2008.
Neff, Roni, editor. *Introduction to the US Food System: Public Health, Environment, and Equity*. San Francisco: Jossey-Bass, 2015.
Pollan, Michael. *The Omnivore's Dilemma: A Natural History of Four Meals*. New York: Penguin, 2007.

REFERENCES

Anderson, Molly. "Ecological Threats to and From Food Systems." In *Introduction to the U.S. Food System: Public Health, Environment, and Equity*, edited by Roni Neff, 51–78. San Francisco, CA: Jossey-Bass, 2015.
Angelo, Mary Jane, and James F. Choate. "Agriculture and the Clean Water Act." In *Food, Agriculture, and Environmental Law*, edited by Mary Jane

Angelo, Jason J. Czarnezki, and William S. Eubanks, 147–161. Washington, DC: ELI Press, 2013.

Beam, Christopher. "Organic Panic: Michelle Obama's Garden and Its Discontents." Slate.com. 2009. Accessed January 11, 2018. Available at http://www.slate.com/articles/news_and_politics/politics/2009/06/organic_panic.html.

Bosso, Christopher J., and Nicole E. Tichenor. "Eating and the Environment: Ecological Impacts of Food Production." In *Environmental Policy: New Directions for the 21st Century*, edited by Norman J. Vig and Michael E. Kraft, 194–214. Washington, DC: CQ Press Sage, 2015.

Burros, Marian. "Obamas to Plant Vegetable Garden at White House." *The New York Times*. March 19, 2009. Accessed December 4, 2017. Available at http://www.nytimes.com/2009/03/20/dining/20garden.html.

CDC. 2018a. Accessed February 13, 2018. https://www.cdc.gov/nchs/fastats/obesity-overweight.htm.

———. 2018b. Accessed February 16, 2018. https://www.cdc.gov/foodsafety/index.html.

———. 2018c. Accessed February 16, 2018. https://www.cdc.gov/foodsafety/cdc-and-food-safety.html.

Christaldi, Joanne, and Diana Cuy Castellanos. "Child and Adult Food Insecurity in the United States." In *The Intersection of Food and Public Health: Current Policy Challenges and Solutions*, edited by A. Bryce Hoflund, John C. Jones, and Michelle C. Pautz, 15–31. New York: Routledge, 2018.

Clemmer, Teresa B. "Agriculture and the Clean Air Act." In *Food, Agriculture, and Environmental Law*, edited by Mary Jane Angelo, Jason J. Czarnezki, and William S. Eubanks, 163–184. Washington, DC: ELI Press, 2013.

Confessore, Nicholas. "How School Lunch Became the Latest Political Battleground." *The New York Times Magazine*. October 7, 2014. Accessed March 2, 2015. Available at https://www.nytimes.com/2014/10/12/magazine/how-school-lunch-became-the-latest-political-battleground.html.

Danilova, Maria/Associated Press. "Trump Administration Halts School Lunch Salt Reduction." *Bloomberg News*. November 29, 2017. Accessed December 4, 2017. Available at https://www.bloomberg.com/news/articles/2017-11-29/trump-administration-halts-school-lunch-salt-reduction.

Evich, Helena Bottemiller. "Michelle Obama Sets Her Garden in Stone." *Politico*. October 5, 2016. Accessed December 4, 2017. Available at https://www.politico.com/story/2016/10/michelle-obama-garden-changes-white-house-229204.

Food and Nutrition Service. U.S. Department of Agriculture. "Supplemental Assistance Program—National Level Annual Summary." 2018a. Accessed February 23, 2018. Available at https://www.fns.usda.gov/pd/supplemental-nutrition-assistance-program-snap.

————. "WIC Program—National Level Annual Summary." 2018b. Accessed February 23, 2018. Available at https://www.fns.usda.gov/pd/wic-program.

————. "National School Lunch Program." 2018c. Accessed February 23, 2018. Available at https://www.fns.usda.gov/nslp/national-school-lunch-program-nslp.

Hamblin, James. "A Brewing Problem: What's the Healthiest Way to Keep Everyone Caffeinated?" *The Atlantic.* March 2, 2015. Accessed February 23, 2018. Available at https://www.theatlantic.com/technology/archive/2015/03/the-abominable-k-cup-coffee-pod-environment-problem/386501/.

Jones, Jeffrey M. "Worry About Hunger, Homelessness Up for Lower-Income in U.S." *Gallup.* March 30, 2017. Accessed February 23, 2018. Available at http://news.gallup.com/poll/207521/worry-hunger-homelessness-lower-income.aspx.

Lee, Courtney Hall. "Grocery Store Inequity: Why Fresh Food Is Often a Scarce Commodity for Low-Income People." *Sojourners.* April 2017. Accessed February 23, 2018. Available at https://sojo.net/magazine/april-2017/grocery-store-inequity.

Levine, Susan. *School Lunch Politics: The Surprising History of America's Favorite Welfare Program.* Princeton, NJ: Princeton University Press, 2008.

Moshfegh, Alanna. "Food Consumption in the United States." In *Introduction to the U.S. Food System: Public Health, Environment, and Equity,* edited by Roni Neff, 373–398. San Francisco, CA: Jossey-Bass, 2015.

Nestle, Marion. *Food Politics: How the Food Industry Influences Nutrition and Health.* Berkeley: University of California Press, 2002.

NIDDK. 2018. Accessed February 13, 2018. https://www.niddk.nih.gov/health-information/health-statistics/overweight-obesity.

NPR Staff. "The First Lady Cultivates 'American Grown' Gardening." National Public Radio. May 29, 2012. Accessed December 4, 2017. Available at https://www.npr.org/2012/05/29/153705721/the-first-lady-cultivates-american-grown-gardening.

Paarlberg, Robert. *Food Politics: What Everyone Needs to Know.* 2nd edition. New York: Oxford University Press, 2013.

Park, Timothy, Mary Ahearn, Ted Covey, Kenneth Erickson, J. Michael Harris, Jennifer Ifft, Chris McGath, Mitch Morehart, Stephen Vogel, Jeremy Weber, and Robert Williams. *Agricultural Income and Finance Outlook.* A Report from the Economic Research Service, U.S. Department of Agriculture. December 2011. Accessed February 7, 2018. Available at https://www.ers.usda.gov/webdocs/publications/35822/12822_ais-91_3-1-12.pdf?v=41055.

Pautz, Michelle C., John C. Jones, and A. Bryce Hoflund. "On the Front Lines in School Cafeterias: The Trials and Tribulations of Food Service Directors."

In *The Intersection of Food and Public Health: Current Policy Challenges and Solutions*, edited by A. Bryce Hoflund, John C. Jones, and Michelle C. Pautz, 121–131. New York: Routledge, 2018.

Reilly, Katie. "Melania Trump Plans to Preserve Michelle Obama's Vegetable Garden." *Time*. 2017. Accessed December 4, 2017. Available at http://time.com/4668035/melania-trump-michelle-obama-vegetable-garden/.

———. "When Is Food (not) Functional?" In *The Intersection of Food and Public Health: Current Policy Challenges and Solutions*, edited by A. Bryce Hoflund, John C. Jones, and Michelle C. Pautz, 93–106. New York: Routledge, 2018.

U.S. Department of Agriculture. "Farms and Land in Farms 2016 Summary." February 2017. Accessed February 7, 2018. http://usda.mannlib.cornell.edu/usda/current/FarmLandIn/FarmLandIn-02-17-2017.pdf.

USDA. 2018a. Accessed January 31, 2018. https://www.ers.usda.gov/topics/food-markets-prices/food-service-industry/market-segments.aspx.

———. 2018b. https://www.ers.usda.gov/data-products/ag-and-food-statistics-charting-the-essentials/ag-and-food-sectors-and-the-economy/.

———. 2018c. Accessed February 13, 2018. https://www.cnpp.usda.gov/myplate.

———. 2018d. Accessed February 16, 2018. https://www.ers.usda.gov/topics/food-nutrition-assistance/food-security-in-the-us/key-statistics-graphics.aspx.

Wilde, Parke. *Food Policy in the United States: An Introduction*. New York: Routledge, 2013.

Environmental Policy in Action: Past, Present, and Future

Contents

Our approach to environmental policy goes further than discussions of the politics of making policy decisions and emphasizes how those decisions are implemented. Understanding environmental policy requires going beyond the creation of it and exploring the day-to-day realities of implementing policy. It is this approach that requires us to look past the role of politicians and political institutions and examine the work of regulators, activists, and members of the regulated community. The efforts of all of these actors—official and unofficial—constitute environmental policy in action and these efforts signal what we want and what we do not want when it comes to the role of government in environmental

© The Author(s) 2019
S. R. Rinfret and M. C. Pautz, *US Environmental Policy in Action*,
https://doi.org/10.1007/978-3-030-11316-2_11

matters. These actions demonstrate whether the United States wants to be a leading force in the global response to environmental issues.

As we have seen throughout this volume, where we are today and where we head tomorrow, is a function of learning from our past. In our final chapter, we consider environmental policy past, present, and future. By appreciating the historical evolution of environmental policy, we come to know and grapple with environmental policy of the present, thereby enabling us to look to the future of US environmental policy. This structure will then enable us to ponder some of the normative questions associated with environmental policy leadership in the twenty-first century.

ENVIRONMENTAL POLICY PAST

A good portion of the preceding pages has been devoted to understanding environmental policy and its implementation in the past. Without a knowledge of the history of major environmental laws or the actions of previous presidential administrations, it is difficult to comprehend present-day environmental policy. Our experience with environmental policy is dominated by the few dozen major environmental laws passed in the 1960s and 1970s, and these laws have achieved laudable results. As discussed earlier, these laws have brought about major reductions in air pollution and improved air quality, for instance. The nation's rivers do not catch on fire, and toxic waste is, generally, not intentionally dumped with little regard for the environmental impacts. Although these achievements should not be diminished, they are widely considered low-hanging fruit. In other words, these are the efforts that are the easiest to accomplish, and the simplest situations to rectify. Devising procedures for disposal of hazardous waste took time, for example, but the challenges of these issues pale in comparison to the environmental issues we face today, such as climate change.

Our environmental laws largely deal with pollution after it has happened, and, often, only pollution that is traceable to a particular source (point-source pollution). Now, we have come to understand that point-source pollution is only part of the issue, and pollution with less discernible sources (non-point pollution) is significant. For example, the pollution coming from a waste pipe at a plant is easily noted; however, the runoff from agricultural fields into the nation's streams and waterways is harder to trace, although the effects are no less significant. This reminder of where we have been leads to the first of three summary points about our past: we have made significant progress in the United States addressing environmental issues, but much of that work has been reactive rather than proactive. Put differently, our approach to environmental problems has been to deal with it after it happens. By contrast, a more proactive approach would entail preventing pollution from happening in the first place.

Second, the creation, passage, and implementation of these environmental laws that have achieved the results we discussed have built a large regulatory apparatus. Many government agencies at the federal, state, and local levels have been created to implement these regulations. From the rule-writers and environmental compliance inspectors to the work of politicians and interest groups, there is a multitude of actors and organizations involved in environmental policy. The growth of the environmental profession—both in government and the private sector—has been tremendous. There is an enormous cadre of specially trained professionals, both inside and outside of government, whose work is dedicated to implementing and monitoring compliance with environmental regulations.

The significant number of environmental professionals coincides with thousands and thousands of pages of federal environmental regulations. Although there are only a few dozen major environmental statutes, the corresponding pages of regulations are ever growing. In more than four decades, the size and scale of government's regulatory structure has become significant. On the one hand, it is impressive that such a structure has been established so quickly to ensure environmental protection and realize major environmental achievements. On the other hand, the enormity of government bureaucracy surrounding environmental protection can easily lead to inefficiencies, overlap, inflexibility, and dampen opportunities for innovation. And as we see with the Trump administration, the structure leaves ample opportunity for critics to upend the government's approach to dealing with environmental problems.

The regulatory structure and the laws it was tasked with implementing are indicative of a third point: in the past, there was widespread agreement that government has a role in protecting the environment. Broadly, speaking, mainstream society evolved from a debate over whether the government should be involved in protecting the nation's environment to a general acceptance of the need for government in this policy arena. The debates centered around to what extent the government should have a role in protecting the environment and what level of government (e.g., state or national government) should be in charge.

Of course, there was plenty of debate about the appropriate balance between economic and environmental concerns. However, these were not partisan debates with one political party supporting government's role in environmental protection and the other party not supporting it. Ultimately, the government's role—if evidenced by nothing other than the size of the regulatory structure it commands—was clearly established in this policy arena. And there was agreement that the federal leadership role to assume in protecting the environment.

It is important at this juncture to emphasize that these are just some of the major characteristics of our environmental policy past. These characteristics are not necessarily positive or negative—as most things are never so easily defined—but they are simply our past. Understanding these attributes of environmental policy helps us explain the present state of environmental policy and enables us to look to the future and what it might entail.

ENVIRONMENTAL POLICY PRESENT

The characteristics of environmental policy today are quite different than they were even a decade ago. The foundation of some of these characteristics were already in place when the first edition of this volume was written and some have emerged only in the last few years. Regardless of the origins of these characteristics, environmental policy today is uncertain. We focus here on three characteristics: (1) hyper-partisanship, (2) gridlock at the national level, and (3) emerging questions about the role of government in environmental protection.

Intensifying Partisanship and Political Polarization

Some of the explanation for the inertia around environmental policy is due to the intensifying partisanship and polarization of political parties (Kraft 2017). Despite a multitude of recent media reports detailing increasing partisanship and political rhetoric surrounding the Trump administration, this is neither a new phenomenon in American politics, nor will it be the last time the nation experiences an era of hyper-partisanship that is debilitating for the work of policymakers. Citizens noted the growing divide in exit polls after the 2018 midterm elections; in one exit poll, 77% of respondents said the nation is becoming more divided (Langer and Siu 2018). As we have noted throughout this book, the two major political parties are increasingly standing in opposition to the objectives of the other party. Furthermore, the political parties are seemingly focused on the outcomes of elections and less on building consensus to govern in the interim. Given this entrenchment of views and positions on issues, various stances on key policy issues are surging in importance, including views on science and environmental policy.

Action to protect the environment was, at one time, a bipartisan effort that brought with it consensus from most sides of the political world; however, this is no longer the case as positions on environmental issues are, more frequently, a key litmus test for politicians (cf. Klyza and Sousa 2013). In the late 1970s and throughout the 1980s, we saw Republicans, in keeping with their conservative principles of a smaller, less intrusive government, wanting to reduce the government's role in environmental protection and, at the very least, give more power over environmental issues to lower levels of governments, notably the states. Today, however, we are witnessing a tendency to move beyond that position to one that fundamentally questions scientific knowledge and our understanding of environmental issues.

For instance, more and more Republican politicians and their appointees, including President Trump and his selections for environmental agency heads, are questioning the science behind climate change. Decades ago, Republicans would have argued about the government's response—if there should even be one—but were far less likely to question widespread scientific consensus. Moreover, the vitriol directed toward environmental protection has exacerbated as more and more Republicans, particularly the 2016 field of Republican presidential candidates (including Rick Perry, now Secretary of Energy), have called for the abolishment of the US EPA.

In keeping with entrenched political stances, Democrats maintain positions that the government should be involved in environmental protection and do not, typically, question scientific consensus. Consider then President Obama's clear position during the 2014 State of the Union address in which he stated, "Climate change is a fact. And when our children's children look us in the eye and ask if we did all we could to leave them a safer, more stable world, with new sources of energy, I want us to be able to say yes, we did" ("Obama's 2014 State of the Union" 2014). However, with the bickering between political parties and emphasis on election outcomes, Democrats are increasingly unwilling to take firm positions on environmental issues, and they are not as apt to advocate vociferously for policy action, as evidenced by Hillary Clinton's unwillingness to push for major environmental reforms during her bid for the presidency. Moreover, many Democrats, despite occasional speeches or introduction of legislation that is unlikely to see any movement (e.g., Climate Protection Act of 2013), seem to prioritize other issues over environmental concerns for political and pragmatic reasons.

Legislative Gridlock at the National Level

Another reason for a lack of environmental policy action is legislative gridlock, notably at the national level. The last two sessions of Congress—the final two years of the Obama administration and the first two years of the Trump administration—have struggled to pass legislation in most policy areas, not to mention legislation surrounding environmental issues. With the Republican control of the White House and of the 115th Congress (in session from January 2017 to January 2019), one might have expected more legislative action, but we saw that the Congress could not even pass a repeal of "Obamacare" despite years of Republicans promising just such action if they gained control of the institution. With the Democrats taking control of one chamber of Congress after the 2018 midterm elections, the divided control of the legislative branch is even less likely to see legislation pass. Of course, tabulations of the number of laws passed assumes that such a figure indicates desirable performance.

Some of the inability to pass laws is evidenced in changes to congressional rules and the increased use of the Senate filibuster (or, at the very least, the threat of filibusters), which enables individual members of the Senate to wield sizable power in stopping any legislative action. As a result, cloture votes—those votes that stymie filibusters or the threat of them—are becoming essential to governing and require 60 votes, instead of the simple majority that we all associate with Senate procedure (Zeleny and Saenz 2013).

With gridlock in the halls of Congress and the polarization of lawmakers, other avenues of policy action are being sought in policy arenas, including environmental protection. Klyza and Sousa (2008, 2013) coined the term "green drift" to explain the nation's evolving approach to environmental policy. Essentially, as a result of legislative gridlock, Klyza and Sousa document how environmental policy is still being made via non-legislative pathways. For example, environmental policymaking is still happening in the halls of administrative agencies as we have repeatedly noted through this book, as well as through the work of civil servants and their exercise of discretion; the courts are still creating environmental policy via their decisions; and state governments are taking an increasingly prominent role in the pursuit of environmental goals.

These realities led Klyza and Sousa to conclude that, although environmental policy is not being made via more traditional means, it is still being made via non-legislative pathways, despite political rhetoric to the contrary. They term these less traditional means, which are achieving objectives, but not in dramatic ways, as "green drift." Green drift is hardly an encouraging label for continued progress in protecting the nation's environment; nevertheless, it is likely the only means of pursuing environmental policy for the foreseeable future.

Legislative gridlock only exacerbates a downward spiral of trust in government. More and more Americans express disgust with government, as approval ratings of Congress hover at their lowest recorded levels. This disapproval, coupled with the inability of lawmakers to come together and pass legislation, leave most citizens cynical about the government's ability to accomplish anything, and especially deal with issues that are less paramount in the minds of Americans such as environmental concerns. In July 2018, according to a Gallup Poll, 62% of Americans are dissatisfied with the direction of the nation and only 35% are satisfied, which is about how Americans have responded to such questions for years ("Direction of Country" 2018). When asked how much confidence Americans have in Congress in a January 2018 NBC News/Wall Street Journal Poll, only 10% reported a great deal or quite a bit of confidence while 48% said they have very little confidence or none at all ("Congress: Misc. Questions" 2018).

Altering the Role of Government in Environmental Protection?

The hyper-partisanship that we have experienced in the country for a number of years now, along with the legislative gridlock, and the administration of Donald Trump has brought about a debate over the role of government in environmental protection more broadly that is surprising. For the first time since the establishment of our modern environmental laws and regulatory structures to implement those laws, questions are beginning to swirl over whether or not the government should be involved. Some of this debate may simply be political and fit with President's Trump rhetorical style of being assertive and desirous of causing a stir—particularly on Twitter. But some of this debate may signal fundamental realignment of the government's—or at least the national government's—role protecting the environment. Since the creation of the EPA in 1970, there have been presidents of both political parties and their leadership has often had different views on the environment, however, no administration to date has tried to undo so many environmental laws so quickly and to gut the agencies tasked with their implementation and oversight the way President Trump has tried to do. President Reagan wanted to curb the federal government's role in environmental protection and was very concerned about the implications for the economy of environmental regulations, but there was not rhetoric that questioned the fundamental need for environmental protection and the agencies tasked with implementation. As a presidential candidate, Trump was asked on Fox News Sunday what agencies he would cut and he named the EPA, calling the agency's actions a "disgrace" (Fox News 2015). When anchor Chris Wallace asked who would protect the environment if the agency was cut, Trump replied "They—we'll be fine with the environment. We can leave a little bit, but you can't destroy businesses" (Fox News 2015). Trump's rhetoric as a candidate has been followed up with actions as president.

In addition to directing the undoing and rolling back of any number of actions, and proposed actions, ranging from the Clean Power Plan to the Mercury and Air Toxics Standard to the Paris Climate Agreement and Endangered Species protections, the administration has overseen major cuts to the EPA. In 2017 alone, more than 700 people have left the agency—mostly scientists and environmental protection specialists— and the aim is to cut staffing by 50%, from 15,000 employees to less than 8000 by 2021 (Kaufman 2018). These cuts are already much more significant than those under the Reagan administration (Ebbs 2018). More broadly, President Trump signed an executive order on January 30, 2017 implementing a one for two regulatory cuts—meaning that for every new regulation, an agency must cut two (Farber 2018). At the EPA, 2017 saw only one new regulatory action—regulating toxic materials used by dentists—and 16 deregulatory actions (Farber 2018). These actions exceed the usual efforts of a new administration representing a different political party than the last administration. These actions—and particularly the speed of these actions—could very well be indicative of a fundamental reset of what the government should be doing regarding the environment. It is up to each individual citizen to decide what the government should or should not be doing around any particular issue, and those decisions should be made as part of a national dialogue about what the citizens want for their country. Much of this debate is elusive at present and what it means for the future is unclear.

ENVIRONMENTAL POLICY FUTURE

In light of the present assessment of environmental policy, projecting the future of environmental policy in the United States is difficult. Some of the challenges we face today, including an aging regulatory infrastructure and the very nature and complexity of environmental issues, have been present for some time. And some of the challenges we encounter now are more recent, such as questioning the role of the government in environmental protection. These conditions make discussions of the future hard. The environmental problems the nation—and, indeed, the world—faces in the first decades of the twenty-first century are unlike the issues that were a prominent fixture of the environmental agenda more than fifty years ago. Today, climate change and energy concerns dominate much of the discussion. The extent of the changes our climate is undergoing and the effects on humans are at the forefront of much debate. And decades ago, the focus was on cleaning up pollution, whereas now we are increasingly focused on minimizing pollution before it happens and finding alternative energy sources in an effort to mitigate environmental effects. The differences in these challenges beget changes in our approach to environmental policy.

As we look to the future, two points inform those considerations. First—and as is often the case when we look to the future—uncertainty abounds. The uncertainty is particularly striking with environmental policy because we see with the Trump administration significant efforts to fundamentally change course of environmental protection, at least at the national level (with spillover effects to subnational governments even less clear). Will the current administration continue to dismantle decades of environmental regulations and structure? Will the Congress and the courts permit these actions to continue? Will the American public push back on these changes, as they did in the 1980s? Will states endeavor to take action, especially with the election of more Democrats to governors' mansions, to the extent they are permitted to do so in our federal system? Will the international community respond to US actions? Hazarding answers to any of these questions is virtually impossible. And uncertainty is difficult for anyone in any circumstance, but think about the implications in this policy arena. Companies that are subjected to environmental regulations do not know if the regulations are going to go away or be very different from what they are accustomed to—and this makes planning for firms very difficult. And this brings added costs no matter what happens. State and local governments do not know if the federal government's role will change and what the effects may be for these subunits of government, and especially if and how funding structures will evolve. After all, the federal government provides a lot of the funds state and local governments use to implement environmental regulations. And citizens do not know how environmental protection will change and the effects they may see on their lives. For example, the vehicle emissions standards put in place during the Obama administration, which required average fuel economy to reach 54 miles per gallon by 2025, have been altered by the Trump administration. By 2021, under the proposed plan, average fuel economy should be 34 miles per gallon with the explanation from government officials that people will be safer because if they have less fuel-efficient vehicles, they will drive less (Plumer 2018). These changes will directly affect the kinds of vehicles we can buy and how much they cost. Only time will help us understand the future. Many previous EPA administrators are warning that "...it could take anywhere from a few years to three decades for future administrations to restore the EPA where it was [in 2017], before the regulatory rollbacks, mass attrition, and budget cuts" (Kaufman 2018).

Second, whatever the government does or does not do, that will not alter the progression of environmental issues. Put differently, the effects of pollution and the degradation of the environment continue while we debate what should or should not be done to curb the ill effects. And new environmental challenges continue to emerge as we learn more and science furthers our understanding of complex issues. As is always the case in public policy, inaction is a choice and one that has lasting effects. If we take another ten years to devise a strategy to address climate change, that means there are another ten years of ill effects of climate change and untold other consequences. But it may take us ten more years to put together workable policy action too.

Regardless of our assessments of government and its ability to function as we would like, these are the realities that environmental policy—and other areas of policy—must contend with. As we look forward, we identify five needs for environmental policy in the future.

First, more holistic training is needed for environmental professionals. An enduring theme in environmental policy is the sheer complexity of the issues and the interdisciplinary nature of them. Many of our environmental professionals are trained in specific areas of environmental concerns. For example, environmental inspectors, often, have backgrounds in particular areas of the natural sciences or engineering. Then, these individuals become inspectors and spend a career focusing on a particular aspect of environmental regulation such as hazardous waste management (cf. Pautz and Rinfret 2013). This narrow focus creates a cadre of experts in specific areas, but it hampers efforts to work across environmental media. Moreover, those individuals who pursue careers in advocacy need a more robust background in the various dimensions of environmental concerns—not just the scientific and technical, but the policy, the organization, and the communication of such issues. Many universities offer students environmental studies programs that are multidisciplinary and serve to foster more holistic training, but we would advocate further expansion of such programs even beyond the traditional college environment. Whatever one's predilections about environmental issues may be, a broad and diverse background is essential for effectively understanding and advocating one's viewpoints and deriving solutions.

Second, the public needs to be able to discuss the challenges of various environmental issues effectively. Decades into the information age, the average person has an incredible amount of information available at his/her fingertips because we no longer have to wait for the evening news to hear about the latest current events. However, with the explosion of the Internet and the emergence of numerous forms of information dissemination, including social media, we are frequently overwhelmed with information. As a result, digesting all this information and ascertaining its credibility proves challenging. Instead of engaging a print copy of the newspaper and reading an article from start to finish because there was only a finite amount of news in the daily paper, we now scan and click and read bits and pieces of many more news stories. However, we end up with a much broader knowledge of what is going on without the depth. Just think for a moment about how you scan news stories, Facebook, and Twitter: you quickly glance through and read what you deem interesting; however, in many of those formats, content is distilled down to the fewest possible characters or even simply images.

This is not necessarily bad or good, but it begs the question, how do we consume information and how comprehensive is it? Further, anyone with minimal technological skills can post information on the Internet and claim it is accurate. Then, that information only needs to be duplicated, reposted, or retweeted. With the viral nature of information, particularly sensational stories, the vast amount of misinformation is unsurprising.

Given the nature of information dissemination and consumption, understanding of complex social and political issues is distilled to slogans and sound bites. Again, without passing judgment on the merits of information transmission, one does have to reflect on the implications for discussion in the public square of these complex issues. With these technological changes and the dramatic increase in available information, the nature of public debate has changed. The issues for debate in the public square, related to the environment or any number of other pressing matters, are no less complex, but our ability to discuss them in comprehensive ways seems to be waning. Society has much to contend with and the multitude of issues result in a crowding effect, and society's ability to look beyond slogans, especially with the information at its disposal, seems to be absent. Instead, we succumb to slinging slogans that may or may not accurately reflect the facts or represent the complexity of the issue. Ultimately, frustration abounds, but little seems to be done about it.

We urge all citizens to get beyond the slogans and the political rhetoric jostled about and dig deeper to search out facts about issues and then make reasoned arguments about the issues. Public discussion needs to be elevated so we, as a nation, can more productively debate the pressing matters before us and make collective decisions about what should be done. It is easy to blame the politicians for these ills, but we contend that the ultimate responsibility lies with the public and its obligation to check rhetoric that distorts and fails to capture the various sides of any issue. The public needs to hold its leaders responsible for what they say and ensure accountability in that debate. This extends to voting and participating in electoral politics.

Third, more study and information gathering is needed. Aristotle is credited with saying "the more you know, the more you don't know" and this old adage could not be more appropriate in the realm of environmental policy. We have come to understand that environmental issues are usually more complicated than we initially think, and the same could be said for politics. Therefore, although it may seem trite, we need more research and information about any number of environmental issues. A better understanding of the multifaceted nature of the issues is essential, and we must find ways beyond sound bites and slogans to talk about these issues.

Arguably, we have seen the complexity of issues increase whereas our appetite for robust and informed debate seems to be declining. We must rectify the situation because the complexity of issues demands a commensurate level of engagement. Moreover, we need information and research from multiple disciplines, not just science and engineering, but from the health sciences, social sciences, and even the humanities. Our arguments have to be better informed, for example, by the moral and ethical arguments philosophers bring. The desire for information must be balanced with an understanding that decisions must be made and perpetually deferring action in the name of more information is disingenuous and irresponsible. How to strike this balance, though, is invariably the challenge, but it is one we must not shrink from.

Fourth, in an effort to ensure forward momentum in terms of environmental progress, we must recognize that information and solutions can come from all sides in the environmental debate. We must move beyond an "us versus them" mentality when it comes to these concerns. Advocacy groups are not necessarily the good guys, and industry groups are not necessarily the bad guys. Throughout this text, you have seen the complexity of environmental issues and that reductionist views about who is "good" and who is "bad" reflect a cursory understanding of these issues. In every category of actor in this policy arena, there are good guys and bad guys; therefore, it is too simplistic to say simply that it is one side versus the other. Instead, we should move beyond the preconceived notions of "hippie tree-huggers" and "evil, profit-driven corporate executives" and devise ways to see beyond stereotypes and labels in an effort to engage all stakeholders as we strive for solutions for the planet.

Fifth, and finally, we need a regulatory system that fosters collaboration because we are all dependent on the health and the well-being of the environment, and that requires us to work together. As we engage in thoughtful debate about the issues, we must rid ourselves of misinformed stereotypes and be able to work together. This means that environmentalists, governmental regulators, the regulated community, and citizens must come together. Our regulatory system, which was designed to thwart innovation and collaboration due to fears of regulatory shirking, must evolve. Our history with environmental regulation has demonstrated that much of this fear is unfounded—or at least overstated—so, we need to move forward. We need a regulatory system that allows for collaboration and flexibility when appropriate because the best science and information 10 years ago may not be the best information to base a course of action on today. Perhaps, we even need to go so far as embracing, more fully, the next generation of regulatory strategies discussed here.

ACTION IN THE FUTURE

From the preceding discussion, you have likely gleaned that the role the United States has played in environmental matters has varied over time. At some points in the history of modern environmental policy, the United States has been at the forefront of change and leadership, and at other times, the nation has lagged. Looking to the future, we see a new generation of leaders emerging. With the United States's announced withdrawal from the Paris Climate Agreement, among other steps, young people are building a movement to compel action on climate change and other environmental issues. Zero Hour is one example of a youth-led organization that is calling for action on climate change and pursuing environmental justice all while they are demonstrating to adults that young people are "taking heed of what they see as the greatest crisis threatening their generation" (Yoon-Hendricks 2018). And a lawsuit filed by the non-profit Our Children's Trust in 2015 demanding government action on climate change on behalf of 21 children is headed to trial after the Supreme Court ruled in favorite of the suit proceeding and against federal government efforts to stop the trial (*Juliana v. United States*) (Greshko et al. 2018). Remember what we discussed about government action throughout this volume—citizens can and do influence the course of action. Rulemaking requires public notice and comment and citizens and organizations should participate. The courts are available to citizens to compel action or to stop action. And we the people select our elected officials at the federal, state, and local levels.

With our discussion of environmental policy drawing to a close, a few final thoughts on the themes and areas of focus are warranted. As we established from the outset, the focus of this approach to environmental policy has been how this area of policy is actually done on a day-to-day basis and the roles of those on the front-lines. Here, we have conveyed stories of front-line regulators, government rule-writers, and activists, among others.

With this approach, we demonstrated the complexity of environmental issues and the challenges facing government, industry, and society as we enter the second decade of the twenty-first century. If anything, environmental issues are even more involved than we understood them to be just a few decades ago. Not only are environmental issues technically complex and involve a multitude of actors, but also it is often difficult to acquire the necessary information in a time frame that coincides with political realities. The current state of political rhetoric further reduces issues to their least common denominator and bumper sticker slogans that do a disservice to all perspectives on the issue and thwart dialog.

Finally, it is imperative that we remember that inaction is action. Our inability to take steps—whatever those might be—regarding the environment is having, and will continue to have, a significant impact. Environmental problems are not going to wait, and they will only intensify while we choose to debate them or push them aside. The United States used to be an environmental leader, but now we lag behind.

The readers of this text constitute the future of environmental action. You will be the environmental professionals, the regulators, the activists, and the citizens who engage these issues. Jobs in this area of the economy continue to hold promise under the heading of green jobs. Furthermore, even if the job is not seemingly related to environmental concerns, the environment touches all facets of life and will, therefore, permeate professions. We hope that you have come to see the complexities of these challenges, the significance of the individuals who work on these issues daily, and the need to continue forward movement.

SUGGESTED RESOURCES

Readings and Websites

Fiorino, Daniel J. *The New Environmental Regulation.* Cambridge: MIT Press, 2006.

Klyza, Christopher McGrory, and David Sousa. *American Environmental Policy: Beyond Gridlock.* Cambridge: MIT Press, 2013.

Kraft, Michael E., Mark Stephan, and Troy D. Abel. *Coming Clean: Information Disclosure and Environmental Performance.* Cambridge: MIT Press, 2011.

Layzer, Judith. *Open for Business: Conservatives' Opposition to Environmental Regulation.* Cambridge, MA: MIT Press, 2012.

Rabe, Barry G. *Greenhouse Governance: Addressing Climate Change in America.* Washington, DC: The Brookings Institution, 2010.

Films or Videos

Avatar. Directed by James Cameron. 2009. Twentieth Century Fox, Dune Entertainment, Ingenuous Film Partners.
Chinatown. Directed by Roman Polanski. 1974. Paramount Pictures. DVD.
Wall-e. Directed by Andrew Stanton. 2008. Disney. DVD.

REFERENCES

"Congress: Misc. Questions." Polling Report. 2018. Accessed August 10, 2018. http://www.pollingreport.com/congress.htm.
"Direction of Country." Polling Report. 2018. Accessed August 10, 2018. http://www.pollingreport.com/right.htm.
Ebbs, Stephanie. "Trump EPA Spends First Year Rolling Back Environmental Regulations." *ABC News*, 2018. Accessed August 10, 2018. https://abcnews.go.com/Politics/trump-epa-spends-year-rolling-back-environmental-regulations/story?id=52162794.
Farber, Daniel A. 2018. "Trump, EPA, and the Anti-Regulatory State." *The Regulatory Review*, January 24. Accessed February 6. https://www.theregreview.org/2018/01/24/farber-trump-epa-anti-regulatory-state/.
Fiorino, Daniel J. *The New Environmental Regulation.* Cambridge: MIT Press, 2006.
Fox News. 2015. "Donald Trump Talks Taxes, Trade, 9/11 and Why He Takes Personal Shots at Political Rivals." *Fox News Sunday.* Accessed August 10, 2018. http://www.foxnews.com/transcript/2015/10/18/donald-trump-talks-taxes-trade-11-and-why-takes-personal-shots-at-political.html.
Greshko, Michael, Laura Parker, Brian Clark Howard, and Daniel Stone. "A Running List of How President Trump Is Changing Environmental Policy." *National Geographic*, August 2, 2018. Accessed August 10, 2018. https://news.nationalgeographic.com/2017/03/how-trump-is-changing-science-environment/.
Kaufman, Alexander C. "Scott Pruitt's First Year Set the EPA Back Anywhere from a Few Years to 3 Decades." *Huffington Post*, January 20, 2018. https://www.huffingtonpost.com/entry/pruitt-one-year_us_5a610a5ce4b074ce7a06beb4.
Klyza, Christopher McGrory, and David Sousa. *American Environmental Policy 1990–2006.* Cambridge: MIT Press, 2008.
———. *American Environmental Policy: Beyond Gridlock.* Updated and Expanded Editions. Cambridge: MIT Press, 2013.
Kraft, Michael E. *Environmental Policy and Politics.* 7th edition. New York: Routledge, 2017.
Langer, Gary, and Benjamin Siu. "Election 2018 Exit Poll Analysis: Voter Turnout Soars, Democrats Take Back the House, ABC News Projects."

ABC News, November 7, 2018. Accessed November 8, 2018. https://abc-news.go.com/Politics/election-2018-exit-poll-analysis-56-percent-country/story?id=59006586.

"Obama's 2014 State of the Union Address." *CBS News*. Accessed February 18, 2014. http://www.cbsnews.com/news/obamas-2014-state-of-the-union-address-full-text/.

Pautz, Michelle C., and Sara R. Rinfret. *The Lilliputians of Environmental Regulation: The Perspective of State Regulators*. New York: Routledge, 2013.

Plumer, Brad. "Trump Officials Link Fuel Economy Rules to Deadly Crashes. Experts are Skeptical." *The New York Times*, August 2, 2018. Accessed August 10, 2018. https://www.nytimes.com/2018/08/02/climate/trump-fuel-economy.html.

Yoon-Hendricks, Alexandra. "Meet the Teenagers Leading a Climate Change Movement." *The New York Times*, July 21, 2018. Accessed July 30, 2018. https://www.nytimes.com/2018/07/21/us/politics/zero-hour-climate-march.html.

Zeleny, Jeff, and Arlette Saenz. "Senate Goes 'Nuclear,' Changes Nominee Filibuster Rules." *ABC News*, November 21, 2013. Accessed February 18, 2014. Available online http://abcnews.go.com/Politics/senate-nuclear-filibuster-rules/story?id=20964700.

INDEX

© The Editor(s) (if applicable) and The Author(s) 2019   365
S. R. Rinfret and M. C. Pautz, *US Environmental Policy in Action*,
https://doi.org/10.1007/978-3-030-11316-2

CPSIA information can be obtained
at www.ICGtesting.com
Printed in the USA
LVHW031819250419
615550LV00014B/1034